FOURTH EDITION

The Longman Writer's Companion

CHRIS M. ANSON
North Carolina State University

ROBERT A. SCHWEGLER
University of Rhode Island

MARCIA F. MUTH
University of Colorado at Denver

Longman

New York San Francisco Boston
London Toronto Sydney Tokyo Singapore Madrid
Mexico City Munich Paris Cape Town Hong Kong Montreal

Acquisitions Editor: Lauren A. Finn
Senior Development Editor: Anne Brunell Ehrenworth
Senior Supplements Editor: Donna Campion
Executive Marketing Manager: Megan Galvin-Fak
Production Manager: Bob Ginsberg
Project Coordination, Text Design, and Electronic Page Makeup:
    Nesbitt Graphics, Inc.
Cover Designer/Manager: John Callahan
Senior Manufacturing Buyer: Dennis J. Para
Printer and Binder: Quebecor World/Taunton
Cover Printer: Coral Graphic Services, Inc.

For permission to use copyrighted material, grateful acknowledgment is made to the
copyright holders on page C-1, which is hereby made part of this copyright page.

Library of Congress Cataloging-in-Publication Data
Anson, Christopher M., 1954-
    The Longman writer's companion / Chris M. Anson, Robert A. Schwegler, Marcia F.
Muth. -- 4th ed.
        p. cm.
    Includes index.
    ISBN-13: 978-0-205-74181-6 (alk. paper)
    ISBN-10: 0-205-74181-9 (alk. paper)
    1. English language--Rhetoric--Handbooks, manuals, etc. 2. Report writing--
Handbooks, manuals, etc. I. Schwegler, Robert A. II. Muth, Marcia F. III. Title.
    PE1408.A61848 2007
    808'.042--dc22   2007023359

This book includes 2009 MLA guidelines.

Longman
is an imprint of

ISBN-13: 978-0-205-74181-6
ISBN-10:   0-205-74181-9

1 2 3 4 5 6 7 8 9 10—QWT—12 11 10 09
Visit us a **www.pearsonhighered.com**

PREFACE FOR STUDENTS AND INSTRUCTORS

We've prepared this book for people who will be called on to write for different audiences and purposes—in short, for all writers. We know from experience and research that the demands of writing situations vary in important ways. We know, too, that writers need a range of concrete strategies in order to work successfully with the expectations and possibilities posed by each writing situation.

In response, we have produced a handbook filled with advice about writing and revising, creating correct and effective sentences, researching and reasoning, documenting and evaluating sources, representing yourself as a writer and speaker, and navigating the electronic world—all within three important communities: academic, public, and work. We hope that you'll find this handbook to be just what its title promises—a true writer's companion.

Hallmark Features

Through four editions *The Longman Writer's Companion* has been known for the following hallmark features.

Emphasis on writing in three communities: Academic, public, and work

Within different communities—academic, public, or work—the kinds of writing employed are likely to vary considerably. So, too, are expectations about style, reasoning, diction, correctness, and documentation.

Recognizing broad differences among communities is important for the many choices you need to make as you write. These differences are explained and highlighted throughout the text.

- **Community Boxes.** These at-a-glance reference boxes depict succinctly how the writing task at hand may differ if the writer's audience is in an academic, public, or workplace community.

The complete list of these boxes follows for your easy reference.

- **Chapters geared toward writing for particular audiences.** Part 4, "Writing for Specific Communities," encourages students to consider the audience and purpose of their writing—and adapt their style and form—depending on whether they are writing for academic (Chapters 15–17), public (Chapter 18), or workplace (Chapter 19) settings. Concrete strategies and sample documents are offered for the summary, annotated bibliography, literature review, essay exam, short documented paper, review, position paper, literary text analysis, visual text analysis, abstract, informative report, lab report, research report, public flyer, letter to the editor, business letter, business memo, résumé, and application letter.

- **Strategies.** Strategy sections appear throughout the handbook, placing special emphasis on concrete, practical strategies that writers can employ immediately in their work. See pages 4, 30, and 371 for a few examples of this feature.

Unique approach to correcting errors: Recognize and revise

It is hard to correct an error if you don't first recognize it as a problem. We have designed *The Longman Writer's Companion* to help writers develop the ability to recognize problems in their own writing by viewing their work as readers do. This unique approach to grammar and usage organizes the chapters in Parts 9–12.

- **Reader's reactions.** These comments, following examples of errors, convey possible responses to confusing or irritating sentences or passages, helping to explain errors or flaws in terms of their effects on readers.

- **Ten Serious Errors.** We asked college instructors about the errors that are most likely to confuse readers and undermine their confidence in writers. Throughout Parts 9–12, sections discussing any of the "Ten Serious Errors" are highlighted with marginal icons. In addition, a table on the flap of the back cover of this book summarizes these errors.

- **ESL Advice.** This tool, designed for nonnative speakers, is interspersed throughout the text. For a complete list of ESL advice in *The Longman Writer's Companion*, see the page following the index at the back of the book.

Discussion of reading, writing, and critical thinking

- **Writing for readers.** Specific strategies help writers develop the ability to keep communities of readers and their likely responses in mind during planning, drafting, revising, and editing (Parts 1, 2, 4, and 9–12).

- **Critical thinking and reading.** Reading, thinking, and audience are intertwined in discussions of the roles and expectations of readers, analytical and critical reading, and critical thinking (Parts 1–2).

- **Collaboration and feedback.** We offer practical advice about giving and receiving constructive criticism and about collaborating with other writers (4b, 5c, 5f, and Chapter 60).

Focus on technology

Because most students routinely use computers and the Internet, we offer realistic advice throughout the text on writing and conducting research in technologically enhanced environments.

- **"Writing in Online Communities"** (Chapter 13) includes information on writing email and participating in online communities through blogs, newsgroups, and IMs.
- **"Web and Internet Resources"** (Chapter 22) and **"Library Resources and Research Databases"** (Chapter 21) include strategies for finding and evaluating electronic resources.
- **Comprehensive online and electronic source citations** model accurate Works Cited and References pages (see pp. 221–231 and 254–260).

New to This Edition

Writing in the academic community coverage is greatly expanded and reorganized.

- **Greater emphasis on writing across the curriculum** provides more support for students in all their general education courses.
- **New chapter on writing in the natural and social sciences (Chapter 17)** encourages students to consider how disciplines require different ways of thinking, different research questions, and different writing styles.
- **Revised chapter on general academic writing (Chapter 15)** includes essential information on analyzing assignments in order to help

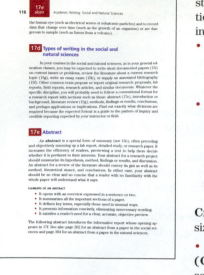

students understand instructors' expectations and develop their writing accordingly.

- **New sample student papers modeling CMS and CSE documentation styles (Chapters 28–29)** join the sample MLA and APA student papers.
- **Revised chapter on writing about literature is expanded to include other humanities (Chapter 16).** In addition to coverage and a sample student literary analysis, this edition includes discussion of visual text analysis.

Critical thinking is increasingly emphasized and coverage expanded.

- **A new chapter on assessing writing (Chapter 60),** designed to help students assess their own writing and understand how others read and evaluate it, also guides students in making informed comments on peers' papers.
- **Coverage of critical thinking, reading, and arguing has been consolidated and moved earlier in the book (Chapters 8–11)** so that students use these concepts to inform their writing throughout the term.
- **New chapter on visual argument (Chapter 11) explores visual rhetoric,** showing students how visuals (informative and persuasive) add to the range of evidence they can include in their papers.

Research and documentation coverage has been expanded and updated.

- **Newer mediums such as blogs and podcasts** are modeled in the in-text citations, works cited, and references for MLA and APA documentation, showing students how to cite sources not often covered in other handbooks (Chapters 26–27).
- **Avoiding Plagiarism and Integrating Sources are now combined** into a new Chapter 24 to better demonstrate their relationship to students.
- **"Library Resources and Research Databases"** (Chapter 21) includes new material on using libraries as research locations, guidance on how to utilize different types of databases, and new material on evaluating library and research database resources.
- **MLA documentation style** (Chapter 26) has been updated according to the guidelines in the *MLA Style Manual and Guide to Scholarly Publishing*, 3rd ed. The *MLA Handbook*, 7th ed., is expected to follow these same new guidelines.

- **Source samples for both MLA and APA** styles (Chapters 26–27) show students where to find information for their citations in exactly those sources students struggle with the most.
- **Updated and new screen shots** accompany text discussions in all research chapters.

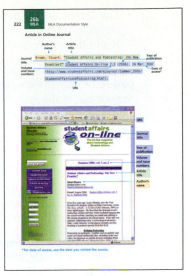

The connections between technology and writing are updated and strengthened.

- **Writing in digital environments** has been added to chapters on planning (Chapter 2), drafting (Chapter 4), and revising (Chapter 5).
- **Distance learning and online courses are addressed in Chapter 13,** with advice on learning in these increasingly prevalent environments.
- **IMing, text messaging, and blogging** are discussed in terms of how audience expectations and format conventions influence content coverage and style issues, encouraging critical thinking about these newest of writing spaces (Chapter 13).

Supplements

For Students

- **mycomplab** **MyCompLab** offers dynamic tools for improving grammar, writing, and research skills with comprehensive results tracking so students can gauge their progress. Highlights include an E-book of the text; interactive video tutorials on key grammar, writing, and research topics; **ExerciseZone** for grammar; Citation Diagnostics and Exercises; Evaluating Sources tutorial; and more!

- **vango notes** Study on the go with VangoNotes. Just download chapter reviews from your text and listen to them on any MP3 player. Now wherever you are—whatever you're doing—you can study by listening to the following for each chapter of your textbook.

  - Big Ideas: Your "need to know" for each chapter
  - Practice Test: A gut check for the Big Ideas—tells you if you need to keep studying

- Key Terms: Audio "flashcards" to help you review key concepts and terms
- Rapid Review: A quick drill session—use it right before your test

VangoNotes are flexible; download all the material directly to your player, or only the chapters you need. And they're efficient. Use them in your car, at the gym, walking to class, wherever. So get yours today. And get studying. VangoNotes.com

- The **Exercise Booklet** offers practice exercises in hard-copy format.

For Instructors

- *Diagnostic and Editing Tests and Exercises* aids in analyzing common errors and can supplement the handbook's exercises. (Available in both print and electronic formats.)

- **The Instructor's Resource Manual,** by Robert A Schwegler, University of Rhode Island, Michelle Niestepski, University of Rhode Island, and O. Brian Kaufman, Quinebaug Valley Community College, offers guidance on how most students use their handbooks, advice specifically tailored to adjunct instructors and graduate teaching assistants, strategies for teaching online with the handbook, and tips for designing courses with *The Longman Writer's Companion.*

- The **Answer Key** provides answers to all practice exercises published in the Exercise Booklet.

Acknowledgments

The fourth edition of *The Longman Writer's Companion* reflects important improvements in a book that has experienced nearly a decade of development. We are grateful to a number of people for helping to move the book forward.

First we wish to thank the students who have generously allowed us to present their writing as an inspiration to others: David Aharonian, Sarah Andrea, Summer Arrigo-Nelson, Anne S. Bloomfield, Amy Braegelman, Jeanne Brown, Justine Buhl, Amy Burns, Pam Copass, Melanie Dedecker, Jennifer Figliozzi, Daisy Garcia, Jen Halliday, Shane Hand, Tammy Jo Helton, Jenna Ianucilli, Jenny Latimer, James Newlands, Jennifer O'Berry, Paul Pusateri, Sharon Salamone, Brian Schwegler, Ted Wolfe, and Tou Yang. Marcia Muth also thanks the students in her writing workshops, which she offers through the School of Education at the University of Colorado at Denver and Health Sciences Center.

Our special thanks go to the following reviewers: Kelly Belanger, University of Wyoming; Laura J. Bird, Northern Illinois University; Linda Breslin, The American University in Cairo; Stuart Brown, New Mexico State

University; Terry Brown, University of Wisconsin, River Falls; Zisca Burton, University of Miami; J. Lee Campbell, Valdosta State University; Laura Carroll, Abilene Christian University; William Carroll, Texas A & M University; Patricia Connors, University of Memphis; Erika Deiters, Moraine Valley Community College; James H. Donelan, UC Santa Barbara; Leona Fisher, Georgetown University; Sara Garnes, Ohio State University; Patricia Gordon, Central Carolina Technical College; Loretta Gray, Central Washington University; Carolyn Grimstead, Long Island University-CW Post Campus; Darrin L. Grinder, Northwest Nazarene University; Charles Hill, University of Wisconsin, Oshkosh; Rebecca Moore Howard, Texas Christian University; Sandra Jamieson, Drew University; Kathleen Kelly, Northeastern University; Winney Kenney, Southwestern Illinois College-Belleville; John Connors Kerrigan, Fort Hays State University; Yolanda Kirk, California State University, Northridge; Carolyn Kuykendall, Saddleback College; Bill Lamb, Johnson County Community College; Leslie Lydell, University of Minnesota; Jeanne McDonald, Waubonsee Community College; Michael Moghtader, University of New Mexico; Patricia Moody, Syracuse University; Marti L. Mundell, Washington State University; Deborah Mutnick, Long Island University; Susan Smith Nash, University of Oklahoma; Catherine Packard, Southeastern Illinois College; Robbie C. Pinter, Belmont University; Laura Bearrie Pogue, Hardin-Simmons University; Mary Prindiville, University of Wisconsin, River Falls; Donna Qualley, Western Washington University; Star Rush, Western Washington University; Mary Sauer, Indiana University Purdue University Indianapolis; Myra Seaman, College of Charleston; Nancy Shapiro, University of Maryland, College Park; Matt Smith, University of Saint Francis; Susan Taylor, University of Nevada, Las Vegas; Deborah Coxwell Teague, Florida State University-Tallahassee; Marcy Trianosky, Hollins University; Kurt Van Wilt, St. Leo College; Richard White, Edison Community College; Debbie Williams, Abilene Christian University; and Patricia Zukowski, University of Massachusetts, Amherst.

Thank you also to those who worked with us as consultants in the development and revision of selected chapters in previous editions of *The Longman Writer's Companion*—Stevens Amidon; Daniel Anderson, University of North Carolina, Chapel Hill; Ellen Bitterman, SUNY, New Paltz; Mick Doherty and Sandye Thompson; Jim Dubinsky, Virginia Tech; Elizabeth Ervin, University of North Carolina, Wilmington; Mary Finley, University Library at California State University, Northridge; Christina Haas, Kent State University; Eric Pappas, Virginia Tech; Gladys Vega Scott, Arizona State University; Charlotte Smith, Adirondack Community College; and Victor Villaneuva, Washington State University. We remain grateful for the advice, expertise, and creativity of all these writers and teachers.

We wish to thank Lauren Finn, acquisitions editor, for overseeing this complicated project and attending to its many details with an imaginative eye and an innovative spirit. We are especially grateful to Anne Brunell Ehrenworth, our truly esteemed development editor, for guiding with clarity and wisdom such a complicated project and for fitting together the many pieces, large and small, textual and visual, typographical and personal. Our thanks to Marion Castellucci for her help in coordinating and reviewing the manuscript. On each page of the text, we can see the contributions of Lois Lombardo, and we thank her for her patience and care. We acknowledge, too, the guidance and care of Bob Ginsberg, who took us from manuscript to printed book.

Chris Anson thanks Geanie, Ian, and Graham for enduring yet another book project and for always being understanding (well, almost always) when long phone calls, hours at the computer, or thickets of manuscripts got in the way of backyard soccer, a leaking faucet, or something more than thirty minutes for dinner. Your patience has been my inspiration.

Bob Schwegler would like to acknowledge above all Nancy Newman Schwegler for sharing her understanding of readers, reading, and writers. "And I'll be sworn up 'y that he loves her; / For here's a paper written in his hand, / A halting sonnet. . . ." He would also like to thank Brian and Tara Schwegler for their advice, Christopher for his smiles, Ashley Marie for her inspiration, Lily for hope, and Kira for style.

Marcia Muth thanks her family: Anderson and Liz, whose friends, crises, inspirations, and inventive writing continue to enlighten her about the rich and varied lives of student writers, and her husband, Rod, who remains the most patient, steadfast, and inspirational of friends, advisors, and companions.

CHRIS M. ANSON
ROBERT A. SCHWEGLER
MARCIA F. MUTH

PART 1

Writing for Readers

▼ *TAKING IT ONLINE*

WEB EXHIBITS
http://webexhibits.org
Browse this site for links to interesting reading and visuals on widely varied topics, academic and otherwise.

GENERAL WRITING CONCERNS (PLANNING/WRITING/REVISING/GENRES)
http://owl.english.purdue.edu/owl
Click on the options on this page for valuable advice about writing processes from the popular Online Writing Lab at Purdue University.

VIRGIL
http://projects.uwc.utexas.edu/virgil/
Visit *virgil* to get handouts on many writing topics as well as advice for writing essays, research papers, application essays, résumés, and other documents.

OVERCOMING WRITER'S BLOCK
http://leo.stcloudstate.edu/catalogue.html
Can't get started? Try the ideas on this page, or turn to the other suggestions available at *The Writing Center*.

WORKING WITH TOPICS
http://writing.colostate.edu
Here's advice across the academic disciplines for finding, narrowing, and working with topics.

DEVELOPING A THESIS STATEMENT
http://www.english.uiuc.edu/cws/wworkshop
Click on "Writing Tips" for advice from the Writers' Workshop at the University of Illinois, Urbana-Champaign.

PART 1

Writing for Readers

1 Writers, Readers, and Communities

The Web page you browsed yesterday was not made by a computer. Someone wrote its text, planned its design, and anticipated readers' reactions. Someone else wrote the newsletter in your mailbox, the forms for your car loan, and the waiver you signed before the technician X-rayed your ankle. Writing and reading surround us, shaping our lives, choices, responsibilities, and values. This book looks at the roles of writers and readers in contemporary culture. It offers concrete strategies for writing, for critical reading and thinking, and for understanding your readers' expectations.

Whether you're drafting a psychology paper, an email message at work, or a neighborhood flyer, try to envision a **community of readers and writers**, people with shared—though not necessarily identical—goals, settings, preferences, and uses for verbal and visual texts. This book will help you develop your skill at recognizing different needs and expectations of writers, readers, and speakers in the academic, public, and work communities in which you may be active throughout your life.

1a Academic, public, and work communities

In a Denver suburb, pets have been disappearing. The culprits have been coyotes or other predators, crowded by new homes and technology parks. Alarmed local residents wonder if a young child will be the next victim.

In such situations, problem solving often begins with written and oral presentations. City officials and citizens may turn to the **academic community** for studies of the habitat and feeding habits of coyotes and other predators. Their research documents may sound like this:

> This report summarizes and compares data from two studies of the habits of predators in areas with significant population growth and urbanization over the past ten years.

The scientific reports focus on one question: how do coyotes behave in a shrinking habitat? But parents, pet owners, and others in the **public community** are likely to ask a different question: how can we protect our children and pets without harming local wildlife? Tips posted on the Colorado Division of Wildlife Web site apply scientific knowledge to residents' concerns.

1

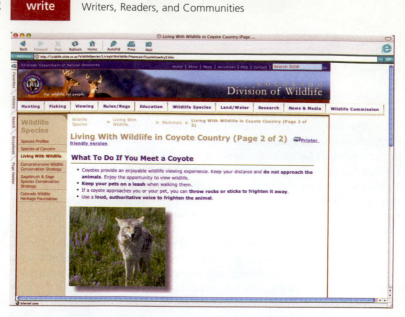

Neighborhood groups might distribute leaflets and organize meetings.

COYOTE ALERT!

Are your children safe in their own backyards? Coyotes attacked
seven dogs and cats last summer. Find out what we can do.
Join the Committee to Safeguard Our Children on
Tuesday, October 2, at 7:00 p.m. in the high school gym.

Other reports might circulate in the **work community**, analyzing the frequency
of complaints, summarizing business perspectives, or presenting policy options
to help people, pets, and coyotes live in balance.

Participating in academic, public, and work communities means
talking, listening, reading, and, especially, writing. Your immediate academic challenge—responding to assignments—helps prepare you to write
more thoughtfully in other communities. In the same way, writing at work or in
public situations can stimulate or enrich your writing for academic readers.

To communicate effectively within a community of readers and writers,
pay attention to its roles, goals, forms, and writing characteristics. (See the
chart on page 3.) These considerations can help you recognize both readers'
expectations and your choices as a writer.

Communities of Writers and Readers		
Academic	**Public**	**Work**
ROLES Students	Residents or group members	Coworkers
Teachers		Supervisors
Researchers	Possible supporters	Organizational work groups (management, accounting, public relations)
Committees gathering expert opinions	Public officials or agencies	
	Community activists	Clients and customers
Readers interested in specialized knowledge	Local groups	Government agencies
	Readers interested in an issue	Public target groups
GOALS Creation or exchange of knowledge	Persuasion in support of a cause or issue	Provision of information
	Participation in democracy	Analysis of problems
		Proposal of solutions
	Provision of issue-oriented information	Promotion of organization
TYPICAL FORM Analysis of text or phenomenon	Position paper	Description of object, event, situation, or problem
Interpretation of text, artwork, or event	Informative report	
	Letter to group, supporters, officials, or event agency, organization, or publication	Proposal
Research proposal		Report of findings
Lab report		Memos, letters, agendas, or minutes of meetings
Scholarly article	Flyer, newsletter, pamphlet, or fact sheet	
Annotated bibliography	Action or grant proposal	Guidelines or instructions
Grant proposal	Guidelines, charter, or principles	Promotional materials
Policy study		Meeting presentation
Classroom presentation	Comments in public forum	
WRITING CHARACTERISTICS Detailed reasoning	Focus on shared values and goals	Concentration on task, problem, or goal
Critical analysis		
Fresh insights or conclusions	Advocacy of cause	Accurate and efficient presentation of problem or issue
	Fair recognition of others' interests	
Extensive evidence		Concise, direct prose
Accurate detail that supports conclusions	Relevant evidence that supports positions	Promotion of product or service
Balanced treatment	Concentration on own point of view or on need for information	Attention to corporate image and design standards
Acknowledgment of other viewpoints		
Thoughtful, stimulating exploration of topic	Orientation to actions standards	

1b Electronic communities

The broad academic, public, and work communities all cohabit the intriguing world of the Internet. A click of a mouse connects you with large and small electronic communities, each organized around a shared interest in a topic, point of view, or issue.

STRATEGY **Use TASALS to help you recognize electronic communities.**

TOPIC. On what subject does the site focus? Do contributors belong to any organization or share any other affiliation?

ATTITUDE. Does the site have a clear point of view or set of values? Do contributors have similar perspectives or values?

STRATEGIES. Does the site use a particular written style or visual design?

AUTHORITY. Does the site support claims or information? Do contributors reason carefully, offering evidence rather than opinion?

LINKS. Do postings or links refer to related online resources?

SUMMARIZE. How can you sum up the qualities of the community, its expectations of participants, and its conventions?

1c Myths and realities about writing

Effective writers know about the realities of the composing process. They know successful writing is almost never a matter of just recording your thoughts in finished form. Instead, it begins with a response: to an idea or a reading, an experience, or a problem. It calls for planning, defining a purpose and thesis, considering community and readers, drafting, revising, editing, and proofreading. And it rarely moves in a straight line. Revising may mean further drafting, or editing may mean collaborating with readers.

Replace the myths that breed self-defeating habits with reliable strategies that increase your impact as you write in different communities.

Myth: People easily succeed in the real world without having to write.
Reality: It's a popular myth that executives don't need to write because their assistants do this work. In Fortune 500 companies, however, over half the employees spend between eight and forty hours writing each week. As more employees carry laptops, their writing time is likely to increase.

Myth: Writing is easy for people born with the knack.
Reality: If we looked over other writers' shoulders, we'd know what researchers know: good writers draft and redraft, succeeding through hard work.

Myth: You can be a good writer without doing much reading.
Reality: It's not likely. The more you read, the better you understand the writing that works in specific communities and your options as a writer.

Myth: It's cheating to ask others to read your paper before you turn it in.
Reality: It certainly is cheating if you have someone else write a paper or parts of it and then claim the work as your own. But successful writers always depend on readers for feedback. Especially at work and in civic groups, key documents are likely to be written collaboratively.

Myth: Good writing is effective for all readers.
Reality: All good writing is clear, coherent, and correct, but what works in one community may not work as well in another. Your sociology research paper will differ in tone, style, and content from the proposal you write at work or the email you send to your running group.

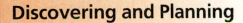

ESL ADVICE: EFFECTIVE WRITING

Another myth is that you can't be an effective writer if English is not your first language. Of course, the more you read and write, the more your English will improve. But effective writing takes hard work whether you're a native or nonnative speaker. And powerful writing from the heart moves readers no matter what the writer's language background.

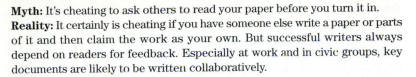

2 Discovering and Planning

Imagine trying to build a house without drawing up any plans beforehand or going into the playoffs without a team strategy, just to "see what happens." Success would depend on luck, not design. The same is true for writing. For almost any formal project—in college, for a civic group, or on the job—you need to generate ideas and "rough out" a structure before you really get started. **Planning** before you write a full draft—often called **prewriting**—gives you a map of where you want to go in your writing.

2a Generating ideas

Whatever your writing task, you will want to ask, "Why am I writing? What do I know about what I'm writing? What else do I need to know?" Gather ideas from your existing resources—your journal entries, readings annotated with your responses, class or meeting notes, your assignment sheet or job description, and any similar projects. (See also 3a.)

Freewrite. Write by hand or at the computer for five or ten minutes *without stopping*, even if you only repeat "I'm stuck." As such empty prose bores you, you'll almost magically slip into more engaging ideas. Or begin **focused freewriting** with an idea you already have—"I guess I support antigambling laws"—to start productively exploring the topic.

List. Lists can help you draw out your own knowledge, create ideas through association, and generalize from details. For her history paper on Soviet espionage during the Cold War, Annie Hanson listed her main points and, under her final point, key supporting details.

1. Cold War background from Yalta to Berlin Wall
2. Western vs. Soviet technology
3. Role of KGB training operatives and recruiting
4. Espionage examples (Fuchs, De Groot, Philby)

Write your topic at the top of a page, and then list ten thoughts, facts, impressions, ideas, or specifics about it. For example, begin with a general idea or a major part of your project, and list supporting details and new associations. Repeat the process with your other ideas or parts.

Ask strategic questions. Strategic questioning can pull information from your memory and direct you to other ideas to pursue. Begin with *what, why,* and *why not.* Ask *who, where, when,* and *how,* if they apply. Continue to ask questions as you probe more deeply. Brian Corby asked questions as he began his letter to the zoning board opposing a high-rise apartment by a public park.

What?
- Proposed high-rise apt.—18 stories, 102 units
- East side of Piedmont Park by Sunrise Ave
- Planning by Feb., groundbreaking by June, done in a year

Why?
- Developers profit
- Provides medium-cost housing in growing area
- Develops ugly vacant lot by park

Why Not?
- "Citifies" one of the few green patches in town
- Traffic, crime rate, park use
- New zoning opens the door to other high-rises

ESL ADVICE: CLEAR AND FORCEFUL DETAILS

Most writing in English tends to be direct rather than abstract. Especially in the academic and work communities, a writer often makes a clear assertion about a topic, a problem, or an event and then supports that idea with facts, details, or research. In a sense, the writer must "prove" the point, as readers won't accept it on faith or by virtue of the writer's authority. If readers find your writing too broad, indirect, or poorly supported, compare their expectations with those of readers in your first language. American teachers and workplace supervisors generally want writers to ask questions about writing projects and are used to explaining what they expect.

2b Organizing information

Ideas and information alone will get you started, but most writing and speaking projects require **structure**—a pattern, outline, or plan to shape and organize. Use a structure readers expect in projects such as reports, or create a structure from the ideas you've generated.

Clusters. Draw a cluster by circling a concept, idea, or topic in the center of a page. Then jot down associations with this kernel topic, circling and connecting them with lines to the center, like the spokes of a wheel, or to each other. To create clusters in cycles, use each subsidiary idea as a new kernel topic. As she began her argument paper, Marianne Kidd used clustering to relate her ideas about censoring music lyrics. (See Figure 2.1 below.)

FIGURE 2.1 A simple conceptual cluster

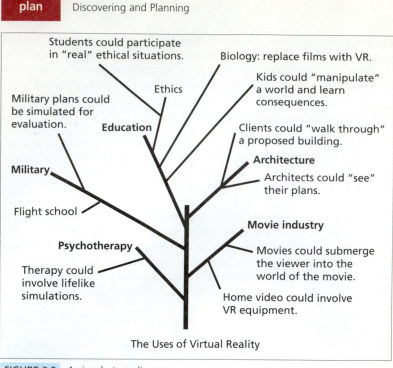

The Uses of Virtual Reality

Students could participate in "real" ethical situations.

Biology: replace films with VR.

Ethics

Kids could "manipulate" a world and learn consequences.

Military plans could be simulated for evaluation.

Education

Clients could "walk through" a proposed building.

Military

Architecture

Architects could "see" their plans.

Flight school

Movie industry

Psychotherapy

Movies could submerge the viewer into the world of the movie.

Therapy could involve lifelike simulations.

Home video could involve VR equipment.

FIGURE 2.2 A simple tree diagram

Tree diagrams. A tree diagram resembles a cluster, but the branches tend to be more linear and hierarchical. Start with your topic as the trunk. Create main branches for central points and smaller branches for related ideas. Then "revise" your diagram into a working plan or outline for the paragraphs or sections of your project. Each main branch of Bill Chen's diagram became a "chunk" or section in his paper on possible uses of virtual reality. (See Figure 2.2.)

Time sequences. If your project involves chronology, use a time sequence. For example, in planning a self-guided tour of a museum exhibit, James Cole drew a time sequence detailing Andy Warhol's artistic life. When you build a time sequence, frame each event along a line, noting dates, ages, or other time markers. If you wish, add thick connecting lines to mark pivotal events that led to or caused other events and thin lines to show simple time links.

Problem-solution grids. Position papers, business reports, and other persuasive pieces often follow a problem-solution sequence, outlining a problem, offering workable solutions, or advocating one solution rather than another. Paula Masek used a problem-solution grid to plan her editorial exploring temporary ways to feed the homeless. Later she discussed each boxed item in a

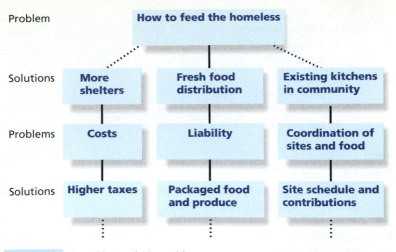

Problem — How to feed the homeless

Solutions — More shelters | Fresh food distribution | Existing kitchens in community

Problems — Costs | Liability | Coordination of sites and food

Solutions — Higher taxes | Packaged food and produce | Site schedule and contributions

FIGURE 2.3 A problem-solution grid

separate section of her draft. (See Figure 2.3.) To create a problem-solution grid, first state the problem. Underneath, in boxes or columns, identify possible solutions. Below these, identify problems each solution might create and then their solutions. Generate as many layers as you wish.

Outlines. The best-known planning technique is the trusty outline, complete with Roman numerals. The traditional outline may help you to label or arrange ideas but doesn't do much to help *generate* them. A **working outline**, however, can help you generate information or identify missing pieces. As you arrange ideas in an outline (or outline a draft to check its logic), consider whether your higher-level generalizations, interpretations, or conclusions are followed by enough supporting details and specifics to inform or persuade a reader. If you spot gaps or unbalanced coverage, consider breaking up a large topic, combining smaller points, expanding ideas, or adding more details or examples.

With a simple topic as your main heading, commit yourself to three second-level headings by writing *A*, *B*, and *C* underneath. (Leave a lot of space in between.) Then fill in the subheadings. Now develop third-level headings by writing *1*, *2*, and *3* beneath *each* letter. Fill them in, too.

Mitch Weber used a working outline to plan a brief history of the non-profit organization where he had a summer internship.

CREATION OF THE FAMILY HEALTH CENTER
   A. Founding Work of Susan and Roger Ramstadt
      1. The "vision"
      2. Finding the money
      3. Support from the Crimp Foundation

2c Planning in digital environments

Whether you are working on a simple word-processed document or creating a complicated multimedia Web page, planning can save you a lot of time and frustration. Fortunately, new technologies offer electronic methods for planning for conventional papers as well as online documents. However, experiment with these technologies to see whether they work as well as paper-and-pencil strategies.

Outlining options. Many word processors have simple outlining programs that prompt you to create a map or plan for your text. You can see and then manipulate the parts or headings of a draft as you consider more effective alternatives to your current design. Such programs also let you view your presentation in outline form to help you write, assemble, and deliver it effectively.

Mapping programs. Some programs allow you to represent your plan for a text in your own map or chart, or in forms it provides. *Inspiration*, for example, gives you many different templates for conceptual maps, such as flowcharts, bubble diagrams, and clusters. Some are designed to match common writing and reasoning processes in specific disciplines (such as cause-effect charts in the sciences and social sciences).

Web outlining features. When creating multimedia documents such as Web pages, visual planning is crucial because your reader will be using hyperlinks to navigate. Most Web design programs such as Macromedia *Dreamweaver* provide an outline or map view of your site so that you can see how the pages link together.

STRATEGY Try electronic planning.

- Use your computer for planning so that you can easily reorganize and develop your ideas into a draft.
- Try interactive questions or prompts from your software, the Web, or the campus computer lab or tutoring center.
- Use a search engine to browse for Web sites on your topic.
- Skim links, gathering possible ideas from varied sites.

3 Purpose, Thesis, and Audience

Think about what writing actually *does*. It helps communicate ideas, develop policies, provide services, or make things work. It can sell, buy, or negotiate. It can be coolly informative or passionately persuasive. It can do public good or make private profit. And it can produce knowledge.

3a Identifying your focus and purpose

Given all that writing *can* do, one of your early steps is to decide just what a particular piece of writing *needs* to do.

1 Define the focus of your task

In many writing situations, someone hands you a task or assignment, and it's your job to produce effective writing. First think about the focus your assignment or task requires. Then concentrate on how to narrow your focus until you find the kernel or core that will lie at the center of your paper. Meg Satterfield began this process by underlining a key noun phrase in her assignment.

> Most of us have volunteered at some time—helping family or friends or joining a service-learning project. Tell your audience (our class) about some unexpected outcome of your experience as a volunteer.

Meg decided that her assignment left the topic open but valued something ("an unexpected outcome") that would surprise or engage readers.

STRATEGY   **Target your topic.**

On your assignment sheet or job description, underline any nouns or noun phrases; use them to invent and narrow possibilities (see 2a).

2 Define the purpose of your task

Focusing on a topic—a noun—gives you a clear sense of what your writing is *about*. But nouns don't act, and your writing needs to *do* something, too. Its **purpose** usually takes the form of an action statement—a verb or verb phrase like these two in Cory Meta's assignment.

> Find a magazine ad that catches your attention. Analyze the ad for its hidden cultural assumptions, being sure to describe exactly what is happening in the ad. Note techniques such as camera angle, coloration, and focus.

> **STRATEGY**　**Pinpoint what you need to *do*.**
>
> On your assignment sheet or job description, underline any verbs or verb phrases that tell you what to do. (See the chart on p. 13 for a list of verbs frequently used in academic writing situations.) Then use planning strategies to generate material related to these verbs (see 2a).

3 Rough out a purpose structure

State briefly the purpose of each section of your writing. A sequence such as "1-2-3-4" or "beginning-middle-ending" can help you decide what each part should do. Use verbs that clarify your purpose: *show, explain, build up to*. In planning a student housing guide, Carol Stotsky specified her purposes by developing a tentative order for her section on housing options.

BEGINNING	Show students why housing options are important for them.
MIDDLE	Explore advantages and disadvantages of each in detail.
ENDING	Recommend that traditional students move gradually from security (home or dorm) to independence (off campus).

3b Creating a thesis

Readers may expect you to clarify your point right away in a college paper, just as they may look for an executive summary with a report or an abstract before a professional article. For this reason, a thesis statement often ends the first paragraph in college writing. The **thesis**, generally expressed in a single sentence, is the controlling idea that you then explore, support, or illustrate using specific examples or arguments. You may draft a paper with a clear thesis in mind, discover your thesis later on and revise accordingly, or modify your thesis as you look for evidence or ideas to back up your assertions.

1 Develop a rough thesis

To begin developing a thesis, first narrow the topic to some specific angle or perspective. Then begin turning the topic from a noun (a "thing") into a statement that contains a verb (an "action"). Notice how Lynn Tarelli developed a thesis for her brochure for a parenting group.

VAGUE TOPIC	Ritalin
STILL A TOPIC	Ritalin for kids with attention-deficit disorder (ADD)
STILL A TOPIC	The problem of Ritalin use for kids with ADD
ROUGH THESIS	Parents should be careful about using medicines such as Ritalin for kids with ADD.

KEY VERBS USED TO SPECIFY WRITING PURPOSES

Analyze: Divide or break something into constituent parts so you can observe, describe, and study their relationships.

Analyze the relationships between form and color, light and shadow, and foreground and background in one of Titian's paintings.

Argue: Prove a point, or persuade a reader to accept or entertain a position. (See Chapters 8 and 10.)

In a letter to the College Senate, argue your position on a campuswide smoking ban.

Compare and contrast: Show similarities and differences for two or more things.

Compare and contrast costs at local hospitals for ten surgical procedures.

Describe: Show how something is experienced through sight, sound, taste, touch, or smell.

Describe obstacles in local historic homes met by visitors in wheelchairs.

Discuss: Provide an intelligent, focused commentary about a topic.

Discuss current transit needs in the metropolitan region.

Evaluate: Reach conclusions about something's value or worth, using substantiating evidence based on observation and analysis.

Evaluate the effectiveness of camera technique in Hitchcock's *The Birds*.

Extend: Apply an idea or concept more fully.

Extend last year's production figures to account for the April slowdown.

Inform: Present facts, views, phenomena, or events to enlighten your reader.

Inform homeowners about the hazards of lead paint.

Show: Demonstrate or provide evidence to explain something.

Show how Pip, in his later years, is influenced by Joe's working-class values in Dickens's *Great Expectations*.

Synthesize: Combine separate elements into a single or unified entity.

Synthesize this list of facts about energy consumption.

Trace: Map out a history, chronology, or explanation of origins.

Trace the development of Stalinism.

Use: Focus on the designated material, selecting specifics from it to explain and illustrate your broader points.

Use the three assigned poems to illustrate contemporary responses to death.

Lynn progressively sharpened the topic and brought the fourth version to life by expressing an assertion about it, seeing it from a specific perspective.

2 Complicate, develop, or modify your thesis

Lynn's thesis still didn't make a clear suggestion to parents about Ritalin: Should it not be used for kids with ADD? Should it be used judiciously?

FINAL THESIS Although Ritalin is widely used to treat children with ADD, parents should not rely too heavily on such drugs until they have explored both their child's problem and all treatment options.

Lynn *complicated* her rough thesis by accepting Ritalin as a legitimate treatment for ADD; her cautions about overreliance and other options *developed* and *modified* it to create a clearer, more complex statement.

As your ideas evolve, be ready to modify or change your thesis. After outlining his contribution to a library publication on computer literacy, Joel Kitze modified his thesis to give readers more to consider.

THESIS In spite of expanding technology, computers will never replace books as the chief medium of written literacy.

SUPPORTING IDEA 1 Books are more democratic, since not everyone can afford a personal computer.

SUPPORTING IDEA 2 Books can be enjoyed anywhere--on a bus or beach, in bed.

SUPPORTING IDEA 3 Children enjoy the physical comfort of reading with adults, a comfort harder to achieve with computers.

MODIFIED THESIS Although computer technology allows masses of information to be stored and conveyed electronically, it will never replace the bound book as the most affordable, convenient, and magical medium for print.

STRATEGY Develop and modify your thesis.

Help your reader anticipate and organize information in your writing, fitting separate chunks—paragraphs and sections—into your larger purpose. Use planning strategies (see Chapter 2) or research (see Part 5) to create a series of points that support, expand, or illustrate your thesis. Then develop and modify your thesis by asking *why, how,* and *for what reason.*

3 Choose an appropriate kind of thesis statement

Not all thesis statements take the same form. Choose the kind of thesis most appropriate for your purpose or readers. (See also 20d and 25c.)

Argumentative thesis. Readers will expect you to indicate your opinion on an issue and perhaps to acknowledge other views.

> Although bioengineered crops may pose some dangers, their potential for combating hunger and disease justifies their careful use in farming.

General thesis. Readers will expect to learn your conclusions or special perspectives and perhaps understand their importance as well.

> Sooner or later, teenagers stop listening to parents and turn to each other for advice, sometimes with disastrous results.

Academic thesis. Readers will expect to learn both your specific conclusion and your plan to support it, using terms appropriate to the field.

> My survey of wedding announcements in local newspapers during the last three decades indicates that religious background and ethnicity have decreased in importance in mate selection but education and social background remain significant factors.

Informative thesis. Readers will expect to learn why information is interesting or useful and how you'll organize or synthesize it.

> When you search for online advice about financial aid, you will find help on three very different kinds of Web sites.

3c Understanding your readers

As you write, you need to shape ideas and information to guide your readers' understanding and accomplish your purpose(s). To do this, you should identify your actual or potential readers as well as their likely perspectives, needs, and expectations. (See Figure 3.1.)

1 Analyze your audience

Begin your audience analysis by asking *Who are my readers? How many readers can I anticipate?* and *How well do I know them?*

STRATEGY Ask questions about your readers.

- **Size and familiarity.** How large is your audience? How familiar or close to you? Are audience members known or unknown to you?
- **Community.** Which expectations of readers are typical of the community in which you are writing? Which are specialized or local? What roles in the community do your readers play or expect you to play?

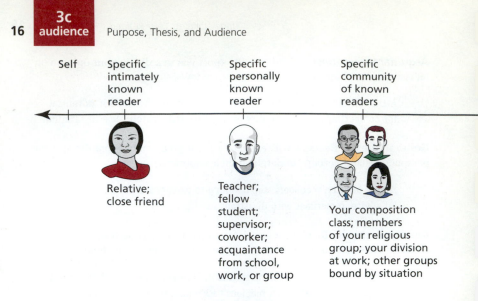

FIGURE 3.1 The audience continuum

- **Knowledge.** What do readers already know about your topic? Are they novices or experts?
- **Social context.** What characterizes your readers socially, culturally, and educationally? How do they spend their time?
- **Intellectual disposition.** How do your readers think? Are they conservative? radical? apathetic?
- **Conditions of reading.** Under what conditions will they read?
- **Power.** What is your status relative to readers? Are they peers or superiors? Do you expect them, or do they expect you, to do something?

2 Respond to your audience

Determine your readers' needs and expectations by asking *What do my readers expect?* Take into account any particular community of readers—academic, public, or work—that you are addressing.

- **Select the genre readers expect.** The type of text you choose to write—the **genre**—depends on your purpose and likely readers. If you request funds for a volunteer project, readers will expect a grant proposal, not a poem.
- **Shape your content to the context.** If you're explaining how to remove mildew for a neighborhood newsletter, skip the history of mildew unless it's relevant to the remedies.
- **Adjust your structure to the situation.** In a letter to your investment firm's client whose stock has tumbled, you might lead up to this

Specific publicly known reader	Specific unknown reader	Specific community of unknown readers	General community of unknown readers

| Senator Kennedy; president of your college; editor of your local newspaper | Personnel director at Inland Chemicals; editor of the *Journal of Economics*; chair of the university committee on using animals in research; others known by name and affiliation | Board of directors at Inland Chemicals; the choir's electronic mailing list; readers of *Hunting Magazine;* other groups with shared interests | Democrats; educated Americans; readers of popular fiction; concerned citizens; working parents |

news with the circumstances of the loss. A lab report, however, should move directly to the conventional sections.

- **Anticipate possible responses of readers.** Will readers expect you to be clinical and detached, informal and chatty, or in between? How might they react if you're emotional, hostile, or legalistic?

4 Drafting

If planning resembles storyboarding a movie, then drafting begins the filming, even though you may retake entire scenes and cut lots of footage. **Drafting** is the challenging process of stringing words together into sentences and paragraphs that make sense to a reader.

4a Moving from planning to drafting

Although all your planning (see Chapters 2–3) prepares you for drafting, you may not know how and where to begin writing. As Amy Burns reviewed a cluster she drew for her paper on superstition, she began jotting notes on "rabbit's foot," one of her "cases of superstition." Using these notes, she began drafting simply with a series of phrases.

> Rabbit's foot—common lucky charm. Omen of good fortune. Brasch says thumping noise from hind paws = communication. Thought to have magical powers. Newborns brushed to chase evil spirits.

Using a simple three-part scheme, Amy then developed a preliminary structure for grouping her ideas on superstition.

INTRODUCTION Fear, people who believe, origins

BODY Examples (black cat, #13, ladder, rabbit's foot, etc.)

CONCLUSION Truth and falsity, mystery of superstitions

Amy used her plan as a way to start, writing an introduction about how superstitions originate in a fear of the unknown.

Group your ideas. Use your planning material to place ideas, topics, or terms into one of three categories: introduction, body, and conclusion. If your project has a required or expected structure, use it to define your groups. If you have made a rough outline, assign chunks of it to these parts. You might set up separate computer files so that you can work on these parts one section at a time. Later you can cut and paste the files into a single text.

As you draft, consider whether you're achieving your general purposes (persuading someone or explaining something) or your more specific purposes for different parts (enlivening a paragraph or illustrating a point). Given her specific purpose, to "grab my readers' attention and interest them in superstition," Amy moved some specific examples into her opening paragraph.

> Do you knock on wood after making a prediction? shiver when a black cat crosses your path? consider 13 unlucky? If so, you have already been swept into the world of superstitions. Many people practice some of the bizarre rituals of superstition, but few know why.

What readers expect first, second, and third may help you determine how to organize to achieve your purpose. You'd probably arrange a local history of a ballpark chronologically but organize an argument for its preservation logically, using your paragraphs to support your assertions.

Write about your writing. Begin not by writing your paper but by writing *about* it. What concerns you most? What do you hope to do? How might you start? As you jot notes, you'll be less anxious about starting—after all, you *have* started. As you continue, don't worry about choosing perfect words or crafting perfect sentences and paragraphs. Just write as much as you can quickly. When momentum develops, keep going.

Try semidrafting. Write full sentences until you're about to stall out. Then simply write *etc.* in place of the full text, and continue with your next point. Or add directions to yourself in brackets, noting what to do next. For documented projects or research papers, use semidrafting to note what you need to integrate from sources, as Kavita Kamal did when writing about "wild children" (supposedly raised by animals in the woods).

> The first case was that of Victor, the "Wild Boy of Aveyron." Victor first appeared in a village in southern France in January 1800. His age was estimated at eleven or twelve years. [Explain his adoption by Itard and Guerin and their subsequent studies.] People assumed that he was a mute because he did not speak. [Now go into the stuff from Shattuck about no malformation of the tongue, mouth, etc.]

ESL ADVICE: SEMIDRAFTING AND PHRASING

If you find composing in English difficult, type *XXX*, draw a circle, or make a note in your first language where you need to rework your phrasing. Continue semidrafting so that you get your main ideas down on paper, and fill in the small points later.

4b Drafting collaboratively

When you write with classmates, a civic group, or a work team, look for collaborative strategies that suit the group and the context.

- Organize **parallel drafting**, dividing up the project, perhaps by group members' specialties, so that each is responsible for drafting a particular section. You can exchange drafts as you revise and edit, but one person may need to act as editor, integrating the drafts.
- Try **team drafting** when writers share similar ideas and approaches, assigning two writers for each section. The first writer drafts until he or she gets stuck, and then the second begins where the first stopped. Recirculate the drafts when revising and editing.
- Consider **intensive drafting** when working with a close friend or colleague. Assemble materials in a space where you can work undisturbed. Decide where each will begin drafting, and exchange sections at a certain time or as you finish segments. Continue exchanging drafts, or vary your pattern by having one person compose aloud as the other types.
- Use the "track changes" feature in most word-processing software to try **collaborative drafting** in an electronic file. This function shows changes to the original draft in a different color onscreen. Every member's changes will appear in the draft for review.

4c Drafting in digital environments

When you are creating simple texts on a computer, you can easily revise and edit as you write. Digital texts, especially Web pages and multimedia documents, may require different drafting strategies because of their less linear organization.

Work in chunks or sections. Multimedia documents, such as Web pages, are often structured by hyperlinks to other text, images, and media. You can therefore draft one page, section, or chunk at a time and then link the pieces together later. As you create each piece, however, keep referring to your visual outline of the entire site. Be ready to change the organization if you notice specific problems with the display of content or the way that one piece links to the others.

Use annotation features. Check your program for a "notes," "comments," or annotation feature. This can be especially helpful during your drafting process. For example, Paul Rutz has added some notes to himself in his draft. Later, he can easily delete the notes as he continues to revise his text.

Playing league hockey as a kid in North Dakota was more than a recreational sport; it was a family occupation and a community obsession. First there were the grueling schedules. You couldn't do real practices on the lakes in the winter; you still needed a rink. With all the teams competing for ice time, the only fair way for the rinks to accommodate everyone was to create a rotating schedule. For at least a few weeks during the season, that meant getting up at 4 a.m. and driving, sometimes for up to forty minutes, to a distant rink to practice.

Comment [PR1]: Include difficulty for parents of kids in younger leagues.

Comment [PR2]: Maybe describe what that's like in North Dakota in the dead of winter.

Some programs now include the option to record voice comments in your draft, which can save you time as you (or your readers or collaborators) insert notes and reminders for your next drafting session.

5 Revising, Editing, and Proofreading

Because so much of what we read is in final, published form, we forget the hours the author has spent **revising**—reconsidering content and structure in terms of community expectations, redrafting whole sections, and struggling to find just the right words. Revision is more than fine-tuning style, grammar, and sentence problems (**editing**) or searching for missing apostrophes and typographical errors (**proofreading**), important though these activities are. Instead, revision means *reading* your draft critically and *reworking* it to make effective changes. It means stepping outside the draft to assess its strengths and weaknesses and then deciding what to expand, clarify, reword, restructure—or just plain cut.

REVISING, EDITING, AND PROOFREADING	
Major revision	Focus on sections and chunks as part of the whole. Redraft, reorganize, add, and delete.
Minor revision	Focus on passages and paragraphs. Revise for sense, style, and economy.
Editing	Focus on paragraphs, sentences, and words. Edit for correctness and conventions (grammar, sentences, wording, punctuation, mechanics). Edit for clarity, style, and economy.
Proofreading	Focus on details and final appearance. Proofread for spelling, punctuation, typographical errors, and missing words.

5a Making major revisions

Concentrate first on **major revisions**, large-scale changes that make your draft as a whole more effective. For example, if your report seems too informal for your work community, you may decide to redraft its introduction, delete an anecdote, or add more alternative solutions. Think critically about content, structure, tone, style, appeals to audience, and purpose.

1 Redraft workable material

Rework ineffective parts, as Jessica White did with her opening.

ORIGINAL DRAFT I was a cheerleading captain and I loved basketball. I put a lot of work into my cheerleading season. We had great team spirit between the cheerleaders and the teammates. We led our crowd to great enthusiasm and spirit.

> **WRITER'S ASSESSMENT: I want people to feel what it was like after the state quarter-finals. This doesn't even say where I was or what was happening.**

REVISED DRAFT There we were, a bunch of cheerleaders packed into Rebecca's car. Everyone's spirits were soaring; we had won the quarter-final game of the state basketball championship. It was a bitterly cold night, but we laughed, joked, and endlessly replayed the highlights of the game.

> **STRATEGY**   **Use question marks.**
>
> Let your draft sit for a few hours or a day, and then read it (preferably aloud). Place a question mark next to any ineffective section. After you finish reading, go back to each question mark, and bracket the passage where the writing loses vitality or meaning. Ask yourself what you want to accomplish there, start a new page or file, and say it again.

2 Reorganize paragraphs or sections

An early draft may reflect your process of discovery instead of the best order for your readers or subject. Keyshawn Williams drafted a memo from a committee looking for ways to cut company expenses. He originally opened with the committee's conclusions, but the group revised the memo to give readers more context—concise background on the committee's task, a clear statement of the problem, and then the recommendations.

> **STRATEGY**   **Summarize your paragraphs.**
>
> Number the paragraphs in your draft, and write a phrase or sentence to sum up the main point of each. Use this list to spot paragraphs that you could combine or reorganize to create a clearer flow of ideas. Consider whether points at the end belong at the beginning. (See 2b and 6f.)

3 Add new material

An addition can develop a paragraph (see 6f), enliven a dull passage, clarify or extend a point, or supply missing detail. When Gina Giacomo revised her Web page explaining the transfer to a new email system, she added the underlined material to clarify the transition for readers.

Your new email address is listed below. It should be easy to remember because it consists of the first six letters of your name. You may send your new address to people or groups that send you messages, but you don't need to. Our server will automatically forward any mail directed to your old address.

> **STRATEGY** **Highlight paragraph openings and closings.**
>
> Highlight the first and last sentence in each paragraph. Read through these highlighted sentences, identifying any gaps where a paragraph doesn't connect clearly to the one before or after it or where information or detail is missing within the paragraph. (See 6d.)

4 Delete unnecessary material

Don't be afraid to slash away large chunks if they're unnecessary, illogical, or redundant, as Brian Corby did in his letter to the zoning board.

With eighteen stories, Regency Towers will cast a long, wide shadow over Piedmont Park. ~~The building will be quite tall and very wide.~~ For several hours a day, the toddler play area will be darkened. On summer afternoons, the shadow will cut across the baseball diamond. ~~This could be dangerous.~~

> **STRATEGY** **Make 10 percent cuts.**
>
> Imagine that your draft will be published if you trim at least 10 percent of the fat. Mark sentences where you can cut or paragraphs where you might merge the essentials. (See 44b.)

5b Making minor revisions

Minor revisions are fairly small changes, mostly refining and polishing passages for three reasons: *sense*, *style*, and *economy*.

1 Revise for sense

When you're immersed in your writing, you may forget what your reader *doesn't* know or think, leading to illogical or puzzling statements. Read your draft to see whether each passage *makes sense* in the context of the whole project. Try to look at the text as your readers might, not in your own way. If possible, ask peer readers to place question marks by any confusing text.

Paul Tichey asked his peer group to read his draft on Nevada's environmentally threatened wild mustangs. Paul revised after his readers said that they couldn't tell whether the Air Force was helping or harming the animals.

The Air Force *, which* was partly responsible for the ~~reduction in the~~ *demise*

~~number~~ *the* of~ wild mustangs on the Tonopah missile range /. ~~The Air~~ *has now*

joined forces with

~~Force is part of a team that also includes~~ the Bureau of Land

Management and a group of wild-horse preservationists. ~~All three~~

~~groups have banded together~~ to help~ *save* the wild mustangs~ *from dehydration and* ~~in this~~

death during the duration of the drought. ~~period of drought and dehydration.~~

2 Revise for style

Consider how your prose "sounds"—its rhythm and complexity. In any rough paragraph, place a +, √, −, or ? next to each sentence to indicate whether you feel positive, neutral, negative, or uncertain about it. Rewrite what you don't like; try to get readers' advice on questionable sentences. When in doubt, try an alternative. (See 42b, 45b, and 47c–d.)

Paul placed a minus sign next to the sentence below. He decided that too many words began with *d*, and *during the duration* seemed redundant.

The Air Force, which was partly responsible for the demise of

the wild mustangs on the Tonopah missile range, has now joined

forces with the Bureau of Land Management and a group of wild-

horse preservationists to help save the mustangs from~ *fatal*

dehydration~ *while the drought persists.* ~~and death during the duration of the drought.~~

3 Revise for economy

Cut what you can without losing sense or coherence. Paul reduced seventy-eight words to thirty-six—a cut of over 50 percent!

SECOND DRAFT A serious problem confronting groups who want to manage wild mustangs on military sites in Nevada is the relative inaccessibility of the sites, since many require security passes or are fenced off, and environmentalists can't come and go as they please, as they can on public or even some private land. It's simply harder to study or help horses on restricted military installations. Open rangeland has easier access, and inspectors can simply move in and out at will.

THIRD DRAFT (REVISED FOR ECONOMY) Restricted access to Nevada military sites presents a serious obstacle to successful horse management. Unlike open rangeland, where inspectors can come and go as they please, military sites are often fenced off and require security clearance.

Count your words.

Count the words in a passage that lacks economy. Then start cutting. See what percentage you can trim without changing meaning. (See 44b.)

5c Revising collaboratively

Honest feedback from a reader can refresh your perspective on your writing. When you act as a peer reader—or ask someone to read for you—first establish the writer's purpose, audience, and concerns.

- What sort of project is it? What is the writer trying to do?
- For what community is it intended? What do readers expect?
- What does the writer want to learn from a reader?

Mix praise and criticism.

Jot notes that balance praise with helpful criticism. Don't simply say, "It was really good," or give directions like "Move this to page 2." Instead, offer diplomatic advice: "What would happen if you moved this to page 2?"

Accept constructive comments from an honest reader gracefully. If you are defensive, your reader is unlikely to give you more feedback. But if a reader questions something you like, remember that you have the final say.

- Give your readers a list of your specific concerns about the draft.
- Minimize apologies. Everyone feels anxious about sharing a draft.
- If time is limited, consider taping reactions, meeting briefly to take notes on responses, emailing, or exchanging comments on the drafts.

5d Revising in digital environments

Keep a junk file. Unlike multiple versions of paper documents, texts revised on a computer leave no trace of their earlier versions unless you save your work and create a new, duplicate copy each time you revise.

A good way to preserve deleted material as you revise is to open a "junk" file with a name similar to that of your document (such as "hockey-paperjunk.doc"). When you cut material, paste it into the junk file and give it a label. Your junk file can also contain extra material, ideas, or references that you have not yet used in your project.

Track your changes. Many programs allow you to turn on a "track changes" feature that shows your changes as you make them, usually in a different color. Tracking changes can be useful when you want to document your revision or when several people work on a single text. You can save the version that displays the changes, make a copy, and then accept all the changes to see the revised version.

Compare documents. To compare two versions of the same document side by side, first save a copy of your draft. Then make revisions on the second copy. When you ask your word-processing program to compare the two versions, it will display all the changes you made. You can then decide which changes are most effective.

5e Editing

Editing means adjusting sentences and words for clarity, style, economy, and correctness. You can improve your editing skills each time you prepare a college paper, a public communication, or a work project. Allow plenty of time to read carefully, and shift your attention from content (what's said) to form (how it's said). Noticing readers' reactions during class or meetings can alert you to their individual and community sensitivities. Check your writing for both the problems readers identify and the features they admire. As you edit, focus on one issue at a time—commas, perhaps—while you scour your text for specific cases. Repeat the process for the next issue.

Many computer programs claim to offer shortcuts for editors. Some can identify features like passive voice verbs or calculate the average length of sentences. Nonetheless, they are no match for careful human readers and editors. They may skip errors or question correct sentences, and they can't help you adjust to different audiences or communities of readers and writers.

1 Edit for clarity, style, and economy

Most writing profits from final cosmetic surgery. If your grant proposal, oral presentation, letter to the editor, or other project has a length limit, edit ruthlessly to meet this expectation. Ask these questions as you edit.

- **Are my sentences clear and easy to read?** Try reading out loud. Whenever you stumble over the wording, rephrase or restructure.
- **Do I repeat some sentence structures too often?** If too many sentences begin with nouns or *I*, start some with prepositional phrases (see 31b-1) or subordinate clauses (see 31c and 43b–c).
- **Do any words seem odd or inappropriate?** If so, reword. Turn to a dictionary or thesaurus for help. (See 45b, 47d.)
- **If I had to cut ten words per page, which could I drop?** Cut, but avoid new problems (such as short, choppy sentences). (See 44b.)

DRAFT   The aligned pulleys are lined up so that they are located up above the center core of the machine.
READER'S REACTION: **This seems repetitive and boring.**

EDITED   The aligned pulleys are ~~lined up so that they are located~~ positioned ~~up~~ above ~~the center core of~~ the machine's core.

SERIOUS ERROR

2 Edit for grammatical problems

Editing for grammatical problems challenges you first to *recognize* the problem and then to *edit* to repair or eliminate it. The chart inside the back cover lists ten errors identified by academic readers as likely to irritate readers and call into question a writer's skills. The sections that discuss these errors are marked by an icon as seen in the margin here. In addition, this handbook's editing advice uses the recognize-revise pattern to help you identify errors and select a useful editing strategy.

> **STRATEGY**   Read for errors.
>
> - Read your paper from start to finish, circling or marking any errors in grammar, punctuation, and sentence logic. If you can quickly correct an error, do so. Otherwise, finish identifying problems, and then look up the relevant advice in this handbook or other references.
> - Read your paper again, this time marking all suspected problems in your text. Follow your instincts if you feel that a sentence is weak or flawed. Then look up the pertinent advice, and edit the errors or flaws. Ask a teacher, tutor, peer editor, colleague, or friend for advice as needed.

Paragraphs from Jim Tollefson's newsletter for his local nature conservancy show his circled errors and his edited version.

DRAFT WITH
ERRORS
MARKED
Critics of the endangered species act think it is too broad. Because some specie's may be less vital to environmental balance than others. They want to protect species selectively, however, scientists do not know which species are more important.

caps
fragment
apostrophe
who?
comma splice

EDITED   Critics of the Endangered Species Act think it is too broad because some species may be less vital to environmental balance than others. Our critics want to protect species selectively. However, scientists do not know which species are more important.

Look for patterns—repeated errors—that you recognize or that readers point out. Then you can make many corrections simply by identifying and repairing a specific type of error.

- Analyze your papers, keeping track of your repeated errors.
- Ask a teacher or expert writer to identify your *patterns* of error.
- Use the strategies in this book or create your own for *recognizing* and *editing* your errors. Collect them in a personal editing checklist.
- Use your checklist; replace items you master with new ones.

After editing her report on the effects of loud music, Carrie Brehe added this item to her editing checklist.

A lot sounds like one word but is actually two. Think of its opposite, a little. From the noise paper: "Alot of teenagers do not know how their hearing works." Strategy: Search for alot.

3 Edit for conventions

Writing correctly means recognizing and using the **conventions**—the options for grammar, sentence structure and style, word choice, punctuation, and mechanics—that readers expect you to use. Some conventions don't vary much across communities, such as using complete sentences or standard spelling in formal prose. In these cases, most writers try to avoid challenging readers' strongly held expectations. After all, a reader irritated by errors isn't likely to give you a high grade, promote you, join your civic crusade, or view you as an attentive writer.

Other conventions, however, vary with the context. For example, newspaper readers wouldn't be surprised to find only one comma in this sentence: *The suspect jumped from the car, evaded the officers and ran into the motel.* But many academic readers would expect a second comma to follow *officers*, perhaps citing the well-known guides of the Modern Language Association (MLA) and the American Psychological Association (APA) as authorities on this comma issue (see Chapters 26–27). Likewise, a chemist would use numerals (such as *12* or *84*) in a lab report, while an art historian might spell out *twelve* and *eighty-four* in an interpretive paper. Effective writers learn how to recognize and edit for various conventions to meet readers' expectations.

5f Editing collaboratively

When you edit collaboratively, you identify and talk about specific problems with "consulting readers," usually friends, peers, or colleagues who help you improve a particular writing project while you learn to identify and repair errors on your own. (See the guidelines on p. 29.)

> ### COLLABORATIVE EDITING GUIDELINES
>
> #### GUIDELINES FOR WRITERS
>
> - Revise content and organization first to prepare for editing. (If necessary, ask your reader for feedback on larger revisions instead. See 5c.)
> - Supply a clean draft; don't waste your reader's time on sloppiness.
> - Share your requirements or writing concerns with your reader.
>
> #### GUIDELINES FOR READERS
>
> - Use familiar labels and symbols for comments. (The terms in this handbook are generally accepted in academic, public, and work communities. See the list of symbols at the end of the book.)
> - Just note possible errors. Let the writer use a dictionary, a style guide, or this handbook to identify and repair each problem.
> - Be specific; *awkward* or *unclear* may not tell the writer exactly what's wrong. Briefly tell why something does or doesn't work.
> - Identify outright errors, but don't "take over" the draft. Rewriting sentences and paragraphs is the writer's job.
> - Look for patterns of error, noting repetition of the same mistakes.

5g Proofreading

After you've edited as thoughtfully as possible, it's time for **proofreading**, your last chance to make sure that errors in presentation don't annoy your reader or undermine your ideas and credibility as a writer. If mistakes accumulate in a college paper or project at work, these errors can lead to a poor assessment or hinder your advancement.

STRATEGY Focus your attention.

- Read out loud or even backwards from the last sentence to the first.
- Look for missing words, incorrect prepositions, missing punctuation marks (especially half of a pair of commas or parentheses), and accidental duplicates.
- Consciously fix your eyes on each word to be sure it doesn't contain transposed letters, typographical errors, and the like.

Your careful editing and proofreading will help ensure that your final version is clear, concise, and consistent.

6 Paragraphs

Every time you indent to begin a new paragraph, you give readers a signal: watch for a shift in topic, another perspective, or a special emphasis. Whether you are writing a history paper, a letter to the editor, or a memo at work, readers will expect your paragraphs to guide them. Revising paragraphs to increase *focus*, *coherence*, and *development* helps readers figure out what's important, how ideas and details logically connect, and what's coming up.

6a Unfocused paragraphs

When you concentrate on a main idea throughout, you create a paragraph that is **focused** because it doesn't stray into unrelated details. A paragraph is **unified** when all its sentences directly relate to its point. Ask questions to help you recognize unfocused paragraphs.

STRATEGY Ask questions for paragraph focus.

Use these questions to identify focused or unfocused paragraphs.

- What is the main point (or topic) in this paragraph?
- How many different topics does this paragraph cover?
- Is the focus announced to readers? Where? How?
- Does the paragraph elaborate on the main point? Do details fit the topic?

Jeanne Brown used questions to analyze a paragraph on color analysis.

UNFOCUSED

A color to look at is the color red. Red is often considered a very fast and sporty color for cars. Porsches that are red are likely to be chosen over blue ones. Red ties are often called "power ties." Red can also be a very daring color to wear. A woman who wears a long red dress and has painted fingernails to match is not a shy woman. She is going to be noticed and will revel in the attention.

READER'S REACTION: *My main point?* I want to talk about the effects red can have on people. I don't think that the focus on red's power is clear. *Focus announced to readers?* Not really. I need to say that I am discussing the effects red has, not simply that it is a color worth looking at. *Elaboration on the point?* No, not much. I need to help readers understand how each example explains my view of red's effect on moods and attitudes.

REVISED

Red is a color that can affect how people feel and react. Red makes heads turn, and the person associated with the color often ends up feeling important and influential. A red Porsche draws more attention than a blue one. A red tie, or "power tie," can be bold and assertive. Worn with a blue or gray suit, the touch of red makes the wearer stand out in a crowd and builds self-confidence. A woman wearing a long red dress with nails painted to match is probably not shy. She is going to be noticed and will revel in the attention because it reinforces her positive self-image.

6b Revising for focus

Help your readers recognize a paragraph's focus by stating your topic and your main idea or perspective in a **topic sentence**. Begin with this sentence when you want readers to grasp the point right away.

When writing jokes, it's a good idea to avoid vague generalizations. Don't just talk about "fruit" when you can talk about "an apple." Strong writing creates a single image for everyone in the crowd, each person imagining a very similar thing. But when you say "fruit," people are either imagining several different kinds of fruit or they aren't really thinking of anything in particular, and both things can significantly reduce their emotional investment in the joke. But when you say "an apple," everyone has a *clear picture*, and thus a feeling.

—JAY SANKEY, *Zen and the Art of Stand-Up Comedy*

Experiment with other topic sentence options: placing it at the end of the paragraph, repeating it at the end from a different perspective, implying it if your point is unmistakably clear, or adding a limiting or clarifying sentence to narrow your point. Supplement your topic sentences with section headings if readers expect them in a report or proposal.

STRATEGY Highlight topic sentences.

Skim your draft, using a highlighter (or bold type) to mark each topic sentence. When you note that one is missing or inadequate, read critically to decide whether to revise the topic sentence or refocus the paragraph. Skim your topic sentences again, tracing your explanation or argument through the draft as a whole.

6c Incoherent paragraphs

A paragraph is **coherent** if each sentence clearly leads a reader to the next or if the sentences form a recognizable, easy-to-understand arrangement.

Paragraphs may lack coherence if sentences are out of logical order or change topic so abruptly that readers must struggle to follow the thought.

STRATEGY **Questions for paragraph coherence.**

Use these questions to check paragraph coherence.

- What words name the topic and main points? Are they repeated?
- What transitions alert readers to relationships among sentences?
- What parallel words and structures highlight similar or related ideas?
- Does the arrangement of ideas and details clarify their relationships?

LACKS COHERENCE

Captain James Cook discovered the island of Hawaii in 1779. Mauna Kea, on Hawaii, is the tallest mountain in the Pacific. Cook might have noticed the many mountains on the island as he sailed into Kealakekua Bay. The island also has five major volcanoes. Mauna Loa, another mountain on the island, is a dormant volcano that last erupted in 1984. Kilauea is the most active volcano on earth. It continues to enlarge the land that makes up this largest island in the Hawaiian chain. The volcano sends forth lava continuously.

READER'S REACTION: This paragraph provides lots of information, but it's hard to follow because the ideas don't seem connected.

REVISED

In 1779, Captain James Cook sailed into Kealakekua Bay and discovered the island of Hawaii. As he entered the bay, did Cook **notice** the many **mountains** on the island? Perhaps he **noticed** Mauna Kea, the tallest **mountain** in the Pacific. Perhaps he **spotted** one or more of the five major **volcanoes**. **One of these,** Mauna Loa, is a dormant **volcano** that last erupted in 1984. **Another**, Kilauea, is the most active volcano on earth. It sends forth lava continuously. **In addition**, it keeps adding to the landmass of what is already the largest island in the Hawaiian chain.

6d Revising for coherence

By repeating key words, phrases, synonyms, and related words that refer to your topic and main point, you keep readers aware of your focus.

According to recent research, **people married for a long time** often develop similar **facial features**. The **faces** of **younger couples** show only chance resemblances. As **they** share emotions for many years, however, most **older couples** develop similar **expressions**.

Place key words prominently, beginning or ending sentences. Avoid burying them in the middle of sentences.

> ### USEFUL TRANSITIONS FOR SHOWING RELATIONSHIPS
>
> | | |
> |---|---|
> | **Time and Sequence** | next, later, after, while, meanwhile, immediately, earlier, first, second, shortly, in the future, subsequently, as long as, soon, since, finally, last, at that time, as soon as |
> | **Comparison** | likewise, similarly, also, too, again, in the same manner, in comparison, equally |
> | **Contrast** | in contrast, on the one hand . . . on the other hand, however, although, even though, still, yet, but, nevertheless, conversely, at the same time, despite, regardless |
> | **Examples** | for example, for instance, such as, specifically, thus, to illustrate, namely, in fact |
> | **Cause and Effect** | as a result, consequently, accordingly, if . . . then, is due to this, for this reason, because, as a consequence of, thus |
> | **Place** | next to, above, behind, beyond, near, here, across from, to the right, there, in front, in the background, in between, opposite |
> | **Addition** | and, too, moreover, in addition, besides, furthermore, next, also, finally, again |
> | **Concession** | of course, naturally, it may be the case that, granted, it is true that, certainly, though |
> | **Conclusion** | in conclusion, in short, as a result, as the data show, finally, therefore |
> | **Repetition** | to repeat, in other words, once again, as I said earlier |
> | **Summary** | on the whole, to summarize, to sum up, in short, therefore, in brief |

Transitional expressions like *in addition, therefore,* and *on the other hand* also alert readers to relationships among sentences.

Many people still consider your college choice your most important career decision. These days, **however**, graduate school is the most important choice **because** the competition for jobs has grown fiercer. **For example**, business positions at the entry level often go to people with MBAs and law degrees. **In addition**, many good jobs require advanced training and skills. **Moreover**, employers pay attention **not only** to the presence of an advanced degree on your résumé **but also** to the program of study **and** the quality of the school.

You can also link elements by using **parallelism**—repeating the same grammatical structures to highlight similar or related ideas (see 42b).

6e Poorly developed paragraphs

Paragraph development provides the examples, facts, concrete details, explanations, or supporting arguments that make a paragraph informative enough to support your ideas, opinions, and conclusions. Short paragraphs are not always underdeveloped, nor are long paragraphs always adequate—yet length can be an important cue. More than two sentences are generally necessary for a paragraph to explore a topic and support a generalization.

UNDERDEVELOPED

Recycling is always a good idea—or *almost* always. Recycling some products, even newsprint and other paper goods, may require more energy from fossil fuels and more valuable natural resources than making them over again.

READER'S REACTION: I'd like to know more before I agree with this. What are these products? How much energy does it take to recycle them? What natural resources do they consume?

STRATEGY Check paragraph development.

- Does the paragraph present enough material to *inform* readers?
- Does the paragraph adequately *support* any generalizations?

6f Revising for development

Examples, whether brief or extended, help clarify a concept, explain a generalization, or provide reasons to support your position. They help a reader see an idea in action and its consequences.

BRIEF EXAMPLES

All kinds of products have been included in the fast-track recalls. For example, a major manufacturer recently recalled tens of thousands of humidifiers that could potentially overheat or catch fire. A leading manufacturer of children's products recalled tens of thousands of baby monitors that could smoke and flame. A prominent clothing retailer recalled more than 100,000 children's jackets with zipper pulls containing unacceptable levels of lead. A well-known company recalled tens of thousands of gas grills because a defective hose could leak gas or cause fires.

—"Fast-Track Recalls," *Consumer Product Safety Review*

EXTENDED EXAMPLE

One day in 1957, the songwriter Johnny Mercer received a letter from Sadie Vimerstedt, a widowed grandmother who worked behind a cosmetics counter in Youngstown, Ohio. Mrs. Vimerstedt suggested Mercer write a song called "I Want to Be Around to Pick Up the Pieces When Somebody Breaks Your Heart." Five years later, Mercer got in touch to say he'd written the song and that Tony Bennett would record it. Today, if you look at the label on any recording of "I Wanna Be Around," you'll notice that the credits for words and music are shared by Johnny Mercer and Sadie Vimerstedt. The royalties were split fifty-fifty, too, thanks to which Mrs. Vimerstedt and her heirs have earned more than $100,000. In my opinion, Mercer's generosity was a class act.   —John Berendt, "Class Acts"

STRATEGY **Add details and specifics to develop paragraph content.**

- **Examples.** Use brief or extended illustrations.
- **Concrete detail.** Recreate sights, sounds, tastes, smells, movements, and sensations of touch.
- **Facts and statistics.** Offer precise data from your fieldwork or authoritative sources, perhaps in numerical form.
- **Supporting statements.** Explain your own interpretations, or quote people or sources that readers will trust.
- **Summaries.** Present other people's opinions, conclusions, or explanations in compressed form (see 20g), showing how your conclusions agree with, disagree with, or supplement theirs.

Patterns of development help you accomplish familiar tasks so that readers can readily recognize the purpose and arrangement of a paragraph or a cluster of paragraphs.

Narrating. Turn to **narration** to recount past or present events, recreate an experience, tell an anecdote, or envision the future.

Describing. You can create images of a place, an object, or a feeling or sketch a person's character through **description**, emphasizing emotional impact (**subjective description**) or physical details (**objective description**).

Comparing and contrasting. Paragraphs that **compare** and **contrast** can evaluate alternative policies or products, examine pros and cons, or compare qualities and explanations. A **point-by-point organization** examines each comparable feature for first one subject and then the next.

PATTERNS FOR PARAGRAPH DEVELOPMENT

TASK	DEVELOPMENT STRATEGY
Tell a story; recreate events; present an anecdote	Narrating
Provide detail about a scene or object; portray someone's character; evoke a feeling	Describing
Explore similarities or differences; evaluate alternatives	Comparing and contrasting
Provide directions; explain the operation of a mechanism, procedure, or natural process	Explaining a process
Separate a subject into parts; explore the relationships among parts	Dividing
Sort things or people into groups; explain the relationships among the groups	Classifying
Explain the meaning of a term or concept; explore and illustrate the meaning of a complicated concept or phenomenon	Defining
Consider why something did happen (or might); explore possible causes and results	Analyzing causes and effects

TOPIC SENTENCE   But biology has a funny way of confounding expectations. Rather than disappear, the evidence for innate sexual **Feature 1** differences only began to mount. In medicine, researchers documented that heart disease strikes men at a younger **Feature 2** age than it does women and that women have a more moderate **Feature 3** physiological response to stress. Researchers found subtle neurological differences between the sexes both in the brain's **Feature 4** structure and in its functioning. In addition, another generation of parents discovered that, despite their best efforts to give baseballs to their daughters and sewing kits to their sons, girls still flocked to dollhouses while boys clambered into tree forts. Perhaps nature is more important than nurture after all.   —CHRISTINE GORMAN, "Sizing Up the Sexes"

A **subject-by-subject organization** considers each subject in its entirety, within a paragraph or a series of paragraphs.

Topic sentence   For everyone, home is a place to be offstage. But the **Subject 1** comfort of home can have opposite and incompatible meanings for women and men. For many men, the comfort of home means freedom from having to prove themselves and impress through verbal display. At last, they are in a situation where talk is not required. They are free to **Subject 2** remain silent. But for women, home is a place where they are free to talk, and where they feel the greatest need for talk, with those they are closest to. For them, the comfort of home means the freedom to talk without worrying about how their talk will be judged.

—DEBORAH TANNEN, "Put Down That Paper and Talk to Me!"

Explaining a process. To give directions, show how a mechanism or procedure works, or explain other processes, label the steps or stages clearly. Arrange them logically, usually chronologically. Devote a paragraph to each part of the process if you wish to emphasize its stages.

Dividing and classifying. To divide a subject, you split it into parts, explaining it and the relationships of its parts. To classify, you sort several subjects into groups, exploring similarities *within* groups and differences and relationships *between* groups.

CLASSIFICATION

Men all have different styles of chopping wood, all of which are deemed by their practitioners as the only proper method. Often when I'm chopping wood in my own inept style, a neighbor will come over and "offer help." He'll bust up a few logs in his own manner, advising me as to the proper swing and means of analyzing the grain of the wood. There are "over the head" types and "swing from the shoulder" types, and guys who lay the logs down horizontally on the ground and still others who balance them on end, atop of stumps. I have one neighbor who uses what he calls "vector analysis." Using the right vectors, he says, the wood will practically *split itself.*

—JENNIFER FINNEY BOYLAN, "The Bean Curd Method"

Defining. When you introduce a term or concept to your readers, you may need to stipulate the meaning it will carry in your writing or want to contrast its definition with others.

You can eat lunch at a food court, as in any other restaurant, but a food court has some special traits. Go to a food court to see but not be heard. The open space jammed with tables will give you a chance to see and be seen; yet the clatter and bustle will make real conversation impossible. Food courts are world tours—Thai, Mexican, Chinese, and Italian with a side of sushi—where you can buy hot dogs, nuggets, and chocolate chip cookies. The quality beats a fast-food outlet but not a good restaurant. For two dollars more than a burger and fries and seven dollars less than a tablecloth and a waiter, food courts deliver a meal that comes somewhere in between.   —BIPIN ROY, College Student

Analyzing causes and effects. You may explain why something has occurred (causes), explore consequences (effects), or combine both.

> Television used to depress me with forecasts of stormy weather, losers on game shows, and dramas of failed love. Then I learned to control the future. What caused me to acquire this skill? One day, upset with my favorite team's losing ways, I turned the television off and sat on the couch imagining a great comeback. Now when people ask me why I turn off the set before the end of a show, I tell them that this way my imagination can reunite long-separated lovers, help contestants with prize-winning answers, and create an upcoming week of warm, sunny days without a drop of rain.
>
> —DAZHANE ROBINSON, College Student

6g Special-purpose paragraphs

Introductory paragraphs build your relationship with readers, motivating them to continue reading. They can establish the tone, approach, and degree of formality expected by readers in an academic, public, or work community. They typically should answer questions like the following.

- What is the main idea or purpose of this writing project?
- What precise topic, problem, or issue will this text address?
- Why should readers be interested in this topic?

This opening paragraph introduces a discussion of the special relationship of past and present, for people as well as places, that characterizes Las Vegas's culture.

> Las Vegas, perhaps more than any other city in the world, promotes a culture of reinvention. It's a place where people come to start over, but it's also a place where buildings never get old—they simply get demolished.   —"Vegas Implosions," *http://www.vegasimplosions.com*

Concluding paragraphs may remind readers of key ideas and encourage them to think about information presented or actions proposed.

> So if it's any consolation to those of us who just don't manage to fit enough sleep into our packed days, being chronically tired probably won't do us any permanent harm. And if things get desperate enough, we just might have to schedule a nap somewhere on our busy calendars.   —DANIEL GOLEMAN, "TOO LITTLE, TOO LATE"

Linking paragraphs work together to form a coherent whole. Add links to clarify their relationships within a cluster or section. Key words and transitional expressions (see 6d) identify connections between paragraphs just as they do between sentences. Specific sentences and paragraphs also can connect sections in a paper—supplying previews, bridges, and summaries.

CREATING INTRODUCTORY PARAGRAPHS

Provide background, context, or history.

Explain an issue.

Present the sides in a controversy.

Use an extended example.

Quote from an authority.

Compare another situation, time period, or issue.

Describe a mysterious or interesting phenomenon.

Tell an anecdote or story, or recall an event.

Supply a definition.

Ask a question.

Offer an intriguing analogy.

Quote someone's opinion.

Provide statistics to define the issue or problem.

Cite pertinent or little-known facts.

Avoid obvious generalizations, shopworn phrases, apologies, and references to your own title.

CREATING CONCLUDING PARAGRAPHS

Summarize main points briefly.

Restate the thesis, or repeat proposed recommendations.

Echo the introduction.

Use a quotation.

Offer a striking example, anecdote, or image.

Predict future events or speculate.

Avoid apologies, overstatements, new ideas, and simply rewording your thesis statement.

STRATEGY Link paragraphs to guide readers.

- Announce your purpose to help readers anticipate your reasoning.
- Provide a **boundary statement**—a sentence beginning one paragraph but acting as a bridge from the paragraph before. Remind the reader of material covered earlier as you present the topic sentence.
- Add a short **planning paragraph** to help readers anticipate the arrangement of the upcoming discussion.
- Create a **signal paragraph** to alert readers to a major change in direction or the beginning of a new section.
- Use a brief **summary paragraph** to mark the end of a discussion or to review main points for readers.

7 Effective Sentences

Most people would find the following sentence hard to read.

INDIRECT OR EVASIVE   It is suggested that employee work cooperation encouragement be used for product quality improvement.

READER'S REACTION: Who is suggesting this? What is "employee work cooperation encouragement"?

CLEAR   We will try to improve our products by encouraging employees to work cooperatively.

You can make sentences easier to read by creating clear subjects and verbs as well as direct sentence structures.

7a Unclear sentences

A clear sentence answers the question "Who does what (to whom)?" When a sentence doesn't readily answer this question, try to make its subject and verb easy to identify. (See 31a.)

                   subject   verb   object
CLEAR   The research team investigated seizure disorders in infants.
                   who?   does what?

                   subject   verb
CLEAR   The seizures often become harmful.
                   who?   does what?

You can create complex yet clear sentences by making the main elements— especially subjects and verbs—easy for readers to identify.

UNCLEAR   One suggestion offered by physicians is that there is a need to be especially observant of a child's behavior during the first six months in order to notice any evidence of seizures.

CLEAR   Physicians suggest that parents watch children carefully during the first six months for evidence of seizures.

7b Revising for clear sentences

As you edit for clarity, work on any recurring sentence features identified as unclear by your readers, or use the strategies that follow.

1 Concentrate on subjects

Sentences whose subjects name important ideas, people, topics, things, or events are generally easy for readers to understand.

STRATEGY Ask questions to clarify significant subjects.

- Who (or what) am I talking about here?
- Is this what I want to emphasize?

UNFOCUSED You run the greatest risk if you expose yourself to tanning machines as well as the sun because both of them can damage the skin.

READER'S REACTION: I thought the focus was the danger, whether sunbathing or tanning. Why are they both buried in the middle?

POSSIBLE REVISION Either **the sun or a tanning machine** can damage the skin, and you run the greatest risk from exposure to **both** of them.

Watch out for nominalizations. When you create a noun (*completion, happiness*) from another kind of word such as a verb (*complete*) or an adjective (*happy*), the result is a **nominalization**, often ending in *-tion, -ence, -ance, -ing,* or *-ness*. Nominalizations usefully name ideas but may obscure information or distract readers from your focus. Be sure each sentence tells who did what (to whom).

USEFUL **Sleepiness** causes accidents at work and on the road.

Replace weak nominalizations with clear subjects.

WEAK Stimulation of the production of serotonin by a glass of milk or a carbohydrate snack causes sleepiness.

READER'S REACTION: Why does this advice on getting a good night's sleep start off with *stimulation*?

EDITED **A glass of milk or a carbohydrate snack** stimulates the production of serotonin and causes sleepiness.

Pay attention to noun strings. Sometimes one noun modifies another or nouns plus adjectives modify other nouns: *sleep deprivation, jet lag, computer network server, triple bypass heart surgery*. Although unfamiliar **noun strings** can be hard to understand, familiar ones can be concise and clear.

To edit confusing noun strings, try turning the key word in a string (usually the last noun) into a verb. Then turn other nouns from the string into prepositional phrases.

CONFUSING   The team did a ceramic valve lining design flaw analysis.

READER'S REACTION: **Did the team analyze flaws or use a special feature called flaw analysis? Did they study ceramic valves or valve linings made of ceramic material?**

EDITED   The team **analyzed** flaws **in** the lining design **for** ceramic valves.

Another option is to turn one noun into the sentence's subject.

EDITED   **Flaws** in the lining design for ceramic valves were analyzed by the team.

Use *I, we,* and *you.* *I, we,* and *you,* although inappropriate in some academic settings, are commonly used in work and public communities. (See 40a.)

VAGUE AND WEAK   The project succeeded because of careful cost control and attention to the customer's needs.

CLEAR AND FORCEFUL   The project succeeded because **we** controlled costs carefully and paid attention to **our** customers' needs.

2 Concentrate on verbs and predicates

Strong verbs can make sentences forceful and clear. Here are four steps you can take to strengthen your verbs.

1. Replace the verb *be* (*is, are, was, were, will be*) with a more forceful verb, especially in sentences that list or identify qualities.

   WEAK   Our agency **is** responsible for all aspects of disaster relief.

   STRONGER   Our agency **plans**, **funds**, and **delivers** disaster relief.

2. Turn nouns that follow forms of *be* into clear, specific verbs.

   WEAK   The new recycling system is a **money saver**.

   STRONGER   The new recycling system **saves money**.

3. Replace **expletive** constructions—sentences beginning with *there is, there are,* or *it is* (see 31a-1)—if they are wordy or obscure. (Keep them if they add variety, build suspense, or usefully withhold information about the doer.)

   WEAK   **There is** a need for more classrooms at Kenny School.

   STRONGER   **Kenny School needs** more classrooms.

4. Eliminate general verbs (*do, give, have, get, provide, shape, make*) linked to nouns; turn the nouns into verbs.

WEAK	Our company **has done a study** of the new design.
STRONGER	Our company **has studied** the new design.

ESL ADVICE: *THERE* AND *IT* AS SUBJECTS

When you use *there* and *it* as the subjects of sentences, these pronouns may not have the object or place meanings usually attached to them. *There* may introduce new, unknown material, while *it* may introduce environmental conditions (including distance, time, and weather).

DRAFT	Although there was snowing, it was dancing after dinner.
EDITED	Although **it** was snowing, **there** was dancing after dinner.

3 Select active or passive voice

When you use a verb in the **active voice** (see 32i), the agent (or doer) is also the subject of the sentence.

> agent   action   goal
> The outfielder caught the towering fly ball.
> subject   verb   object

When you choose the **passive voice** (see 32i), you turn the sentence's goal into the subject. You de-emphasize the doer by placing it in a prepositional phrase or by dropping an unknown or unimportant agent altogether.

> goal   action   [agent]
> The towering fly ball was caught [by the outfielder].
> subject   verb   [prepositional phrase]

Many writers favor the active voice because it is direct and concise, and many readers find too much passive voice weak. On the other hand, the passive voice may be favored in lab reports and other scientific or technical writing in both academic and work communities. It avoids spotlighting the researcher or repeating the researcher's actions; instead it focuses on results—what happens, not who does it. It also may be used ethically to protect the identity of someone such as a child or the victim of crime or abuse. At the same time, it may inadvertently, or even deliberately, conceal a doer (or agent), thus obscuring responsibility for actions.

AGENT DE-EMPHASIZED	Federal tax forms have been mailed. [By the IRS, of course.]
AGENT CONCEALED	Hasty decisions were made in this zoning case. [By whom?]

Rewrite sentences in the passive voice that add extra words, create inappropriate emphasis, or omit the doer (see 40c).

	subject
PASSIVE VOICE (15 WORDS)	**Three thousand people** affected by the toxin were interviewed agent by **the Centers for Disease Control**.
	agent (subject)
ACTIVE VOICE (13 WORDS)	**The Centers for Disease Control** interviewed three thousand people affected by the toxin.

7c Revising for variety and emphasis

If you feel that editing for clarity produces too many similar sentences, try some of the following options to direct the attention of your readers.

- Emphasize material by shifting it to the places where a reader's attention gravitates—the **sentence opening or closing**.
- **Repeat key words and ideas** within a sentence or cluster of sentences to draw attention to them. (Avoid too much repetition that calls attention to itself rather than your ideas.)
- Try **climactic sentence order**—sentences that build to a climax—to create powerful emphasis. Such sentences can stress new information at the end or focus on the last element in a series.
- Try an occasional **periodic sentence**. By piling up phrases, clauses, and words at the start, create suspense by delaying the main clause.
- Consider creating a **cumulative sentence**. Start with the main clause, and then add, bit by bit, details and ideas in the form of modifying phrases, clauses, and words to build a detailed picture, an intricate explanation, or a cluster of ideas and information.
- Vary your **sentence length**. Add short sentences for dramatic flair. Use longer ones to explore relationships among ideas and build rhythmic effects. Use middle-length sentences as workhorses, carrying the burden of explanation, but don't use too many in a sequence.
- Vary your sentence types (see 31d-2). **Declarative sentences** present, explain, and support ideas or information. An occasional exclamation (**exclamatory sentence**), a mild order (**imperative sentence**), or a question (**interrogative sentence**) can change your pace.
- Surprise your readers on occasion. Add **key words** to summarize and redirect a sentence. **Extend a sentence** that appears to have ended, adding new information or twists of thought. Use parallelism (see 42b) to highlight a contrast in a witty, dramatic, or ironic **antithesis**.

PART 2

Critical Reading, Thinking, and Argument

▼ TAKING IT ONLINE

CRITICAL THINKING CONSORTIUM
http://www.criticalthinking.org/
This Web site provides a variety of resources, including materials on critical thinking in academic and business contexts.

CRITICAL THINKING ADVICE
http://www.canberra.edu.au/studyskills/learning/critical/
This Australian site is an excellent resource for information about, and strategies for, all aspects of critical thinking.

READING YOUR TEXTBOOKS EFFECTIVELY AND EFFICIENTLY
http://www.dartmouth.edu/~acskills/success/reading.html
Follow the links here for techniques that can help anyone be a more effective reader.

THE BASIC PRINCIPLES OF PERSUASIVE WRITING
http://www.writingcentre.ubc.ca/workshop/tools/argument.htm
Review logical, emotional, and ethical appeals along with the characteristics of sound evidence for persuasive writing.

GUIDE TO THE LOGICAL FALLACIES
http://www.nizkor.org/features/fallacies
Author of a Macintosh tutorial gave permission for his work to appear at this site. Forty-two fallacies are described and explained with examples.

TECHNICAL VISUALS
http://www.umaine.edu/ptw/techvisuals/tip3.htm
Provides advice for constructing effective drawings, diagrams, flowcharts, tables, and graphs.

PART 2

Critical Reading, Thinking, and Argument

8 Reasoning Critically

What convinces people to accept your conclusions, to share your views, to follow your recommendations, or to trust your explanations? An important factor is your **critical reasoning** or **critical thinking**: the careful, logical, insightful thought your writing (or speaking) embodies.

WRITER **1**   Foreign language classes are a waste of money. Anybody with a brain knows that all our kids need is English.

   READER'S REACTION: **Don't children need language skills for business or travel—or for talking with family or others who don't speak English? And why attack people without giving any reasons or evidence?**

WRITER 2   Although foreign language requirements motivate some students, others are discouraged by required courses. For example, a survey of recent graduates showed . . .

   READER'S REACTION: **I'm not sure about this, but the writer notes several views and sounds reasonable. Let's see the evidence.**

Writer 1 opens with an opinion—and then simply restates it while attacking others. In contrast, Writer 2 begins to reason—presenting a point of view, recognizing other views, providing reasons and evidence. When you write or speak, the quality of your thinking contributes to your **persona**, the representation of yourself that you create for an audience. Do you present yourself as thoughtful, informed, fair—hence persuasive? Or do you seem illogical, careless, imprecise, or uninterested in other views?

8a Recognizing critical reasoning

Critical reasoning, a process of thinking through a problem, asking a question, or explaining, has four major characteristics.

- Reaches logical or reasonable conclusions supported by evidence
- Questions assumptions and tries to see differing outlooks
- Draws on precise information and clearly defined ideas
- Desires to go beyond the superficial to reach fresh insights

Good critical thinking means that you search for better evidence, consider alternatives, and check your logic to confirm, modify, or even reverse your conclusion. (See also Chapter 10.)

Critical Reasoning in Academic, Public, and Work Communities

	Academic	Public	Work
GOAL	Analysis of text, phenomenon, or creative work to interpret, explain, or offer insights	Participation in democratic processes to contribute, inform, or persuade	Analysis of problems to supply information and propose solutions
REASONING PROCESS	Detailed reasoning, often explained at length, with tight logic leading to conclusions	Plausible reasoning, not ranting, focused on supporting own point of view	Accurate analysis of problem or need with clear explanation of solution
SPECIAL INTERESTS	Crucial citations of others as well as insights beyond common knowledge	Shared values and goals, often local, that support a cause or policy	Sharp focus on task, problem, or goal that promotes organization
EVIDENCE	Specific references to detailed evidence, gathered and presented to support conclusions	Relevant evidence, often local or interest-oriented, to support claims and substantiate probabilities	Sufficient evidence to show the importance of the problem and to justify an appropriate solution
VIEWPOINT	Balanced treatment recognizing and explaining other views	Fair recognition of other views, interests, and goals	Awareness of alternatives and likely results of actions

---

STRATEGY   Use insights of others to improve your reasoning.

- Use face-to-face or electronic discussions (see 13b–c) to identify issues, conclusions, evidence, and possible objections to your view.
- Put your tentative thoughts on paper, and then read what others say in order to identify gaps in your evidence or logic.
- Ask others to read your drafts critically and to identify reasonable objections so you can address them as you revise.
- Put your work aside for a while; then read it as your readers might. Note any gaps that undermine clarity, persuasiveness, or credibility.

8b Building a chain of reasoning

Critical thinking works toward a **chain of reasoning**, the path you take in linking observations, interpretations, conclusions, and evidence as you explore an academic topic, recommend a change at work, or urge people to take a stand. Some links in your chain may supply *information*: examples, facts, details, data. Others may offer *ideas*: reasons, comments by authorities, other views, analysis, logical argument. (See 10d.)

1 Reach conclusions

The important end point of a chain of reasoning—your **main conclusion**—is likely to be stated in an argumentative or academic thesis (see 3b-2). You may even offer multiple conclusions, such as adding work-stations *and* upgrading software to track inventory.

TYPES OF CONCLUSIONS YOU MIGHT DRAW

- **Interpretations** of meaning (experience, film, literature), importance (current or past event), or cause and effect (problem, event)
- **Analyses** of elements of a problem, situation, phenomenon, scientific topic, academic subject, issue, or disagreement
- **Propositions** about an issue, problem, policy, or disagreement
- **Judgments** about "right" or "wrong" (action, policy), quality (perfor-mance, creative work), or effectiveness (solution, proposed action)
- **Warnings** of consequences of action or failure to act
- **Recommendations** for guidelines, policies, or solutions
- **Plans** for further study, direct action, or involvement of others

TYPES OF INFORMATION THAT CAN SUPPORT CONCLUSIONS

- **Background** to supply the scope and substance of an issue, subject, or problem through history, context, or consequences
- **Evidence** to provide reasons for accepting conclusions as accurate, valuable, or important
- **Subject knowledge** to provide in-depth understanding

STRATEGY **Focus on your conclusions.**

- List all your conclusions (interpretations, opinions, and so on). Use an outline, colored highlighters, a cluster or tree diagram, or two columns to identify and relate main and supporting conclusions.
- Review your conclusions. Do others come to mind? Are any important ones missing? Do you need to develop them?
- Think as readers might. Will they see any assertions as interpretations or judgments? Will they expect—and accept—your conclusions?

2 Provide supporting information

A chain of reasoning needs both information and inferences. **Information** includes facts of all kinds—examples, data, details, quotations—that you pre-sent as reliable, confirmable, or generally undisputed. Information turns into

evidence when it's used to persuade a reader that an idea is reasonable. **Inferences** or **generalizations**, often stated in a thesis (see 3b), are your conclusions based on and supported by information.

Review your work to make sure you have distinguished between information and inference.

- List the key facts about your subject. Which will readers see as undisputed? Which can you confirm with observation or reliable sources? If facts are disputed, what reasons support your presentation?
- Next list your inferences. Which reflect your understanding? Which do the facts imply? Which *might* happen as a result of the facts?

TYPES OF EVIDENCE

Examples of an event, idea, person, or place, brief or extended, from personal experience or research

Details about an idea, place, situation, or phenomenon

Information about times, places, participants, numbers, surroundings, consequences, and relationships

Statistics, perhaps presented in tables or charts

Background on context, history, causes, or effects

Quotations from experts, participants, or other writers

---

3 Assess evidence and reasoning

Readers expect you to select evidence carefully and to link it reasonably with assertions—that is, to proceed logically. (See also 10d and 10f.) Ask yourself questions to evaluate evidence as you read and write.

- How *abundant* is the evidence? Is it *sufficient* to support your claim?
- Does it *directly* support the claim?
- How *relevant, accurate,* and *well documented* is the evidence?

Proceeding logically is complicated when evidence persuades one audience but not another. Consider, for example, how two citizen groups might respond to a proposed greenway between parks in two neighborhoods, one in economically depressed Coolidge and the other in wealthy Lake Stearns. Starting from the assumption that the generally law-abiding residents of Coolidge are deprived of shopping and services that have left the area because of a high crime rate, the Coolidge Consortium logically supports the greenway because it will give residents access to recreation and shopping in Lake Stearns. In contrast, starting from the assumption that the balance of a peaceful, low-crime neighborhood can easily be upset, a Lake Stearns group argues logically that, although most Coolidge residents are law-abiding, the greenway will draw habitual criminals who will undermine the quality of life in both neighborhoods. Each side reasons logically, but each starts with different assumptions and arrives at different conclusions. (See also 10f.)

> **STRATEGY**   **Evaluate your assumptions.**
>
> Ask questions like these to identify and evaluate your assumptions.
>
> - How do I view the groups of people on each side of this issue?
> - What will my readers want in a plan that addresses this problem?
> - What do specialists in the field see as questions worth investigating?
> - What might my peers suggest about my answers to these questions?

4 Review your assumptions

Some of your assumptions and values are easy to identify, but others are unspoken. After hearing the talk at work about efficiency, you might think your readers there want only to cut costs. But saving jobs and offering a quality product are also goals. The success of your reasoning may depend on how closely your assumptions match those of your audience.

- List your assertions that identify cause-effect links, classify, compare, connect generalizations and examples, or define (see 6f). Delete or rethink any that are weak or possibly illogical (see 10d).
- To spot weak reasoning, imagine a skeptical reader's reactions.

> WEAK   Violence in schools is rising because of increased violence in movies and on TV.
>
> READER'S REACTION: **Is this true? My kids watch TV, but they aren't more violent than I was as a kid when TV was far less violent.**

8c Representing your reasoning

How you present yourself and your reasoning to readers can do much to shape their willingness to accept your reasoning.

1 Be well informed

Issues, ideas, and insights are embedded in social, occupational, historical, or disciplinary contexts around a topic. (See also 10b–d.) List what you know about your topic and its context. Note key areas, given your purpose. Define what's unclear, and strategize about how to fill the gaps.

2 Include readers' perspectives and likely reactions

If you fail to acknowledge other views, contrary arguments, conflicting evidence, or different solutions, your readers may find your presentation one-sided and question your credibility. By anticipating such reactions, even in a thesis (see 3b), you complete your chain of reasoning and build readers' confidence in your conclusions. (See 10d.)

3 Be balanced and reasonable

Emotional language may be just right for urging public action. The same language might irritate, even offend, coworkers or academic readers expecting critical analysis. As you pick the words and tone to represent your thinking, you create an image of yourself—a **persona**—whose qualities may make readers trust you, dislike you, or find your views rash.

4 Assess the appropriateness of strong bias

Writing effectively means knowing when to be cool and logical and when to show emotion. At work, bias is expected when you represent an organization but not when you write objective reports. In public, your devotion to a cause generally will be accepted as such, but your academic writing should favor unimpassioned reasoning.

9 Reading Critically

When you read, you almost always respond, and responding can turn into critical understanding as well as writing of your own. **Critical reading**—interacting with a text and developing your own ideas, often in the form of notes—is a rich source for further writing. Whatever you read, including essays, articles, memos, reports, and Web pages, pay attention both to understanding the text and to developing your own critical perspective.

9a Reading to understand

Like most people, you probably begin to read by going to the first page and plunging into the text. By starting "cold," however, you may have too much to do at once: understand the details in the text, grasp the writer's conclusions, and develop your critical responses. Instead, you may want to "warm up" by previewing a text and developing a reading plan.

1 Preread

Begin by figuring out the "big" features that shape a text's meaning, ideas, or relationship to readers before you jump right into the text.

> **Preview the form.** Locate features that suggest the text's approach: long paragraphs or short, opening abstract, headings, sidebars, frames, glossary, references, links, visuals, one column or more.
>
> **Preview the organization.** Skim a book's table of contents. Look for headings in articles, reports, or memos. Click on the site map.
>
> **Examine the context.** Consider the author's background, the original readers and situation, the place and date of first publication, or a Web site's sponsor.
>
> **Sample and predict.** Scan the text to activate your own knowledge and prepare for interpreting unfamiliar words and examples in context. Look up baffling words before you read. Recall similar texts; try to predict where the reading will go.
>
> **Learn some background.** Talk to peers, coworkers, or others who know a difficult subject. Find an encyclopedia entry on key concepts.
>
> **Plan ahead.** When you read Web pages or library articles, consider printing or duplicating the text so you can write on your own copy.

2 Follow a reading plan

As you read, look for the generalizations and conclusions that will help you make sense of unfamiliar material. Focus on beginnings—the thesis that guides the introduction, general statements that open sections, and topic sentences that begin paragraphs (see 3b, 6b, and 6g). Look for paragraphs that supply an overview of the main ideas and the organization. In addition, set aside extra time for sections devoted to new information and insights.

> **Find what's important.** Read first—*without highlighting*—to capture the essentials. Go back again to note what's *really* important.
>
> **Read the visuals.** Examine graphs, charts, diagrams, or other illustrations; analyze what they say and how they relate to the written text.
>
> **Pause and assess.** Where are you? What have you learned so far? What confuses you? Jot down your answers; then skim what you've just read.
>
> **Summarize in chunks.** Glance back over a section, and state the main point so far. Guess where the reading will go next.
>
> **Share insights.** Meet with classmates or coworkers to discuss a text. Compare reactions, considering how the others reached their interpretations.

52

9b
read

Reading Critically

3 Respond after reading

When you read carefully, you respond to the content and evaluate it according to your purposes and the standards of the community of readers and writers to which a text is addressed.

Record main ideas. Use a file card, journal, or computer file so you can review without leafing through copies, printouts, or books.

Add your own responses. Note what you already know as well as your own views about the topic. Don't simply accept what the author says.

Reread and review. Reread difficult material, first skimming more quickly and then studying the passages you've highlighted.

Write in your text. If a book or other text isn't yours, don't write in it. If it—or a photocopy or printout—is yours, annotate it.

STRATEGY   **Annotate a text.**

Write brief responses like these, perhaps in the margins.

- **Interpretations:** What does the author or speaker mean?
- **Confusions:** At what points are you puzzled?
- **Questions:** What more do you need to know?
- **Objections or counterarguments:** Where do you disagree?
- **Restatements:** How can you say it in your own words?
- **Evaluations:** What do you like or dislike about the reading?
- **Applications:** What can you use for class, work, or activities?
- **Expectations:** How does this reading resemble or differ from others typical in your academic, public, or work community?

9b Reading to respond and evaluate

Your purposes and context shape your responses as a reader. If you are gathering details for an essay or oral presentation, your **analytical reading** will focus on *understanding* the content—the ideas, purposes, information, organization, perspective, and approaches. (See 20g.)

These activities can help guide your analytical reading of a text.

- **Summarize:** How can you sum up or restate its key ideas?
- **Paraphrase:** How can you state its main points in your own words?
- **Synthesize:** How can you connect its information with that in other texts?
- **Quote:** Which of the text's exact words make powerful statements?

Next, your **critical reading** will focus on *interacting* with the text, adding to it your knowledge and insight, analyzing what it does—and doesn't—

address, relating it to other texts within the community, and assessing its strengths and limitations. Your critical reading will be active, engaged, and responsive as you ask questions, look for answers, and develop your own perspective.

- **Question:** What answers do you still want or need?
- **Synthesize perspectives:** How can you relate it to other views?
- **Interpret:** What do you conclude about its outlook and bias?
- **Assess:** How do you evaluate its value and accuracy?

The example below illustrates both analytical and critical comments.

ANALYTICAL COMMENTS		CRITICAL COMMENTS
Compares health care choices to grocery shopping	How is health care like going to the grocer? The more you put in the cart, the higher the bill. But unlike your grocery expedition, where all you pay for are the items in your own cart, with health care the other customer's cart is on your tab, too.	*Sounds good, but is it fair overall? Need to read more*
Admits benefits but claims costs will increase *Supplies supporting evidence*	Nor will the tab get any better with the patient protection legislation being considered in Washington. Sure, Americans will get guaranteed access to emergency rooms, medical clinical trials and specialists. Senate legislation even provides the right to sue your insurer and be awarded up to $5 million in punitive damages. . . .	*Lots of coverage problems–like my emergency room bill*
Projects costs and effects	The litigation costs, and the efforts by some employers to avoid liability, could lead to an additional 9 million uninsured Americans by 2010.	*Does everyone agree on estimates?*
	—"Restrict Right to Sue or We'll Pay in the End," *Atlanta Journal-Constitution*, July 19, 2001.	*What's this paper's usual viewpoint?*

9c   Using journals

A **journal** is a place to explore ideas, develop insights, experiment with your writing, and reflect on your reading. You may want to organize entries around a writing task, a reading assignment, a research question, or a regular schedule for recording observations. Unlike a diary, where you record daily activities, a journal encourages interpretation and speculation as you develop your voice as a writer. (See also 20e–f.)

You can keep an informal journal in whatever form you prefer—an electronic file, a three-ring notebook, or a small binder—although you may appreciate being able to remove or reorganize pages. Stick to a regular schedule for writing because an abandoned journal soon withers away.

STRATEGY   **Make your thoughts visible in a journal.**

Nurture your own voice as a writer, and cultivate your creative insights as you turn reading, listening, and thinking into writing.

- Translate new ideas into your own words, clarifying and speculating about them for an imaginary reader or for yourself.
- Brainstorm, letting one thought lead to the next without immediate criticism or evaluation.
- Extend ideas, developing implications, applications, or solutions.
- Take issue with what you read or hear, flexing your critical thinking muscles as you challenge and critique other views. Then look for balance—areas where you respect or agree with others, too.

10   Arguing Persuasively

Argument can persuade a foundation to support an academic research grant, encourage a production team to alter a process at work, or convince a county airport to curtail expansion in the public community. Because value judgments, policy questions, and proposed actions seldom lend themselves to proof or absolute certainty, readers are aware of other opinions and evidence. They'll expect you to argue with good reasons, logic, evidence, and attention to other opinions before they'll agree with you. You'll need to encourage them to share your perspective, convincing them that your line of reasoning—your argument—is fair and justifiable. (See also Chapter 8.)

10a Recognizing an issue

Argumentative writing begins with an *issue*—a subject or situation about which opinions clearly differ. Such disagreements are common in public settings, where people with different values, cultures, and perspectives meet to address problems. Differences about policies, interpretations, and solutions are frequent in academic and work settings, too. Your argument develops around *your* opinion, that is, the value judgment, action, or interpretation you propose and wish your readers to endorse. Your aim initially is to answer two questions: What issue am I arguing about? What, precisely, is my opinion? To find (or focus) an issue that interests you, look for significant problems, judgments, and disagreements.

1 Identify an existing issue

Many arguments you construct will address existing issues. Some, such as gun control or global warming, will have broad relevance. Others will concern a specific audience, for example, proposals for a new campus drinking policy or limitations on business and residential development. Issues of this sort come to you partly formed; other people have already identified the dimensions of disagreement, gathered supporting ideas and information, and taken stances, pro and con. You need to focus more sharply, looking for significant problems, judgments, and disagreements.

> **STRATEGY** **List issues and get involved.**
>
> - **List current issues.** Make a list of disagreements you encounter in various settings—academic, public, and work—to help you focus your own response to the issues.
> - **Read.** Turn to news and opinion magazines (such as *The Nation* or *National Review*); editorials in local and national newspapers (in libraries or online); or periodical databases indexing a range of articles on civic, professional, academic, and business controversies.
> - **Interview.** Talk with people about issues that inspire strong opinions.
> - **Write.** For each possible issue, write a one- or two-sentence summary of at least two different opinions. Look for a focused subject, even a limited or local issue such as parking policies or garbage problems.

2 Recognize a potential issue

When you focus on a problem others have not identified, offer an opinion or evaluation likely to be controversial, or propose a change in a long-agreed-upon policy, you address a potential issue.

Use these techniques to recognize potential issues.

- **Review the consequences.** Question and evaluate the consequences of policies or actions.
- **Question the "taken-for-granted."** Challenge common beliefs or routine policies; explore contrasting views or alternative approaches.
- **Offer an evaluation.** When you state a judgment about the quality of a performance, policy, work of art, or product, you create an issue, at least to the extent that you are trying to convince others to share your opinion and are not simply stating your personal preferences.

3 Assess the issue

A problem is not automatically an issue, nor is every opinion worth arguing about. Drunk driving, for example, is certainly a problem but is not in itself an issue. Anyone advocating drunk driving would seem foolish, but reasonable people do disagree about how to discourage it.

Issues in Academic, Public, and Work Communities		
	Academic	**Public**	**Work**
GENERAL	Standardized testing Affirmative action in college admissions	Genetically altered foods Violence and sex on television	Child care at work Ethnically targeted marketing
LOCAL	Housing regulations at Nontanko River State University	A local crusade against a television series	Discipline policies at Abtech's Child-Care Center

Sometimes you'll identify an intriguing topic but need to investigate it to decide whether it's an arguable issue. For example, when Paul Pusateri heard about fast food restaurants being sued for causing obesity, he thought that the complainants had no case. After doing a bit of research, however, he discovered a debatable issue: Are fast food restaurants at least partly responsible for growing rates of obesity? Some people argue that consumers are responsible when they choose to eat fattening foods. Others argue that the practices of fast food chains encourage unhealthy diets, thus affecting the lives of millions of people.

Ask yourself these questions to evaluate the issue.

- Is the issue clearly debatable? Are there two or more reasonable contrasting opinions? Is there evidence to back opinion?

- Is the issue more than individual preference or personal taste? Reasoning generally can't change likes and dislikes.
- Does the issue avoid deeply held assumptions that cannot be argued? Social and political issues are arguable unless they rest on systems of belief such as religion.

10b Developing your stance

A good argument is positive: you try to persuade people to accept your opinion, but you don't attack them for having another point of view. To do this, you need a clear idea of your own opinion and the reasons why you hold it, and you need to anticipate readers' arguments. (See 8b.) Opinions can take three different forms. Each commits you to a different purpose for argument.

Value judgment. Do you want to argue that some activity, policy, belief, performance, book, or situation is good or bad, healthful or harmful, effective or ineffective, desirable or undesirable?

> College students who eat regularly at fast food restaurants may invite a lifetime of health problems.

Policy. Do you want readers to accept or follow a course of action?

> The Caraway College Health Services Center should initiate an extensive campaign to educate students about the possible long-term consequences of eating unhealthy fast food.

Interpretation. Do you want readers to agree that one point of view about a subject is better or weaker than alternatives?

> Although customers are responsible for placing their fast food orders, their unhealthy choices are often heavily influenced by advertising strategies, unclear information, and other practices of fast food chains.

STRATEGY Explore your stance.

- **Write informally** about an issue. Do you feel scornful, fearful, indignant, or outraged? Why?
- **List** key elements of your issue, summarizing your responses.
- **Add** facts, examples, and ideas that support your reactions.
- **Think about** other perspectives. Read, talk, and listen. Make a preliminary research plan, or test your views on friends or online.

10c Creating an argumentative thesis

To organize your writing and help readers focus on your outlook and your evidence, state a **proposition** or **claim**—a **thesis** (see 3b) specifying the issue and your opinion. As you refine your rough thesis, look for blurred or illogical propositions, especially in a complex thesis.

BLURRED AND
ILLOGICAL
Police should stop conducting unconstitutional roadblocks to identify drunk drivers and substitute more frequent visual checks of erratic driving.

READER'S REACTION: **This proposition seems to assume that roadblocks are unconstitutional. Is the writer supporting this value judgment or proposing a policy?**

Make sure your thesis either focuses on one proposition or identifies related propositions you will argue in an appropriate order.

SINGLE
PROPOSITIONS
Roadblocks to identify drunk drivers are unconstitutional. Police should make more frequent visual checks of erratic driving.

RELATED
PROPOSITIONS
The current practice of using roadblocks to identify drunk drivers is unconstitutional; therefore, police should use another procedure such as visual checks for erratic driving.

10d Developing reasons and evidence

As you consider your issue or research it, develop reasons supported by varied, sound evidence that your particular audience will find persuasive (see 8b). For example, your field study of recycling attitudes might well enlighten academic readers, but readers at work might want evidence of recycling's cost-effectiveness. In a public forum, detailing conditions at the local landfill might help influence a policy change.

Details. Look for statistics, technical information, surveys, interviews, and background or historical information for text or visuals (see 11a–b). Be prepared to justify the validity and authority of your sources, especially if they come from the Web. (See 22d.)

Comparisons. You can compare a particular issue, problem, policy, or situation about which you are uncertain to one about which you (and your readers) are more certain, but avoid far-fetched or unreasonable comparisons.

Quotations and ideas from authorities. The words of experts can lend support, but readers will expect them to be fair and authoritative.

Examples. Events, people, ideas, objects, feelings, stories, images, and texts drawn from your own or others' experience all can be used as brief or extended examples to support a thesis. Supply both *explanation* to make your point and *concrete detail* to give it power.

Logical links. To use your evidence effectively, you'll need to link it logically to a series of reasons that support your viewpoint. Try using a word such as *because*, *therefore*, or *consequently* in your rough thesis to establish this connection.

> **Claim or Opinion Stated in a Rough Thesis:** New classroom teachers should be required to continue coursework because it will improve the quality of their teaching, support their motivation to succeed as teachers, and help to address teacher shortages.
>
> **Reason 1:** People master a skill or activity best by doing it.
>
> **Evidence:** Comparisons with medical internships, examples and data from research on innovative teacher preparation programs
>
> **Reason 2:** Practicing teachers are often more motivated than preservice teachers.
>
> **Evidence:** Information from scholarly article comparing outcomes of preservice and inservice courses
>
> **Reason 3:** Reducing the time required for preservice preparation would help increase the number of new teachers available in a time of teacher shortages.
>
> **Evidence:** Interviews with teacher interns, federal employment statistics, postings from a teacher preparation discussion group
>
> **Reason 4 (Possible Counterargument):** New teachers will still be effective in the classroom, especially if they are supervised and mentored by administrators in the schools that hire them.
>
> **Evidence:** Newspaper profiles and reports on new teachers, interview with principal and associate superintendent

10e Acknowledging other perspectives

Traditional argument resembles debate: you imagine an adversary and try to undermine that person's points or **counterarguments**. Most contemporary approaches to argument, however, expect you to acknowledge other people's perspectives yet still try to convince them of your views. Especially within a workplace or in public where your opponents on one issue may be your allies on another, treat others respectfully. (See 8b–c.)

STRATEGY **Anticipate counterarguments.**

Divide a sheet of paper into three columns. On the left, list the main points supporting your opinion. Write opposing points in the middle. On the right, counter the opposing points.

10f Arguing logically

Strategies of argument are ways to organize and check the logic of your opinions and supporting evidence (see 8b).

1 Use data-warrant-claim (Toulmin) reasoning

In *The Uses of Argument* (1964), Stephen Toulmin proposes **data-warrant-claim reasoning**, which draws on several kinds of statements reasonable people usually make when they argue: statements of data, claim, and warrant. A statement of **data** corresponds to your evidence and **claim** to your conclusion or proposition. **Warrant**, however, refers to the mental process by which a reader connects the data to the claim, answering "How?"

In constructing a line of reasoning, you present the data or indisputable facts that lead to your claim, but you also present the warrants, the probable facts and assertions that will encourage readers to accept your claim. This approach does not assume that an argument can provide absolute proof of a proposition. It aims instead at showing readers that an opinion or proposed action is plausible, grounded on good evidence and reasons, and worth their endorsement.

Suppose you are examining the relative safety of cars. As data, you have a study on the odds of injury in different models of cars. To argue effectively, you need to show readers *how* the data and your claim are connected, what patterns (probable facts—warrants) link the data to your claim.

DATA	WARRANT	CLAIM
Ratings of each car model by likelihood of injury (scale: 1 to 10)	• The cars in the ratings fall into three easily recognized groups: small, medium, large. (probable fact) • The large cars as a group have a lower average likelihood of injury to passengers than either of the other groups. (probable fact) • Although some other cars have low likelihood of injury, almost all the large cars seem safe. (assertion + probable fact) • Few consumers will go over the crash ratings to see which models get good or poor scores. (assertion)	For the average consumer, buying a large car is a good way to reduce the likelihood of being injured in an accident.

2 Use Rogerian argument

Effective argument requires a relationship between you and your reader, an issue that **Rogerian argument** considers, based on the theories of psychologist Carl Rogers. Rogers argues that people are more easily persuaded when an opponent seems an ally, not an enemy. To practice Rogerian strategies, imagine the views of someone opposed to your opinion. What is that person's frame of reference? What assumptions are behind those views?

Once you understand the other person's ideas, you may wish to work a **concession** into your argument, acknowledging an opposing view. A concession doesn't have to be so strong that it undermines your argument. But placed strategically, it can show your effort to be fair and help persuade a reader to listen. Highlight brief concessions with *although* or *of course*.

3 Use deductive and inductive reasoning

A **deductive argument** states and then supports an explicit premise (assertion or claim) using syllogistic reasoning as its basic logical format. A **syllogism** includes a major premise, a minor premise, and a conclusion.

MAJOR PREMISE   All landowners in Clarksville must pay taxes.

MINOR PREMISE   Gary Hayes owns land in Clarksville.

CONCLUSION   Therefore, Gary Hayes must pay taxes.

A flawed syllogism can often pinpoint faulty reasoning.

MAJOR PREMISE   All Ferraris are fast.

MINOR PREMISE   That car is fast.

CONCLUSION   Therefore, that car is a Ferrari.

In a complex argument your reasoning will be more elaborate, but the syllogistic pattern can frame and test your reasoning.

An **inductive argument** does not explicitly state the premise; rather, it leads readers through accumulated evidence to a conclusion. It usually begins with a **hypothesis**, more tentative than an assertion, and the ideas the writer wants to consider. The writer has, but withholds, a conclusion until readers are convinced by the supporting points.

4 Use logical and emotional appeals

Adapt your strategies for argument to your readers, arranging reasons and evidence in ways that most people will accept as reasonable and that will enhance your credibility as a writer. Emotional strategies focus on the values, beliefs, and emotions that can motivate readers to care about an issue. However, such appeals are generally best accepted when they are also supported by logical strategies—reasoning based on likely good or bad consequences, relevant comparisons, authoritative experts, trustworthy testimony, pertinent illustrations, and statistics. Watch for **logical fallacies** or flaws in reasoning as you evaluate your evidence and shape your argument.

MISLEADING AND ILLOGICAL REASONING: LOGICAL FALLACIES

Faulty Cause-Effect Relationship (*post hoc ergo propter hoc* reasoning—"after this, therefore because of this"): attempts to persuade you that because one event follows another, the first causes the second.

> The increase in violence on television is making the crime rate soar.
>
> READER'S REACTION: **This *may* be true, but no evidence here links the two situations.**

False Analogy: compares two things that seem, but aren't, comparable.

> Raising the speed limit is like offering free cocktails at a meeting of recovering alcoholics.
>
> READER'S REACTION: **I don't see the connection. Most drivers aren't recovering from an addiction to high-speed driving.**

Red Herring: distracts readers from the real argument.

> Gun control laws need to be passed as soon as possible to decrease domestic violence and accidents. The people who think guns should not be controlled are probably criminals themselves.
>
> READER'S REACTION: **The second sentence doesn't follow logically or add support. It's just a distracting attack on people who disagree.**

Ad Hominem: attacks the person, not the issue.

> Of course Walt Smith would support a bill to aid farmers—he owns several farms in the Midwest.
>
> READER'S REACTION: **I'd like to hear reactions to his ideas, please.**

Begging the Question: presents assumptions as facts.

> Most people try to be physically fit; obviously, they fear getting old.
>
> READER'S REACTION: **I don't see any evidence that people fear aging—or that they are working on their physical fitness, either.**

Circular Reasoning: supports an assertion with the assertion itself.

> The university should increase funding of intramural sports because it has a responsibility to back its sports programs financially.
>
> READER'S REACTION: **So the university should fund sports because it should fund sports?**

10g Writing a position paper

A short **position paper** or documented argument defines an issue, considers its audience, and uses evidence and reasoning to advance its thesis.

Paul Pusateri

Dr. Drept

WRT 101

15 October 2006

Running Uphill

1   Who is at fault? Is it the fast-food chains for putting such fattening items in front of consumers with endless promotions and marketing schemes? Or is it the consumer's fault for eating the unhealthy meals, knowing full well the negative consequences? Suing a fast-food chain for causing your own obesity, as some people have done (Cohen), may be extreme. As one report puts it, "Fast-food litigation has been greeted coolly so far because it appears to run up against a core American value: personal responsibility" (Cohen). At the same time, this does not mean that the fast-food chains are free from significant blame for the rise of obesity and similar health problems that affect many people today (Surgeon General). The truth is that most people know fast food may not be good for them; they simply don't realize just how unhealthy it is. For example, how many of us know that a "quick lunch" at McDonald's including a Big Mac, fries, and a Coke, has 62 grams of fat and 1,500 calories (Barrett 74)? Even though the chains are starting to make their menus healthier, they are still to blame. Their pricing policies, overall menus, and marketing techniques lead people to eat fast food no matter how much fat it contains or how many calories it provides.

2   How are we to know what is good for us and not so good in the food we eat? What standard can we use to judge the meals offered by fast-food restaurants? To maintain a desirable, healthy weight, men need about 2,700 calories per day and women need about 2,000. The American Heart Association recommends less than three hundred milligrams of cholesterol and fifty to eighty

Introduces issue

Cites authorities

Presents position

Establishes criteria for evaluation

grams of fat per day, while the National Academy of Sciences recommends 1,100 to 3,300 milligrams of salt per day (Minnesota Attorney General). In each case, the national average intake for these is higher (Minnesota Attorney General), driven in part, perhaps, by the amount of fast food we eat.

Develops explanation of problem

3   Not all fast food contains excessive salt, cholesterol, and calories, of course, but the items that dominate the menus at a Wendy's, Burger King, McDonald's, and other fast-food restaurants and that appear frequently in advertising generally do. For example, a report by the Minnesota Attorney General gives these nutrition facts for two staples of fast-food menus, a cheeseburger dinner and a pizza dinner.

Provides supporting examples and detail

1. Quarter-pound cheeseburger, large fries, 16 oz. soda (McDonald's)

This meal:	*Recommended daily intake:*
1,166 calories	2,000-2,700 calories
51 g fat	No more than 50-80 g
95 mg cholesterol	No more than 300 mg
1,450 mg sodium	No more than 1,100-3,300 mg

2. 4 slices sausage and mushroom pizza, 16 oz. soda (Domino's)

This meal:	*Recommended daily intake:*
1,000 calories	2,000-2,700 calories
28 g fat	No more than 50-80 g
62 mg cholesterol	No more than 300 mg
2,302 mg sodium	No more than 1,100-3,300 mg

Discusses convenience and price

4   The information in these charts is probably astonishing to most of us. Even though restaurants make nutrition facts available to customers and publish them online--for example, at a McDonald's Web site (McDonald's USA)--the "need for speed" and convenience that makes us turn to fast-food restaurants in the first place means that most of us do not consult the lists of nutritional facts. Instead, we order foods prominently displayed on

menus or we order by price, from a value menu or a promotional special, both of which in my experience feature familiar and relatively unhealthful choices. In so doing, we often pass by the better choices, the small fries rather than the large, for example. At McDonald's, instead of a quarter-pound cheeseburger and large fries, we might choose a hamburger and small fries with 481 calories and 19 grams of fat, a healthier solution (Minnesota Attorney General).

5   Admittedly, fast-food chains have been adding healthier options to their menus. Arby's Light Roast Chicken has 276 calories and only 7 grams of fat; Wendy's has a healthy chili with 210 calories and 7 grams of fat. Burger King and McDonald's have a vanilla shake with 5 grams of fat and a chicken salad wth only 4 grams of fat, respectively (Minnesota Attorney General).

Makes concession

6   These items often do not receive adequate emphasis in advertising or menu placement, however. In addition, the lack of adequate emphasis frequently means that customers end up thinking that some kinds of food are healthy when they are not. As Kelly Frey points out in "Salad Not Always Healthiest Fast-Food Choice," a Crispy Chicken Salad with ranch dressing at McDonald's has 8 more calories and 19 more grams of fat than a Big Mac. Salads from Wendy's and Burger King may also have more fat and calories than the burgers. Even a Cobb salad with low-fat dressing at McDonald's would take a 150-pound person sixty minutes to walk off all the 320 calories it contains (Barrett 74).

Discusses menu placement

7   Even television ads that pass certain tests for truthfulness can be misleading. The ads for Subway, for example, leave the impression that the chain's sandwiches are healthful. Some are, yet many are not. Subway's advertising is factually true. The specific sandwiches advertised as healthful actually are; it is the others that are not, but they tend to fall within the general impression of healthfulness created by the advertising. At Subway, a 6-inch BMT

Discusses marketing techniques

10g
arg

Arguing Persuasively

Italian sandwich has 39 grams of fat, the same as a Big Mac from McDonald's and a Bacon Double Cheeseburger from Burger King (Diet Riot). A Quarter Pounder or a Whopper Jr. would be a better choice for me than the Cold Cut Trio I commonly eat at Subway.

Refines position

8   The blame may lie with the fast-food chains, but the responsibility for making healthier choices is ours as well. There are ways we can do this, but even the available healthy choices are

Advocates course of action

outside the range of those usually marketed by the chains. Nonetheless, an article like Jo Licten's "Healthiest Fast Food for Busy Travelers" can be a guide. From it I learned that Burger King's Mustard Whopper Jr., which replaces mayonnaise with mustard, decreases calories by 80. I thought that Mexican fast food could not taste good and be healthy, but I found that a Bean Burrito from Taco Bell can be a complete meal with only 370 calories and 12 grams of fat (Licten). It's like running uphill, but it is possible to begin reversing the unhealthy practices for which fast-food chains are still to blame.

[New page]

Works Cited

Barrett, Jennifer. "Fast Food Need Not Be Fat Food." *Newsweek* 13 Oct. 2003: 73-74. *Academic First Search*. Web. 21 Oct. 2006.

Cohen, Adam. "The McNugget of Truth in the Fast-Food Lawsuits." *New York Times* 3 Feb. 2003: A24. Print.

"Diet Riot." *DietRiot.com* 14 Oct. 2003. Web. 19 Oct. 2006.

Frey, Kelly. "Salad Not Always Healthiest Fast-Food Choice." *ThePittsburghChannel.com*. WTAE, 15 May 2003. Web. 19 Oct. 2006.

Licten, Jo. "Healthiest Fast Food for Busy Travelers." *roadandtravel.com*. Road and Travel Magazine, 2003. Web. 5 Oct. 2006.

"McDonald's USA Nutrition Information." *mcdonalds.com*.

McDonald's USA, 21 Oct. 2006. Web. 31 Oct. 2006.

Minnesota Attorney General's Office. *Fast Food Facts*. N.d. Web. 19

Oct. 2003. <http://www.olen.com/food/book.html>.

Surgeon General of the United States. *The Surgeon General's*

Call to Action: Prevent and Decrease Overweight and Obesity.

Washington: GPO, 2006. Print.

11 Creating a Visual Argument

Suppose you want to convince readers that your ideas for an ecologically sound yet student-friendly dorm were worth serious consideration. You could argue with words alone, but pictures and drawings or plans would be more informative and more persuasive. Figures 11.1 and 11.2 show two visuals a student created as part of *EcoDorm: An Independent Student Project* at the University of Idaho.

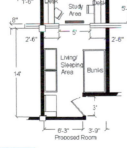

FIGURE 11.1   Drawing of proposed dormitory room
Source: <http://www.uidaho.edu/ecodorm>.

FIGURE 11.2   Computer-generated picture of proposed dormitory room
Source: <http://www.uidaho.edu/ecodorm>.

Visuals can't substitute for careful reasoning and detailed supporting evidence. However, visuals can be a critical component of argument. They can help explain an issue or problem. They can clarify supporting evidence. They can draw on emotions and values to make your argument especially persuasive.

11a Presenting an issue

Even if an issue is complex and detailed, you need to introduce it clearly and concisely before you can move on to supporting your perspective. Visuals can emphasize the importance of the issue while providing details at a glance (or two).

1 Graphs and tables

When you want readers to grasp an issue or problem in terms of numbers, statistics, or facts, a table or graph (12e) can substitute for sentences loaded with detail.

COMPLICATED   A recent survey showed considerable support for noise reduction efforts in the town. Of the respondents, 45% strongly supported the efforts, 20% gave moderate support, 15% gave mild support, and 20% offered no support.

CLEAR
AT A GLANCE

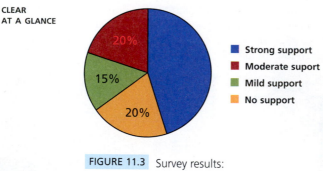

FIGURE 11.3   Survey results:
Support for noise-reduction
laws

2 Pictures and drawings

Pictures can help readers understand complicated physical settings or problems such as dorms with fire hazards or decaying neighborhoods. They can present social relationships or issues, including those involving values or emotions. Save the Children, for example, uses photographs integrated with text to emphasize the poverty and need of the children it serves as well as the urgency of the problem. The photos also support the agency's appeal for contributions.

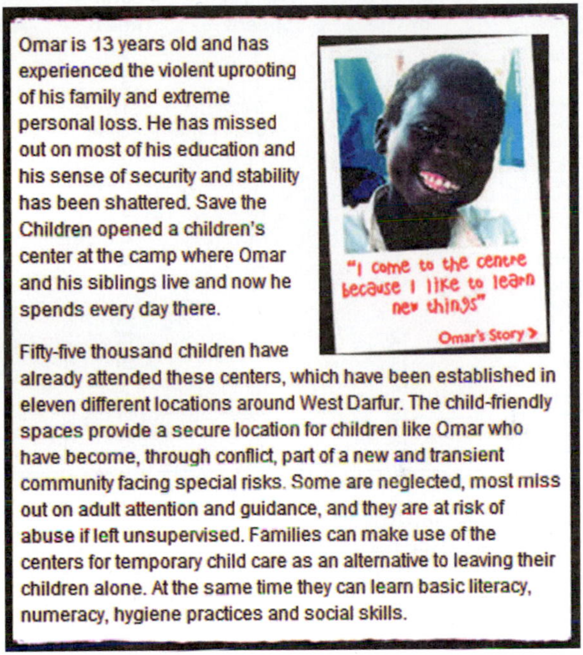

Omar is 13 years old and has experienced the violent uprooting of his family and extreme personal loss. He has missed out on most of his education and his sense of security and stability has been shattered. Save the Children opened a children's center at the camp where Omar and his siblings live and now he spends every day there.

"I come to the centre because I like to learn new things"

Omar's Story ▶

Fifty-five thousand children have already attended these centers, which have been established in eleven different locations around West Darfur. The child-friendly spaces provide a secure location for children like Omar who have become, through conflict, part of a new and transient community facing special risks. Some are neglected, most miss out on adult attention and guidance, and they are at risk of abuse if left unsupervised. Families can make use of the centers for temporary child care as an alternative to leaving their children alone. At the same time they can learn basic literacy, numeracy, hygiene practices and social skills.

FIGURE 11.4   Omar's story: Save the Children
Source: <http://www.savethechildren.org/campaigns/rewrite-the-future/omars-story.html>.

11b Providing evidence

Visuals can add depth and detail to reasoning and evidence you present in words. Although they need to be referenced in your text, often they can stand more or less on their own. Visual evidence is of two kinds: (1) details, facts, and statistics presented in graphs, tables, or other figures, and (2) photographs or drawings that are evidence in themselves. Facts and statistics presented as columns of figures (tables) or in graphs and charts can simplify the presentation of complex evidence. They can also highlight key points. They make evidence easier to understand and more persuasive. For example, comparative data about the relative pace of life in different countries is efficiently summarized in the following selection from an extensive table.

THE PACE OF LIFE IN 31 COUNTRIES				
Country	Overall Pace of Life	Walking Speeds	Postal Times	Clock Accuracy
Switzerland	1	3	2	1
Ireland	2	1	3	11
Germany	3	5	1	8
Japan	4	7	4	6
Italy	5	10	12	2
England	6	4	9	13
Sweden	7	13	5	7
Austria	8	23	8	3
Netherlands	9	2	14	25
Hong Kong	10	14	6	14
France	11	8	18	10
Poland	12	12	15	8
Costa Rica	13	16	10	15
Taiwan	14	18	7	21
Singapore	15	25	11	4
USA	16	6	23	20

FIGURE 11.5 The pace of life in 31 countries
Source: Levine, Robert. "The pace of life in 31 countries." *American Demographics*, 19 (1997): 20–29.

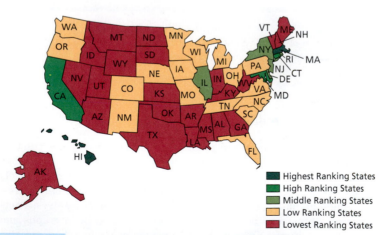

- ■ Highest Ranking States
- ■ High Ranking States
- ■ Middle Ranking States
- ■ Low Ranking States
- ■ Lowest Ranking States

FIGURE 11.6 A comparative survey of state firearm laws
Source: Gun Control in the United States: A Comparative Survey
<http://www.soros.org/initiatives/justice/articles_publications/publications/gun_report_20000401/GunReport_Chart1.pdf>.

Visual presentations can also appeal to values and emotions, as does the map on the previous page, in which the color red indicates states with what the author considers fewer or inadequate gun control laws. (Using such strategies to add emphasis to weak or questionable evidence is, of course, unethical.)

Visuals can also help explain complicated reasoning, as in the following graph highlighting the consequences of failing to decrease birth rates in less developed countries.

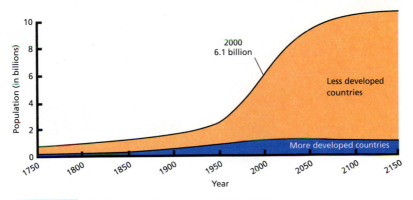

FIGURE 11.7 World population growth, 1750–2150
Source: <http://www.prb.org/PrintTemplate.cfm?Section-Population_Growth&templates-/ContentManagement/HTMLDisplay.cfm&ContentID+5602>.

As these examples indicate, well-selected examples can add depth and concrete detail to an argument.

PART 3

Presenting Your Work

▼ TAKING IT ONLINE

SPINNER AND RAYZER'S GUIDE TO NETTIQUETTE

http://pixel.cs.vt.edu/class1/spinners/InternetSpeak/nettiquette.html

Use this concise summary of appropriate Internet behavior to guide your online communication.

A PERIODIC TABLE OF VISUALIZATION METHODS

http://www.visual-literacy.org/periodic_table/periodic_table.html

Do you wish that you could figure out how to present ideas and information in visual form? The color coding and the symbols on this page can help you identify the type of visual display you might want to develop. Then use your mouse to pop up examples of the methods listed in the table. For more about visual literacy, explore the other advice and tutorials at this site.

USABILITY FIRST: WEBSITE DESIGN

http://www.usabilityfirst.com/websites/index.txl

This page provides links to advice about text and website design, writing, and presentation of information.

PRESENTATIONS

http://www.rpi.edu/dept/llc/writecenter/web/presentation.html

Review the solid advice here on oral presentations.

TEN TIPS FOR SUCCESSFUL PUBLIC SPEAKING

http://www.toastmasters.org/tips.asp

These tips from Toastmasters International can boost your confidence before an oral presentation.

PART 3

Presenting Your Work

12 Designing Documents

How can you prepare a report, a portfolio, or a visual that's clear and easy to read? How can you create a memorable document that engages readers and represents you as an effective writer? The answers often lie in document design—how you present your text on the page and integrate visual aids.

12a Goals of document design

Here's how document design can help you convey ideas, information, and conclusions effectively.

- Emphasize key points or ideas.
- Help readers readily locate and visualize information.
- Let readers know you've considered their needs.
- Signal readers about your knowledge and perspective.
- Create a positive, persuasive image of you (a persona).

For well-designed documents, consider both how the printed page (or computer screen) looks and how readers process information. If a document is crowded or hard to understand, a reader may not bother to read it. If it's easy to follow, with clear headings, graphics, and other design elements, readers will respond positively. Visual elements include layout, space, headings, type, and cues provided by letters or numbers on a page as well as any visual aid (such as a photo, chart, or graph).

12b Format choice

Readers need different things from documents. The same reader approaches an essay about air pollution quite differently from a set of instructions about the operation of a chain saw. Equally true is the fact that two people might approach either document differently. An engineer for a chemical plant working to comply with EPA guidelines will read the essay about pollution very differently from a homeowner who lives downwind from the plant.

1 Formulate the elements of your plan

Your design plan should answer these questions.

- What format or document type will I use?
- What medium will I use (print, electronic, Web, multimedia)?

- How will I divide the document into sections and make the organization visible to readers (table of contents, headings, color, paper choice, dividers, artwork)?
- What typeface and type size will I use?
- How will I highlight important information and ideas (type treatment, underlining, color, boxes, visual aids, marginal comments)?
- How will I use visual aids, and which kind will I employ (graphs, tables, charts, photographs, drawings, video)?

2 Prepare a design document

A design document is a statement of your plan for creating a report, Web site, article, or other document. If your project takes more than a few pages and includes a variety of design elements, take time to create a plan.

1. Begin your design document by writing down the purpose and audience for your text. State the purpose for each of the major design decisions you have made, including format, layout, sections, type, visuals, medium, and color. Indicate the main ideas, information, and insights you wish readers to take with them after reading your document.
2. Outline the content of your paper (informally), indicating where you will place major design elements such as headings, visuals, or columns. Annotate your outline, indicating where you intend readers' attention to be focused and what reactions you want them to have. Your concern here should be with the **readability** (ease of reading) and **usability** (usefulness) of your document.
3. Conclude with a list of the resources you need to produce your document, such as software, paper, fresh cartridges for a printer, photographs, graphics, and clip art.

12c Layout

Layout is the arrangement of words, sentences, headings, lists, tables, graphs, and pictures on a page or computer screen.

1 Use visual cues

To increase readability, supply visual cues but avoid using too many elements. Typographic devices such as **boldface**, *italics*, shading, boxes, and divider lines signal distinctions; they emphasize items and parts. Use *italics*, **boldface**, CAPITALS, and exclamation marks (!!) sparingly to create emphasis. Limit underlines (especially online where links are underlined).

Connotations of colors may vary with the context and reader.

COLOR	ENGINEERING	MEDICINE	FINANCE
blue	cold/water	death/not oxygenated	reliable/corporate
red	danger	healthy/oxygenated	loss
green	safe/environmental	infection	profit

Use color to communicate rather than decorate.

- Accomplish specific goals (such as warning or caution).
- Prioritize and order; readers go to bright colors first.
- Symbolize, based on your knowledge of your readers.
- Identify a recurring theme, or connect a sequence.
- Show a pattern or relationship in a chart or graph.
- Code symbols or sections to simplify finding information.

2 Arrange information effectively

Use **white space**, open space not filled by other design elements, to organize text into chunks and guide the reader's eye. Consider the spaces around graphics and between letters, words, lines, or paragraphs. Note the margins (usually one inch to an inch and a half at the top, bottom, and sides). Try **lists** to break up dense text, emphasize points, itemize information, and group items, making it easy for readers to absorb ideas quickly. Consider highlighting items with bullets or numbers.

Headings, brief phrases that forecast or announce upcoming content, often are larger and darker than the rest of the text. Use them to move readers along so they see the organization and quickly find information.

- Use a consistent font and style for headings.
- Allow white space between headings and text.
- Position your headings consistently (for example, centering first-level headings and beginning second-level headings at the left margin).
- Focus headings for your specific content, task, or reader: *Deducting Student Loan Interest* rather than *Student Loans*.
- Make comparable headings parallel in structure (see 42a).
- Avoid clutter by using only the headings you need.

Depending on the audience you're addressing and the document you're writing, readers may expect specific features. Academic papers often use MLA or APA conventions (see Chapters 26–27). Newsletters, Web sites, letters, memos, and other documents all follow their own visual conventions (see pp. 126–128, 131, and 133–135 for examples). Images prepared for presentations, often using software such as *PowerPoint*, require special attention to size, color, and clarity so that your listeners can easily see what's projected. (See 14b-3.)

12d Type choice

Take judicious advantage of the fonts, typefaces, and type sizes available to highlight, organize, or connect text elements. A few—two or three fonts in a document—are generally better than too many.

Type size and weight. Select a readable typeface or font that enhances content. Type smaller than 8 point is hard to read; both 10- and 12-point type are easy to read. The latter is most common in academic texts. The larger the type, the more important the ideas will seem, but save sizes above 12 point for special purposes and documents, such as overhead transparencies.

8 point   10 point   12 point   16 point

Because some fonts have thicker or wider letters, you can use type weight to highlight without changing type style (**boldface**, *italics*, shadow).

Typefaces. Serif typefaces have little "feet" or small strokes at the end of each letterform. Sans serif typefaces lack them.

N serif   **N sans serif**

Readers tend to find serif typefaces easier to read in long documents but sans serif effective in titles, headings, labels, and onscreen material. Serif typefaces include Times New Roman, Courier, Garamond, and Century Schoolbook. Sans serif typefaces include Arial, **Impact**, and Futura.

Fonts. Use decorative fonts and symbols with discretion. *Mistral*, **Sixpack**, **Cooper Black**, or *Siglight* can add engaging or emotional touches to brochures, invitations, or posters. Symbol fonts (such as those in Zapf Dingbats, Monotype Sorts, or Wingdings) can direct a reader's attention, emphasize a point, identify comparable items, or add simple graphic flourishes. Your software may supply symbols and icons like these.

✿ → ✳ ❄ ♥ ✖ ✿ ✓ ✁ •❍ ☎ ♦

12e   Visuals

Sometimes words aren't as efficient in making a point as tables, graphs, charts, photographs, maps, and drawings. Memorable visuals entice readers, are absorbed quickly, and communicate what words cannot.

1   Use tables, graphs, and charts to organize information

Tables concisely present information—usually text or numbers in columns and rows (see Table 1). **Graphs** rely on two labeled axes (vertical and horizontal) using **lines** (see Fig. 1) or **bars** (see Fig. 2) to compare items or relate variables. **Pie charts** show percentages of a whole (see Fig. 3 on p. 78). Title, number, and label tables as such in your text; number and label all other graphics as figures, and supply a brief caption. In MLA style, abbreviate a label (Fig. 1); in APA style, spell it out (Figure 1).

2   Use other visual devices

Drawings and diagrams can show physical features, connect parts, and illustrate spatial relationships so readers *see* what to do or how something works. Photographs or illustrations record reality, as in newspapers and magazines. Simple drawings called "clip art," from software or the Web, are easy to paste into a document to enhance a point.

Table 1 Web Site Services, 2005 (percentages, by sector)					
	PUBLIC UNIVERSITY	PRIVATE UNIVERSITY	PUBLIC 4-YR. COLLEGE	PRIVATE 4-YR. COLLEGE	COMMUNITY COLLEGE
Undergraduate Application	99	90	95	96	96
ePortfolio	32	27	37	28	10
Journals & Reference	92	96	92	94	84
Course Reserves	78	81	66	67	35
Course Registration	97	94	97	80	97
Online Course	95	67	88	54	94
E-Commerce Capacity	92	81	87	57	85

Source: "The Campus Computing Project," www.campuscomputing.net

- Choose simple, appropriate visuals, not decorative filler.
- Use each visual to illustrate one main point that it clearly supports.
- Set off visuals with white space. Don't crowd them.
- Position graphics close to pertinent text. Supply verbal cues (labels, numbers, and captions) to link visuals and text.
- Credit sources for graphics. (Get permission to borrow, if needed.)
- For an oral presentation, use short phrases, bulleted points, and large type to keep your visuals simple, direct, and easy to read.

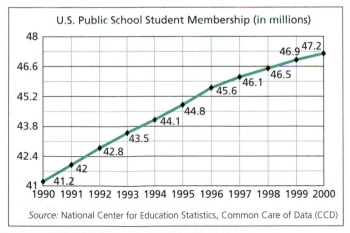

U.S. Public School Student Membership (in millions)

Source: National Center for Education Statistics, Common Care of Data (CCD)

Fig. 1. Number of students enrolled in public schools.
Source: <http://nces.ed.gov>.

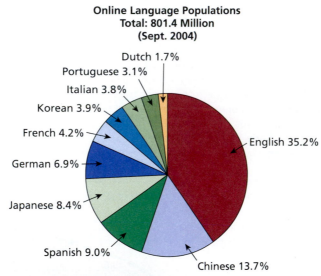

Citrus fruit	27
Fish	26
Vegetables	20
Dairy	17
Sugar	16
Beef	15
Processed potatoes	8

Percent increase in quantities consumed, 2000–2020

Fig. 2. U.S. projected consumption growth, 2000–2020.
Source: <http://nationalatlas.gov/articles/agriculture/a_consumerAg.html/>.

**Online Language Populations
Total: 801.4 Million
(Sept. 2004)**

Dutch 1.7%
Portuguese 3.1%
Italian 3.8%
Korean 3.9%
French 4.2%
German 6.9%
Japanese 8.4%
Spanish 9.0%
English 35.2%
Chinese 13.7%

Fig. 3. Online population by language group.
Source: GlobalReach <http://global-reach.biz/globstats/index.php3>.

12f Sample documents

The following sample documents—an academic paper, a technical document, a newsletter with a varied layout, and a Web site—show how the principles of document design work in different situations. Each document has been annotated to point out its features and layout.

Sample page from student paper on the World Trade Center memorial with an integrated photograph

Daisy Garcia
Professor L. Miles
HPR 101
15 December 2006

Rebuilding

September 11, 2001, marks a day when your feelings of shock and loss of direction matched with others across the country no matter where you were or what you were doing when the twin towers of the World Trade Center collapsed. Deciding what, if anything, to build on the site has been a process of differing emotions, perceptions, and plans. The various proposals have been ambitious, breathtaking, moving, and, above all, quite different in perspective and style.

. . .

Freedom Tower is designed to stand as the tallest building in the world in its completion at a symbolic height as a 1,776-foot spire. The antenna structure will be the home of various channels in the New York area and have a representational design

relating to the Statue of Liberty. David M. Childs is collaborating with Libeskind as the design architect. It will contain a vertical garden known as "Gardens of the World," observation decks, and programs for recreational commercial use. The commercial buildings are going to be designed by the other three architects chosen by Silverstein. There are about 10 million square feet of office space in five towers and 880,000 square feet of retail space. The Wedge of Light is an area designed and aligned with the heavens so that on September 11 of each year, it is lit.

1 Positions illustration next to discussion in text

2 Refers to content of illustration in related text

Technical document with headings and a figure

1 *Introduction*

Simply defined, a pump is a hydraulic machine (variously constructed) used for raising, compressing, or transferring fluids. Pumps are one of the most basic and essential pieces of industrial equipment. They are used in nearly every process plant to do what the definition entails: raise, compress, or transfer fluids. The pump has applications in the areas of potable water distribution, wastewater transfer, the pumping of chemicals, slurries, pulp and seawater. Pumps pressurize sprinkler and standpipe systems, circulate purified water for pharmaceutical applications, deliver feed water to boilers, and pump steam condensate.

2 The Radial Centrifugal Pump **3**

The most common type of pump is called a dynamic pump. A dynamic pump adds momentum to a fluid as it passes through the pump's impeller. The dynamic pump category can be subdivided into radial and axial pumps. The centrifugal radial pump, the apparatus examined in this experiment, involves fluid leaving the pump impeller in the radial direction. The centrifugal pump converts the energy of an electric motor or turbine first into kinetic energy and then into pressure energy by means of a rotating impeller and a static boundary casing called a diffuser. Below is a diagram of a simple centrifugal pump, similar to the one used in this experiment.

4 **5**

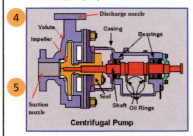

6 Fig. 1. Centrifugal Pump Apparatus--similar to the setup used in this experiment.

In this picture it is easy to see that the fluid leaves the pump apparatus perpendicular to the axis on which it entered. This constitutes a radial motion.

1 Uses large, bold font to indicate A-level head

2 Uses smaller font to indicate B-level head

3 Uses spacing to create readable document

4 Places diagram by corresponding text

5 Adds color and descriptive labels

6 Labels figure appropriately

Student project with variety in layout

Thursday
July 8, 2003

Volume XX
Issue 2

The Daily Moose

North America's Only Newspaper Devoted to Moose Lovers Everywhere. Twenty-Two Years and Growing.

④ ①

Big Moose Comes From Small Dreams

Staff Reporter: Andrea White

Growing up, your favorite animal may have been a cat, dog, or turtle. Even as exotic as parrots, giraffes and elephants. But in areas north of Chicago and Boston, children wish for pets like deer, caribou and even moose. Moose usually occupy areas in the northern United States and Canada, so finding them in southern California is quite unusual. However, traveling to Orange County, California, you might see dozens, even hundreds of these winter-weather giants. Mainly Seconds, a craft/antique store in Orange County, has a display of numerous moose paraphernalia all collected by the "Moose" himself, Mike Bonk.

In 1982, Mike's first store opened and received a gift from his wife and former employees. It was a corduroy moose head with a plaque inscribed "The Moose is Loose." This present hangs on the wall near the entrance next to painted words, *The Moose Museum*. The museum started when Mike put his personal items on display around the store. It seemed that as the store increased and prospered, his collection did also. Soon there were so many moose collectibles, the store formed itself into a museum.

The Moose Museum Located at Mainly Seconds,

②

This museum is not like any other. Set in the back section of the store, it consists of about fifty cases and ten aisles of various products either resembling or being moose associated. "If it's moose, it's in here," Mike said during a recent interview. And it's true. (Cont. on page 2).

⑤

The Moose Museum
Cordially Invites You …

③

To Explore the Wide World of Moose

Come experience the Northern Wilderness in Sunny California.
New Exhibits! More Moose!

789 S. Tustin Avenue   555-9876

Warning: Moose X-ing

Travel columnist: Caroline Cesserta

My family and I always agonize about where to travel for our yearly summer vacation. This year, my daughter and I agreed on a nice mountain lodge in Colorado while my husband and other daughter sided on a tropical getaway to Mexico. To compromise, we decided to tour California starting from the Mexican border up to Oregon. One of my personal favorite spots is very unusual store I discovered when we were stopped at a rest stop and someone noticed my moose decal on the back window. (Cont. Pg. 2)

---

① Uses varied typefaces and sizes for a system of headings

② Integrates photograph and text

③ Encloses highlighted text in oval "box"

④ Uses single column for lead story

⑤ Uses double column for additional text

Web site about mountain lions with appealing photos and buttons

1. Highlights beauty of animal and calls attention to the site
2. Provides site map and access to information categories and a video
3. Emphasizes elusive nature of the animal with ghosted profile of mountain lion
4. Uses white background to make text easy to read

13 Writing in Online Communities

Technology has many sounds—hums, pings, whirs, and clicks. However, the most important sound is still that of your own personal or professional "voice" as you represent yourself in electronic communities.

TOO CASUAL   Hiya, Prof.! Sorry I slept late and missed your test. I really, really hope I can do the makeup this week. —Drake
READER'S REACTION: Sounds like a goof-off to me.

REVISED   Prof. Jones: Unfortunately, I missed the test today in Physics 130. Is it possible for me to do a makeup this week at your convenience? —Drake Long

Some online environments are like libraries: you visit to read and retrieve materials. But many others are interactive, involving exchanges among community members as you email, chat, send **instant messages** (IMs), reply to messages from an electronic list, or respond to a blog—a "Web log." Each online community has accepted standards for group members, language and customs to help you represent yourself appropriately.

13a Online expectations

Expectations of participants may be as specific as the shared interest uniting an online community. Briefly "lurking" (reading without participating) is a good way to discover who participates, what rules govern participation, and whether your expectations match the community's.

1 Identify the type of online community

The **domain name** in an electronic address identifies an organization or other entity on the Internet, indicating the origin of material you access. For instance, the National Association for the Advancement of Colored People maintains the domain name *naacp.org*, which follows *www* in its Web site address and @ in its email addresses. Some suffixes also identify material from other countries (such as *.ca* for Canada, *.no* for Norway).

COMMON DOMAIN SUFFIXES IN INTERNET ADDRESSES

.com	commercial sites	.edu	educational groups
.gov	governmental sites	.net	network sites
.org	nonprofit organizations	.mil	military sites

---

2 Use netiquette as a guide to community standards

Netiquette defines the behavior and politeness expected online. It's your responsibility to observe the commonsense guidelines that apply across nearly all Internet communities as well as a specific group's standards.

- **Think before you act.** Once sent or posted, a message or blog is open to friends, relatives, instructors, or employers.
- **Learn the norms.** Read a site's FAQ (frequently asked questions) page, and lurk before you participate.
- **Respect a group's interests.** Avoid personal attacks ("flames"), off-topic messages, hoaxes, inappropriate jokes, spamming (sending unsolicited email to groups), irrelevant replies, and tedious copies of previous messages. When a topic is not of general interest, request or supply responses "off list" through email rather than the list address.
- **Use conventional grammar and usage.** Avoid creating a sloppy persona with careless wording, a rude one with ALL CAPS, or an inappropriately casual one with IM abbreviations.

- **Remember the Golden Rule of netiquette.** Real people receive your email or access your Web site. Be considerate of them.

13b Email conventions

Flexible and fast, email can create so much information that others may be irritated if you ignore conventions or lack purpose (see 3a).

1 Use the elements and functions of email

Online readers expect conventional elements in messages.

- **From.** State your identity in this line. Your email program may automatically show your address or your screen name.
- **Sent.** The date and time you send can help you track correspondence.
- **To.** Record the names of primary recipients. For copies sent to others, use the lines for **Cc:** (carbon copy) and **Bcc:** (blind carbon copy, sent without the knowledge of the main recipients).
- **Subject.** Use a short, clear subject line, like a news headline. If you're replying or forwarding from another message, keep this line current.
- **Message body.** Be concise. In a reply, clarify your topic, but follow the community's convention about including previous messages.
- **Signature or sig file.** Sign email for a reader's benefit. If you use a sig file to add your full name and contact details, consider your credibility and your readers before adding clever sayings, lyrics, or jokes.
- **Reply and reply-all.** Select "Reply" to answer the sender and "Reply-All" to include everyone who got the original. To avoid posting a personal note, check the "To:" and "Cc:" lines before hitting "Send."
- **Forward.** Use discretion if you send messages on to others.
- **Attach.** If you attach files, spreadsheets, or video clips, remember that not all recipients will be able to open these documents.

2 Tailor your messages to the community

Individual email is like a letter; you specify who receives your message. List-based email, like contributions to printed newsletters, goes to all the list's subscribers. Individual mail isn't necessarily more "personal" or list mail more "professional." Recipients may expect different levels of formality, but most appreciate specificity, relevance, and brevity.

- Identify your *most essential* point. Present it early and briefly.
- Clarify what you want readers to do or think about as they respond.
- Break long blocks of text into short, readable paragraphs. Separate paragraphs with a blank line; consider adding headings.
- Replace detailed explanations with sources or an attached file.
- Reply economically, repeating only key material from prior messages.

Casual exchanges may use shortcuts such as **emoticons** (*emotion* + *icon*) that are inappropriate in professional or academic writing.

:-)   grin   :-(frown   ;-)   wink   8-0   bug-eyed surprise

Abbreviations and **acronyms** (pronounceable abbreviations for common phrases) may also speed up casual communication. (See 58a-2.)

BTW   by the way   F2F   face-to-face   FYI   for your information

13c Online communities

To join an **electronic mailing list** or newsgroup, email the host service. You'll then automatically receive all posted messages—individually or grouped in the day's "digest"—at your email address. Popular in the academic community, these lists allow private, focused discussion by a group of subscribers. In contrast, you access a **newsgroup** directly, and messages are immediately posted for anyone to read. These popular resources for public and civic groups generally welcome participants.

Web-based forums allow access to sites where users converse about shared interests. Some are moderated, many ask you to set up a user name and password, and a few charge fees. Interactive **blogs** (for "Web logs") are sites where owners post and encourage responses to information, reflections, news, and political or social commentary. A **wiki** is an electronic information source that allows users to add or modify information.

Real-time discussion takes place instantly; words appear on each participant's screen as they are typed. The most popular real-time communities are **chat rooms**, informal conversations hosted by private Internet services or available via the Internet Relay Chat (IRC) network. More simply, instant messaging (IMing) or texting on a cell phone allows immediate, simultaneous electronic conversation—and, like other online exchanges, requires that you consider how to represent yourself and that you respect conventions expected by your readers.

Class conferences and exchanges are regular parts of courses offered partially or entirely online. If you don't routinely use the communication functions expected, allow time to learn how they work. Find out the purposes of online exchanges, conventions expected, ways to submit questions or post responses, resources required (online or print), deadlines for postings, and methods of assessment (numbers or types of postings, quiz scores). (See also 60c.) If you attach a file for others to read, use the required format so that everyone can access it.

Some instructors use electronic courseware to post assignments and schedules, track student progress, supply links to course-related sites, provide a discussion board and chatroom for scheduled discussions, develop a bulletin board to organize postings by topic, and give everyone access to an "internal" email system. Explore the site fully so that you can meet course requirements and enhance your learning.

STRATEGY **Get engaged in online learning.**

Apply your long-standing classroom skills online even though you don't see your classmates or go to class at a set time.

- Instead of "surfing," slow down. Read everything posted, especially introductory information. Print important guidelines.
- Learn the rules and procedures. Online courses, like their face-to-face counterparts, have due dates, late penalties, discussions, quizzes, and assignment guidelines.
- Present yourself as a member of a learning community. Join group discussions, exchanges, and projects. Treat your classmates respectfully, and do your share of the online work.
- If you tend to procrastinate, pace your work. Schedule your reading and writing so you meet all the due dates. If you prefer informal discussion to essay production, use your exchanges to generate ideas and plan your writing assignments.

13d Web pages

Web pages offer many different types of writing.

TYPES OF WEB SITES

- **Personal home pages** sponsored by individuals to present personal, family, hobby, or special-interest news
- **Commercial sites** sponsored by corporations, businesses, or other enterprises to promote shopping or to explain products and services
- **Educational sites** sponsored by schools, colleges, libraries, scholarly journals, and other groups to supply access to resources or information
- **News or entertainment sites** sponsored by newspapers, magazines, and other media to supply breaking news or information archives
- **Search engines** dedicated to indexing Web pages for users

1 Design your Web page for readers

When building a Web page, first consider its format and purpose. Is it a class project on coral reef preservation, designed as a resource for those with similar interests? Is it an "online business card" limited to background and contact listings? Is it an autobiography for your friends and family?

Before you begin building, search for sites with similar purposes. Analyze how they work, listing what you like or dislike. Politely contact authors of notable pages for advice. Ask peers or colleagues for ideas, too.

Then consider how you want to present yourself. How will you establish your credibility? How will you react if an outsider visits a site for fellow students or an employer or instructor visits your personal site? What might readers want to find? How are they likely to navigate? How will they expect its pages to relate? Finally, name your site carefully because search engines index words in the title and text. When your site is ready, visit the home pages of major search engines to register it so people can find your work.

2 Organize and manage your site

Maintain your site so that you engage readers and encourage visits.

- **Keep content key.** Web users want information, not "cool" graphics. Don't overcrowd pages; allow ample "white space." When appropriate, list information. Use visuals to reinforce your topic, not fill space.
- **Stay updated, not outdated.** Publish when ready; update as needed.
- **Check your links.** Regularly test any links to supporting documents, data, or related sites to make sure they still work.
- **Consider visitors.** Use multiple platforms and browsers to test user interfaces. Include contact details, preferably an automatic email link.

13e Avoiding plagiarism and behaving ethically online

The Internet gives you access to nearly limitless texts, images, music, streaming video, and other media, but you need to be careful to behave ethically online. Because you can easily download such material to your own computer—and then to CDs or disks—it's tempting to see all of it as yours, free for the asking. But it's not. In fact, it's not always clear whether online material is copyrighted and thus whether you're doing anything wrong when you copy or distribute it. Downloading songs, stories, cartoons, or other materials may violate federal copyright laws and result in fines (or worse) if you're caught. Avoid plagiarism and illegal or unethical practices that can create suspicion or provoke investigation. (See also Chapter 24.)

Online communication also requires that you work ethically and professionally. When you use a school email account—even if you access it away from campus—you are responsible for abiding by the institution's policies and regulations. You are also obligated by the terms of a public Internet service provider's contract. If you use your employer's Internet account, your employer may monitor what sites you access, and you probably have no legal expectation of privacy for anything you write or post. You may also be accountable under local, state, federal, or international law.

Aside from possible institutional or legal penalties, your own credibility as a writer rests on your careful use of online materials. Evaluate your sources to assure their credibility in your community, identify and credit what you use, and request permission when needed to copy images, quote from postings, or use similar materials. (See also Chapter 24.)

14 Speaking Effectively

Surveys show that people fear public speaking more than almost anything else, including losing a relative or being fired. Fear often comes from too little preparation—trying to "wing it" and hoping for the best.

SPEAKER I can't get the computer to project the latest sales figures, but most of them are going up.
LISTENER'S REACTION: **What a disorganized waste of time—especially with our supervisor here.**

Good speakers use practice and experience to turn apprehension into energy, presenting themselves and their ideas enthusiastically and clearly. (See 15l on group, 18g, on public, and 19h on committee presentations.)

14a Oral presentations

Oral presentations aren't limited to formal occasions when someone stands on a stage to deliver a polished address. You might present your portfolio to your class, sum up a project's status at work, or speak from the audience at a town meeting. In such settings, listeners expect speakers to follow accepted patterns. Ask yourself questions like these.

- How long do others speak?
- How formal is the usual style?
- What evidence and what persuasive strategies do others use?

14b Preparing an oral presentation

You can greatly improve your performance—and your confidence—if you prepare in four stages: *planning, practice, delivery, reflection.*

1 Plan ahead when you speak formally

Keep a list of information about your presentation; let it shape your plans. For example, your time limit will help you decide what details, points, and materials (such as handouts) to include. (See 3a and c.)

Analyze your speaking situation. Consider where, when, and how you'll speak as well as what your purpose will be.

Speaking in Academic, Public, and Work Communities

	Academic	Public	Work
AUDIENCE EXPECTATIONS	Explore, advance, or exchange knowledge	Support position, policy, or proposal	Advance product, service, or mission
	Develop clear topic with solid, logical evidence	Present position with compelling reasons and evidence	Present clear information on problem, task, or situation
GOALS OF ORAL EXCHANGES	Develop and exchange information or interpretations	Publicize issue, promote views or position, or reach compromise	Make decisions or solve problems to improve product or service
	Reflect on and respond to shared interests	Explore issues and options	Inform about products and services
TYPES OF INFORMAL ORAL EXCHANGES	Class, peer, or collaborative discussion	Civic exchange, board discussion, or committee discussion	Work group, client, or committee discussion
GOALS OF ORAL PRESENTATIONS	Present creative, applied, or theoretical work	Advocate position, policy, or proposal	Analyze problems and recommend solutions
	Analyze, synthesize, or interpret sources or findings	Inform group, officials, or community about issue or proposal	Promote product development, assembly, marketing, or delivery
	Engage intellectual interest of group	Motivate others to care or act	Inspire employees or customers
TYPES OF FORMAL ORAL PRESENTATIONS	Description, explanation, interpretation, or demonstration	Public statement or appeal on issue, action, or proposal	Progress report, analysis, proposal, or recommendation
	Conference panel, poster session, lecture, or address	Interviews or press statements on issue	Telephone, video, Web, and in-person presentations

- What's the occasion? Who—and how many—will be there?
- How long is the event? How long will you speak?
- What place or space will you speak in? Where will you be?
- How will you know when to speak?
- What do you hope your presentation will accomplish?
- What will your audience expect to find out or experience?
- What do you know—or need to find out—about your topic?

Begin organizing your remarks. Group your remarks or create an informal outline. Write out powerful opening and key sentences.

1. *Introductory remarks*: introduce yourself and give your audience a preview of what you'll say, show, or cover.
2. *Content or substance of the presentation*: present your main ideas, illustrations, and supporting material (see 6f).
3. *Conclusion*: sum up, restate your purpose, and remind your audience of what you have shown or offered.

Develop your talking points. Write out your **talking points**—key phrases, words, visual cues, or other reminders to guide you as you speak.

- Jot down both your main points and signals to help you coordinate your talk: "Check time," "Show overhead."
- Use transitions (*next* or *to sum up*; see 6d) to link the parts and guide your audience: "As we've seen, the Valdez oil spill initially devastated the Alaskan shoreline. I want to turn now to its long-term impact."
- Match your style to your situation, audience, and topic.
- Estimate the time for each group of talking points. If necessary, consolidate, trim, or use a handout.
- Transfer your final talking points—content and cues—to 3" × 5" cards. Write out your first and last sentences to begin and end confidently.
- Number your cards so you always know where you are. At the top of every fifth card, estimate the time used by that point.

To involve your listeners, have them read a handout, view a slide, talk in pairs, or tackle an activity—but allow the *time* for participation.

2 Rehearse your presentation

Try to anticipate the physical conditions of your talk—body position, foot placement, breathing, eye movements. Rehearse alone first; then invite a few trusted listeners. Ask for advice on pacing, volume, body movements, transitions, and the like. Videotape or record a rehearsal to spot problems, distracting habits, or unclear points. Keep rehearsing until you know every transition, dramatic pause, and reminder to look around.

3 Deliver your presentation

Although reading a printed paper aloud is common in some fields, most audiences prefer speakers to *present* their ideas instead of *read* them. This type of **extemporaneous** or **conversational speaking** encourages greater interaction among the speaker, audience, and ideas.

- Use your talking points to recall what to say, not to read out loud.
- Speak loudly and clearly, projecting your voice over the audience.

- Vary pitch and cadence for emphasis; don't exaggerate emotions.
- Avoid distracting verbal habits—"um," "like," or "you know."
- Move around if you wish, but don't pace, drum on the podium, or jingle your keys.

Vary your eye contact so you don't favor the same person, group, or part of the room. Look directly at listeners (for only a few seconds unless you're answering a question). Glance at your visuals, but focus on your audience. Don't make them wait while you write out a transparency. (See Chapter 11.)

STRATEGY **Use visuals to enhance your speech.**

- Prepare your visuals ahead, whether you use a chalkboard, flip chart, overhead transparency, or audiovisual projection.
- Try to rehearse with any equipment to figure out how to run it, where to stand, and how to coordinate your visuals with your remarks.
- Use a large readable font, or pass out copies of your visuals to simplify taking notes.
- If you use software such as *PowerPoint*, practice with the technology, avoid too much glitz, and always bring backup overheads.
- Let listeners read visuals for themselves. Paraphrase, note, or sum up in bulleted points what you present in detail.

4 Assess your results

Look for feedback on what you did well and what you can improve. If possible, ask someone to attend and honestly appraise your presentation. Your instructor may provide a scoring guide, evaluation sheet, or advice. Write out a self-assessment to strategize about future problems. (See Chapter 60.)

14c Managing speech anxiety

Like pilots with thousands of flight hours, experienced speakers have learned to control their apprehension. Giving oral presentations in college provides you with experience and confidence. These techniques can help reduce and control your anxiety.

- Write down your fears; look for strategies to overcome them.
- Before presentations, rest and eat well despite your anxiety.
- Sweaty palms and butterflies don't predict the quality of your talk.
- Take long, deep breaths to slow your heart rate, calm your nerves, and provide oxygen to your brain. Deliberately relax any tense spots.
- Focus on your ideas, not your looks or your worries.
- Move confidently to your speaking position. Face your audience, and organize your materials or adjust a microphone before you begin.
- Don't panic if you get lost or distracted: pause, breathe, cope.

14d Fielding questions

Presentations often end with a dialogue with listeners. Anticipate likely questions, plan brief answers, and remain flexible. Ask for clarification if you don't understand a question. Respond directly, not evasively. If you don't know an answer, say so; don't make one up. Answer hostile questions diplomatically, with "Yes," "No," or "I'm not sure," and move on.

Writing for Specific Communities

▼ *TAKING IT ONLINE*

TAKING AN ESSAY TEST: DR. K'S TAKE ON HOW TO DO IT RIGHT
http://www.personal.psu.edu/faculty/k/x/kxk30/essaytst.htm
This site offers concrete advice and strategies for preparing for essay
exams as well as tips and techniques for answering essay questions
effectively.

11 WAYS TO IMPROVE YOUR WRITING AND YOUR BUSINESS
http://www.editorialservice.com/11ways.html
These tips, written for participants in a business writing seminar,
can help you write memos, business letters, reports, and news releases.

OCCUPATIONAL OUTLOOK QUARTERLY
http://stats.bls.gov/opub/ooq/ooqindex.htm
Check the index or search for articles (with examples) on job
alternatives, applications, résumés, and interviews.

DEVELOPING A LETTER OF APPLICATION
http://www.techwhr-l.com/articles
At this site for technical writers, you will find articles on job hunting,
letters of application, résumés, and interviews.

CIVNET: A WEBSITE OF CIVITAS INTERNATIONAL
http://www.civnet.org
Follow the links here to many sites on civic involvement and
volunteer organizations.

PART 4

Writing for Specific Communities

15 Academic Writing: General Education

General academic writing is common in introductory college courses (general education courses), which require similar kinds of thinking and working with information and texts. In such courses you might be asked to write summaries, research papers, or short documented papers, writing that often asks you to weigh two sides of an issue, analyze why something happens, or summarize the main ideas in an article. What differs is the content and subject matter you're writing about.

In more advanced courses and in your academic major, you'll do more discipline-based writing. This kind of writing draws on forms, styles, and structures shaped by the community of people who work within a field, such as architects, music historians, or engineers. It's still academic writing, but it shares some features with the writing of professionals working in the field. (See Chapters 16–17.)

15a Goals of general academic writing

Academic assignments may be designed for practice or for specific learning. They may ask you to convince someone about a point, to share information with interested readers, or to reveal your understanding of a text, a phenomenon, an object, or a process. These purposes are usually revealed by specific nouns and verbs in an assignment (see 3a).

Assignments also may have specific **learning goals** (such as gaining knowledge in an area or practicing a skill like researching), **rhetorical goals** (such as presenting information or arguing a point), or **assessment goals** (such as showing how well you've accomplished the assignment). Sometimes these goals are clear and specific, as in the following psychology assignment.

> The two main goals for this assignment are to give you practice summarizing the main points of a journal article that reports original psychological research and to help you to critique research by asking questions about its design and conclusions.

When the learning goals aren't so clear, look at the grading criteria to figure out what the instructor is emphasizing in the task.

15b General academic audiences

The "default" audience for college writing is the instructor, but instructors often put aside their own tastes and opinions to play the role of a wider, "educated" college audience as they read your work. Some assignments will ask you to share your writing with your peers or to address a specific audience such as readers opposed to your views or members of a disciplinary group.

15c General academic writing tasks

College writing begins with an assignment, often generally announced in a course syllabus or specifically explained by the instructor when you begin the task. To understand your writing tasks, list the names and due dates of assignments. Jot down any explanation of their nature, purpose, complexity, or relationship to the course material. Note any sequence, patterns, or changes in the type of writing.

In the syllabus for her history of science course, Amanda Loh noted the increasing complexity of her assignments.

> You will write frequent informal response papers of about one page, both to reflect on the material and to show your understanding of it. In addition, three formal essays of 800–1500 words each will be explained in class and in handouts: a document comparison (describing and analyzing differences in two historical documents), a change essay (explaining how a scientific concept or process changed over time), and a comparative analysis (analyzing how two cultures viewed or developed a particular scientific approach or method).

Whether your assignment is handed out, described in class, or posted on the Web, you need to analyze it carefully, noting its purpose, any particular audience, and any specific or unusual expectations.

STRATEGY Analyze your assignment.

- What is the task called? Does it seem to be a name that's common in the field of study, or is it your instructor's own creation?
- What are its length and its level of formality? (Usually, the longer an assignment, the more formal it is.)
- What freedom does it allow, and what constraints does it impose in subject matter, information used, or specific questions asked?
- What key word and verbs signal what you need to do? Are you to report information "neutrally" or take a position and argue a point? Check any description, assignment guide, or grading scale for clues about the structure, style, voice, or content of the task.

15d Types of general academic writing

General academic writing can be categorized by the activity in which you engage—drawing on sources, reflecting, interpreting, observing or experimenting, or testing (though some assignments combine several activities). These activities are useful in academic writing across many disciplines and will strengthen your writing regardless of your field of interest. (See the table below.)

Your academic writing also can be divided into two types based on your approach to the material. **Information-driven** assignments ask you to report information objectively. For these, you are like a reporter gathering, distilling, and presenting information in objective summaries, annotated bibliographies, literature reviews, essay exams, reports, documented papers, or Web pages. Instead of selling ideas to readers or sharing opinions with them, treat your audience as clients who want you to supply thorough, objective, and clear information that's interesting or useful.

Types of Academic Writing		
Type	**Characteristic Activities**	**Common Forms**
DRAWING ON SOURCES	Summarizing, paraphrasing, synthesizing, analyzing, comparing, compiling, evaluating	Summaries and abstracts, reviews and syntheses (research, ideas, or information), book reviews and reports, annotated bibliographies, informative research papers, poster presentations, analyses of issues or controversies
REFLECTING	Responding, reacting, speculating, exploring, inquiring	Reading journals, logs (data observations and insights), personal essays, reaction papers, autobiographies, reflexive writing (self-observing and self-critical)
INTERPRETING	Analyzing, defining key ideas and meanings, identifying causes and effects, describing patterns, applying a theory, drawing a conclusion, taking a stand on an issue	Interpretations of a text or work of art (documented or not), analyses of phenomena (historical, social, or cultural), "thesis" papers taking a stand on scholarly issues, documented arguments drawing on research
OBSERVING/ EXPERIMENTING	Making observations; designing surveys and experiments; collecting, synthesizing, and analyzing data; recognizing patterns	Scientific reports and articles, logs of observations and experiments, lab reports, field research reports, project evaluations
TESTING	Explaining, supporting, defining, presenting information and ideas, offering conclusions	Essay tests, take-home exams, tests requiring sentence- or paragraph-length answers, written responses to readings

STRATEGY **Find an internal logic for information-driven writing.**

Try informal grouping and outlining to find an internal logic to help readers process and understand information (see also 2b).

- Identify chunks. List the main areas you want to cover, and fit your information into these chunks. Add or revise categories as needed.
- Look for patterns. For example, if you compare or contrast two events, divide your paper into two large sections (one for each event) or into subtopics (each covering both events). If you use classification, give each category or part a section (see 3b).
- Organize a sequential order, perhaps spatial (describing physical features in relationship with each other), chronological (discussing events over time to explain a history or process), or hierarchical (establishing the relative importance of features or parts).

Point-driven assignments ask you to argue the case for your own interpretation or evaluation. For these, you begin in the role of a reporter, collecting information, opinions, or data. Then you change to the role of an arbitrator, jurist, or judge who critically analyzes and weighs the issues, evidence, or opinions. Your writing supports your point: the commentary, opinion, analysis, or arguments that you present to readers in your persuasive review, essay, exam, or position paper.

STRATEGY **Find a persuasive logic for point-driven writing.**

Focus on your issue to analyze reasons, evidence, and alternatives in order to convince readers to respect your position (see 10b–f).

- Based on your assignment, identify an academic or social issue that allows various points of view. State your view in a thesis.
- Identify the reasons for your view, and use them as the areas you want to cover. Fit your supporting evidence into these areas.
- Investigate what others think, and incorporate these views into your paper with reasoned responses. As you acknowledge or counter them, you'll show readers your thoughtful analysis.

15e Summary

A **summary** concisely presents the key elements and content of a longer text (or of an event) using your own words. It can help you grasp and record the content of a source (see 20g) or convey the key points about your own original research (see also 17e).

ELEMENTS OF A SUMMARY

- It begins with a one- to two-sentence compressed overview of the work or event.
- It provides enough detail to convey the general substance or identify the main ideas without extra embellishment.

- It may note major subpoints either chronologically, as presented in the text, or hierarchically, from most to least important.
- It is presented objectively, without personal comments or evaluation of the text's coverage, accuracy, or value (unless assigned).

Here is the opening of Jen Halliday's summary of an article reporting changes in students' racial attitudes, written for a sociology paper.

> In this article, the authors report on a study of the change in racial attitudes of a sample of White college students when they had increased interracial contact with Black students and were exposed to increased information about racial issues. The authors randomly selected a group of 10 White college students between the ages of 18 and 23 at a midsized Midwestern university. To gauge participants' existing attitudes and feelings toward African Americans, they used a combination of surveys and interviews . . .

States central point first

Moves next to the method, findings, and discussion

15f Annotated bibliography

An annotated bibliography is just like a regular bibliography (see Chapters 26–29) except that each entry adds a description or summary of the work's aim, purpose, or contents. Annotations are usually a paragraph or two but may use an abbreviated sentence structure like this:

Summarizes research on the development of the Cherokee syllabary.

Annotated bibliographies are commonly assigned to help students survey and report on a body of scholarship or prepare for a longer research paper.

ELEMENTS OF AN ANNOTATED BIBLIOGRAPHY

- It briefly introduces the topic of the bibliography and perhaps the kinds of works it covers.
- It refers accurately to the literature cited and follows the expected documentation style (see Chapters 26–29).
- It follows each reference with a clear description or summary, briefly but accurately representing the work.
- It arranges entries alphabetically, sometimes grouped in sections by date or by general topic or focus.

Following is a sample entry from an annotated bibliography which consists of an introduction to the topic followed by twelve entries.

Annotated Bibliography on Bilingualism

by Ian Preston

Glazer, Nathan. "Where Is Multiculturalism Leading Us?" *Phi*
    Delta Kappan 75 (1993): 319-24. Print. This article describes
    the Center for the Study of Books in Spanish for

Cites source

Sums up viewpoint

Children and Adolescents, an organization that promotes the positive aspects of bilingualism. Unlike other organizations that portray their ethnic groups as victims, the Center, Glazer argues, ought to be followed as a model of a bilingual program.

15g Literature review

The literature review, sometimes called a survey paper or a review of the literature, is usually one section of a longer paper but may be assigned as a paper in itself. In a psychology paper reporting the results of an experiment, for instance, the literature review is typically the first section after the introduction. Its purpose is to synthesize the existing research on your topic and thus provide a backdrop and justification for your own research. It may concentrate on current studies that define a problem or establish a need for further research. Most literature reviews present the findings of others in a fair and balanced manner, summarizing the literature instead of critiquing it.

ELEMENTS OF A LITERATURE REVIEW

- It specifies the topic, issue, or problem that is the focus and typically organizes information chronologically or thematically.
- It accurately identifies and concisely summarizes other researchers' work, noting influential contributions.
- It includes major points of agreement or disagreement among the other studies, generally without critiquing them.
- It synthesizes information from prior studies, noting overlaps while crediting each researcher.
- It establishes a context for justifying and shaping your own study based on the current state of knowledge.

The following selection from a literature review was orginally part of an APA-style paper studying how the human perspectives of cat owners affect their pets' health and longevity. The literature review, which provides scientific background for the study, opens by giving readers an idea of the problem the paper addressses and the general conclusion it reaches. Note how the writer connects her sources to each other.

A Healthier Diet for Cats

by Sarah Andrea

Focuses on problem

Provides glimpse of overall conclusion

1   In the wild, animals innately know to avoid excessive consumption, eating only to maintain themselves. At the same time, 25% of this country's domesticated cats are morbidly obese or diabetic. Studies suggest that the diet of most domesticated cats is

to blame. With a digestive tract much simpler than a human's, a feline is not able to metabolize vegetable protein and does not have a dietary requirement for carbohydrates. Cats have thus evolved with an ability to digest food high in protein and low in carbohydrates. The diet of a wild cat is dependent on mainly one element, animal protein, such as a mouse, made up of 3% carbohydrates, 40% protein, and 50% fat (Riond, 2003; Russell, 2002).

Summarizes important information

2   Dry cat foods, often purchased because of their lower cost, contain high percentages of carbohydrates from cereal grains. According to studies conducted by Appleton (2001) and Mazzabero (2003), a cat's inability to adapt to the drastic change in the dietary ingredients of dry food causes high blood glucose and an overall exhausting of beta cells, leading to diabetes mellitus. Studies by Rand (2002, 2003) of dry, wet, and raw meat feline diets demonstrate the contribution of dry foods to feline diabetes and obesity.

Groups related studies

[The paper continues, ending with a list of references.]

15h Essay exam

When you work on an essay exam, even a take-home exam, you have only a short time to write. Read the question carefully, and jot down a working thesis and specific evidence. Organize information in clear chunks so your instructor will quickly see your knowledge of the topic. State your points clearly, especially beginning each paragraph. Watch your time.

ELEMENTS OF AN ESSAY EXAM ANSWER

- It addresses all parts of the exam question directly.
- It follows directions about the approach (such as comparison or explanation) and covers the number of points or examples expected.
- It uses references—quotations, facts, and other information—efficiently, illustrating the point without overloading the essay.
- It connects references and synthesizes material to show significance.
- It interprets, supporting a point, not merely listing details.
- It may be information-driven, providing an objective explanation such as a description or definition, or point-driven, presenting a position or arguing for an interpretation.

Here are selections from an open-book essay exam that asked students for a point-driven response: to identify a common theme running through a survey of American literature and to discuss their interpretation of this theme in two stories.

Moral Perfection in "Young Goodman Brown"

and "The Birthmark"

by Ted Wolfe

States theme selected

1   Hawthorne's "Young Goodman Brown" explores the conflict between good and evil. Young Goodman Brown has his religious faith tested during a journey into the woods. In what may or may not be a dream, he is shown by the devil

Refers to events in story

that everyone he believed to be good is evil. . . . When the devil is about to baptize him, Brown calls out for

Interprets events and character's name

Faith, his wife, telling her to resist the temptation. He is really calling out for faith, as in faith in God. When he does this, the hellish vision passes, and he is alone in

Draws conclusion about story

the woods. From this, I think we can conclude that Hawthorne believes that people should try to resist temptation and live moral lives.

Uses short supporting quotation

2   But Goodman Brown is never the same after the experience, be it dream or reality. He becomes "a stern, a sad, a darkly meditative, if not a desperate man." In his heart he doubts the goodness of Faith/faith, Deacon Gookin, Goody Cloyse, and everyone else. . . . Symbolically, the experience in the woods causes him to give up his faith.

Develops conclusion further

The overriding message that Hawthorne is trying to convey is that one should try to keep one's faith, to believe in others' inherent goodness, and to live morally. If one doesn't, life becomes as barren and miserable as it became for Goodman Brown.

Follows directions to discuss two stories

3   Hawthorne's "The Birthmark" also addresses . . .

[The paper continues with second short story.]

Concludes essay

4   . . . Hawthorne's point is that one should not get so caught up in trying to be morally perfect that it ruins one's life. People must learn to "find the perfect future in the present."

15i Short documented paper

In many courses, you may write a short paper that draws on a few sources and argues, interprets, or simply presents information.

ELEMENTS OF A SHORT DOCUMENTED PAPER

- It summarizes or synthesizes others' views, results, or positions.
- It presents information fairly in your own words.
- It may provide reasoned conclusions or interpretations based on cited sources but may allow readers to apply these to their actions or beliefs.
- It is well organized and easy to read.

Following are excerpts from an informative short documented paper. Although the paper cites facts and statistics from four articles, it also has its own thesis that presents a conclusion based on its synthesis of research studies.

Desperate Times for Teachers

by David Aharonian

1   There is a major controversy regarding teacher salaries presently in this country. Many people feel that teachers are overpaid because they have summers off from work. They feel that teachers do not truly work year-round and therefore are either getting a fair rate of pay or getting too much. Many teachers, however, disagree with this assessment. They feel that they are underpaid for the work that they do. Most teachers find it very difficult just to make ends meet on a teacher's salary, and often they resort to moonlighting.

Synthesizes opposing positions

States thesis

2–6   Moonlighting means that a person holds another job in addition to his or her career. . . .

Defines key term

[Four additional paragraphs supply information and data from two sources on moonlighting teachers.]

7   But there really are no easy solutions to the problem. One obvious answer would be to increase teacher salaries (Alley 21). This would lead to less moonlighting and allow teachers to concentrate more on their primary occupation. But there are still plenty of people who oppose raising teacher salaries. Many times teachers may go two or three years without any raise in their pay. Then when the teachers do get a raise, it may only be 2 or 4

Presents alternatives, leaving reader to decide

Supplies detail

percent. This certainly lowers the morale of the teachers and can

Concludes with pertinent quotation

cause teachers to become frustrated (Henderson 12). As one teacher in Oklahoma put it, "It's hard to look across the hall and see a teacher who's taught 14 years, making only $4,000 more than you are" (Wisniewski and Kleine 1).

[The paper ends with a list of works cited.]

15j Review

A **review** is a critical appraisal of an event, an object, or a phenomenon, such as a sculpture show, dance performance, concert, film, play, book, or product. Reviews help people make decisions or test their judgments against someone else's. In a review, you describe, analyze, and evaluate your subject from an informed but opinionated perspective, ranging from fairly objective and descriptive to strongly judgmental. A **critique**, a similar assignment, summarizes a text and offers a subjective critical reaction to it, explaining how and why the text was written as well as how readers might look at it from fresh perspectives.

ELEMENTS OF A REVIEW

- It describes or summarizes its subject at the start, providing the background a reader needs to grasp the subject.
- It offers a reasoned, supported evaluation of the subject's main elements, often introduced as an opening thesis or as the point of the second of two parts, following a description of the subject.
- It demonstrates the writer's knowledge of the subject so that readers are more likely to respect the conclusions presented.
- It supports its conclusions with details and examples so readers will respect its points even if they do not agree with the evaluation.
- It establishes clear standards or criteria for assessing the work's success, value, or significance.

Note how Amy Braegelman, a student in an introductory linguistics course, prepares readers for the subject of the book she is reviewing before she moves into the review itself.

Introduces general subject of book reviewed

1   The preservation of a language, though the community that uses it may be small, is crucially important. Language is not just a communicative amenity--it is a reflection of (and an influence on) a specific culture. Not only does a language allow a culture to flourish, but it allows the people within that culture to flourish. In some cases, a language is particularly well suited to a specific culture because it is all that allows its users to function in society. To allow or force a language so tailored to die is to leave the culture with no ef-

fective means of communication, only whatever its people have managed to acquire, usually by bare necessity, of the surrounding, dominant language.

2   Cathryn Carroll's book *Laurent Clerc: The Story of His Early Years* (Washington: Gallaudet UP, 1991) gives the reader a broader platform on which to base these convictions. Beginning with the early nineteenth century, Clerc's story raises questions about the beliefs, stereotypes, and attitudes surrounding the deaf and their language. . . .

Identifies book and explains its focus

[The paper continues with five paragraphs on the book's contents.]

8   Carroll's fascinating book illustrates the folly of expecting one mode of communication, one language, to suffice for every member of society. Her book portrays the struggle of the deaf to gain equal standing in a greater society that had so much trouble accepting them. . . .

Concludes with evaluation of book

15k Position paper

When you write a position paper, you present a position on an issue or controversy and then support that position. Sometimes you'll draw supporting material from the course or from internal logic, personal experience, or anecdote, and sometimes you'll do outside reading or research. Your topic must be one on which others hold different opinions, not simply your likes or dislikes, matters of indisputable fact, and beliefs based on conviction rather than empirical evidence (including most religious beliefs). (See also Chapter 10.)

ELEMENTS OF A POSITION PAPER

- It states and supports a clear position on a genuine, arguable issue.
- Its introduction explains the issue, supplies a thesis or position statement, and leads into paragraphs supporting the position with appropriate evidence.
- It uses factual knowledge, statistics, logical reasoning, or carefully selected anecdotes to support the writer's opinion, perspective, interpretation, or solution.
- It discusses alternative points of view to demonstrate that its reasoning is careful and thorough (see 10f).
- It cites any sources using the expected documentation style. (See Chapters 26–29.)

For an example of a position paper, see the annotated sample in 10g.

15l Oral presentation

Planning a presentation with a partner or team takes time but provides valuable experience for work and public communities. (See 18g and 19h.)

STRATEGY   **Work together as a speaking team.**

- Split up research responsibilities; collaborate as you create and exchange talking points; rehearse as a group (see 14b).
- Unify around your purpose, theme, and organization.
- Coordinate all contributions, and divide the time evenly; plan how to monitor and cue each other on time limits.
- Have the first presenter introduce the team; then have each speaker create a transition to the next. Create a single presentation that reveals differences in the subject, not oppositions in the team.

16 Academic Writing: Humanities and Literature

The humanities include literature, history, languages, philosophy, classics, art history, music, performing arts, cultural studies, and related fields. In these fields, you will interpret texts, performances, and works of art, looking for their meaning, the relationship of their various elements, and their techniques. Writing in the humanities develops theories to understand our lives and cultures, looks for patterns of meaning in past events and ways to deal with the future, and evaluates texts, performances, ideas, and interpretations.

16a Goals of writing in the humanities

Research in literary, film, or cultural studies and similar fields focuses on texts—verbal, aural, or visual. It attends to the action of the people represented there, the ideas conveyed, the visual images and patterns, and the techniques employed. Researchers try to interpret how these elements are related and what they convey (intentionally or not) about ideas, culture, society, or history.

16b Audiences in the humanities

In a humanities course, your primary audience is your instructor, although you sometimes may be asked to address other specific audiences or to share your writing with your peers. These readers are likely to expect detailed analyses, clear interpretations, and well-supported conclusions. Outside the academic community, the interests of researchers in the humanities are shared by the broad public audience that reads novels, attends film festivals, consults music reviews, visits art museums, or enjoys creative performances.

16c Writing tasks in the humanities

As these examples suggest, much of the writing in the humanities **analyzes** (to understand the elements of a work) and **interprets** (to understand the relationship of the elements and the overall meaning of the work itself or of the culture or society it embodies). When you analyze, you break a subject into its components and study the relationships among the parts—how they affect or relate to each other, how they work together, how they fit within a larger system, how they are in turn divided into a smaller system. You look for connections, patterns, and relationships within the larger whole. When you interpret, you try to discover in a text the patterns of meaning, presented or embodied, that help link its various elements more or less into a significant whole.

16d Types of writing in the humanities

Although the subjects and methods of inquiry in the various fields of the humanities may differ, many courses require the kinds of evaluative writing expected in general education courses, especially reviews or critiques (see 15j). Besides appraising creative work, writing in the humanities is also likely to analyze and interpret it, especially imaginative literature (fiction, poetry, drama, and often film).

When you analyze and interpret, you often call attention to the work's characterization, plot, symbolism, or figurative language. In addition, imaginative literature may convey its meanings through a fictional representation of some situation or human activity: the events of a story, a confrontation between characters, a monologue or dialogue revealing thoughts and emotions, or a scene or setting in which events take place. The next sections explain strategies for reading in the humanities and illustrate how to analyze and interpret literary and visual works, advice that readily transfers to related humanities fields.

16e Ways of reading literary texts

When you read a novel, short story, or poem or view a drama or film, you often pay attention both to meaning and to artistic technique.

1 Read through "lenses"

Your perspective as a reader may determine your strategies for reading and interpreting. From a psychological view, you might note how a character tries to overcome feelings of childhood abandonment. Or, through a feminist lens, you might examine the portrayal of women in a novel. How particular groups or communities see the world may be refracted through the lenses of academic fields such as psychology or feminist theory or those of other groups bound by occupation, race, culture, or social status.

STRATEGY   Shift your reading lens.

After reading a literary work, recall the key events, characters, and settings through a series of lenses appropriate to the work. What happens when you use the lens of economics or, more specifically, capitalism or socialism? What happens if you shift to the lens of technology? or religion? or biology? Test as many lenses as you can to see what insights you gain.

2 Read for theme

For many critics and students of literature, to read for meaning is to read for theme. You can view **theme** as an idea, perspective, insight, or cluster of feelings that a work conveys or that permeates a work, organizing the relationships among its parts. Or you can view theme as the insights readers are likely to derive from their reading experience.

As you read, write down your ideas, responses, or clusters of feelings. Note the techniques writers use to convey meaning (see 16e-3). Look especially for repeated words and ideas, contrasting characters or events, and patterns of images, which can signal possible themes.

In reading a short poem, Sevon Randall notes repetitions and contrasts that reveal a cluster of feelings and ideas (a theme).

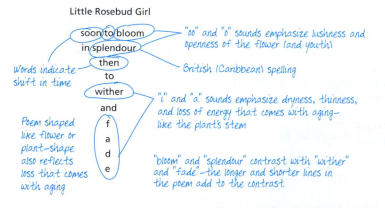

Little Rosebud Girl

soon to bloom

in splendour

"oo" and "o" sounds emphasize lushness and openness of the flower (and youth)

Words indicate shift in time

then

to

British (Caribbean) spelling

wither

and

"i" and "a" sounds emphasize dryness, thinness, and loss of energy that comes with aging— like the plant's stem

Poem shaped like flower or plant—shape also reflects loss that comes with aging

f
a
d
e

"bloom" and "splendour" contrast with "wither" and "fade"—the longer and shorter lines in the poem add to the contrast

—ANSON GONZALEZ, "Little Rosebud Girl" (1968)

3 Read for technique

When you read for meaning, you inevitably read for technique. A writer can't create events, portray characters, represent scenes, or elicit a reader's reactions without using techniques of characterization, plot, setting, or imaginative language.

Look for these key elements as you read.

Character. Who are the major and minor characters? What are their traits? Are the characters complex or one-dimensional? How do they change—or fail to change—in response to events? How self-aware are they? Which ones are presented positively, which negatively?

Plot. Are events presented in chronological order, or have they been rearranged? What is the role of conflict in the plot? Do events spring from the characters' personalities or serve mainly to reveal character traits? Is there a main conflict, a chain of conflicts, or a climax?

Setting. Where and when do events occur? Does the setting help explain characters' actions or convey a mood that shapes readers' reactions?

Point of view. Who tells the story? Is the narrator a character or a persona, a voice adopted by the writer or poet? Is the story narrated in the first person (*I*) or in the third person by a narrator who is not identified as *I* but speaks of the characters as *he* or *she*? Is the narrator *omniscient* (all-knowing)? limited in knowledge? reliable?

Language. How does the work use imaginative language—simile, metaphor, understatement, paradox, or irony? Does it use vivid description, unusual wording, rhythms, rhymes, or other sound patterns?

Genre. What's its form: novel, short story, poem, drama, or film? Is it a specific *type* of one of these, such as a novella or allegory? Do its characteristics define a specific genre (such as cinema verité for film)?

16f Literary text analysis

When you write about a literary text, you often analyze and interpret its meaning or its technique. Either way, you reach reasonable conclusions—observations and judgments—supported by evidence from the text or secondary sources.

To write about meaning, you explain and support your conclusions about the text's theme, or you focus on your insights using a particular perspective (historical, feminist, and so forth). Consider two common schemes as you organize your paper. You can separate your thesis into parts or subtopics and take up each of these in a different section. Or you can divide your paper to correspond to different segments of the work (beginning, middle, end) or different elements (characters, language, symbols). Then, in each section of your paper, show how the particular segment or element supports your thesis.

To write about technique, you typically highlight the author's use of language, setting, or characterization. Then you draw conclusions about how technique shapes the work's meaning and readers' likely responses. If you examine one technique, try dividing your essay into parts corresponding to sections of the work, showing how and why the technique is used in each section. If you treat more than one technique, try devoting a part to each different technique.

As you are writing, recall the academic conventions for verb tense (see 32b); use present tense to summarize a text ("Falstaff *acts* . . .") or to discuss what an author does ("Toni Morrison *gives* her characters . . ."); use past tense for historical context ("During the Vietnam War, Levertov's poetry *took on* a political tone").

ELEMENTS OF A LITERARY TEXT ANALYSIS

- It often states its thesis early to establish its conclusion about a work's theme or to reflect its dual purpose of describing and analyzing technique and then relating technique to meaning.
- It presents carefully selected evidence such as details, examples, and passages quoted, paraphrased, or summarized from the text.
- It analyzes passages presented as evidence to show how they support the paper's analysis and interpretation.
- It cites all text material and outside sources using MLA or another documentation style (see Chapters 26–29.)

In the following literary analysis, notice how the writer backs up her interpretation of the meaning of a short story. She uses quotations from the story but does not allow them to dominate. She also mentions details from the story and refers to its characters, events, and plot as she develops her interpretation.

Images of Self in "The Yellow Wallpaper"

by Jennifer O'Berry

Identifies context and literary work

1   During the 1800s the idea of the "new woman" was appearing. Women began to realize that they were seen only as their husbands' and society's "property." They began to pursue their independence and create their own identities. In Charlotte Perkins Gilman's short story "The Yellow Wallpaper," a nameless woman is searching for her personal identity and freedom from the oppressive childlike treatment inflicted on her by her doctor/husband. Gilman presents an elaborate metaphor about the images seen by the woman within the wallpaper found in her nursery/bedroom. This metaphor and the images the woman finds in the wallpaper play a significant role in the woman's achievement of finding her true self. Her state of insanity at the end of the story serves as a

States thesis about theme

safe mask for her newly found freedom from alienation and oppression.

2   Gilman presents the woman in her story as a somewhat
unstable character who believes that she is sick, although
John, her doctor/husband, believes that she is only
suffering from a "slight hysterical tendency" (416). This
characterization seems intentional on the part of Gilman
because it makes the reader see clearly that the woman's
ideas are oppressed, even from the beginning, by her
husband. John thinks that all his wife needs is a strict
rest schedule in which she is "absolutely forbidden to
'work'" (416) until she is "well" again. Gilman seems to
suggest, by putting *work* in quotation marks, that the duties
of the woman, and all women at that time, were not truly
considered work. She was forbidden to write and to have
visitors. Early in the story, when the "rules" for her
recovery are stated, the woman begins to comment on her
disagreement with her husband, but she stops abruptly, as
if she does not dare to have such thoughts. She believes
that she would recover more quickly if, instead of being
quarantined and forbidden from such pleasures as her
writing, she "had less opposition and more society and
stimulus" (416).

3   The woman tells the reader that "Mary is so good with
the baby" (417), implying that she herself does not want to
spend time with the baby. The child is also never mentioned
by the woman as being with her or spending time with her.
This seems to suggest that she may actually be experiencing
a type of postpartum depression, causing her to want to
abandon her child. The thoughts that lead her to feel that
she may be ill may actually be due to her desire to abandon
her role of wife and mother which was so rigidly demanded
by society at that time. She gets "unreasonably angry"
(416) about the condition of things sometimes, but she

Interprets characters using quotations and summaries for support

Deepens interpretation of woman's condition in terms of theme

blames this anger on her "nervous condition" (416). She tries to dismiss these thoughts because she feels that they are not proper. Therefore, she feels that she must be ill.

Identifies imagery related to theme

4   Gilman uses many images to enlighten the reader about the childlike treatment of the woman by her husband. The woman is directed by her husband to rest in a bedroom that used to serve as a nursery. Gilman chooses this room to show how John thinks of his wife. When referring to his wife, John commonly chooses names such as "blessed little goose" (418), "blessed child" (420), and "little girl" (421). This shows that he does not see his wife as an equal but rather as a helpless child who is solely dependent on him. As the woman begins to realize that she has been a subject of this type of oppression, she begins to be "a little afraid of John" (422) and to "wish he would take another room" (424), which exhibits her awareness of this treatment and the desire to be free from it, and from him.

Focuses on imagery in wallpaper

5   Because of her rigid rest schedule, the woman is forced to spend most of her time in her nursery/bedroom, where she begins to explore the "worst [wall]paper" (417) she has ever seen in her life. Since she is not allowed to do much else, she commits herself to "follow that pointless pattern to some sort of conclusion" (419). She finds many images in the pattern, all of which aid in her "improvement" (423) "because of the wallpaper" (423) out of her mother/wife roles. She describes the pattern as images that will "plunge off at outrageous angles, [and] destroy themselves in unheard-of contradiction" (417). These "contradictions" seem to be referring to the contradictory treatment of her by her husband and society's contradictory expectations of her to be the perfect wife and mother. She becomes entranced by the wallpaper and "follows the

pattern about by the hour" (419). With each second, the images become more numerous and complex. She begins to see "a broken neck and two bulbous eyes" (418), a woman behind the pattern in wallpaper. This woman "is all the time trying to climb through . . . but nobody could climb through . . . it strangles so" (424). She begins to identify with the woman and decides that she will stop at nothing until the woman is released from her entrapment.

6   At the end of the story, the woman is simultaneously on the brink of self-identity and insanity. On the last night she is to stay in the house, she is left alone in the room where she finally frees the woman in the wallpaper. When the woman in the wallpaper begins to "crawl and shake the pattern" (425), the main character "[runs] to help her" (425). Through the night, the two women pull and shake the bars and are able to "peel off yards of that paper" (425). She breaks down some of these cultural bars with the help from the woman in the wallpaper. When morning arrives, there is only one woman--the two have merged, and the woman's true identity has been found. In the remaining wallpaper are "many of those creeping women" (426). This symbolically represents the great number of women who also desire to be freed from the bars put up by society. She wonders if those women will ever "come out of the wallpaper as [she] did" (426). This shows her symbolic escape and her desire for other women to experience this personal freedom.

Interprets climax of plot

7   John returns at the end of the story to discover his wife in a state of insanity. When he sees her as the woman in the wallpaper, creeping around the room, he faints. She "had to creep over him" (426) because he was blocking her path. This strongly symbolizes the conquering of her husband because of her dominant position

Contrasts main characters at story's conclusion

over him. She tells him that he cannot "put [her] back" (426) because she is finally free. Her creeping, which is like that of an infant, seems to represent a birth of her new self. At the same

Points out irony

time, she has become completely insane. It is rather ironic that she must move into this state in order to be free from oppression. This seems to represent society's view of a liberated and self-identified woman. John believes that his wife is not ill before she begins her pursuit of self-discovery. When this discovery is complete, he sees her as insane. The opposite is true for the woman herself. She sees herself as ill before her process of identification and fully healthy afterward.

8   The woman in Gilman's short story uses the yellow wallpaper as a tool to find her true self. The color of the wallpaper itself seems to represent the brightness and hope of a new horizon, yet at the same time, it is a reminder of the "old, foul, bad yellow

Returns to thesis and restates theme

things" (423), like a fungus that grows and decays. This is representative of the woman's life. She can never truly be free because society's views and ideas will never acknowledge that a liberated woman can achieve her own identity.

[The paper ends by citing the text where the story appears.]

16g Visual text analysis

Visual texts as films, paintings, videos, architecture, photographs, and sculpture call for a different approach than novels, poetry, or drama do. Visuals differ in technique: films and videos, for instance, draw on photography and animation. Visuals also differ in space and time: photographs, paintings, sculpture, and architecture occupy space but don't unfold in time as novels or films do.

When you analyze visual texts, note features and qualities like the following.

- **Arrangement.** How are the visual elements placed with regard to each other? Where are the figures in a picture, the objects in a photograph, or the parts of a building situated?
- **Color.** What color scheme dominates the visual: pastels, sepia, or shades of gray? Which patterns in the use of color are apparent?

- **White space.** How much of the work is left empty or "white"? For example, is a central figure surrounded by white or neutral space, or is the entire painting, photograph, or film scene filled with people, objects, and background material?
- **Cinematography or Photographic Style.** What film or video techniques (such as fading, quick cuts, or slow motion) does the work employ? How are lenses (close-up, long distance, sharp, blurry, grainy) or recording material (film, tape, digital) used?
- **Realism or Abstraction.** Are people, objects, or scenes presented in realistic detail (a still life of fruit) or abstract form (the shape of a human figure or masses of color and form)?
- **Sound.** Does the work include speech and sound, or does it consist simply of form, shape, or volume occupying space (paintings, sculptures, buildings, photographs)?
- **Eye movement.** Do the eyes of viewers move around based on the ways characters look at each other (**gaze movement**)? Or do their eyes move around according to geometric or structural relationships among objects and colors (**structural movement**)?

ELEMENTS OF A VISUAL TEXT ANALYSIS

- It states a thesis analyzing the visual's elements or interpreting its cultural, psychological, social, or philosophical insights.
- It presents detailed evidence from the visual, drawing on qualities such as arrangement, color, style, or sound, and then interprets this evidence to show how it supports the paper's thesis.
- It organizes information into chunks or sections, each covering a quality, feature, or point to help a reader follow the explanation.

The elements of the visual on page 113—a Web page—are organized to interest viewers to enter the site. Bright, colorful images, coupled with sleek design and use of vibrant hues, encourage viewers to take a closer look at the products offered and potentially make a purchase.

17 Academic Writing: Social and Natural Sciences

Academic writing in the social and natural sciences inquires and reports about the world around us. The fields in the social sciences are as varied as psychology, sociology, political science, economics, education, and business. Research in such fields examines individual and group characteristics, behaviors, and relationships. The natural sciences include broad and narrow scientific and medical fields: biology, physics, and chemistry as well as pharmacy, anatomy, oceanography, and meteorology. Research in such fields investigates the rocks, oceans, stars, chemicals, and atoms of the natural world as well as the physical dimensions of its inhabitants from tiny organisms to complex humans.

17a Goals of writing in the social and natural sciences

Writing in the social and natural sciences reports the findings of scientific inquiry: field observations, surveys and interviews, microscopic study and experiments in labs, clinical notes and trials in hospitals, or experiments in facilities like wind tunnels. Through such study researchers strive to understand the workings of the human and natural worlds.

17b Audiences in the social and natural sciences

In a course in the social or natural sciences, your primary audience is your instructor and possibly the members of your lab, your research team, your course peers, or some other specific audience. These readers will expect you to report detailed information clearly and accurately, often following conventional formats. They're likely to expect you to justify and explain your research from its background, theoretical grounding, hypotheses, methods, and findings to its conclusions.

Outside the academic community, the interests of researchers in the social and natural sciences are shared by people in many careers—social workers, forensic anthropologists, engineers, physical therapists—as well as teachers and other researchers whose work may be influenced by research findings. Many informative accounts in magazines, newspapers, and professional publications are directed at general audiences and provide a bridge to understanding technical discussions.

17c Writing tasks in the social and natural sciences

Because the social and natural sciences are so wide-ranging, many fields address clinical and applied needs through specific writing tasks such as grant proposals, engineering reports, clinical notes, individual educational plans, or nursing care plans. Even so, these fields share common expectations about the need to report clearly and accurately. Research writing also carefully presents the theory, background, and prior work that justify or shape a study and then reports the study's procedures and findings. Given the complexity of both human behavior and natural phenomena, research projects tend to focus only on small parts of the whole. Both the research questions asked and the opportunities for investigation shape the research design.

Typically, social scientists gather data by observing human behavior or soliciting information from individuals or groups. Studies may report on individual or small-group behavior over an extended period (**case studies**) or on behavior characteristic of a location (rural town, city neighborhood, manufacturing plant) or a group of people (elementary school students, restaurant workers, athletes) (**ethnographies**). Methods of study can include gathering responses from a number of people (**surveys**), examining behaviors and attitudes of individuals or small groups (**interviews, observations**), or comparing behaviors in normal situations (**control groups**) with those in altered situations (**experimental groups**).

Typically, natural scientists gather data through observation and collection in order to study changes, physical dimensions, or components of a subject. They look for relationships among events, materials, or matter and energy, especially for mathematical correlations or likely causes and effects. They often use sophisticated equipment to measure phenomena invisible to the human eye (such as electrical waves or subatomic particles) and to record data that change over time (such as the growth of an organism) or are dangerous to sample (such as fumes from a volcano).

17d Types of writing in the social and natural sciences

In your courses in the social and natural sciences, as in your general education classes, you may be expected to write short documented papers (15i) on current issues or problems, review the literature about a current research topic (15g), write an essay exam (15h), or supply an annotated bibliography (15f). Other common texts propose or report original research: proposals, lab reports, field reports, research articles, and similar documents. Whatever the specific discipline, you will probably need to follow a conventional format for a research report with sections such as these: abstract (17e), introduction or background, literature review (15g), methods, findings or results, conclusions, and perhaps applications or implications. Find out exactly what divisions are required because the expected format is a guide to the pattern of inquiry and credible reporting expected by your instructor or field.

17e Abstract

An **abstract** is a special form of summary (see 15e), often preceding and objectively summing up a lab report, detailed study, or research paper. It increases the efficiency of readers, previewing a text to help them decide whether it is pertinent to their interests. Your abstract for a research project should summarize its hypothesis, method, findings or results, and discussion. An abstract for a review of the literature should convey its gist as well as its method, theoretical stance, and conclusions. In either case, your abstract should be so clear and so concise that a reader with no familiarity with the whole paper will understand what it says.

ELEMENTS OF AN ABSTRACT

- It opens with an overview expressed in a sentence or two.
- It summarizes all the important sections of a paper.
- It defines key terms, especially those used in unusual ways.
- It presents information concisely, eliminating unnecessary wording.
- It satisfies a reader's need for a clear, accurate, objective preview.

The following abstract introduces the informative report whose opening appears in 17f. See also page 262 for an abstract from a paper in the social sciences and page 304 for an abstract from a paper in the natural sciences.

ADD/ADHD Misdiagnosis

by James Newlands

Most misdiagnoses of ADD/ADHD result from similarities with other disorders. The disorder most often confused with ADD/ADHD is childhood bipolar disorder. Misdiagnosis is due both to similarities between the diseases and to lack of widespread knowledge of childhood bipolar disorder. In addition, females are often misdiagnosed with depression because they frequently display inattentiveness rather than the hyperactivity generally associated with ADD/ADHD. Misdiagnosis also may mean that medications with potentially serious consequences are prescribed for children.

Opens with overview

Sums up major points covered in report

17f Informative report

Often assigned in the social sciences, the informative report gathers research-based details, ideas, and conclusions relevant to a problem, solution, or policy. In it, you address a need of readers for practical knowledge, a desire for greater understanding, or even simple curiosity. You also make clear your sources: articles, books, newsletters, or research databases. In most cases, however, an informative report is not arranged like a literature review that systematically surveys the sources and their conclusions (see 15g). Instead, you need to develop an effective organization that supplies the information your readers need.

ELEMENTS OF AN INFORMATIVE REPORT

- It draws on recent, reliable research and other sources.
- It identifies a need for information and responds to it.
- It provides clear explanations and presents information in ways that are accessible to readers.
- It may include visuals such as pictures, tables, and graphs to explain complicated information.
- It organizes information to emphasize important facets of the subject, highlighting what is most useful or interesting to readers.

For a course in the health sciences, James Newlands wrote a paper on ADD/ADHD misdiagnosis, explaining the problem and emphasizing its seriousness. Here are the opening paragraphs of his paper written in APA style. (See 17e for his abstract.)

ADD/ADHD Misdiagnosis

by James Newlands

Introduces problem of misdiagnosis   The last 10 years have seen a considerable increase in the number of ADD/ADHD cases diagnosed along with a marked increase in medication prescribed. In 2000, more than 19 million prescriptions for ADHD drugs were filled, a 72% increase since 1995 (Lebelle, 2000). The increase is due both to increased awareness of the disease and to misdiagnosis. Increased awareness among teachers

Identifies need of parents for information   means that the school usually approaches parents to have an assessment for ADD/ADHD, and parents often feel pressured to use drug treatment to "correct" their children's behavior (Lebelle).

Emphasizes difficulty of diagnosis   There is no valid independent test for ADD/ADHD. Instead, health professionals rely on a list of behaviors (inattention, hyperactivity, impulsivity, academic underachievement, or behavior problems), diagnostic interviews, and anecdotal information from family and school staff (Lebelle, 2000). The lack of an objective test leaves diagnosis open to interpretation by the doctor. Combined with pressure from schools to "correct their child's behavior," diagnosis by a doctor causes many parents to allow their

Previews organization of paper   children to go on medications such as Ritalin. What effects do these medications have on children? How and how often are children being misdiagnosed? In this paper I discuss the main causes of misdiagnosis and the consequences of medication for children.

[The paper continues, ending with a list of references.]

17g Lab report

In fields like biology, chemistry, or engineering, you are likely to write lab reports on experiments. Lab reports need to be clear and concise, describing exactly what you did and what happened as a result.

Lab reports vary in style and format, depending on the field. Check with each instructor about requirements, such as section numbers and headings. A typical structure begins with an overview or abstract of the focus or goal (why it was done), introduces the problem or principles (what it shows), describes the methods (how it was done), explains the results (what happened), discusses the outcomes (what the results mean), and states a conclusion (what it shows).

ELEMENTS OF A LAB REPORT
- It strictly follows the format required by the instructor or field.
- It focuses on the objective description of cause and effect during the experiment.
- It does not digress into unnecessary commentary on the experiment.
- It uses specific terminology and unambiguous language.
- It presents data and results accurately, without distortion.

Typical sections of a lab report include the Abstract, Introduction, Experiment (Materials and Procedure), Results, Discussion, and Conclusion. Here is a selection from the closing section of a chemistry lab report.

Butane: Determining Molecular Weight from Vapor

by Melanie Dedecker

[The report follows the brief assigned format, beginning with Materials, Procedure, and Calculations.]

Conclusion. The purpose of this experiment was to determine the molecular weight of butane gas through the use of the ideal gas law and to learn how to write an accurate procedure. In order to determine the molecular weight of butane gas, a lighter was weighed and then lighted underneath a graduated cylinder full of water. The gas that was emitted from the lighter displaced the water in the graduated cylinder. From this data and the mass of used butane gas, the density of the gas was determined. This value was used in an altered form of the ideal gas law to ascertain the molecular weight of butane gas. Although the actual molar mass of butane gas is 58 g/mol, this experiment determined the molar mass of butane to be 61.4 g/mol, resulting in a 5.86% error.

Includes required section headings

Uses specific terms

Supplies detailed results

[The report ends with possible reasons for this result.]

17h Research report

A research report in either the social or natural sciences typically follows a conventional arrangement (see the elements listed below) to report on a tightly focused study that aims to answer a particular question. Reading current research in your field will help you develop appropriate questions and understand the ongoing research "conversation" of the field. Further, you'll learn its usual ways of reporting research and the standard headings (and thus the standard sections) expected.

In the social sciences, for example, you'll generally explain who or what you studied, how you conducted your inquiry (interview, observation, survey, or experiment), what you learned, and how your findings answer your original question. For a case study or long-term observation, you may add narrative or descriptive evidence. In the natural sciences, you're also likely to describe your materials and laboratory procedures.

ELEMENTS OF A RESEARCH REPORT

- **Introduction.** Explain your investigation, survey and summarize prior research, and state your research question (or questions) or the hypothesis that you will test through your experiment.
- **Methods.** Describe your research design, methodology, and any laboratory procedures, materials, or measuring tools. Justify these if necessary. Mention problems or notable events during your study. Include survey or interview questions in the report or an appendix.
- **Results.** Present your results, the detailed data from the study, in your written discussion and in tables or graphs that make the information easy to grasp.
- **Discussion.** Explain your results—what the data mean and how they are related—including the extent to which you have answered your research questions or supported your hypothesis.
- **Conclusion.** Finish your report by highlighting the broad results of your study and suggesting directions for further research.

In a course on American folklore, Justine Buhl read about beliefs and superstitions that persisted through generations of college students. She conducted a survey to study the phenomenon on her own campus and presented the results of her (admittedly limited) survey in a research report. Following are brief portions of her report.

Food Folklore: Still Alive on Campus

by Justine Buhl

Introduces research topic   1   On any given day, in one of the many colleges around the country, students are, as they say, "grossed out" by the food served in their college dining halls. If you listen carefully, you will most likely hear students asking, "What is that? It looks disgusting!" or "Is this even real chicken?" Many of the things students say are similar to, or even the same as, things students have been saying for many years. These stories and beliefs, passed down by word of mouth from generation to generation, are a kind of college folklore of dining hall food.

[The paper briefly reviews relevant research on college folklore.]

2   I have encountered beliefs and stories about dining hall food enough times to be curious about them and about their similarities to the food folklore on campuses other than my own. I therefore decided to interview students at my own university and to do some research on college folklore in order to answer two questions: What are stories and beliefs about dining hall food that circulate among students at the university? How similar are these stories and beliefs to those that circulate on other campuses?

States research questions

Method

Uses heading to identify section

3   To answer these questions, I interviewed twenty students from the university and asked each six questions.

1. What are some of the stories you have heard about the food in our dining halls?
2. What similar stories (if any) have you heard from students at other colleges?
3. What special names have you heard to describe dining hall food on this campus?
4. What similar names (if any) have you heard from students at other colleges?
5. What are some of the common myths you have heard about dining hall food on this campus?
6. What similar myths (if any) have you heard from students at other colleges?

Includes questionnaire

[The paper next describes the interviewing procedure and minor difficulties during the research process.]

Results

Presents results in text

4   In response to question 1 about food stories (see Fig. 1), eight people said they thought laxatives were put in the food. One each responded that "They put poison in the food," "They spit in the food," and "They put pills in the food."

[Continues summarizing the results for each of the other questions.]

Shows results in graph

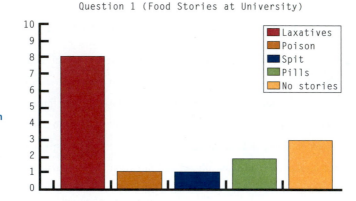

Fig. 1. Responses to question 1.

Discussion and Conclusion

Relates results to research questions

5   Students at the university have clearly encountered stories about dining hall food ("laxatives") and names for the food ("mystery meat"). They have also heard some gruesome urban myths about the food. They have heard these from their friends at other colleges as well. What is particularly interesting, however, is that all three forms of folklore have been in circulation for generations at American colleges.

[The paper continues by drawing on scholarship on campus folklore and suggesting that the stability reflects enduring concerns of students.]
[It ends with a list of references.]

18 Public Writing

In every public and civic context, people write to inform, express their views, organize collective efforts, and challenge injustice. Such writing improves your skills and flexibility as it helps you become a better-informed citizen.

18a Goals of public writing

When you address a public audience, you're likely to think of yourself as a volunteer, an activist, or a committee member, not as a writer. Your first concern will be to organize a beach cleanup or elect a mayor. You'll write to achieve your civic goals: to motivate others to support your cause, to influence policy, and to promote democratic processes.

18b Public audiences

When you prepare a meeting reminder for your book club or a newsletter for neighbors, you will know your readers personally. They expect clear information and may appreciate motivation, but they often already agree about issues or activities. But when you begin publicity for the track club's dinner—its big fund-raiser—you'll need to address a wider circle, readers you don't know personally and who won't support the dinner unless you persuade them that your cause is worthwhile. Use questions like the following to connect your readers with your goals.

- Why are you writing? What do you hope to accomplish?
- Who are your readers? What do they value? How much do they know or care about your project or issue?
- Do you primarily want to inform or to motivate? Do you want readers to agree with you or to take action—go to a meeting, contribute time or money, vote "yes" or "no," call an official, or join your group?
- What appeals to your readers' passion, anger, or fear might persuade them to do what you want—your sincerity, testimonials from others, information, or tugs on their interests or community values?
- How might you approach these readers? Will they respond best to impassioned appeals, logical analyses, or combined strategies? Will they expect a neighborly letter, a flyer, or a polished brochure?
- How can you contact prospective readers—through flyers at a meeting, appeals by mail or email, or letters in the newspaper?

18c Public writing tasks

Community members who are motivated by a cause or by strong civic values are likely to belong to groups of like-minded people. As a result, public writing is often collaborative, prepared by a committee and revised, as time allows, in accord with responses from a wider group. For example, the file for an electronic newsletter from an organization may be managed by an individual, but both the text and the layout probably have been composed and revised by several people. Exactly how such materials are written often depends on the urgency of the time schedule and the motivation of collaborators. Your writing task is likely to require juggling your individual objectives, your group's goals, and your readers' expectations. (See 4b, 5c, and 13c for collaborative strategies.)

STRATEGY Focus your public writing.

Work with others to answer these questions and make appropriate decisions.

- What is your task? Who will do what as you work on it?
- What's your deadline? How soon will recipients need information? How much time should you allow for printing, mailing, or other steps?
- What type of material should you prepare? What is the usual format? Do you have models or samples of past materials?
- Does your material require approval from anyone?
- Do you need to reserve a meeting room, coordinate with another group, or make other arrangements before you can finish your text?
- How will you distribute your material? Do you need to arrange duplication, mailing, or volunteers to deliver or post materials?

18d Types of public writing

Many types of public writing—letters, flyers, pamphlets, newsletters—are flexible documents. They can be directed to different readers, such as group members, newspaper readers, officials, or residents. They can address different, or multiple, goals by informing, building support, motivating to action, or promoting participatory democracy.

18e Public flyer

A common form of public writing is the flyer informing people about a meeting, activity, or event. Flyers also supply directions, advice, and information to residents, citizens, and other groups. (See also Chapter 12.) Sometimes they are prepared as companions to posters—which may supply similar information as they promote events.

Types of Public Writing		
Type	**Characteristic Activities**	**Common Forms**
PROVIDING INFORMATION	Gathering information, exploring issues, examining other views and alternative solutions, comparing, summarizing, synthesizing, and presenting material	Flyer, newsletter, fact sheet, informative report or article, letter (to group supporters, interested parties, officials, residents, or community in general), pamphlet, poster
BUILDING SUPPORT	Reaching consensus within a group, articulating a stance, defining a problem, proposing a solution, appealing to others with similar or different values, presenting evidence, finding shared values, advocating, persuading	Position paper, letter (to prospective supporters, officials, newspaper, or others concerned or involved), policy guidelines, statement of principles
MOTIVATING TO ACTION	Defining action, orchestrating participation, supplying information about involvement, motivating participants	Action proposal, grant proposal, flyer, letter, call to action in newsletter or other publication
PARTICIPATING IN DEMOCRATIC PROCESSES	Attending public meetings, meeting with officials, understanding legislative processes and timing, advocating civic involvement, distributing information on public or civic actions	Meeting minutes, committee report, legislative update, letter to officials, letter to group members, call to participate in newsletters or other publications, summary or analysis of public actions, petitions

ELEMENTS OF A PUBLIC FLYER

- It may open with its topic ("Hostetler Annual Reunion"), a general appeal ("Light a candle for peace!"), or a greeting ("Dear Choir Members").
- It clearly presents the essentials needed to attend or participate: date, time, place, directions, plans, equipment or supplies, contact and emergency telephone numbers, rain date, and so forth.
- It sticks to essentials and omits long explanations or background.
- It uses visual features, headings, graphics, and white space to highlight the most crucial information. (See 12c–d.)
- It may be informal or formal, depending on the group and the topic.

The flyer on page 126 announces a group's special event—a meeting to collect signed petitions for presentation to the school board.

18f Letter to the editor

Both partisans and interested citizens submit letters to the editor to comment on current issues or engage in topical debate. Check the opinion

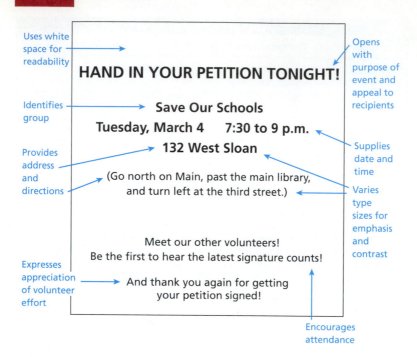

Uses white space for readability

Identifies group

Provides address and directions

Expresses appreciation of volunteer effort

Opens with purpose of event and appeal to recipients

Supplies date and time

Varies type sizes for emphasis and contrast

Encourages attendance

HAND IN YOUR PETITION TONIGHT!

Save Our Schools
Tuesday, March 4   7:30 to 9 p.m.
132 West Sloan
(Go north on Main, past the main library, and turn left at the third street.)

Meet our other volunteers!
Be the first to hear the latest signature counts!
And thank you again for getting your petition signed!

section of your local or campus paper, in print or online, to read current letters and to locate directions for submitting your own letter.

ELEMENTS OF A LETTER TO THE EDITOR

- It respects the length limit set by the newspaper or publication.
- It clearly identifies its topic and its point of view or proposal.
- It briefly supplies reasons and evidence that may persuade readers to consider or agree with its point of view. (See Chapter 10.)
- It treats other views and writers respectfully, even if it disagrees with their opinions.

Following are two letters to the editor (pp. 127–128), both providing reasons, evidence, and counterarguments while advancing the writers' perspectives on the particular issues.

18g Oral presentation

People gather daily to exchange opinions about local concerns. Citizens lobby officials for actions. Campus forums draw students, faculty, and administrators to discuss policies. Interest groups engage members and visitors. (See Chapter 14, 15l, and 19h.)

Letter to the Editor
April 16, 2007
Greeks Wrong in Punishing Critics

I am writing in response to the recent letter from Jillian Soares (April 14, 2007). As president of the Pan-Hellenic Council, she claims that the Council has the right to fine a fraternity or sorority if any of its members "speak publicly in ways that undermine the integrity or reputation of the Greek societies at Central Range State University." She uses this passage from the Pan-Hellenic Council's bylaws to justify fining Nina Campbell's sorority for statements she made in a recent Snowcap Advocate column. In it, Campbell criticized lack of fraternity and sorority support for the University's "All Campus Diversity Initiative."

As a sorority member myself, I think Campbell's criticisms were inaccurate and overstated. Certainly the Greeks can do a better job of promoting diversity—but then everybody can. After all, would a "Diversity Initiative" be necessary if everyone were doing a good job? But I think the Greeks have done more than most others on campus and that Campbell simply ignores all sorts of positive evidence. Campbell's opinions aren't the real problem, however. The proposed punishment is, along with the policy that makes it possible.

In her letter, Soares claims that the issue isn't a question of free speech because no one is trying to prevent Campbell from stating her opinion. She says that Campbell can avoid the fine for her sorority by resigning from the organization. She also states that the Council is not trying to prevent any Pan-Hellenic members from criticizing fraternity or sorority activities—the policy is only for statements that "distort the facts" or that are "needlessly insulting." But who is to determine the "facts"? When people don't like what they are hearing, they often claim that critics have "got the facts wrong."

The biggest problem with the policy is that it might discourage people from speaking out about actions that are truly discriminatory, unjust, or illegal. Soares says that anyone who wishes to speak out without violating the policy can resign from the fraternity or sorority. The policy might not prevent people from making reasonable criticisms, but it would certainly discourage them. Even when a person knows she is right to criticize, she might not want to cause trouble or expense for her "sisters."

Do we really want to force people to resign when they are speaking from the heart about things they believe are wrong—even if we disagree with them or even if they see the "facts" differently? Isn't this discriminatory?

Rebecca Fala

Sorority Circle

STRATEGY **Prepare to speak in a public forum.**

- Attend meetings, listen, and read to get informed about issues.
- Plan and rehearse (see 14b), even to speak for a minute or two.
- Be reasonable; don't alienate those who are undecided or disagree.
- Use facts, details, and other evidence—not emotion—for support.
- Stay calm at a tense meeting so that fear and nervousness don't lead you to speak angrily, make accusations, or even cry.

Letter to the Editor
February 18, 2007
"Balanced Education" Limits Diversity in Ideas

Last week at the South Valley School Board meeting, Concerned Citizens for a Balanced Education made a proposal that ought to be voted down at the next meeting. Concerned Citizens is critical of student government at South Valley High for sponsoring a talk by Malcom Zindt, who disapproves of the current president and many of his policies. They want to ban any speakers who "do not offer students a balanced perspective on issues or current events" in order to guarantee that "a South Valley education is a balanced education."

I believe that there are three important reasons for voting against this proposal.

(1) The proposal requires that any speakers present a "balanced" view. Speakers worth listening to generally present their own views, however. We want to listen to them because they offer special insights or because they are strong representatives of a point of view. Speakers who offer balanced perspectives are often less interesting—even boring. As a result, fewer students will attend their presentations and fewer will have a chance to encounter challenging ideas.

(2) By requiring that each speaker provide a balance of ideas, the proposal will eliminate the possibility of a set of lectures that create balance by presenting speakers with very different points of view. The student government has already set up a talk by Rose Azavone, a well-known critic of Zindt's and a supporter of current government policies. Concerned Citizens opposes this proposal because it would "require spending extra money for a job that one speaker could do." I believe Concerned Citizens is less interested in balance than in making sure students do not get to hear ideas the Citizens don't like!

(3) Concerned Citizens makes it clear that its idea of "balance" is pro versus con, left versus right. They seem to think that each issue has only two sides. This view is too simple. As a college student, I have come to realize that there are usually more than two ways of looking at an issue.

I hope the Concerned Citizens proposal will be defeated. I would like students at my former high school to get a chance to hear many voices and then make their own conclusions.

Ken Park, S.V.H.S., Class of 2004

19 Workplace Writing

Whether you work for a major corporation, run your own small business, join a government agency, or serve in a nonprofit organization, much of your work life will be spent communicating with others. As technology increases the pace and quantity of written exchanges, your ability to write is likely to become even more critical to your success.

19a Goals of workplace writing

Although workplaces vary greatly, their goals tend to be similar—to meet the needs and expectations of readers by providing and promoting the organization's products or services. Use questions like the following to help analyze workplace writing situations.

- What is my purpose? What do I want to accomplish?
- What type of document am I writing?
- What do readers expect me to do: provide information? identify a problem? analyze alternatives? propose a solution?
- What level of information do I have? what level of responsibility?
- How does my organization handle writing processes, file exchanges, document templates, or technical specifications?
- How are collaborative writing teams organized?
- How do the editing and text approval processes work?

19b Workplace audiences

Your writing may address very different readers, from your colleague at the next desk to the government official who processes your forms. Because your busy readers value clear, accessible documents, try to meet different needs simultaneously—providing a summary for your overloaded supervisor along with detailed charts in the appendix for the sales team. These questions can help you assess what your readers expect and need.

- How large is my audience? Who does it include? a coworker? a supervisor? a committee? a customer or client? an outside agency?
- Do readers expect a draft or a finished product? Will they implement my recommendations? Will they rely on my technical data?
- How much time do my readers have? Do they need detailed analysis or focused summary? Will they read carefully or skim the headings?
- What do my readers need to do with my writing? Will they revise it? approve it? implement it? incorporate it in their own writing?

19c Workplace writing tasks

You'll want your clarity, tone, and language to represent you and your organization well. Many writing tasks will be similarly structured because you'll supply comparable information about comparable situations. For example, using the standard form for a status report or evaluation simplifies your task and aligns your writing with readers' expectations.

When your project is complex or no form or template is specified, ask others how similar materials have been prepared. Keep samples of well-regarded

Types of Workplace Writing		
Type	**Characteristic Activities**	**Common Forms**
PROVIDING INFORMATION	Gathering information; exploring issues; comparing competing products or services; tracing background information; summarizing, synthesizing, compiling, and presenting information	Report, study, agenda, minutes, instructions, employee manual, procedural manual, policy guidelines, memo, email message, summary, technical description, organizational chart, brochure, letter (of transmittal, response, adjustment, acknowledgment, good news, bad news, or application), position description, résumé, visuals
REQUESTING INFORMATION OR ACTION	Identifying an issue or a problem, identifying objectives or operational goals, identifying gaps in data or other information, identifying and evaluating potential sources and resources	Memo, email message, directive, letter (of request, inquiry, commitment, or complaint), sales letter, marketing material, advertisements, order form, other forms, letter of application, contract
IDENTIFYING ALTERNATIVES OR RECOMMENDING SOLUTIONS	Analyzing, evaluating, or selecting alternatives; comparing and contrasting; organizing supporting evidence; clarifying implications; advocating	Proposal, report, study, analysis, letter, email message, memo, summary, abstract, projection, evaluation, recommendation

documents that might be useful models. Notice what characteristics and structures your readers favor in other written materials.

19d Types of workplace writing

Reports, memos, and letters can serve many different purposes. For example, an engineer writes technical reports, while a teacher writes progress reports (or, indeed, report cards). Proposals are adapted to internal and external purposes; memos, however, tend to be used internally and letters externally. Ask advice, and observe existing communication patterns to determine preferred forms. (See also 12b–f, 13b.)

19e Business letter

The formal business letter serves many ends but generally follows the practices and format expected by readers. The first sample letter included here is a sales contact (see p. 131); the second focuses on a job applicant's accomplishments and abilities (see p. 134).

Acme Technical Products

3515 Lansing Road/Jackson, Michigan 49203
(517) 555-6651
www.acme.com

Uses letterhead paper

February 15, 2007

Ms. Janet Anderson
Purchasing Agent
Everett Batteries
15 Johnstown Boulevard
Westerly, RI 02891

Supplies full address of recipient

Dear Ms. Anderson,

Identifies recipient in salutation

Thank you for using Acme products in your lithium-ion battery research and development program. Acme is ready to support you with your future needs as you transition from this developmental battery into a manufacturable consumer product. We are ready to provide you with volume discounts and to work with you to develop a "just-in-time" inventory control, which will save you inventory and storage costs.

We also would like to provide you with information on our new separator materials designed specifically for lithium-ion battery development. The enclosed catalog provides you with pricing and technical data on a number of different separator products designed for a variety of battery needs.

I look forward to working with you in the future.

Sincerely,

Steve Adams

Steve Adams
Sales Associate

Supplies writer's name and position

Enclosure (1)

Notes enclosure, typist, and copies

SA: rd
cc: Sales Manager

- **Stationery.** The best is 25 or 50 percent white cotton bond, usually twenty-pound weight. Avoid colors and fancy paper.
- **Print quality.** Use a laser printer or a letter-quality impact printer. Your credibility will be damaged by fuzzy print or nonstandard fonts.
- **Format.** In **modified block format**, often used for longer letters, the return address and the closing and signature are aligned at the page center, but paragraphs are not indented from the left margin (see p. 134). In **block format**, often used for short letters, all paragraphs (including the greeting and signature) are flush at the left margin (see above).

- **Salutations.** Use the recipient's first name only if you are already on a first-name basis. Use the full name if you don't know the person's gender. Avoid male-specific greetings such as *Dear Sir.* If you don't know which person to address, use salutations such as *Dear Credit Manager.*
- **Notations following the signature.** Place any notations flush left, including initials for writer and typist: *RL: gw, Enc.* or *Enclosure, cc: Nancy Harris* (naming a person who is sent a copy).
- **Longer letters.** Use letterhead stationery only for the first page. For subsequent pages, use plain paper of the same weight.
- **Envelope.** Match the letter in color, weight, and type.
- **Electronic transmittal.** If you are expected to email or fax your letter, adapt its features for easy scanning or conversion to a company's word processor. Avoid multiple typefaces and type sizes, underlining, bullets, boxes, columns, or other features that might scramble.

ELEMENTS OF A BUSINESS LETTER

- It follows conventional form, identifying sender and recipient.
- It is prepared carefully, using appropriate visual features (see 12c–d).
- It has a few well-written paragraphs, each clarifying a specific point.
- It summarizes and synthesizes, respecting the reader's time.
- It specifies what the writer wants, whether information, service, agreement, or employment.

19f Memo

Most companies use a corporate memo template or a standard word-processing template. The organization's name and logo or letterhead may appear at the top. Unlike letters, which circulate externally, memos circulate internally and need no address. In many organizations, the convenient email message often functions as a memo. Even for routine messages, be sure to compose and proofread as carefully online as off. Check the address line to avoid sending a message meant for an individual to an entire group. Use an accurate subject line so the topic is clear to recipients. If you have doubts about a sensitive message or a hasty exchange, wait a day to gain perspective. Then revise your message as needed before sending it.

ELEMENTS OF A MEMO

- It precedes the message with the words *To, From, Date,* and *Subject,* efficiently identifying the readers, writer, topic, and date.
- It typically distills its message into a few concise paragraphs, briefly outlining the situation or topic.
- It generally identifies any action or response required, including deadlines for replies.
- It follows the same conventions for spacing, any enclosure notations, attachments, and copies as letters do.

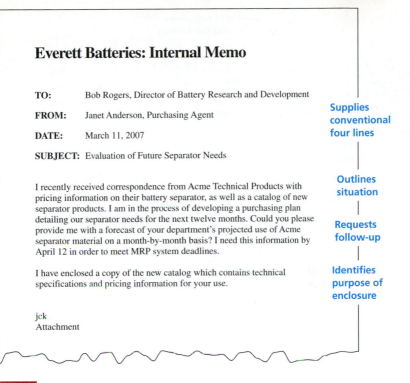

Everett Batteries: Internal Memo

TO: Bob Rogers, Director of Battery Research and Development

FROM: Janet Anderson, Purchasing Agent

DATE: March 11, 2007

SUBJECT: Evaluation of Future Separator Needs

I recently received correspondence from Acme Technical Products with pricing information on their battery separator, as well as a catalog of new separator products. I am in the process of developing a purchasing plan detailing our separator needs for the next twelve months. Could you please provide me with a forecast of your department's projected use of Acme separator material on a month-by-month basis? I need this information by April 12 in order to meet MRP system deadlines.

I have enclosed a copy of the new catalog which contains technical specifications and pricing information for your use.

jck
Attachment

Supplies conventional four lines

Outlines situation

Requests follow-up

Identifies purpose of enclosure

19g Résumé and application letter

Your résumé and cover letter sell your most important "product," you and your accomplishments. Develop your résumé around categories: your career objective, education, work or volunteer experience, activities or skills, awards, and references. Arrange information by time order or major skills. Use your cover letter to discuss, highlight, or add to your résumé; to connect the job requirements to your skills; and to express your spirit and interest. (See p. 134.)

Edit, proofread, and design your final documents carefully (see 12b–d). Prepare both for print or electronic submission (plain text without formatting but with searchable keywords). Turn to your campus career center, job-hunting Web sites, or books for advice and samples.

ELEMENTS OF A RÉSUMÉ

- It complements your letter of application by concisely presenting your background, education, experience, skills, and achievements to a prospective employer.
- It uses headings to identify sections or categories to organize details.
- It generally arranges the specifics in each section in reverse chronological order, placing the most current information first.
- It is carefully designed and printed for clarity and easy reading.

½" margin at top above writer's complete address

550 Sundown Ct.
Dayton, OH 45427
June 12, 2007

1" margin on each side

Jennifer Low, Director of Personnel
Marshall School
232 Willow Way
Huber Heights, OH 45424

Recipient's complete address

Salutation with colon

Dear Ms. Low:

Identifies job sought

I am seeking employment in elementary education, grades one through eight, and Jan Blake informed me of your junior high opening. During the past year as a student teacher, I have met many people at Marshall School, and I would love the opportunity to work with such a wonderful teaching staff.

Highlights recent training

My recent schooling at Wright State University has equipped me with many strategies that I am excited about implementing into my teaching. One strategy I am ready to try is the use of procedures. If students know what is expected of them, I believe that they can and will live up to those expectations.

Single-spaced text with double-spaced ¶s

My greatest strengths as a teacher are my creativity and time management skills. Both are assets when planning my lessons and keeping students interested while using class time wisely. During one past teaching experience, my task seemed impossible until I designed learning centers to combat time constraints.

Identifies special skills that supplement résumé

I firmly believe in inquiry teaching, a technique that always worked well during my student teaching. One of the joys of working with children has been seeing their eyes light up when they begin to understand new information.

Explains benefits of experience

I feel that I would be an asset to Marshall School and hope to start my career in your district next fall. I can be reached at 453-555-5555 and look forward to an interview with you.

Supplies contact information

Sincerely,
Tammy Helton
Tammy Helton

Notes enclosure (résumé)

Enclosure

Tammy Jo Helton

550 Sundown Ct., Dayton, OH 45427

453–555–5555   TJ@mailnow.com

CERTIFICATION

Elementary Education (grades 1-8)

Bachelor of Arts, August 2007, Wright State University,

Dayton, Ohio

EDUCATION

Wright State University, 2004-2007, College of Education

Sinclair Community College, 2003-2004, general education

Wayne High School, 2002 graduate, college preparatory

AWARDS

Phi Kappa Phi National Honor Society 2006, 2007

Dean's list 2005, 2006, 2007

TEACHING EXPERIENCE

Student Teaching

Seventh grade physical science, L. T. Ball Junior High, Tipp City, Ohio

Planned and implemented lessons while maintaining classroom control.

Observation

Shilohview, Trotwood, Ohio

Implemented preplanned lessons.

Teaching

Sixth-grade religious education class, Dayton, Ohio

Currently responsible for planning and implementing lessons.

WORK EXPERIENCE

Goal Line Sports Grill, 2004-present: Server, cash register, supervisor

Frisch's Big Boy, 2002-2004: Server, inventory, preparation

Shilohview Park, 2001-2003: Park counselor, activity planner

INTERESTS AND ACTIVITIES

Took dance lessons for ten years; played drums in the school band.

References available on request.

Centers name, address, phone, and email address

Begins with required teaching credential

Summarizes education and awards

Uses capitals for main headings

Organizes experience to show skills

Uses reverse chronological order

Adds optional information

ELEMENTS OF A LETTER OF APPLICATION

- It follows a traditional business letter format.
- It begins by identifying the job and conveying to readers your enthusiasm about it.
- It complements your résumé by adding details and examples that show the pertinence of your experience.
- It ends by looking forward to an interview, supplying contact and availability information.

19h Oral presentation

Committees and boards have their own conventions for communication, which, if violated, can weaken a member's standing. Observe carefully to figure out whether a group interacts formally (using parliamentary procedure), informally (allowing spontaneous comments), or even ineffectively (needing guidelines). (See Chapter 14, 15l, and 16g.) Plan your participation.

- Study the agenda ahead; read documents, or gather background.
- Plan, rehearse, and prepare any visuals or materials (see 10d).
- Focus in order to time comments well, advance discussion, offer new ideas, and link your remarks to those of others. Don't dominate.
- Adjust to the group's formality and any shifts to social talk.
- Consider how others may react to assumptions you imply. Control your emotions to avoid rash or potentially offensive remarks.

PART 5

Researching and Writing

▼ TAKING IT ONLINE

LIBRARY RESEARCH GUIDES

http://www.library.cornell.edu/services/guides.html

This site offers instruction on how to develop research topics, locate background material, and find and evaluate books, periodical articles, recordings, and Internet resources.

INTERNET TUTORIALS

http://www.lib.berkeley.edu/TeachingLib/Guides/Internet/FindInfo.html

These tutorials explain electronic searches, search strategies and tools, and evaluation techniques.

INTERNET SEARCH STRATEGIES

http://www.rice.edu/fondren/etext/howto/search.html

Try this page for a quick look at types of search engines, search engine evaluations, search techniques, and source evaluation.

WAYS TO SEARCH FOR GOVERNMENT INFORMATION

http://library.csun.edu/Find_Resources/Government_Publications/finddocs.html

For useful advice about locating many types of government documents, turn to this site.

COMMUNITY INFORMATION BY ZIP CODE

http://library.csun.edu/Find_Resources/Government_Publications/zipstats.html

When you're conducting research on your own community, visit this site for sources of local information, accessible by zip code.

TYPES OF SURVEYS

http://www.socialresearchmethods.net/kb/survtype.php

This portion of the online textbook *Research Methods Knowledge Base* explains and illustrates how to use surveys.

PART 5

Researching and Writing

20 Getting Started: Researching and Writing

Research can take many forms, and it can play many roles in your writing. Put simply, **research** means systematic inquiry into a subject. Your research may lead you to written sources (print or electronic), to fieldwork (interviews, surveys, ethnographic observations), or even to a systematic examination of your own experience. Along the way, you are likely to encounter **research conversations**, exchanges among writers, readers, and speakers investigating certain aspects of a subject. Their shared focus on these aspects or elements of the subject makes it a particular matter of interest—a **research topic**.

You can use the depth of information, ideas, and insights you develop through research for a number of purposes. You might create an **informative** essay, report, or brochure.

> "Everybody's Wheezin': My Generation's Journey with Asthma"
> (informative essay on rising incidence of the affliction)

> "Unions versus Tobacco Growers in Mid-Twentieth Century America"
> (academic paper)

You might create an **argumentative** paper taking a stand on an issue or a **proposal** supporting a particular course of action.

> "Bring the Gray Wolf Back"
> (essay or editorial)

Or you might explain and support an **interpretation** or **analysis**.

> "Rebuilding America: Images of National Identity in Contemporary Popular Song"
> (interpretation of contemporary song lyrics and music videos)

20a Beginning your research

Research is a careful, sustained inquiry into a question, phenomenon, or topic—guided by **research questions** that set goals for gathering and examining information. Managing the process of identifying resources, evaluating them, and integrating them with your own ideas and insights requires considerable attention and detailed recordkeeping. The process usually begins simply enough, however, either with your own experiences and reading or in an assignment in class or at work.

1 Choosing a topic

Your research can grow from a personal interest, an assignment, a strong feeling or point of view, a pressing issue or problem, or the interests and needs of potential readers.

STRATEGY Respond to your assignment.

Begin by reading your assignment carefully, underlining key terms. Then respond to the assignment in these ways.

- If a word or phrase immediately suggests a topic, write it down, followed by a list of synonyms or alternative terms.
- If you can't identify a topic right away, write down key words and phrases, and brainstorm related words and phrases, along with the topics they suggest.
- Consider asking the person or people who gave the assignment what they think of a potential topic—and for further topic suggestions. Consider asking potential readers for their reactions.

In an intermediate composition course, Jennifer Figliozzi and Summer Arrigo-Nelson underlined important words in their assignment to "investigate the psychological or social dimensions of a local or campus problem." They then listed some campus problems.

| canceled classes | student fees | date rape | parking |
| library hours | role of sports | student alcohol use | crime |

They chose "student alcohol use" because the topic sounded interesting with sources readily available and the field research manageable.

Try to balance your interests with readers' expectations. For example, Jennifer and Summer knew that their audience wanted an academic report using print and electronic sources with field research on a problem. They also considered likely questions and expectations of their audience—the local campus community—as they planned.

AUDIENCE
QUESTIONS

What discoveries or information about student alcohol use might benefit the campus community?

RESPONSE

Our conclusion about local student drinking behavior could help the campus program to reduce student alcohol use.

Recognize your interests. Perhaps you have an interest, a passion, a job you like (or hate), a sport or recreation activity, a curiosity, or some other involvement that is part of your life and might intrigue readers. You don't need to start with a precise opinion or conclusion—simply a strong feeling or interest can help you identify a specific issue worth further study. Here is how two students turned their interests and feelings into research projects.

INTEREST	TITLE OF FINAL PAPER
Curiosity: Why do so many workers in fast-food restaurants seem to be recent immigrants?	Easy to Hire, Easy to Fire: Recent Immigrants and the Fast-Food Industry
Job: I've been working as an EMT, but I'll bet most people don't know anything about the job.	You Won't Meet Us Until You Need Us: What EMTs Do

Read for an issue or problem. So much has been written about topics such as global warming, political bias in the media, or the influence of television violence on behavior that these topics easily exceed the scope of even the most ambitious research paper. A quick bit of browsing, however, can lead you to more focused issues, problems, and topics. Where can you do this browsing? Glance quickly through one or two issues of a magazine or newspaper, scan the entries in a database, or consult informational Web sites. Look for words, phrases, and titles that suggest topics, especially unanswered questions or issues that (for most people at least) remain unresolved.

STRATEGY **Consult academic databases.**

Turn to academic databases such as *PsychINFO*, *First Search*, *ScienceDirect*, and *MEDLINE*, choosing a database that covers a field that interests you. Then type in a subject (such as *breast cancer*) and terms that researchers often use to identify questions worth investigating (e.g., *recent issues*, *controversies*, *discoveries*, *risks*, *new developments*, or *alternatives*).

Draw on your experience. Research can begin with your personal or professional interest in a subject, a question or problem, a puzzling phenomenon, or a community's need for information. For example, if you begin sneezing every time you walk past the perfume area in a department store, you might try informal experiments, perhaps seeing how close you can get without sneezing. You might also seek advice from a Web site such as the *Health and Environment Resource Center* at <http://www.herc.org>. Once you begin searching for an explanation, you're asking a research question: What is the relationship between perfume and sneezing?

Even a few words can spark an interest, as Jenny Latimer describes.

After I had stuffed a couple of red licorice sticks into my mouth in front of my coworker Julie, she picked up the wrapper and said, "I didn't realize they had hydrogenated oils in them. I'll never eat them again!" I started wondering about hydrogenated oils. What are they, and why do they seem to be in everything we eat? When did this start? What do they do to you? Do we need to worry or do something about them?

Your own emotions and attitudes can suggest topics as well.

EMOTION	POSSIBLE TOPIC	TITLE OF FINAL PAPER
Fear	I've never seen a tornado, but I've always feared them. I'd like to explore their dangers (real or exaggerated).	Seven Good Reasons for Fearing Tornados
Sadness	Other students often say, "I'm depressed." I'd like to know whether depression is really a serious problem for college students.	Depression and College Students: How Often and How Serious?
Anger	I lose my temper easily. Friends say I'm just hot-tempered, but I worry I'm out of control. What causes anger to boil up so easily?	Two Views of Anger: Letting Off Steam or Losing Control?

Audience Expectations for Research Writing

	Academic	Public	Work
GOALS	Explain or show, offer well-supported interpretations or conclusions, analyze or synthesize information for use in other settings	Support arguments for policy or course of action, inform or advise for the public good	Document problems, propose a project or course of action, compare information, improve performance
TYPICAL QUESTIONS	What does it mean? What happened? How does it occur? How might it be modified?	How can this policy be made better? What do people need or want to know?	What is the problem? How can we solve it? What course of action will help us achieve our goals?
TYPICAL FORMS	Interpretive (thesis) paper, informative paper, research report, grant report	Position paper, editorial, proposal, informative article, pamphlet, guidelines	Proposal, report, feasibility study, memorandum
AUDIENCE EXPECTATIONS	Detailed evidence from varied sources including quotations, paraphrases, and summaries; documented sources that acknowledge scholarship	Accessible, fair, and persuasive information with evidence; informal documentation	Clear, direct, and precise information; appropriate detail; less formal documentation

Pay attention to your audience. The interests and expectations of your audience can help guide your choice of a topic. The chart on page 140 can help you identify your potential readers' likely concerns and perspectives.

2 Narrowing a topic

Think of a **subject** as a broad field, filled with clusters of information, ideas, and written interchanges—clusters that are often only loosely related to each other even though they fall within the same subject area. A **topic** is a single cluster of ideas and information within a broader subject. Writers interested in questions surrounding the cluster of ideas and information often "speak" to each other through their writing, creating an ongoing conversation you can enter through your own writing.

By limiting your attention to a particular topic, you take an important step toward making your research project manageable. But how can you identify potential topics (or subtopics) that are limited enough to provide a real focus for your writing yet are the subject of enough discussion to provide adequate resources for your work? Pay attention to issues, disagreements, points of discussion, new discoveries, and intriguing ideas or interpretations as you do preliminary research on a subject. These focal points in what others have to say about the subject can suggest ways to narrow your topic choice.

As you browse print and online sources, review your assignment, or talk with an authority on the subject, note key words and phrases they use to identify topics of discussion. Pay attention to questions they raise to identify directions for inquiry and argument. Respond with statements or questions of your own that narrow potential topics to reasonable limits.

Here are some notes Tou Yang made from articles on the topic *athletic dietary supplements* that he found in the database *Academic Search Premier*.

NOTES

"Eat Powder? Build Muscle! Burn Calories!"—creatine monohydrate; lots of
athletes swear by it and claim it has only good effects
"Creatine Monohydrate Supplementation Enhances High-Intensity Exercise
Performance in Males and Females"—controversy over whether creatine
works or not; they claim it does
"From Ephedra to Creatine: Using Theory to Respond to Dietary
Supplement Use in Young Athletes"—understanding why athletes use
dietary supplements even though they are probably not effective

RESPONSES

Some disagreement over whether creatine works or at least over how well it
works—take a position on this?
Or explain how it works and what it seems to add to sports performance?

Research Writing: Informative and Persuasive

Purpose for Writing	Possible Form	Possible Title	Possible Focus
Informative	Documented essay	"Everybody's Wheezin': My Generation's Journey with Asthma"	Exploration of rising incidence of the affliction
Informative	Report	"'Buy U.S. Bonds': How Posters Helped Shape Public Opinion During World War II"	Historical examination of the ways the government employed posters
Informative	Brochure or pamphlet	"What Linux Can (and Can't) Do for Your Computers"	Investigation of both strengths and limitations
Informative	Academic research paper	"Unions versus Tobacco Growers in Mid-Twentieth Century America"	Analysis of conflicts during a specific time period
Persuasive	Documented essay or editorial	"Bring the Gray Wolf Back"	Presentation and support of stand with reasons and evidence
Persuasive	Position paper or *PowerPoint* presentation	"Meeting Objections to Gray Wolf Reintroduction in the Adirondack Region of New York"	Advocacy of position with recognition of alternate views
Persuasive	Proposal	"A Three-Step Process for Reintroducing Gray Wolves to Adirondack State Park"	Presentation and support of proposed actions
Persuasive (interpretation)	Academic essay	"Dream Interpretation: Three Current Approaches"	Explanation and application of three interpretive approaches to one of the writer's dreams
Persuasive (interpretation)	Report on field research	"Diversity on Campus: What Do Western College Students *Really* Think?"	Analysis and interpretation of data gathered on student views
Persuasive (interpretation)	Thesis-and-support essay	"Rebuilding America: Images of National Identity in Contemporary Popular Song"	Interpretation of contemporary song lyrics and music videos

3 Identifying keywords

Keywords—words or phrases identifying important ideas and clusters of information—are often used in library catalogs and by Web or database search engines (21d, 21f, 22b) to link discussions of a subject. As you examine print or electronic sources, make a list of all the keywords, names, or phrases that might refer to your topic. Note synonyms, such as *maturation* for *growth*. These keywords can help you initially define your topic and eventually develop research questions (20c) to guide your research (21a-3).

20b Types of research writing

No matter what subject you investigate, the specific steps you take will be heavily influenced by your answer to this question: Will I use my research to *inform* or to *persuade*?

An **informative** research paper, report, or Web site focuses on your subject: the phenomenon, discovery, process, controversy, question, person, or performance you are exploring. Your research and writing will focus on discovering information and ideas and sharing them with readers. Your efforts will be subject-driven. Taking this approach does not mean that your writing will be a dull recitation of facts. On the contrary, you'll use your understanding, insights, and conclusions to organize information from sources to help readers understand, answer potential questions, and reach substantiated conclusions about the topic.

A **persuasive** research project focuses on your **thesis** (see 3b) or conclusion. You'll concentrate on evidence and explanatory details that logically support your point of view, persuade readers, and explain issues or problems (see 10d and 21c). You'll need to do more than just support your conclusions, however. To convince readers, an argument needs to offer detailed information about the issue or problem and the viewpoints involved. It needs to develop, refine, and support your thesis, proposal, or interpretation.

20c Developing a research question

Research writing, especially informative writing, aims to answer research questions about your subject—both those raised by specialized research and those likely to interest readers.

STRATEGY State your research questions.

Work toward one or two questions early in your research process. Relate your questions to your general and specific goals for gathering and examining possible sources. Design questions to enlighten both yourself and your readers.

For example, Summer Arrigo-Nelson and Jennifer Figliozzi developed the following questions for their academic research project on the relationship of parental behaviors to college student drinking.

- *Will students with permission to drink at home show different drinking behaviors at college than those without permission to drink at home?*
- *Do the students feel that a correlation exists between drinking behaviors at home and at college?*

Research questions can take several forms, depending on your individual preferences and your purposes for writing. Some writers prefer questions that focus on factual or informational matters: *who, what, where, when, why,* and *how.* Other writers prefer questions suggesting both a purpose and an organizational pattern for writing. Jennifer Latimer, for example, arrived at her research questions this way:

> *I looked at the red licorice sticks package, the fruit-flavored candy package, the wheat crackers box, even the pudding pack—all contained hydrogenated oils. I did some preliminary research and developed two questions for my research and my readers:*
> *What effects do hydrogenated oils have on us?*
> *Should I (and we) ever again eat delicious treats containing them?*

20d Developing a preliminary thesis

Research essays, reports, and even Web sites generally use a **thesis statement** (see 3b) to guide readers' attention and state the writer's key idea or theme. Your thesis should grow from and reflect your research questions, of course (see 20c). Creating a rough thesis early on helps you focus and shape your search strategy (see 21a). Later, complicating, developing, and qualifying your thesis in response to your research will help you review or revise the direction of your work.

Thesis statements in research writing help indicate your purpose for writing (inform or persuade, see 20c). They often follow one of these patterns.

- **Issue.** What is the issue, and what is my stand on it?
- **Problem.** What is the problem, and what solution am I proposing?
- **Public question.** What situation do we face, and how should we respond?
- **Academic question.** What is the phenomenon, and what is my analysis and interpretation of it?

20e Creating a research file and a timeline

In a **research file**, you can record and systematically store your activities throughout the research and writing process. It is a good place to accumulate materials and keep them ready for later use. You can build a portable research file in a notebook, in a folder, on note cards, or in a word-processing file in your desktop, laptop, or handheld computer.

1 Building your research file

- Identify your topic, research questions, or rough thesis (see 3b).
- Create a research plan, listing possible resources and assembling a working bibliography (see 21a).
- Divide your file into sections for your main research and writing stages, and keep it with you as you work.
- Take notes, recording relevant ideas and information from sources (see 20f), including summaries, paraphrases, and quotations (see 20f–g).
- Copy or record passages or images with their sources, ready for possible inclusion.
- Document sources (see Chapters 26–29) of all materials in your file.
- Add reactions, chunks, drafts, and revisions integrating your insights with ideas and information from your sources (see 24g–h).

Besides creating a research file for material, you need to stick to a schedule so that you finish on time. Because college research projects require sustained effort over several weeks or months, by planning carefully and using your time efficiently, you can avoid the stress of a looming deadline and the fear of turning in an incomplete or substandard paper.

2 Constructing a timeline

- Use a printed calendar or your computer to record your plans.
- Divide up the work, noting likely activities and due dates.
- Allow several days or a week for activities such as choosing your topic, stating your research questions and rough thesis, beginning your working bibliography, reviewing notes and revising plans, finishing your research, planning or outlining your paper, drafting the paper and source list, getting feedback from peer readers, revising, editing, and proofreading.
- Work backward from the final deadline, scheduling each stage.
- Keep your timeline in your research file, and check it regularly.

20f Reading and note taking

A research project calls for two types of reading—analytical and critical. When you read *analytically*, you try to understand the ideas and information presented in a source. When you read *critically*, you interact with the source, assessing its strengths, limitations, and biases; analyzing its relationships to other texts produced by a research community; and identifying questions or issues it leaves unaddressed. (See also Chapter 9.)

Analytical reading helps you develop much of the content of a report or paper. Critical reading leads to insights you contribute to understanding the topic.

ANALYTICAL READING	CRITICAL READING
What does it say?	What does it mean or imply?
(literal)	(interpretive)
—summary	—interpretation
—paraphrase	—position of author
—synthesis	—nature of publication
—quotation	—use in one's own ideas
—detail	—reception of audience

1 Taking notes

Because analytical reading concentrates on grasping information, **analytical notes** record facts, details, concepts, and quotations from your sources, focusing on what's relevant to your research questions. **Critical notes** often accompany them, adding your comments, interpretations, or assessments of a source in relation to your research questions.

2 Recording notes

Here are three formats for note taking. (See also 21a-4.)

Note cards. Some writers prefer portable, convenient index cards, generally 4" × 6" or 5" × 7". If you identify the card's topic clearly at the top and restrict each card to one kind of note (quotation, summary, paraphrase, synthesis), you can group, add, or rearrange cards as you plan or write.

Research journal. A research journal (usually a notebook) provides space to record information, reflect on new knowledge, and begin assembling your project. Add headings or marginal comments to identify the topics of the notes. Store photocopies or printouts in any pockets or in a folder.

Electronic notes. You can use software designed for note taking or set up word-processing files like a research journal or set of note cards (one page = one card). If you specify a subtopic or research question for each entry, you can use these labels to sort, reorganize, or retrieve material.

STRATEGY Link your notes.

- **Link notes to your keywords or research questions.** At the top of each card, page, or entry, use your keywords, research questions, or subtopics to identify how material relates to your topic.
- **Link notes to sources.** Clearly note the source on each card, page, or entry. Use the author's last name or a short version of the title to connect each note to its corresponding bibliography entry (see 21a-4).

- **Link notes to exact locations.** Include the page numbers of the source, especially for material quoted or paraphrased. If an electronic source uses paragraph, not page, numbers, note them.

3 Recording quotations

When you're using actual books and journals, not photocopies or downloads, be *absolutely certain* that you copy quotations word for word and record the exact page number where each quotation appears. If a quotation runs on to a second page in the source, note both numbers and the place where the page changes. (After all, you don't know what you'll finally quote.)

20g Summarizing, paraphrasing, and synthesizing

Analytical reading and note taking require careful, critical thinking as you draw information and ideas from a source and put them into forms useful in your own writing: quotations, summaries, paraphrases, and syntheses. In a **summary**, you present the essential information in a text without interpreting it. In a **paraphrase**, you restate an author's ideas in your own words, retaining the content and sense of the original but providing your own expression. A **synthesis** brings together summaries of several sources and points out the relationships among the ideas and information.

1 Summarizing

A summary helps you understand the key ideas and content in an article, part of a book, a Web site, or a cluster of paragraphs. You can also create a summary as a concise way of presenting a source's ideas and information in your own writing. In an **objective summary**, you focus on presenting the source's content in compressed form and avoid speculating on its line of reasoning. In an **evaluative summary**, you add your opinions, evaluating or commenting on the original passage.

STRATEGY   **Prepare a summary.**

To summarize information on your topic, follow this process.

- **Read** the selection, looking for the most important ideas, evidence, and information. Underline, highlight, or make note of key points and information that you think should be mentioned in your summary.
- **Scan** (reread quickly) the selection to decide which of the ideas and bits of information you noted during your first reading are the *most* important. Try also to decide on the writer's main purpose in the selection and to identify the major sections of the discussion.

- **Summarize** *each section* of the source (each step in the argument, each stage in the explanation) in a *single sentence* that mentions the key ideas and information.
- **Encapsulate** the *entire passage* in a *single sentence* that captures its main point or conclusion.
- **Combine** your section summaries with your overall summary to produce a draft summary of the main point, other significant points, and the most important information.
- **Revise** to make sure your summary is logical and easy to read. Check against the source for accuracy.
- **Document** clearly the source of your summary using a standard style of documentation (see Chapters 26–29).

In a summary, you can present the key ideas from a source without including unnecessary detail that might distract readers. Summer Arrigo-Nelson and Jennifer Figliozzi used two one-sentence summaries of research to help introduce one of the questions for their academic research paper.

> First, research has shown that adolescents who have open and close relationships with their parents use alcohol less often than do those with conflictual relationships (Sieving). For example, a survey given to students in seventh through twelfth grades reported that approximately 35 percent of adolescent drinkers were under parental supervision while drinking (Department of Education). Based on this research, we are interested in determining if students who were given permission to drink while living with their parents would possess different drinking patterns, upon reaching college, than those who did not previously have permission to drink.

2 Paraphrasing

A good paraphrase doesn't add to or detract from the original but often helps you understand a difficult work. When you want to incorporate the detailed ideas and information from a passage into your own writing but don't want to quote your source because the wording is too dense or confusing, then a paraphrase can be the answer.

To paraphrase part of a source, put the information in your own words, retaining the content and ideas of the original as well as the sequence of presentation. (Many paraphrases contain sentences that correspond with the original except for changes in wording and sentence structure.)

STRATEGY **Paraphrase a source.**

Use these steps in preparing a paraphrase.

- **Read** the selection carefully so that you understand the wording as well as the content.

- **Write** a draft of your paraphrase, using your own words and phrases in place of the original. Rely on synonyms and equivalent expressions. You can retain names, proper nouns, and the like from the original, of course.
- **Revise** for smooth reading and clarity. Change sentence structures and phrasing so your version is easier to understand than your source.
- **Document** clearly the source of your paraphrase using a standard style of documentation (see Chapters 26–29).

As part of her research about alcohol abuse on her campus, Jennifer Figliozzi looked for background information about the issue. She encountered the following passage in Leo Reisberg's article "Colleges Step Up Efforts to Combat Alcohol Abuse" in the June 12, 1998, *Chronicle of Higher Education.*

> The university also now notifies parents when their sons or daughters violate the alcohol policy or any other aspect of the student code of conduct. "We were hoping that the support of parents would help change students' behavior, and we believe it has," says Timothy F. Brooks, an assistant vice-president and the dean of students at the University of Delaware.

Because she wanted to avoid long quotations yet integrate the information smoothly into her discussion, Jennifer paraphrased part of the passage.

> Officials at the University of Delaware thought that letting parents know when students violate regulations on alcohol use would change students' drinking habits, and according to one administrator, "We believe it has" (Reisberg A42).

3 Synthesizing

By bringing together summaries of several sources and pointing out their relationships in a synthesis, you can use your sources in some special ways: to provide background information, to explore causes and effects, to look at contrasting explanations or arguments, or to bring together ideas and information in support of a thesis.

STRATEGY **Synthesize sources.**

To create a synthesis of your source materials, follow this process.

- **Identify** the role a synthesis will play in your explanation or argument as well as the kind of information you wish to share with readers.
- **Gather** the sources you plan to synthesize.
- **Read** your sources, and summarize each of them (see 20g-1).

- **Focus** on the purpose of your synthesis, and draft a sentence summing up your conclusion about the relationships of the sources.
- **Arrange** your summaries in the order in which you will present your sources in the synthesis.
- **Write** a draft of your synthesis, presenting summaries of your sources and offering your conclusion about their relationships.
- **Revise** so that your synthesis is easy to read. Make sure readers can easily identify the sources of the ideas and information.
- **Document** clearly the sources for your synthesis using a standard style of documentation (see Chapters 26–29).

Many academic papers begin with a summary of prior research designed to identify a need for further research and to provide justification for the research questions. The opening section of Summer Arrigo-Nelson and Jennifer Figliozzi's academic research paper uses synthesis for this purpose.

> Research dealing with student alcohol use most often focuses on children's perceptions of their parents' actions and on the relationship between child and parent. Studies conducted with high school students have supported the hypothesis that positive family relationships are more likely to be associated with less frequent alcohol use among adolescents than are negative relationships. Adolescents model the limited substance use of their parents where there is a good or moderate parent-adolescent relationship (Andrews, Hops, and Duncan). Other factors the studies found to be associated with positive family relationships, along with substance use, were academic achievement, family structure, place of residence, self-esteem, and emotional tone (Martsh and Miller; Weschler, Dowdall, Davenport, and Castillo).

Work and public writing often use synthesis similarly to identify a problem to be addressed or a policy to be examined or reconsidered.

21 Library Resources and Research Databases

A good **search strategy** is a plan for locating the variety of resources you need to answer your research question or support your thesis. It will help you to consult sources with varied opinions on aspects of your topic.

21a Developing a search strategy and working bibliography

A search strategy has five elements: resources, search tools, keywords, working bibliography, and timeline.

1 List resources

Your search strategy should include a list of the kinds of resources you plan to use—printed books, scholarly journals, newspapers, Web sites, interviews, and surveys, for example. Draw on your preliminary research (20a–d) to create your initial resource list, and update it as you discover other potential resources. If you have specific titles, Web sites, or people in mind as sources, list them here, too, and update your list periodically.

2 Identify search tools

The most obvious search tools come readily to mind when you begin researching: your library's online catalog and Web search engines such as *Google*. However, more specialized research tools can often lead you to fresh information and ideas worth sharing with your readers.

STRATEGY Try specialized research tools.

- Indexes of magazine and periodical articles: *Readers' Guide to Periodical Literature, New York Times Index, Wall Street Journal Index*
- Indexes of articles in scholarly journals and professional publications in fields such as business, public health, law, or engineering: *Social Sciences Index, Applied Science and Technology Index, MLA International Bibliography, Humanities Index, Education Index*
- Academic and professional databases with built-in search engines (*PsycINFO, MEDLINE, OCLC FirstSearch*) and indexed databases (*Questia, AltaVista, CataList, MetaCrawler, Dogpile*)

3 Use keywords

Many people begin searching for sources using general terms to identify their topic, only to discover that these are not the terms used in an index or search engine. Indexes, databases, library catalogs (21d–f, 22b), and many other reference sources are arranged (or searched) by keywords (see also 20a). Sometimes it helps to have two or three alternative keywords or phrases so that, if a particular database or other resource yields little under one, you can try the others before moving to another resource.

4 Compile references for a working bibliography

Your search strategy should make provision for recording information that will help you or your readers locate a source. A list of sources you have examined and may decide to draw on as you write is called a **working bibliography**. In a working bibliography, you record information you will need to provide in your final paper in a list of works cited, reference list, list of works consulted, or footnotes (see Chapters 26–29). As you are doing research, keep a copy of your working bibliography close at hand so you can make notes about entries to add or delete. (If it is in electronic form, you may be able to make changes right away.)

INFORMATION FOR A WORKING BIBLIOGRAPHY

When you examine a source, record the following kinds of information for your working bibliography and, eventually, for the list of sources for your paper.

PRINTED BOOKS

- Author(s) or editor(s)
- Title
- Publication information: place of publication, name of publisher, date of publication
- Volume or edition numbers, if any
- Call number (to help locate the book in library stacks)

PRINTED ARTICLES

- Author(s) or editor(s)
- Title
- Name of journal, magazine, newspaper, or collection of articles
- Publication information
  - Article in a periodical: volume number, issue number, month or day of publication, page numbers of article (inclusive)
  - Article in a collection: title of collection and editor's name, place of publication, name of publisher, date of publication, page numbers of article (inclusive)

ELECTRONIC OR ONLINE WORKS

- Author(s), editor(s), or group(s) responsible for the document
- Title or name of the Web site and the document
- Information about any corresponding print publication (as above)
- Electronic publication information: date of electronic publication or latest update, date you accessed the document, and complete URL; (for online journal) volume and issue number, publication date; (for databases or CD-ROM) document access number or version number; (for email or post to a discussion list) name of sender, subject line, date of posting, name of list, and date of access

---

Organize your working bibliography.

Choose one of these strategies to organize your working bibliography.

- **Alphabetically**, the way entries will eventually appear in a list of works cited or references. This strategy can save time and effort when you are preparing your final text.
- In **categories** reflecting the parts of your subject or the kinds of evidence they provide for your argument. This strategy can help you identify at a glance areas covered well and those needing further investigation.
- According to the **plan for your paper**. This strategy can help you gather your resources efficiently as you write.

5 Revise and update your timeline

Your timeline should be part of your search plan (see 20e). Revise and update it to reflect changes in direction or emphasis that arise from discoveries or new ideas that emerge from your research.

21b Library resources and databases

Your specific search strategy for library resources and research databases should reflect both the advantages and disadvantages of these forms of research, especially in comparison to the readily available resources on Web sites.

Advantages. Many important resources are available *at* a library (printed books and articles, microforms, CD-ROM databases, for example) or *through* a library (online databases available only through a library's Web site or on library terminals). Scholarly publications, technical and specialized reports, and government publications are more likely to be available at libraries than on Web sites.

Reference librarians can provide considerable help and advice—and are glad to do so. Libraries often provide Internet and Web access so you can follow a strand of research at *one* location, whether it takes you to printed sources, databases, the Web—or back and forth among them.

Disadvantages. Library research may require a substantial time commitment; library schedules may not correspond with your schedule. Library resources can also be difficult to navigate, especially if you are not familiar with the organization of research libraries.

1 Examine different kinds of library resources

In general, library resources fall into three categories, each with its own system for locating specific sources.

- **Books**, **pamphlets**, and miscellaneous resources including photographs, films, and recordings: Use **online catalogs**.
- **Articles** in magazines, scholarly journals, and other periodicals: Use **electronic and print indexes**, often on a library's Web site.
- **Databases** of articles and information: Use **search engines** embedded in the databases, also often on a library's Web site.

2 Move from general to specific resources

Your research will often move from general, less-detailed sources to more specific and detailed ones as you narrow your topic and begin adding depth of detail and specific evidence to your writing. The distinction between general and specific treatment of a topic holds true for online and field resources also, but it is especially sharp for library resources.

Another important distinction to bear in mind is that between **primary sources**, consisting of information and ideas in original or close-to-original form (such as historical records, literary works, raw statistics, and actual documents), and **secondary sources**, consisting of works that analyze, summarize, interpret, or explain primary sources.

21c General resources

You can use general resources to gain a broad overview of a topic, including background information and a sense of relationships to other subjects. General references can also provide names, keywords, and phrases useful for tracing a topic, as well as bibliographies of potential resources. (Many are available both in print and online.)

General encyclopedias, ready references, maps, and dictionaries. These provide basic information on a wide range of topics and are good places to begin research for an overview of your topic.

> *New Encyclopaedia Britannica, Columbia Encyclopedia, World Almanac and Book of Facts, Canadian Almanac and Directory, Statistical Abstract of the United States, National Geographic Atlas of the World, The American Heritage Dictionary of the English Language, Oxford English Dictionary*

Specialized encyclopedias and dictionaries. These provide in-depth coverage of a specific topic or area. The range of resources is wide.

> *Dictionary of the Social Sciences, Current Biography, Who's Who in America, McGraw-Hill Encyclopedia of Science and Technology, International Encyclopedia of Business and Management, Encyclopedia of Advertising, International Encyclopedia of Film, International Television Almanac, Encyclopedia of Educational Research, Dictionary of Anthropology, Encyclopedia of Psychology, Encyclope-*

dia of the Environment, New Grove Dictionary of Music and Musicians, Women's Studies Encyclopedia

Bibliographies. These provide organized lists of books and articles on specific topics within a field of study or interest.

Bibliographic Index: A Cumulative Bibliography of Bibliographies, MLA Bibliography of Books and Articles on the Modern Languages and Literatures, International Bibliography of the Social Sciences, Foreign Affairs Bibliography, Film Research: A Critical Bibliography with Annotations and Essays

21d Books and online catalogs

Library catalogs give you access to books and to many other resources, including periodicals, recordings, government documents, films, historical archives, and collections of photographs. Your library's catalog is most likely an **online catalog**, although **card catalogs** are still occasionally in use in small libraries. You can search under the *author's name*, the *title of a work*, the *subject area*, the title of a *series or periodical containing the work*, and, in some libraries, *words in the title or in a work's description*. Some catalogs list works not only in their home library but also in other libraries in a region or in a consortium, such as a group of college libraries.

Rachel Torres discovered that her library belonged to just such a group when she began her search for resources, especially printed books, on her topic, Afro-Cuban music. She began by typing her topic into the search screen for "words in title or description," and the catalog returned a number of possible sources (see Figure 21.1 on p. 156). She chose the fourth item on the list and moved to the next catalog screen, which provided detail about the book along with a list of copies available in the cooperating libraries (see Figure 21.2 on p. 157).

21e Periodicals, print or electronic indexes, and government documents

Periodicals are publications that appear at intervals and contain articles by different authors. **General-interest magazines** appear once a month or weekly, with each issue paginated separately. **Scholarly journals** generally appear less frequently than magazines, perhaps four times a year, with the page numbering running continuously throughout the separate issues that make up an annual volume. **Newspapers** generally appear daily or weekly and frequently consist of separately numbered sections. Most scholarly journals are still available primarily in printed form, although many colleges and universities have begun subscribing to journals in electronic form, with current and

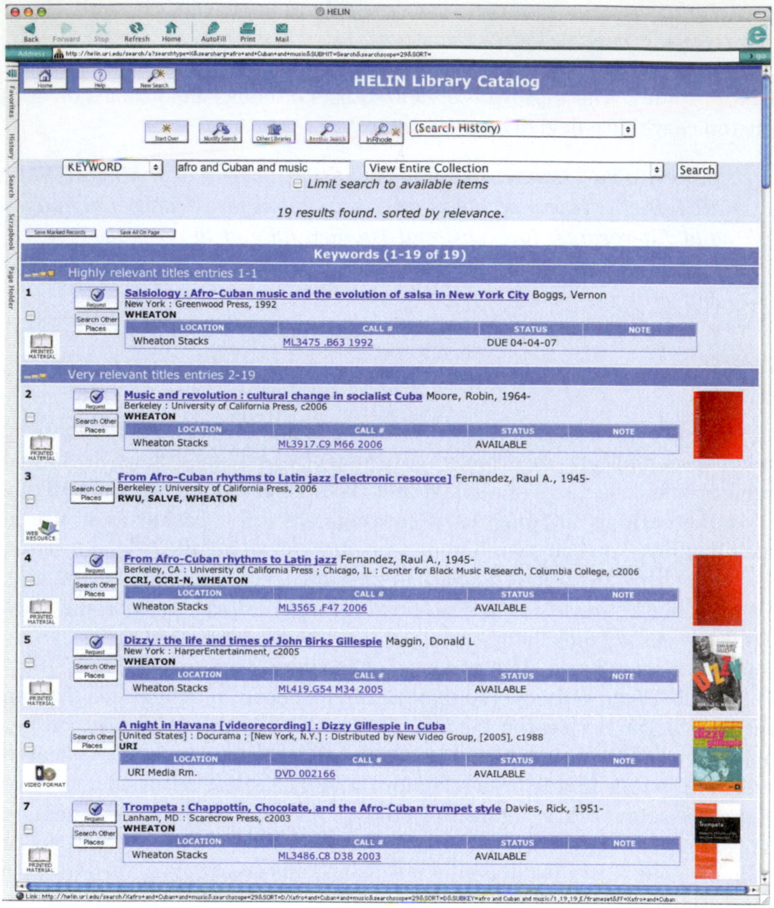

FIGURE 21.1 Sample search results for keywords *Afro-Cuban music*

back issues available online, either through terminals in the library or through the library's Web site. Many general-interest magazines and newspapers are also available in electronic as well as printed form.

1 Indexes

You can locate articles in print (and in electronic form) by consulting some of the many print and online **indexes**.

General and newspaper indexes. These give you a way to search for topics in the news and in other periodicals intended for the general public as well as some intended for more specialized audiences. They include *Academic Index, Readers' Guide to Periodical Literature, Wall Street*

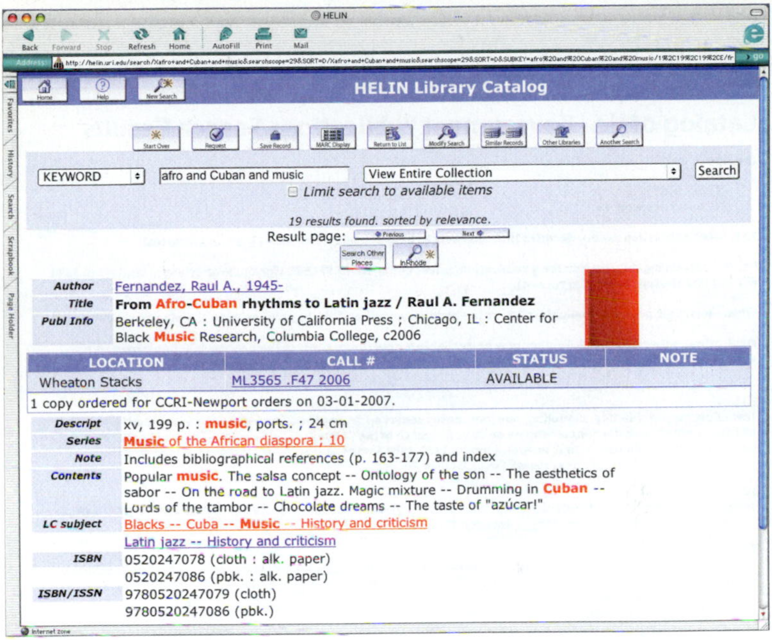

FIGURE 21.2 Detailed information for one entry

Journal Index, Washington Post Index, Expanded Academic, Editorials on File, and OCLC *WorldCat.*

Specialized indexes. These provide ways to search for publications offering more specialized, technical, or academic resources. Among these are *Anthropological Literature, Humanities Index, Music Index, BIZZ (Business Index), EconLit, Education Index, ERIC Current Index to Journals in Education, Index to Legal Periodicals, Social Sciences Index, Applied Science and Technology Index,* and *MEDLINE.*

Abstracts. Collections of abstracts provide brief summaries of articles in specialized fields. They include *Abstracts of English Studies, Biological Abstracts, Dissertation Abstracts International, Historical Abstracts, Newspaper Abstracts, Psychological Abstracts,* and *Sociological Abstracts.*

2 Government documents

Government documents include reports of information and research, records of hearings, pamphlets, public information publications, and regulations issued by Congress, federal agencies, and state and local governments. These rich sources of information, both general and technical, are sometimes housed in separate collections in a library.

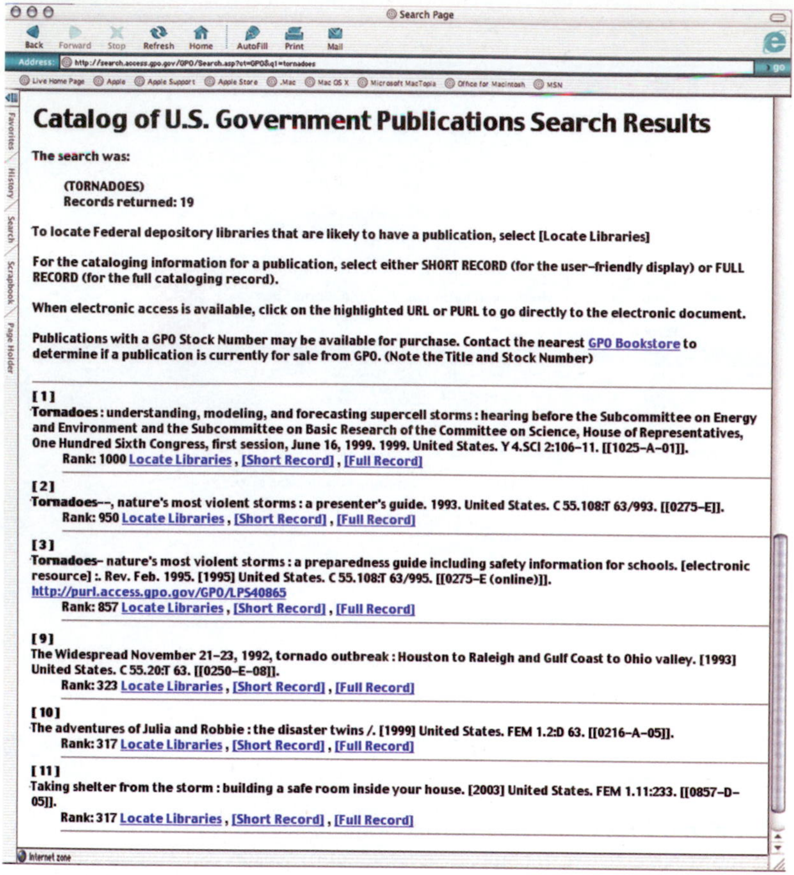

Catalog of U.S. Government Publications Search Results

The search was:

(TORNADOES)
Records returned: 19

To locate Federal depository libraries that are likely to have a publication, select [Locate Libraries]

For the cataloging information for a publication, select either SHORT RECORD (for the user-friendly display) or FULL RECORD (for the full cataloging record).

When electronic access is available, click on the highlighted URL or PURL to go directly to the electronic document.

Publications with a GPO Stock Number may be available for purchase. Contact the nearest GPO Bookstore to determine if a publication is currently for sale from GPO. (Note the Title and Stock Number)

[1]
Tornadoes : understanding, modeling, and forecasting supercell storms : hearing before the Subcommittee on Energy and Environment and the Subcommittee on Basic Research of the Committee on Science, House of Representatives, One Hundred Sixth Congress, first session, June 16, 1999. 1999. United States. Y 4.SCI 2:106-11. [[1025-A-01]].
Rank: 1000 Locate Libraries , [Short Record] , [Full Record]

[2]
Tornadoes--, nature's most violent storms : a presenter's guide. 1993. United States. C 55.108:T 63/993. [[0275-E]].
Rank: 950 Locate Libraries , [Short Record] , [Full Record]

[3]
Tornadoes- nature's most violent storms : a preparedness guide including safety information for schools. [electronic resource] :. Rev. Feb. 1995. [1995] United States. C 55.108:T 63/995. [[0275-E (online)]].
http://purl.access.gpo.gov/GPO/LPS40865
Rank: 857 Locate Libraries , [Short Record] , [Full Record]

[9]
The Widespread November 21-23, 1992, tornado outbreak : Houston to Raleigh and Gulf Coast to Ohio valley. [1993] United States. C 55.20:T 63. [[0250-E-08]].
Rank: 323 Locate Libraries , [Short Record] , [Full Record]

[10]
The adventures of Julia and Robbie : the disaster twins /. [1999] United States. FEM 1.2:D 63. [[0216-A-05]].
Rank: 317 Locate Libraries , [Short Record] , [Full Record]

[11]
Taking shelter from the storm : building a safe room inside your house. [2003] United States. FEM 1.11:233. [[0857-D-05]].
Rank: 317 Locate Libraries , [Short Record] , [Full Record]

FIGURE 21.3 Search results in *Catalog of U.S. Government Publications* for keyword *tornadoes*

To access government documents published after 1976, search the *Catalog of U.S. Government Publications* at <http://catalog.gpo.gov/F>. Many documents are available electronically. For those published before 1976, consult the printed *Monthly Catalog of United States Government Publications*.

After reading several magazine and newspaper articles about tornadoes, Michael Micchie noticed that some of the writers cited government documents and government-sponsored research. He decided to see if any government publications addressed the subject. His search of the *Catalog of U.S. Government Publications* using the keyword *tornadoes* returned sixteen citations, each with a link to a full description of the document and a link to a list of libraries likely to have a copy of it. Figure 21.3 shows part of the response he received.

21f Online databases

Researchers (both student and professional) have come to rely on electronic databases for all kinds of information, especially for texts of scholarly and technical articles and for general-interest periodical articles. College, university, and public libraries offer a wide range of databases.

Online databases are simply files of information available only through the Internet or Web. Most databases, online or occasionally on CD-ROMs, focus on specialized or technical fields and are expensive to construct and maintain. Consequently, most restrict access to paying customers, including students and faculty whose fees are paid by their institutions.

Most databases are also quite specialized, but useful and interesting. Here, for example, is a description of the *Family Index*, which covers a range of topics most people would consider well worth learning about.

> *Family Index.* Indexes articles on the family from approximately 1,500 interdisciplinary journals. Family-related articles include family history and trends; education; economics, public policy and the law; health care; gerontology; religion; diverse families; marriage; parenthood and child development; sexuality; abuse and neglect; and other family problems.

This typical database provides information about articles from a large number of journals, more than would be indexed by a Web search engine (see 22b). Updated regularly, it focuses on contemporary documents from 1995 on, a good choice for the latest work in the field.

Databases vary according to the kinds of information they provide: *full-text databases*, *abstracts databases*, and *indexing* or *bibliographic databases*. They also differ according to field of interest and number or range of resources they contain. They are generally searchable by author, title, and keyword, or by special categories reflecting the scope and emphasis of the collection.

1 Full-text databases

Full-text databases list articles or documents and provide brief summaries of each. In addition, they provide complete texts of most items. As a result, they can save you time and effort locating potential sources. Full-text databases range from extensive collections of scholarly or general-interest articles like *Academic Search Premier* to highly focused collections like *Health & Wellness Resource Center*. Some of the most useful full-text databases include the following.

- **General**
Academic Search Premier (EBSCOhost)
Provides full texts of more than 3,180 scholarly publications in social

sciences, humanities, education, computer sciences, engineering, language and linguistics, arts and literature, medical sciences, and ethnic studies and similar academic fields.

LexisNexis Academic
Provides full texts of articles on news, law, and business information from national and international newspapers and periodicals.

National Newspaper Index (InfoTrac)
Offers indexing, abstracts, and full text of the *New York Times*, the *Wall Street Journal*, the *Washington Post*, and the *Christian Science Monitor*.

InfoTrac OneFile (InfoTrac)
Contains news and periodical articles. Subjects covered include business, computers, current events, economics, education, environmental issues, health care, humanities, law, politics, science, social science, and sports.

• **Specialized**
CQ Researcher (Congressional Quarterly)
Collection of weekly reports, each exploring a single, controversial issue. Each report discusses pros and cons, offers comments from experts, includes charts and graphs, offers a timeline of events, and provides lengthy bibliographies.

National Service Center for Environmental Publications
Database of thousands of EPA documents at <http://www.epa.gov/ncepihom/>.

Health & Wellness Resource Center (InfoTrac)
Contains articles on fitness, pregnancy, medicine, nutrition, diseases, public health, occupational health and safety, alcohol and drug abuse, HMOs, prescription drugs, and similar subjects.

Jenny Latimer was looking for detailed information for her paper about the presence of hydrogenated oils in snack foods, especially candy. She knew her research would involve technical information but didn't know which fields of study would provide what she needed: food science and nutrition, health sciences, chemistry, or biology. In addition, she was worried about being limited to sources that were too technical for her to understand or explain to readers. She decided to consult a database that covered general-interest as well as academic publications and provided both abstracts and full texts so she could sample the available sources online.

First she entered her search terms into the query screen of the database using the terms *hydrogenated oils* and *candy*, but the search engine was unable to identify sources using these terms. She then broadened the search using the terms *hydrogenated oils* and *food* connected by AND to search for documents with both (see 22b-2). This search identified sixteen sources, some of which seemed promising (see Figure 21.4).

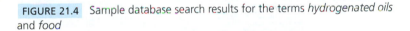

FIGURE 21.4   Sample database search results for the terms *hydrogenated oils* and *food*

Jenny looked at all the articles in abstract and full-text form and took notes on several, including one that provided specific examples she felt might be important for her paper (see Figure 21.5 on p. 162). After reading and taking notes, she decided that the areas of study most likely to provide the information and insights she needed were nutrition studies and health sciences.

2 Databases containing abstracts

Many databases, especially those in academic or technical fields, provide abstracts (brief summaries of a document's content) and sometimes full texts of selected items. (Some databases also link to a library's online subscription to academic and technical journals.)

PsycINFO
Indexing and abstracts of journal articles and books in psychology.

CINAHL (OVID)
Indexing and abstracts of journal articles and other materials in nursing and allied health.

Sociological Abstracts (CSA)
Abstracts and indexing in sociology and related disciplines.

Biological Abstracts
Indexing and abstracts of journals in the life sciences.

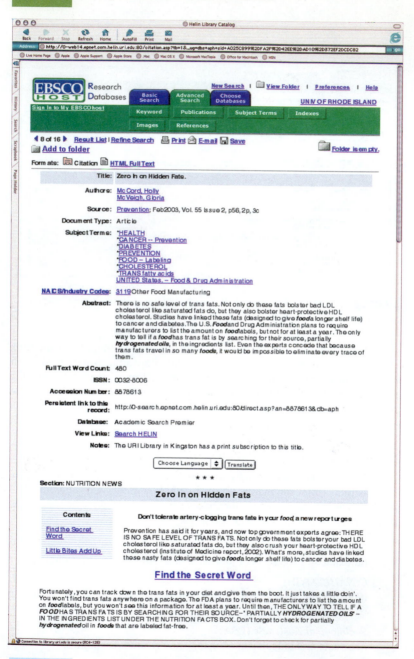

FIGURE 21.5 Detailed information for one entry under *hydrogenated oils* and *food*

America: History and Life (ABC-CLIO)
Indexing and abstracts of journal articles and materials on U.S. and
   Canadian history.

MLA Bibliography
Indexing and abstracts of journals, books, and other materials in language
   and literature.

ComAbstracts (CIOS)
Abstracts of articles published in the field of communication.

MEDLINE
Indexing and abstracts of journals in medicine.

ERIC
Indexing and abstracts of journals and other materials in education.

Jenny Latimer's search for information on the presence and effects of
hydrogenated oils in foods, especially snack foods and candy, led her to research in nutrition and health sciences and to the database *Health & Wellness
Resource Center*, which provides abstracts of scholarly articles and conference presentations. Here she found two abstracts that added breadth and
complexity to her research because they suggested that the dangers of hydrogenated oils are not as clear as many claim (see Figure 21.6 on p. 164).

3 Indexing or bibliographic databases

Many databases identify titles and publication (or access) information
for articles and documents in a specialized field, but you will often need to locate the texts of these sources through some other means. (Some databases
may provide a link to a library's online subscription to a scholarly journal.)

Art Index (OCLC *FirstSearch*)
Indexes over 400 publications in the arts.

GEOBASE (OCLC *FirstSearch*)
Indexes articles on geology, geography, and ecology.

4 Resource databases

Resource databases provide access to information, images, and documents arranged in the form of an electronic reference work, or they offer
tools for researchers. Here are several useful examples.

Web of Science (ISI/Thomson)
Web access to databases (*Science Citation Index*, *Social Sciences
   Citation Index*, and *Arts & Humanities Citation Index*) of citations

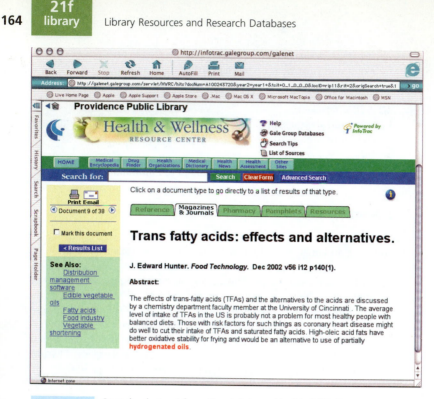

FIGURE 21.6   Sample abstract from the database *Health & Wellness Resource Center*

in research journals. Citation indexes allow you to identify the sources used by researchers and to track the strands of a research "conversation."

RefWorks (CSA)
Web-based, bibliographic management service you can use to create a list of sources by drawing bibliographical information from online databases and automatically creating entries in a variety of documentation styles.

WorldCat (OCLC *FirstSearch*)
Catalog of library holdings and Internet resources worldwide.

STRATEGY   Consult online databases.

1. Use the descriptions of databases in this section only as a *starting point*. Be alert for databases that are even better suited to your needs.
2. Most libraries provide handouts or online directories with up-to-date information on the availability and features of the library's online databases.

3. Move from general databases to more specialized ones.
4. Keep detailed records of the databases you consult as well as possible sources, abstracts, or full texts you locate. Download or print out copies.
5. Pay attention to links and alternative search paths suggested by a database.
6. If the full text of an article is not available online, check your library's catalog to see if it is available. (Many libraries provide links to their catalogs as part of their database programs.)
7. If a database provides only an abstract or a bibliographical reference to an article, check to see if the database will email you the full text of articles you find potentially useful. Some databases charge for this service; others will provide texts for free.

21g Evaluating library sources

Library sources—books from reputable publishers, articles from scholarly or well-known periodicals, government documents—often have been reviewed by experts and produced with editorial checks. Even so, once you locate these sources, you'll need to decide whether they are appropriate for your research community and your questions and whether they support or deepen your thesis.

STRATEGY   Use questions to evaluate your sources.

- Does the publisher, journal, or sponsoring organization have a reputation for balance and accuracy? Is it an advocate whose views require caution?
- Is the author's reputation clear? What do other sources think of the author's trustworthiness, fairness, and importance?
- How accurate is your source, especially if it presents facts as truth? Can you spot obvious errors? Which points are well documented?
- How does the writer support generalizations? Do they go beyond the facts? Are they consistent with your knowledge?
- Are the ideas generally consistent with those in your other sources? If different, do they seem insightful or misleading and eccentric?
- Does the source meet the expectations of your research community?
- Does the source appropriately document information, quotations, and ideas or clearly attribute them to the author?
- Has the source appeared without an editorial or review process? Does it apply only to a specific setting? Is its information outdated? Does it cite experts who have political or financial interests? Does it try to obscure its own bias? If so, consider it questionable; use it with caution.

22   Web and Internet Resources

Many writers begin their research on the World Wide Web or the Internet. They do so because of accessibility and the wide range of current resources available. Email, discussion groups, and, above all, Web sites provide varied interpretations, opinions, and information, ranging from text to data to visuals and audio. To access a Web site, you simply need a **browser**, such as *Internet Explorer* or *Netscape*, and an electronic address, known as a **URL** (uniform resource locator). Or you can follow links embedded in an online document (usually marked by an icon or highlighted line).

Web and Internet resources are rich and varied, but they have limitations, too. The texts are often shorter and less detailed with less development of explanations or arguments than in print texts. The electronic texts have not necessarily been reviewed and edited carefully as many print texts have. And the absence of systematic cataloging and indexing on the Web and Internet makes search tools and a search strategy crucial.

22a   Developing a Web and Internet search strategy

In creating your Web and Internet search strategy, emphasize diversity. Go beyond Web sites to electronic versions of printed texts (books, magazines, scholarly and professional journals, and newspapers), electronic databases and collections of documents (including government publications), discussion groups and newsgroups, visual and audio resources, synchronous devices including Webcams, and the links embedded in Web texts.

STRATEGY   Make a checklist.

Turn your plan for Web and Internet research into a checklist you have at hand while you are working online. Include in your checklist reminders to examine a variety of resources, including the following.

Web sites and Web pages	Online versions of printed texts	Online databases (see 21f)
Synchronous devices	Discussion groups and newsgroups	Visual and audio documents
Embedded links	Collections of documents	Online periodicals

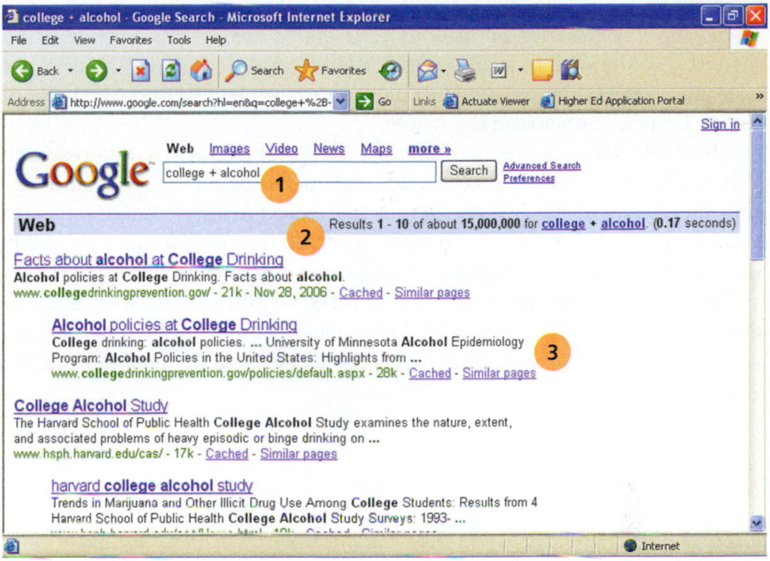

1. Keywords used in search
2. Results of search
3. One source with annotation

FIGURE 22.1   Results of a *Google* search using the keywords *alcohol* and *college*

22b Search engines

To locate Web and Internet resources, use a **search engine**, an electronic tool that gathers data about Web pages and Internet sites such as discussion groups. The sites a search engine identifies, the information it gathers, and the way it selects and organizes information depend on two things: (1) the principles on which it operates and (2) the questions you ask of it.

1 General search engines

General search engines typically search for resources according to keywords or phrases you type into a search box. Results from different search engines may both overlap and differ because each search engine indexes only a selection of the sites on the Web or Internet. Each also uses its own principles of selection and arrangement, identifying different sites and providing different information about them (see Figure 22.1). Using several search engines is worthwhile, although each search may turn up many irrelevant, dated, or untrustworthy sites for every one that is relevant.

Sometimes a search returns disappointing or confusing results. Perhaps the keywords or phrases in your query are not the ones used by some sites, so the search engine passes them by. Your query may be fine, but the results may be disappointing because the search engine finds the parts of a phrase or name rather than the whole.

Rashelle Jackson was working on a project guided by this research question: "What techniques used in hip hop performance make it different from other kinds of music?" She typed the words *hip hop techniques* into several search engines, and each responded with lists of resources including a site with the title "The Phonograph Turntable and Performance Practice in Hip Hop." The descriptions from the first three search engines were uninformative, incomplete, and even misleading. Only the fourth gave her a good idea of the site's contents and its relevance to her search (see Figure 22.2).

The Phonograph Turntable and Performance Practice in **Hip Hop** ...
... This transformation has been concurrent with the invention by the **Hip Hop** DJ of a ... sliding lever which allows the performer to effect certain **techniques** on a ...

The **Phonograph Turntable** and Performance Practice in **Hip Hop** Music
The **Phonograph Turntable** and Performance Practice in **Hip Hop** Music Miles White ... globalization of **Hip Hop** music and culture ... invention by the **Hip Hop** DJ of a new technical ... capabilities of ...

The **Phonograph Turntable** and Performance Practice in **Hip Hop** Music
White. Introduction ...

The **Phonograph Turntable** and Performance Practice in **Hip Hop** Music
The **Phonograph Turntable** and Performance Practice in **Hip Hop** Music Miles White ... globalization of **Hip Hop** music and culture ... invention by the **Hip Hop** DJ of a new technical ... capabilities of the **phonograph**, a process which ... Description: The popularization and globalization of **Hip Hop** music and culture over the past twenty or so years has provided new and refreshing areas of inquiry and research across a number of academic disciplines and critical approaches. The scholarly work ...

FIGURE 22.2   Search engine results for the keywords *hip hop techniques*

2 Advanced searches

If your results for a search seem uneven or unhelpful—too many items, too few items, or mostly irrelevant items—click on the advanced search advice available on most search engines. Find out how to search most productively, using specific words, math signs ($+$, $-$), symbols (* to look for all variations using part of a word), or automatic default combinations.

Word your query to combine, rule out, or treat terms as alternatives. Use the principles of Boolean logic to focus on what you want to know.

OR (expands)	Search for either term (documents referring to either X OR Y)
AND (restricts)	Search for both terms (documents referring to both X AND Y, but not to either alone)
NOT (excludes)	Search for X unless X includes the term Y (documents referring to X, but not those referring also to Y; X NOT Y)

3 Metasearch sites

A **metasearch** site enables you to conduct your search using several search engines simultaneously—and then to compare the results. Conducted early in your research, a metasearch can help you identify which search engines are most likely to be useful for your task. Metasearches can also suggest interesting new directions for your inquiry.

Dogpile	<http://dogpile.com>
Mamma	<http://www.mamma.com>
MetaCrawler	<http://metacrawler.com>

4 Focused and question-oriented sites

Some search sites focus on specific disciplines, fields of inquiry, or content areas. As you narrow your search or look for more complex information or the results of academic studies, these focused search sites will become more useful.

Other search tools allow you to ask questions rather than use keywords, for example, *Ask.com* at <http://ask.com>. Or they may link keyword queries to what (sometimes) are related, relevant resources as does *WebReference* at <http://www.webreference.com>.

22c Web sites and Internet resources

To find appropriate resources you should recognize some important kinds of Web and Internet sites, their content and purposes, and the uses you can make of them.

1 Individual Web sites

Individual Web sites are not necessarily *about* individuals, although they may be, as is the case with *home pages* created by individuals to share events in their lives or to broadcast their opinions. Individuals may share accounts of experiences: white-water rafting, service in Iraq, or work on an oil rig in Northern Alaska. Home pages maintained by researchers often contain links to their research articles, both those in print and in progress.

Blogs are Web sites offering daily or weekly accounts of a person's activity and thoughts. They can be fascinating sources of information from people in war zones, dangerous parts of the world, or important jobs. Others can be just plain boring. Sites such as Blogcatalog <http://www.blogcatalog.com> illustrate the wide variety available.

2 Sponsored Web sites

All kinds of organizations—public, private, corporate, academic, government, religious, and social—sponsor Web sites. The suffixes on the electronic addresses often indicate what kind of organization the sponsor is.

edu	educational institution
gov	government agency
org	nonprofit or service organization
com	business organization (commercial)
net	network organization

A sponsored Web site may be little more than a billboard or marketing device, yet such sites can also be excellent sources of up-to-date information and articulate advocates for a cause. The usefulness and the integrity of a sponsored Web site generally depend on the character of the sponsoring organization and the resources devoted to site maintenance.

3 Advocacy Web sites

Advocacy Web sites explain or defend an organization's actions and beliefs and argue for specific policies. Although they are biased in favor of the organization's position—after all, they *advocate* for the point of view—many are of high quality: explaining positions, answering critics, and providing detailed supporting evidence and documentation along with lists of readings on the topic or issue. Some even provide links to Web sites with opposing points of view as a way of stimulating open discussion.

4 Informational Web sites

Carefully organized informational Web sites provide tables of data, historical background, reports of research, answers to frequently asked questions (FAQs), links, and lists of references. Large Web sites may also provide site maps and allow for keyword searches. Be aware, however, that many informational sites are poorly organized, unevenly developed, and even untrustworthy. Look on the site for details about the sponsor, the way the site's information is gathered and maintained, and the date of the last update.

Informational Web sites may focus on a particular subject such as sleep research, horror movies, or poetry from the Beat Generation of the 1950s or an activity such as developing an environmental project or a healthy lifestyle. Or they may focus on the activities and research projects of the sponsor itself.

5 Research-oriented Web sites

Research-oriented Web sites are broadly informational but more narrowly focused and differently arranged than most informational Web sites. They typically contain one or more of the following.

1. Full texts of research reports (sometimes twenty-five or more pages)
2. Summaries of completed or ongoing research projects
3. Electronic texts of research articles that appeared in print journals or book-length collections
4. Extensive data frequently presented in downloadable tables, graphs, and charts or as texts of field notes and discussions of statistics
5. Reviews of current research
6. Texts of unpublished conference papers and other presentations
7. Announcements of grants, conferences, and forthcoming publications
8. Addresses or phone numbers for researchers
9. Bibliographies of books and articles; links to related Web sites
10. Artistic performances and creations

Universities, research institutes, and professional groups (such as the American Psychological Association) often maintain research-oriented Web sites.

6 Online periodicals and books; electronic versions of print publications

Online magazines, newspapers, and scholarly journals are similar to print publications in many ways. Indeed, many appear in both versions.

Los Angeles Times	<http://www.latimes.com>
Newsweek	<http://www.newsweek.com>
Business Week	<http://www.businessweek.com>
Weekly Standard	<http://www.weeklystandard.com>
The Nation	<http://www.thenation.com>

Many online sites go one step further and make back issues or selected articles available, as is the case with publications like the following.

Scientific American <http://www.sciam.com>
   (General-interest magazine of science and technology)
Salon <http://www.salon.com>
   (General-interest magazine of social and cultural commentary)
The Journal of Popular Culture <http://www.msu.edu/~tjpc/>
   (Academic articles on popular culture)

7 Electronic lists and discussion groups

The Internet and the Web play host to many discussion groups, some focusing on highly specialized topics like beekeeping, small countries in Eastern Europe or Africa, and poetry slams. The postings to such lists vary in quality, from inquiries by novices to discussions and responses from nationally recognized experts. It can be difficult to judge the quality of contributions because the writers may identify themselves only by screen names.

An **electronic list** posts messages from members of a mailing list to all other members and gives them a chance to respond. **Newsgroups** or **bulletin boards** are open sites where you can post messages or questions and read postings from others. Both kinds of sites are good places to gather opinions, possible sources, and ideas about readers' expectations about a topic. Many search engines will help you locate postings, as shown in Figure 22.3.

8 Government publications sites

Government publications on an astonishing range of topics are available in print form in most college and university libraries. In addition, many government agencies have spent considerable effort developing Web sites for access to their reports and documents. Use the following sites to identify government publications relevant to your research.

USA.gov	<http://www.usa.gov>
Catalog of U.S. Government Publications	<http://catalog.gpo.gov/>
FedStats	<http://www.fedstats.gov/>
FedWorld	<http://www.fedworld.gov>

22d Evaluating Web and Internet sources

Web and Internet sources often have not been edited or reviewed by outside readers, so you can't assume that they are credible or reliable.

FIGURE 22.3 Newsgroup message from *Google* requesting research help

1 Examine Web materials

Examine Web sources carefully and ask questions appropriate to the kinds of information and ideas being presented.

- Is the material documentary (films, sounds, images, surveys)? If so, consider authenticity, biases, and relevance to your research questions.

- Is the resource textual (essays, narratives, studies, articles)? If so, consider its authorship, construction, level of detail, support for reasoning, complexity, fairness, sources, and documentation.
- Is the resource peculiar to the Web (personal, educational, corporate, organizational sites)? If so, consider its genre, affiliation, reputation, possible motivation, construction, design, and value in terms of content.
- Is the resource conversational? If so, analyze it as primary material (see 22d-3).

2 Ask critical questions about Web materials

To evaluate the strengths, weaknesses, and credibility of Web resources such as personal pages and organizational sites, ask the following questions developed by Paula Mathieu and Ken McAllister at the University of Illinois at Chicago as part of the *Critical Resources in Teaching with Technology* (CRITT) project.

Who benefits? What difference does that make? On many Web sites, the information presented seems designed primarily for the reader's benefit. Advice about a healthy diet, information about the best product or about lodging and travel, or tips about the best ways to get a car loan may seem unbiased and helpful. Yet no site can offer all the available information, and the selection is likely to benefit someone: producers of a specific kind of food, product manufacturers, or loan companies, for example. Before you decide to use the information from a site, consider who benefits from it.

Who's talking? What difference does that make? If the identity of the group or persons responsible for the site is clear from the pages, you can find out more about them and judge their likely credibility or bias. However, a group whose name makes it sound dedicated purely to the general public interest may actually have a strong bias. Having a set of values and conveying them to readers is perfectly appropriate, of course, but readers need to be aware of these values so that they do not consider the information as purely objective. If the source of the information on a site is not made plain, you may have to search the site for it, looking at the end of the text, the information in the URL, or in any linked files, such as a privacy statement or a page for further information.

What's missing? What difference does that make? Every resource has a point of view that guides its selection and presentation of information. A site promoting milk drinking might mention lactose intolerance only briefly (or not at all). A site devoted to understanding lactose intolerance would probably not spend much time (if any) discussing the benefits of milk drinking.

Because most sites limit some information and focus on other information, be sure to look to other sources to fill in the missing pieces.

3 Evaluate conversational resources

Electronic mailing lists, newsgroups, or Web-based forums can provide you with instant access to firsthand information. However, you need extra vigilance to distinguish authoritative comments, backed by genuine expertise, from unsupported opinions (see 8a–b and 10d–f). One strategy is to treat conversational materials as primary resources, data which you need to analyze and interpret for your readers. Ask critical questions: What do you know about the author's expertise, credibility, fairness, logical reasoning, or supporting evidence? Do other resources substantiate the author's claims? How does the author's view relate to your research thread? How would your research community react to the material?

23 Fieldwork

Field research is firsthand research, gathering material directly from people you interview or survey or from events and places you observe. Your fieldwork addresses your research questions with original, even surprising, findings that are the product of your own investigation, not somebody else's research. Because you may find that your results vary or are more complex than you expected, it's important to plan your field research with an open mind or a "neutral" perspective on what you're investigating. This perspective will help you to avoid leading questionnaires, biased notes during an observation, or data-gathering methods that skew your results, such as interviewing only one social group about food in the student union.

Good field research also involves interpretation. Give the data you collect the same critical "reading" and analysis you give to all other sources. Secondary sources from your research may suggest how to present your findings and what to conclude from your data. Of course, your fieldwork goals and methods depend on your task and research community.

Academic. Field research in sociology, psychology, business, education, or urban planning often means studying people's behaviors or outlooks to find patterns, causes, or effects. In chemistry, engineering, or pharmacy, it inquires into how substances, organisms, objects, or machines work. When you plan your fieldwork, find out about any institutional approval needed for research involving other people (see 23d).

Public. Field research in public settings often gathers (and measures) people's opinions on issues or policies. Government research in the public interest can profoundly affect laws and regulations. Researchers for the Environmental Protection Agency, for instance, sample soil, water, and air across the country to test levels of pollutants or contaminants.

Work. Field research in businesses and organizations often looks at how customers (or staff) act and interact, how problems might be solved, or how quality or efficiency might be improved. Market researchers gauge interest in a product or recruit consumers for taste tests or "focus groups" that respond to products or marketing strategies.

> **STRATEGY** Prepare for your fieldwork.
>
> Do background research, and plan your fieldwork carefully. To identify worthwhile questions or problems, look over research already conducted. Use the methods of others as models for your own.

23a Interviewing

Talk with experts or people with pertinent experiences or opinions to test or supplement your other sources. An interview can be structured or open-ended. As you plan, think about your goals, and shape the interview questions accordingly.

> **STRATEGY** Organize a productive interview.
>
> - List potential interviewees and possible questions. Consider whether you will need a lengthy conversation or just a few short answers.
> - Write out your questions, arranging them logically. Avoid any that could be answered by *yes* or *no* or that are unclear or leading.
> - Use your questions, but don't be shackled by them. In the interview, follow up on new information and ideas that serve your purpose.
> - If you wish to tape-record instead of take notes, always ask permission. Bring backup supplies as well as paper and pen.
> - After an interview, send a thank-you note—both to be polite and in case you need a follow-up interview.

23b Surveying, polling, or using questionnaires

Surveys, polls, and questionnaires gather opinions or information about specific behaviors and possible actions. They can be administered orally (asking questions in a mall or on the phone), on paper (filling out a survey in a restaurant), or, increasingly, in electronic form (responding in a file on the Web). In any case, think through your questions carefully, and test your instrument before you administer it for your study.

1 Use surveys or polls

Surveys and **polls** collect short answers, often in *yes/no* form, providing statistics for charts, comparisons, or support. All can provide basic information, but what they supply in simplicity and speed, they lack in depth and complexity.

STRATEGY Plan and test a survey or poll.

- Decide which people you want to survey or poll. How many do you need to contact? Of what gender, age, or occupation?
- Always draft, test, and revise your questions in advance.
- Consider your location; it may determine who answers your questions.

Shane Hand marked answers to his recycling questions on a tally sheet.

Do you . . .

Use coffee mugs instead of polystyrene cups?	Yes	No
Reuse plastic wrap, foil, and plastic bags?	Yes	No
Recycle newspapers and/or magazines?	Yes	No

Are you willing to . . .

Take your own bags to the store?	Yes	No

2 Use questionnaires

Usually mailed, **questionnaires** can gather in-depth information from many people but need careful preparation for clarity. (See the sample questionnaire at the end of the research paper in 27c.)

STRATEGY Design and test a questionnaire.

- Decide on your purpose (what you want to find out and why), the selection of your participants (the characteristics of the people you will question), and your expectations (possible problems).
- Choose whether to group questions in sections. Decide whether to ask multiple-choice or yes-no questions that supply numerical data, open-ended questions that supply narrative detail, or a combination of these.

- Figure out what respondents might be willing to do (writing, checking, circling, or marking answers) and how you will analyze answers.
- Draft your questions, and test them on several people. Ask your testers to identify where they were confused or lacked information.
- Revise the questionnaire, and prepare it for distribution. Try to fit your questions on one page (front and back), but leave room for comments.

23c Conducting an ethnographic study

You can use **ethnographic research** to interpret practices, behaviors, language, and attitudes of groups connected by interests or ways of understanding and acting. Because an **ethnography**—the written report of this cultural analysis—aims for in-depth understanding, you may use several methods to gather detailed information about your subject, including observations of people, events, and settings; conversations or interviews with **informants** (people who provide information about the group to which they belong); and collection of **artifacts** (characteristic material objects).

Focus your fieldwork on a specific setting, activity, person, or group. Conduct **structured observations** in which you objectively watch a situation, behavior, or relationship in order to understand its elements and processes. For instance, to study how preschoolers use language during play, you might conduct a series of structured observations at a day-care center.

STRATEGY Plan a structured observation.

- Choose the site; if necessary, get permission to observe.
- Decide how to situate yourself (in one spot or moving) and how to explain your presence to those observed.
- Decide what information or artifacts you want to gather and why. Try to anticipate how you will use this material in your report.
- Consider what equipment you will use to record information: tape recorder, camera, notepad, or video camera.
- Anticipate problems, and plan strategies for dealing with them.

The following notes were transcribed from an audiotape for an anthropology study of a person with an unusual occupation.

Dave Glovsky—Palace Playland: Dave's Guessing Stand
(Sound of game, the Striker: hammer swings in background)
[First interchange between Brian Schwegler and Dave Glovsky is inaudible because of background noise.]
BS: So, Dave, can you tell me a little something about how you guess? Can you tell me how you guess?
DG: Ages? I read the lower lids. I read the lower lid. It deteriorates as we get older. The more it gets darker, they get older. Even children

of sixteen can fool me with the deterioration under the eyes. They can have beautiful skin, but I don't check the skin. I check the lower lid of their eyes.

[The interview continues until a customer arrives.]

DG: Hey, come on in, have fun. What do you want me to guess?

Female cust: My age.

DG: All right, that's a dollar. (Holds up one dollar bill.) A hundred dollar bill. Step into the office here. (Points to a patch of pavement.)

When you report ethnographic data, be precise. Offer interpretations that go beyond simply presenting details.

First Draft: Dave the Guesser
by Brian Schwegler

"Come on in, have some fun with the famous guesser of Old Orchard," says Dave "The Guesser" Glovsky. Relying on his voice and personality to attract customers, he seems out of place in this mechanized wonderland. Hand-painted signs covered with cramped writing are his advertisement. . . .

As I stand in front of his stand and read his signs, a young woman approaches Dave.

"Hey, come on in, have fun. What do you want me to guess?" Dave asks.

"My age," says the young woman.

"All right, that's a dollar." Holding up the dollar bill that the woman gives him, Dave examines it the way a jeweler examines a precious stone. "A hundred dollar bill." Pointing to a space on the pavement, Dave says, "Step into the office here." Dave checks her out from all angles, looking for the clue that will let him know her age within two years, his margin of error. . . .

23d Obtaining consent and approval for research on human subjects

Whenever you conduct research on human subjects, even when administering a short questionnaire, you need to abide by certain ethical and legal principles to avoid injuring your subjects. (This is also true of animal research.) "Injury" doesn't just mean physical harm, such as testing a product known to cause cancer. It also refers to possible psychological injury, such as might occur when interviewing children about traumatic events in their lives. Furthermore, participants are protected by privacy laws; although most people know when they become uncomfortable answering questions, they may not always be aware of how the law protects them. Consult with a teacher or a human subjects board member on your campus to ensure that your research meets the proper standards.

Most campuses have a committee, board, or unit that provides information about using human subjects in research. Such groups are responsible for approving research plans after considering their legal and ethical implications as well as the kinds of information that the researcher proposes to gather. The group can approve, disapprove, or return a proposal for revision.

Gaining approval to conduct human subject research is required on most campuses—and has the benefit of protecting the researcher as well as the people who participate. However, whether you need approval for field research involving people will depend on various factors. In some cases, an entire class can receive general approval to conduct surveys, polls, or questionnaires; in other cases, no approval may be necessary. Be sure that you and your instructor know the practices on your campus and follow the requirements accordingly.

STRATEGY　**Follow conventions for informed consent.**

Besides meeting institutional guidelines and regulations, ethical field research involves some commonsense principles.

- Explain your research to participants. You may need to keep the explanation general so that you don't influence their responses, but you should not conceal the purpose and nature of your study.
- Make clear to participants what will happen with the data you gather. Who will see it? How long will it be kept? (Human subject committees have requirements for the collection, use, storage, and disposal of data, and you should follow those requirements.)
- Explain whether you will preserve anonymity or offer an option of anonymity. If you need to use names, will you use pseudonyms?
- Give your subjects the option of seeing the results of your research.

24　Avoiding Plagiarism and Integrating Sources

Does everything you write have to be your own? Of course not. You can draw on other people's words, knowledge, and ideas, and your writing will often be the better for it. Remember to do two things, especially in research writing.

General Attitudes About Plagiarism in Three Communities

	Academic	Public	Work
BELIEFS ABOUT PLAGIARISM	Strongly believes in individual ownership of ideas, texts, inventions, and other products of research and scholarship	Remains relatively unconcerned about the ownership of words produced for wide public or civic circulation, not for profit	Vigorously protects slogans, icons, language, and organizational representations from general use or appropriation by competitors
BELIEFS ABOUT WRITTEN MATERIALS	Views writing as intellectual property of writer (but sometimes owned by institution)	May view materials as part of group identity or mission, but sees public benefit or advocacy, not ownership, as goal	Views written materials as part of mission, products, or services, often owned by organization (not writer)
ATTITUDES ABOUT TEAMWORK	Generally accepts teamwork and team credits (with disciplinary differences)	May expect collaboration to facilitate consensus and efficiency within and among groups	Relies on internal work teams, all expected to defend organization's territory
EXPECTATIONS OF WRITERS	Expects writers to credit original author of almost any written source and to distinguish the writer's words and ideas from the source's	Expects writers to share generously, freely adapting and circulating materials, but to credit local or national authorities who substantiate values, claims, and advocacy	Expects careful protection of organizational materials, but accepts unattributed use of "boilerplate" language of unclear origin or value
REGULATORY MECHANISMS	Codifies and enforces strict plagiarism rules that can lead to paper, course, or status penalties	Generally accepts shared materials such as flyers, bylaws, and brochures, but could resort to legal protection of group identity or integrity	Turns to lawsuits to challenge theft of corporate identity, products, services, or intellectual property

- Acknowledge your borrowings—and in so doing avoid plagiarism.
- Integrate your own work with the material you draw from your sources.

24a Recognizing plagiarism

Consider the following cases. (1) After procrastinating for weeks, Kim can't imagine finishing her research paper on time. Following a friend's advice, she uses her credit card to buy a paper for $50 from an Internet paper mill, puts her name on it, and hands it in. (2) Paul realizes that a research paper he wrote the previous semester also fits the assignment in his spring class. He makes some minor changes and hands it in without mentioning that he originally wrote it for another course. (3) In her research paper, Tisha quotes a paragraph from an excellent source, dutifully citing it in her text and her references. A paragraph later, she adds more from the source but forgets to put quotation marks around the text or include an in-text citation.

Which of these cases is plagiarism? Which falls under "academic dishonesty"? Are they of equal severity? If someone like Tisha just makes an honest mistake while writing a paper, should she be considered guilty of plagiarism and suffer the (increasingly harsh) consequences?

Plagiarism, which comes from a Latin word for "kidnapping," generally refers to the theft of another person's ideas or words. However, plagiarism is part of a system of beliefs and regulations that govern the ways we write and the ways we use people's words. The standards for acknowledging and citing sources vary with the context. In college, you are in a setting where the rules about plagiarism are strict and apply to almost any kind of work you do for a course. Not learning and following those rules can lead to a failing grade for either a paper or an entire course, a special plagiarism notation on your transcript, or expulsion from your college or university. Very serious plagiarism, especially at higher levels of research and scholarship, can result in lawsuits and can ruin a career.

According to the Council of Writing Program Administrators (WPA), plagiarism in an academic setting "occurs when a writer deliberately uses someone else's language, ideas, or original (not common-knowledge) material without acknowledging its source" (<www.wpacouncil.org>). Thus, turning in someone else's paper as your own, taking someone's original idea from a book as your own, and copying passages or even sentences into your paper without noting their source all represent plagiarism.

24b The problem of intention

Some cases of plagiarism are conscious and deliberate. In other cases, the writers are trying to work honestly but haven't learned appropriate documentation practices, or they have come from a culture with different norms. Even so, for many readers and teachers, your naiveté makes no difference at all. If the result *looks* like plagiarism, you may still be found guilty of academic misconduct.

Figure 24.1 represents plagiarism from the perspectives of both the writer and the reader or teacher. At the top of the figure are cases of deliberate plagiarism. For most honest writers, the problem of plagiarism begins somewhere at the bottom of the figure, as they try to acknowledge sources but do so clumsily or incorrectly. But the reader's response is the same.

If you choose to plagiarize consciously and deceptively (placing yourself at the top of Figure 24.1), remember that plagiarism hurts everyone—including you: it cheats you out of your own learning opportunity, it robs oth-

Writer's Intention	Writer's Process	Reader's Response
CONSCIOUS	**CHEATING**	**"PLAGIARISM"**
↓	↓	↓
UNCONSCIOUS	**MAKING MISTAKES**	**"PLAGIARISM"**

FIGURE 24.1 Plagiarism from the perspective of the writer and a reader or teacher

ers (parents, taxpayers) who may be funding your education, it subverts and complicates the work of teachers who are trying to help you learn, it slows social progress by undermining the achievement of higher standards of education and work, and it damages those who put time and energy into producing the work you're now stealing. By using this book to learn how to cite sources carefully and responsibly, you can avoid the situations represented by the bottom part of Figure 24.1.

24c When to document sources

In general, you need to document the words, ideas, and information you draw from another person's work. Keep in mind the three most important reasons for documenting sources.

1. To add support to your conclusions and credibility to your explanations by showing that they are based on careful research
2. To give credit to others for their original work
3. To show your readers where they can obtain the materials you cite (and from there, perhaps others)

Decisions on what needs documenting may vary from audience to audience. If you're writing to a general audience, readers may expect you to cite sources for your discussion of subatomic particles. If you're writing for a physics professor or an audience of physicists, you might assume that such matters are common knowledge. However, in some college classrooms, your instructor may want to know all the works you have consulted in order to see the evidence of your explorations.

YOU MUST DOCUMENT

- Word-for-word (direct) quotations taken from someone else's work
- Paraphrases or summaries of someone else's work, whether published or presented more informally in an interview or email message
- Ideas, opinions, and interpretations that others have developed and presented, even if they are based on common knowledge
- Facts or data that someone else has gathered or identified if they are not widely enough known to be considered common knowledge
- Information that is not widely accepted or that is disputed
- Illustrations, charts, graphs, photographs, recordings, original software, performances, interviews, and the like
- Anything from the Internet that you can reasonably cite, including emails from mailing lists, text from blogs and chatrooms, and so on

BUT DO NOT DOCUMENT

- Ideas, opinions, and interpretations that are your own
- Widely known ideas and information—the sort you can locate in common reference works or that people writing or speaking on a topic usually present as common knowledge
- Commonly used quotations ("To be, or not to be")

24d Working with common knowledge

In every field, researchers share certain kinds of knowledge. Everyone in biological fields, for example, knows what a "double helix" is and would not need to cite a source for such information, which is called **common knowledge**. When your topic or discipline is unfamiliar to you, however, you may not know what counts as common knowledge.

STRATEGY   **Test whether information is common knowledge.**

- Consider whether information seems to be widely accepted and frequently repeated in sources or generally shared by educated readers. If it's not, *cite the source*.
- Consider your composition teacher—who wants to know that you have learned from your sources—as your primary reader. To show your learning, cite what might be regarded as common knowledge in a specialized field.
- Ask several people whether they know a particular fact that might be considered common knowledge. Or ask yourself. If the answer is "no," *cite it*.
- When in doubt, *cite*. It's easier to cut an unnecessary reference when you revise than to have to find it again in your research file.

24e Citing sources responsibly

When you include quotations, paraphrases, and summaries in your writing, you must acknowledge their sources. If you don't, you're treating someone else's work as your own.

- Be sure you enclose someone else's exact words in quotation marks.
- Make sure that paraphrases and summaries are in your own words.
- Be sure to cite the source of any ideas or information that you quote, paraphrase, or summarize.

The following paraphrase is too close to the original to be presented without quotation marks and would be considered plagiarized, even if you had done so without knowing better.

ORIGINAL PASSAGE

Malnutrition was a widespread and increasingly severe problem throughout the least developed parts of the world in the 1970s, and would continue to be serious, occasionally reaching famine conditions, as the millennium approached. Among the cells of the human body most dependent upon a steady source of nutrients are those of the immune system, most of which live, even under ideal conditions, for only days at a time. (From Laurie Garrett, *The Coming Plague*, New York: Penguin, 1994, p. 199)

POORLY PARAPHRASED VERSION

Garrett points out that malnutrition can give microbes an advantage as they spread through the population. Malnutrition continues to be a severe problem throughout the least developed parts of the world. The human immune system contains cells that are dependent upon a steady source of nutrients. These cells may live, even under ideal conditions, for only days at a time.

The writer of the poorly paraphrased version made only minor changes in some phrases and "lifted" others verbatim. It's difficult, therefore, to tell which words or ideas are Garrett's and which are the writer's.

APPROPRIATE PARAPHRASE

Garrett points out that malnutrition can give microbes an advantage as they spread through the population. The human body contains immune cells that help to fight off various diseases. When the body is deprived of nutrients, these immune cells will weaken (Garrett 199).

Because this writer's paper focused on the general threat of global disease, he also could have simply summarized the passage. (See 20g-1, 24h-3.)

APPROPRIATE SUMMARY

It has been suggested that malnutrition can weaken the immune system and make people more susceptible to diseases they would otherwise fight off (Garrett 199).

Inadvertent plagiarism—really a kind of sloppiness in your writing process—often happens when you are working between your source material and your developing paper. You *think* you're using your own words, but the words of your source are so fresh in your mind that they creep in and "become" yours.

STRATEGY **Watch out for inadvertent plagiarism.**

Keep your distance whenever you paraphrase or summarize a source.

- Be sure to look back at the source and compare your words with those of the source.
- If any phrases or sentences are too close to the original, either quote the material directly and exactly (using quotation marks) or revise your summary or paraphrase so that you're not presenting the author's words as your own.

24f Citing sources in context

Academic research usually acknowledges and draws on the work of previous scholars and researchers. Most academic writers indicate where they fit in the tradition of research on a topic and explain any agreements and disagreements with earlier work. As they present their explanations, arguments, and evidence, they also supply precise, formal documentation in the style favored by their academic field. For four common styles used to cite sources as they are mentioned in the text and then listed at the end of the paper, see Chapters 26–29 on MLA, APA, CMS, and CSE documentation. If your instructor does not specify a documentation style, ask what is expected, and follow directions carefully.

The following excerpt from Summer Arrigo-Nelson and Jennifer Figliozzi's research report shows their careful integration (and critique) of a research study, cited in MLA style.

First, although both questions 1 and 4 looked to determine student alcohol use within the home, a discrepancy appeared between the percentage of people who replied that they were offered alcohol at home and those who said that their parents believed alcohol was only for those over twenty-one years of age. This discrepancy could have arisen if the students in the sample were not thorough in their evaluation of their parents' views, in which case, correlations drawn from this data should not be relied upon (Aas, Jakobsen, and Anderssen).

Material from nonacademic settings, however, may follow somewhat different conventions. Work audiences will expect concise treatment of things they already know and extended summaries, tables, graphs, and illustrations—all carefully documented with a recognizable citation system (see Chapters 26–29). Material designed for general public consumption may cite sources in a somewhat informal fashion; texts with many footnotes or academic-sounding references can confuse or put off some public audiences.

The following paragraph is excerpted from page 12 of the *Exxon Valdez* Oil Spill Restoration Plan's Update on Injured Resources and Services <http://www.evostc.state.ak.us/Publications/Downloadable/2002_IRS_update.pdf>, a publication of the *Exxon Valdez* Oil Spill Trustee Council. The excerpt comes from a research report on the recovery of the harlequin duck from the effects of the oil spill. Notice how the writer condenses several important and scientifically complex studies into a research synthesis that is readily understandable by a reasonably educated public audience but does not overwhelm the reader with complex references.

Winter surveys from 1995–1998 found that adult female survival was lower in oiled versus unoiled areas, and a similar survival scenario is suggested from data collected in 2000 to 2002. Oil remained in the subsurface of the intertidal zone through 2001, including under some mussel beds where harlequin ducks could be feeding. Biopsies from harlequin and Barrow's goldeneye ducks continue to show differences in an enzyme indicative of exposure to hydrocarbons between birds from oiled versus unoiled parts of the sound. These differences are consistent with the possibility of continued exposure to spill-derived hydrocarbons in the western sound. The biological effect of this possible exposure has not been established, but the declining trend of female survivability in the oiled areas may be continuing. Although this result cannot be attributed unequivocally to oil exposure, there is reason for concern about possible oil exposure and reduced survival for harlequin ducks in the western sound.

If you cite such work in your own papers or projects, you may wish to "unpack" the general references into specific citations. In more informal and less research-oriented public writing, be sure that you check any quotations or materials that appear to be from a source other than the public document itself. If you encounter an unreferenced quotation, try contacting the organization or author of the document to get the full citation for the source.

In contrast, consider an excerpt from a document at the same oil spill Web site that is clearly intended for other researchers and scholars with technical backgrounds (see <http://www.evostc.state.ak.us/StoreAuth.cfm?doc=/ Store/Proposal_Documents/1609.pdf>). Notice especially how careful the authors are to cite the sources of their information. Notice, too, how specialized their language and terminology are and how they rely on established studies to provide their background information.

> The waves on most PSW [Prince William Sound] beaches where oil is lingering are relatively small. Hence, it is expected that the effect of wave action does not extend too deeply into the beaches. The armoring of beaches further minimizes the effects of waves on oil entrapment and subsequently the washout of oil to sea. Hayes and Michel (1997) and Short *et al.* (2004) report data and present explanations supporting the sheltering of oil due to armoring. This implies that even if a seaward hydraulic gradient due to tide favors the washout of oil to sea, the armoring would entrap some of the oil behind boulders of pocket beaches, near boulder or bedrock outcrops.

24g Integrating sources

You've decided to draw on sources for your essay or report. Now you're surrounded by photocopied pages from books and articles, note cards or slips of paper with quotations on them, and ideas scribbled on a notepad along with references to various sources. You're facing the daunting task of weaving all this information into your own words as you create your paper.

Perhaps you are creating a research paper that is an original contribution to a subject area—something *you* create through your thorough sleuthing for information and your way of pulling all that information together and presenting it for others. Yet it's also about *other people's* work. It's your way of representing what a community of scholars and researchers and commentators has said about a topic or how this community has tried to answer a question. Weaving other people's words and ideas into your own paper can accomplish many specific purposes. The way you integrate outside material into your writing often depends on what you're trying to *do* with the source.

STRATEGY **Consider your paper's goal.**

- As you gather and read your source material, take notes about the possible purposes it might serve in your paper.
- As you write the paper (see Chapter 25), refer to your notes to make strategic decisions about what to incorporate where.

- Avoid trying to "force" a quotation to fit a purpose it doesn't serve; if an author has objectively cited a controversial position, it would misrepresent that author to imply that he or she holds that position as well.
- Be willing to scrap a source or citation if it serves no purpose.
- Avoid the "display for teacher" syndrome—putting in quotations and citations just to show your instructor that you have collected information.

1 Introducing a topic and providing background

Especially as you begin your paper, you may want to use some sources to explain a context, introduce your topic, or provide a history or background.

In his paper on conspiracy theories, Sam Roles decided to use his sources to provide background on why conspiracy theories are hard to refute. He followed the MLA style in documenting his sources (see Chapter 26).

Conspiracy theories arise, according to scholars, for a number of reasons: political fragmentation and suspicion of difference (Pipes); something to occupy the imagination of a bored subculture (Fenster); and fear of more powerful groups (Johnson). For example, in the 1950s and 1960s, communism provided a . . .

2 Summarizing prior research

In some cases, your research paper explores a topic or relationship many others have written about. Instead of trying to provide lots of references, use some sources selectively to give a brief summary of others' work. To introduce his paper about conspiracy theories, for example, Sam Roles summarized the different categories of research on the topic, citing representative references in each category.

Conspiracy theories are studied within several disciplines. Psychologists, for example, consider the relationship between conspiracy theories and disorders such as paranoia (Edmunds). Sociologists examine the formation and spread of conspiracy theories within a culture or group and their underlying causes (Haskins). Political scientists focus on the way that political ideologies can lead to the creation of beliefs about leaders' motives (Argyle). And experts in anthropology consider the cultural bases of myth creation, fear of persecution, or the construction of alternative realities (Lizaro). In my . . .

3 Providing examples and cases

If you begin with generalizations about your topic or question, you will want to provide specific examples to illustrate your points. In the following paragraph, Sam Roles's generalization (in green) is illustrated by three examples. Notice how each example comes from a different source.

Many conspiracy theories surround political figures or political events. The Apollo moon missions, for example, are now questioned by conspiracy theorists as having been staged by the government in a studio (Adams). For decades, it has been thought that Jack the Ripper was actually Prince Albert Victor Christian Edward ("Prince Eddy"), the Duke of Clarence (Evans and Skinner). And theories of who assassinated President John F. Kennedy abound (Posner).

4 Showing evidence or support

When you make a point or state part of your argument, the words of experts can help you support your ideas. To present both sides of the debate over whether a UFO was found in New Mexico in the 1940s and the discovery covered up by the government, Sam Roles incorporated a quotation from a book taking one side of the issue.

But were these sightings really UFOs? As Berlitz and Moore have pointed out, New Mexico in the late 1940s was "the site of the major portion of America's postwar defense efforts in atomic research, rocketry, aircraft and missile development, and radar-electronics experimentation" (18). Such activity, including flashes of light in the sky, could have been mistaken for the presence of UFOs.

In his notes on his sources, Sam had written the following, indicating a specific purpose for the quotation, related to the broader plan for his paper.

Use to begin showing disagreement with UFO claim.

5 Expanding an idea

As you develop ideas, use your sources to help extend, refine, or elaborate on them. This approach is especially useful when you make a transition from one part of your paper to the next. Short quotations, summaries, and paraphrases can serve this purpose when woven together with your words and ideas. Occasionally, a block quotation may be effective, as in the following example. Note that there is no page reference following the quotation because the source is an unpaged Web site.

Joltes (1995) points out how difficult it is to change the views of conspiracy theorists even when there is overwhelming evidence and rational explanation to account for a phenomenon:

> Likewise, when the US Air Force discloses the existence of a weather balloon experiment that offers a rational explanation for the "Roswell incident," a conspiracy buff will claim that records were faked, witnesses bought off or silenced, or whatever else was necessary to conceal evidence of alien contact. The aliens really do exist, but all the evidence has been suppressed, destroyed, or altered; therefore, the conspiracy theorist has had to work diligently to reconstruct what really happened, often producing "evidence" that is obviously contrived and illogical. But this matters not as long as it fits the theory.

6 Taking issue with a claim

You may want to argue against what someone else has said or what some group (of scholars or others) believes. After clearly explaining and citing sources for the opinion or belief, you can refute or "answer" the claim by drawing on other sources. Your artful use of sources can show weaknesses in a line of reasoning, or it can advance your own point of view on a topic, as in the following example.

In summarizing his report of a carefully coordinated 1994 investigation of the Roswell incident, Col. Richard M. Weaver says that "the Air Force research did not locate or develop any information that the 'Roswell Incident' was a UFO event" (1). Records did indicate, however, that the government was engaged in a "top secret balloon project, designed to attempt to monitor Soviet nuclear tests, known as Project Mogul" (1).

Tests of these balloons are the only plausible explanation of numerous UFO sightings and of the desert debris assumed to be an alien spacecraft.

24h Quotations, summaries, paraphrases, and syntheses

You can integrate sources into your paper in several ways: as quotations, paraphrases, or summaries. Furthermore, not all sources will appear in words; for example, you might want to include charts of facts, details, and statistics, or other visuals such as pictures, graphs, and screen shots.

1 Integrating quotations

Quoting someone's words means putting them into your paper or oral presentation in the *exact* way that they appeared in the original text (an obvious reason why it's so important for you to be accurate when taking notes during the research stage of your project). Avoid stringing quotations together or using many long quotations set off in blocks (which may look like padding). Instead, use direct quotations for these purposes.

- To show that you're accurately representing ideas that you want to challenge, modify, or extend
- To preserve an especially stylish, persuasive, or concise statement
- To show vividly and dramatically what other people think
- To provide a jumping-off point for your thoughts or a change of pace

You can set off the exact words of a source with quotation marks as you blend them into your discussion. For example, you can quote entire sentences, interpreting them or linking them to your point.

Yet alcohol awareness campaigns have seen only moderate success. "Although heavy drinking and monthly and daily alcohol use among high school seniors have declined since the 1980s, the decline is less among college-bound seniors, and binge drinking is a widespread problem on college campuses" (Bradley and Miller 1).

Or you can use an **embedded quotation**, weaving in key wording if it is less than a line or two.

EFFECTIVE Yet a 1994 government investigation of the Roswell incident "located no records at existing Air Force offices that indicated any 'cover-up' by the USAF or any indication of such a recovery" of alien debris (Weaver 1).

GENERAL GUIDELINES FOR INTEGRATING SHORT QUOTATIONS

- Follow your introductory line with a colon only if that line is a complete sentence. Use commas to set off a tag such as "X says" that introduces or interrupts a quotation; vary *says* with other verbs (*claims*, *explains*, *shows*).
- When you work a quotation into your own sentence, use the context to decide whether it should be separated with a comma.
- If you leave out words or add to a quotation, use ellipses (see 53d) or brackets (see 53b) to identify your changes.
- Position these punctuation marks *inside* concluding single or double quotation marks: commas, periods, and question or exclamation marks that apply to the quoted material.
- Position these punctuation marks *outside* concluding single or double quotation marks: semicolons, colons, and question or exclamation marks that apply to the whole sentence.

---

2 Using block quotations

A **block quotation** is a longer passage from a source, set off from your own prose because of length. Remember that readers expect you to *do* something with block quotations, not just insert them.

If you quote a passage longer than four lines typed (MLA style) or forty words or more (APA style), set it off from your prose. Begin on the line after your introduction. Indent one inch or ten spaces (MLA style) or 1/2" or five spaces (APA style). Double-space the quotation; do not use quotation marks (unless they appear in the source).

MLA STYLE

> Some psychologists believe that conspiracy theories have their
>
> origins in the public's trust in authority. If that "authority" is not
>
> fully credentialed but appears to be, the public may formulate
>
> beliefs that are not supported by evidence, a point made by Robyn
>
> M. Dawes in an analysis of why people believe in epidemic cases of
>
> child sexual abuse and the presence of satanic cults:
>
> > Asking people to doubt the conclusions concerning
> >
> > widespread childhood sexual abuse and satanic cults is
> >
> > asking them not only to reject the usual bases of authority
> >
> > and consensus for establishing reality, but in addition to

accept principles that violate foundations of everyday functioning. Now in point of fact we do ask people to accept such principles, and they do. Few people, for example, believe that the world is flat, even though it appears to be, or believe that cigarettes and alcohol are good for them, even though both may have very pleasant effects. We return once more to the efficacy of authority. People who have no direct experience of the curvature of the earth believe that it is not flat, and even the greatest devotees of tobacco and alcohol believe that these drugs are harming them. We accept what we have been told by "reputable authorities." (Dawes 3)

APA STYLE

Perez (1998) anticipates profound shifts in staff training.

The greatest challenge for most school districts is to earmark sufficient funds for training personnel, not for purchasing or upgrading hardware and software. The technological revolution in the average classroom will depend to a large degree on innovation in professional development. (p. 64)

Begin the first line without further indentation if you are quoting from one paragraph. Otherwise, indent all paragraphs 1/4" or three spaces (MLA style) or any additional paragraphs 1/2" or five spaces (APA style).

Also present four or more lines of poetry in a double-spaced block quotation. On the line after your introduction, indent ten spaces or an inch from the left margin (MLA style). Do not use any quotation marks unless the verse contains them.

MLA STYLE

Donald Hall also varies line length and rhythm, as "The Black-Faced Sheep" illustrates.

My grandfather spent all day searching the valley

and edges of Ragged Mountain,

calling "Ke-*day*!" as if he brought you salt,

"Ke-*day*! Ke-*day*!" (lines 9-12)

3 Integrating summaries and paraphrases

To make your writing smoother and more sophisticated, be selective in using quotations. Usually you can summarize, even combining several sources, or paraphrase rather than quoting sources directly.

> Yet at first, government officials denied they had any tests under way in New Mexico. Many officials were as baffled as the general public, including Captain Tom Brown, AAF information officer, who told reporters that he and his colleagues were as mystified as everyone else about the phenomena (Rotondo A1).

4 Integrating facts, details, and statistics

You can build entire paragraphs around facts, details, and statistics drawn from your sources as long as you indicate clearly the sources of your information. You may retain some of the emphasis of your source in using these materials; more likely, you'll end up integrating these details into prose that reflects your own purposes.

5 Using visuals

Visuals (drawings, photos, graphs, and the like) can sometimes present or emphasize data better than words. If you copy a visual from print or download it from an electronic resource, you'll need to cite the source, and you may need permission to use it. Whether you create a visual yourself or draw it from your research, make sure it adds to the written text and doesn't simply substitute for it. Visuals that add to a written explanation or extend it imaginatively can increase the credibility and effectiveness of your writing (see Chapter 12).

STRATEGY Use visuals for emphasis or for an imaginative approach.

- Put the visual as near to the relevant written text as you can without disrupting the flow of the text or distorting the visual.
- Don't interrupt the writing in ways that make it hard to read.
- Use visuals of good quality and of appropriate size for the page.
- Ask one or more readers whether your visuals are easy to understand and whether they add to the text's ideas and effect.
- Label each visual (*Figure 1, Figure 2 . . .*; *Table 1, Table 2 . . .*) in a form appropriate to the documentation style you are using (see Chapters 26–29).

25 Writing, Revising, and Presenting Your Research

How do you know when to begin *writing* your research paper? Actually, there's no set time. If you've been recording your responses as a critical reader and assembling material as answers to your research questions, you've already begun drafting. Think strategically about your task as you move toward a more complete text.

25a Reviewing your research questions

You began with a clear research question (see 20c) or rough thesis (see 20d) and developed it as you consulted sources, took notes, and built your research file. Do you still want to *explain* and present detailed information, or is your goal now to *persuade* readers to share the strong opinions you have developed? Are your original research questions still worthwhile, or have you arrived at a new set to answer for readers? Has your research changed your outlook and your thesis, too?

STRATEGY Let your research questions guide your draft.

Arrange your research questions in a logical sequence, adding any others that you now think you ought to address. Answer the questions, and use them to determine the tentative order of material in your draft.

25b Reviewing your purpose

Review your readers' expectations, values, questions, and likely reactions to your project (see 3c and see the chart on p. 140). Try to respond with clear explanations, arguments, and supporting evidence. Also consider the goals that your research questions reflect (see 20c).

> I'm going to tell readers about the three kinds of depression that may afflict college students—"the blues," common depression, and clinical depression. (informative paper)

> I want readers to agree with me that hunting is an acceptable activity when not excessive. (persuasive paper)

> I have a three-step solution to the problem of people downloading music without paying for it. (persuasive problem-solution paper)

You also began with a plan, perhaps a formal outline, a set of notes, or a **purpose structure**, a series of statements briefly describing what you intend to do in each section of your paper, like this one for a paper on the problem of sleep deficits among high school students.

Beginning: Explain what sleep deficits are and how studies show that most high school students' schoolwork suffers because of them. Argue that the solution to the problem is to begin the school day later.

First Middle: Explain the problem that high school students need more sleep than most people think; the early beginning of the high school day robs them of sleep they need.

Second Middle: Explain that the high school day begins early because the buses have to be used by elementary, middle, and high school students; most districts can't afford more buses. Show that most school administrators believe it's OK for high school students to get up early.

Third Middle: Argue that changing starting times is important despite the difficulties. Tell how high schools that have changed their start times show improved student performance linked to overcoming sleep deficits. Explain that they claim the change has been worth the cost.

Fourth Middle: Outline the cost-effective strategies used by districts with later start times. Argue that these strategies should be adopted by almost all districts to help solve the problem.

End: Summarize the solution; urge readers to take action in their districts.

25c   Building from a thesis to a draft

Begin with a thesis statement (see 3b) based on your research questions. Modify it as you draft, perhaps breaking it into several sentences, or organize around its parts, repeated at key points. Instead of a detailed traditional outline, try a working outline, blocking out the general sequence and relating the segments (see 2b). Pull together the materials that belong in each part using whatever method of grouping suits your resources and notes.

STRATEGY   Group your materials in sequence.

- Arrange your cards or notes in relation to one another. As patterns emerge, you may see how other material fits.
- Prepare pieces of paper describing available information—major points from sources, paraphrases, summaries, or ideas to include. Arrange these in relation to each other until you find a workable grouping (see 24g–h on integrating sources).
- Photocopy your research journal if you've written on both sides of the pages or don't want to cut it up. Then cut out the separate entries, arrange them in a sequence, and draft transitions to connect them.
- Use your word-processing program to cut and paste relevant electronic notes into a new file wherever they seem to fit.

Once you have chunks of related materials, move from the largest units to the smaller sections, interweaving notes, source materials, and additions. Write transitions between the chunks, explaining how they fit together. Use your research questions to focus your introduction and conclusion, but direct these key parts to your readers as you draft.

STRATEGY   Design an introduction and a conclusion for readers.

For the introduction, ask, "How can I make readers want to read on?" For the conclusion, ask, "How can I keep readers thinking about my topic?" Try several versions of each, experimenting with style and content.

1 Organize an informative research paper

It's true that an informative research paper follows the shape of its subject. But it also needs to take into account your readers' expectations, knowledge, and values in addition to your desire to make sure that readers understand your insights and conclusions. If you don't have an overall plan in mind, however, consider building your writing around one or more of these familiar informative plans.

- Describe a surprising or puzzling phenomenon; then explain it.
- Outline a challenging task or goal and the ways to accomplish it.
- Explain a common view; then suggest a new perspective.
- Focus on relationships, events, or objects that people consider unimportant. Explain why, to the contrary, they are very important.
- Compare the customs, values, or beliefs of one social or cultural group to those of another. Or explain them to people unfamiliar or (initially, at least) unsympathetic to these customs or beliefs.

- Start with a phenomenon that people have explained differently and generally unsatisfactorily. Then offer your detailed explanation, indicating why you think it is more satisfactory.
- Concentrate on your own insights, explanations, and conclusions. Organize around *your* selection and arrangement of information.

2 Organize a persuasive research paper

A persuasive research essay advances, supports, and defends a thesis. The thesis may be a stand on an issue (an argumentative proposition), a proposed policy or solution to a problem, or an interpretation of a subject. What sets persuasive research writing apart is the acknowledgment of alternative opinions, policies, or interpretations. Thus, your plan needs to account not only for reasons and evidence to support your thesis but also for grounds for preferring it to the alternatives.

- Explain the issue, problem, or object of interpretation—the focal point of differing opinions or interpretations.
- State your thesis, and add other indications of your opinion, proposition, solution, or interpretation.
- Acknowledge and summarize other points of view, and demonstrate why yours is preferable.

Organize logically, perhaps following one of these arrangements.

- *Present alternatives.* Begin by discussing the issue or problem. Then discuss the alternatives in detail, indicating why each is lacking in whole or part. End with your own perspective, which may incorporate parts of the alternatives. This strategy is useful when your research has identified extensive arguments in favor of other opinions or solutions.
- *Summarize the scholarship.* Begin with a detailed analysis of other interpretations, solutions, or policies. Indicate why this prior work is limited, flawed, or inadequate. Then offer your own solution or interpretation that addresses the weaknesses.
- *Find a middle ground.* Begin by outlining other views, interpretations, or solutions that take unsatisfactory, even extreme, positions. Then present your own reasonable middle perspective.

25d Revising and editing

Allow time to revise what you've written based on your audience's needs, the community for which you're writing, your research questions, and your purposes (see 5a–b). Ask others to respond to your draft (see 5c). Carefully edit (see 5e), proofread (see 5g), and design your document (see 12b–e). Make sure that any quotations are accurate and that page numbers and authors are cited correctly (see 24h). Double-check your documentation form (see Chapters 26–29).

25e Presenting your research

Be certain, especially for academic readers, that you supply your paper in exactly the print form or electronic format expected. For a print paper following an academic style such as MLA or APA, be sure to lay out the paper precisely as that style requires. For examples, see the sample MLA (Chapter 26) and APA (Chapter 27) papers. If your document can be submitted electronically, use any required software, and submit the file on a disk or as an attachment. If approved by your instructor or expected by your workplace or public audience, you may want to use a presentation program like *PowerPoint* that encourages the combination of text and graphics.

If you are expected to prepare a Web document in HTML or a similar language, be sure that readers will be able to move around at will and follow links to related documents or sources. A multimedia presentation using a program such as Macromedia *Dreamweaver* enables you to incorporate text, audio, still visuals, and action video. The result can be similar to a television documentary with the option of combining extensive text with detailed information, references, and documentation. Check with your instructor, supervisor, civic colleagues, or others involved to be certain that a particular electronic format will meet their expectations.

PART 6

Documenting Sources: MLA Style

▼ *TAKING IT ONLINE*

MLA STYLE

http://www.mla.org

For reliable information on MLA documentation style and for sample citations that will complement what you'll find in the upcoming section, visit the official site of the Modern Language Association (MLA), an organization that encourages the study of English, American, and other literatures and languages. Click on "MLA Style," and then visit the FAQ (frequently asked questions) page for advice on specific issues such as documenting Web sources.

   For more advice on using MLA style, check the home page of your library or tutoring center, or go to one of the sites below. Be certain that any site you use is updated to reflect the most current MLA style.

MLA CITATION STYLE

http://www.liu.edu/cwis/cwp/library/workshop/citmla.htm

If you appreciate visual learning cues, try this color-coded guide to sample MLA entries for a list of works cited.

MLA CITATION EXAMPLES WRITTEN BY HCC LIBRARY

http://honolulu.hawaii.edu/legacylib/mlahcc.html

This site, sponsored by the Honolulu Community College Library, provides general formats and typical examples for entries for an MLA list of works cited.

MLA FORMATTING AND STYLE GUIDE

http://owl.english.purdue.edu/owl/resource/557/01

One of the many useful documents supplied by the Purdue University Online Writing Lab, this page explains how to lay out your paper and supplies links to sample in-text citations, Works Cited entries, and long and short quotations in MLA style.

PART 6

Documenting Sources: MLA Style

26   MLA Documentation Style

The MLA (Modern Language Association) documentation style offers a convenient system for acknowledging and directing readers to your sources. It consists of an in-text citation (generally in parentheses) that leads a reader to the corresponding entry in a list of works cited (at the end of the text).

STRATEGY   Decide when to use MLA style.

ACADEMIC SETTINGS

When readers expect MLA style or simple parenthetical documentation, especially for writing in the humanities

WORK AND PUBLIC SETTINGS

When your subject and readers would be well served by a simple documentation style that seldom uses footnotes or endnotes

When you need an easy way to identify exact sources of quotations, paraphrases, or summaries

When other writers or publications in your setting use MLA, modified MLA, or a similar informal style

For more on MLA style, see the *MLA Handbook for Writers of Research Papers* (7th ed., New York: MLA, 2009), the *MLA Style Manual and Guide to Scholarly Publishing* (3rd ed., New York: MLA, 2008), or updates posted on the MLA Web site at <http://www.mla.org>.

Each MLA citation has two parts: a brief reference to the source in the text of the essay or report itself and a detailed entry for the source in a list titled "Works Cited" at the end of the text.

IN-TEXT CITATION

We think of the 1800s as the time when large corporations appeared, but at the beginning of the century, "business enterprises were generally small, family affairs" (Yates xv).

—Kevin Park, College Student

ENTRY IN THE LIST OF WORKS CITED

Yates, JoAnne. *Control Through Communication: The Rise of System in American Management*. Baltimore: Johns Hopkins UP, 1989. Print.

26a MLA in-text (parenthetical) citation examples

The MLA documentation style uses a citation in the text (usually an author's name) to identify a source. Readers can easily locate this source, described in full, in the list of works cited that ends the paper. In-text citations follow standard patterns, and many note the exact page in the source where readers can find the particular information mentioned. Note that no comma separates the author's name (or the title of the work) from the page number, and *p.* (or *pp.*) does not appear before the page number(s).

DRAFT   Even costumes convey the film's theme (Dell, p. 134).

EDITED   Even costumes convey the film's theme (Dell 134).

1. Author's Name in Parentheses

You can provide the author's name in parentheses. For a quotation, paraphrase, or specific detail, give the page number in the source.

IN PARENTHESES   When people marry now "there is an important sense in which they don't know what they are doing" (Giddens 46).

2. Author's Name in Discussion

You can include the author's name (or other information) in your discussion, clarifying which observations are your source's.

IN DISCUSSION   Giddens claims that when people marry now "there is an important sense in which they don't know what they are doing" (46).

3. Placement of Parenthetical Citations

Consider clarity and readability as you decide where to place a parenthetical citation. Keep the citation close to what you are documenting, preferably positioned at a pause or at the end of the sentence. (See p. 207.)

Lawson identifies three medical stories repeated in email messages (18). The tale of "the child battling cancer" (Juno 42) also regularly reappears.

4. General Reference

A **general reference** refers to a source as a whole, to its main ideas, or to information throughout; it needs no page number.

IN PARENTHESES   Many species of animals have complex systems of communication (Bright).

IN DISCUSSION   As Michael Bright observes, many species of animals have complex systems of communication.

5. Specific Reference

A **specific reference** documents words, ideas, or facts from a particular place in a source, such as the page for a quotation or paraphrase.

QUOTATION   Dolphins can perceive clicking sounds "made up of 700 units of sound per second" (Bright 52).

PARAPHRASE + FACTS   Bright reports that dolphins recognize patterns consisting of seven hundred clicks each second (52).

6. One Author

Provide the author's last name in parentheses, or integrate either the full name or last name alone into the discussion.

According to Maureen Honey, government posters during World War II often portrayed homemakers "as vital defenders of the nation's homes" (135).

7. Two or Three Authors

Name all the authors in parentheses or in the discussion.

The item appears in a partial list of Francis Bacon's debts after 1602 (Jardine and Stewart 275).

For three authors, do the same: (Norman, Fraser, and Jenko 209).

8. Four or More Authors

Within parentheses, name the first author and add *et al.* ("and others"). Within your discussion, use a phrase like "Chen and his colleagues point out . . ." or something similar. If you name all the authors in the works cited list rather than using *et al.*, do the same in the text citation (see Entry 3 on p. 210).

More funding would encourage creative research on complementary medicine (Chen et al. 82).

9. Organization or Group as Author

When an organization or group is the author, name it in the text or the citation; shorten or abbreviate a cumbersome name such as Committee of Concerned Journalists.

The consortium gathers journalists at "a critical moment" (Committee 187).

10. More Than One Work by the Same Author

When the list of works cited includes more than one work by an author, add a shortened form of the title to your citation and italicize that shortened title.

One writer claims that "quaintness glorifies the unassuming industriousness" in these social classes (Harris, *Cute* 46).

11. Authors with the Same Name

When authors have the same last name, identify each by first initial (or entire first name, if necessary for clarity).

Despite improved health information systems (J. Adams 308), medical errors continue to increase (D. Adams 1).

12. No Author Given

When no author is named, use the title instead. Shorten a long title, as in this version of *Baedeker's Czech/Slovak Republics*.

In 1993, Czechoslovakia split into the Czech Republic and the Slovak Republic (*Baedeker's* 67).

13. Indirect Source

Use *qtd. in* ("quoted in") to indicate when your source provides you with a quotation (or paraphrase) taken from yet another source. Here, Feuch is the source of the quotation from Vitz.

For Vitz, "art, especially great art, must engage all or almost all of the major capacities of the nervous system" (qtd. in Feuch 65).

14. Multivolume Work

To cite a whole volume, add a comma after the author's name and *vol.* before the number (Cao, vol. 4). To specify one of several volumes that you cite, add volume and page numbers (Cao 4: 177).

In 1888, Lewis Carroll let two students call their school paper *Jabberwock*, a made-up word from *Alice's Adventures in Wonderland* (Cohen 2: 695).

15. Literary Work

After the page number in your edition, add the chapter (ch.), part (pt.), or section (sec.) number to help readers find the passage in any edition.

In *Huckleberry Finn*, Mark Twain ridicules an actor who "would squeeze his hand on his forehead and stagger back and kind of moan" (178; ch. 21).

Identify a part as in (386; pt. 3, ch. 2). For a play, give the act, scene, and line numbers, as in (*Ham.* 1.2.76). For poems, give line numbers as in (lines 55–57) or (55–57) after the first case; if needed, give both part and line numbers as in (4.220–23).

16. Sacred Text

Give book, chapter, and verse for the Bible, Koran, or other religious text. Place a period between chapter and verse numbers (Mark 2.3–4). In parenthetical citations, abbreviate names with five or more letters, as in the case of Deuteronomy (Deut. 16.21–22).

17. Two or More Sources in a Citation

Separate sources within a citation with a semicolon.

Differences in the ways men and women use language can often be traced to who has power (Tanner 83-86; Tavris 297-301).

18. Selection in Anthology

For an essay, story, poem, or other work in an anthology, cite the work's author (not the anthology's editor), but give page numbers in the anthology.

According to Corry, the battle for Internet censorship has crossed party lines (112).

19. Electronic or Other Nonprint Source

After identifying the author or title, add numbers for the page, paragraph (par., pars.), section (sec.), or screen (screen) if given. Otherwise, no number is needed.

FILM

The heroine's mother in the film *Clueless* died as the result of an accident during liposuction.

WEB SITE WITH SCREEN NUMBERS

Offspringmag.com summarizes current research on adolescent behavior (Boynton, screen 2).

WEB SITE WITHOUT PAGE NUMBERS

According to *The Royal College of Psychiatrists* Web site, using alcohol to get to sleep often means awakening "half-way through the night."

PDF FILE WITH PAGE NUMBERS

According to *The Royal College of Psychiatrists* Web site, using alcohol to get to sleep often means awakening "half-way through the night" (4).

> **PLACEMENT AND PUNCTUATION OF PARENTHETICAL CITATIONS**
>
> Put parenthetical citations close to the quotation, information, paraphrase, or summary you are documenting.
>
> - At the end of a sentence before the final punctuation
>
>   Wayland Hand reports on a folk belief that going to sleep on a rug made of bearskin can relieve backache (183).
>
> - After the part of the sentence to which the citation applies, at a natural pause in the sentence so that you do not disrupt it, or after the last of several quotations in a paragraph, all from one page of the same source
>
>   The folk belief that "sleeping on a bear rug will cure backache" (Hand 183) illustrates the magic of external objects producing results inside the body.
>
> - At the end of a long quotation set off as a block (see 24h), after the end punctuation with a space before the parentheses
>
>   Many baseball players, especially pitchers, are superstitious:
>
> > Some pitchers refuse to walk anywhere on the day of the game in the belief that every little exertion subtracts from their playing strength. One pitcher would never put on his cap until the game started and would not wear it at all on the days he did not pitch. (Gmelch 280)

20. Informative Footnote or Endnote

Use a note when you comment on a source, provide background details, or supply lengthy information of use to only a few readers. Place a superscript number (raised slightly above the line of text) at a suitable point in your paper. Label the note itself with a corresponding number, and provide it as a footnote at the bottom of the page or an endnote at the end of the paper, before the list of works cited, on a page titled "Notes."

[1]Before changing your eating habits or beginning an exercise program, check with your doctor.

21. Long Quotation

The citation in parentheses follows a long quotation set off as a block (without quotation marks; see 24h). Put the citation after the end punctuation with a space before the parentheses.

In India, cricket has been commercialized like American football and basketball.

> Like other sports figures in the capitalist world, the best-known Indian cricket stars are now metacommodities, for sale themselves while fueling the circulation of other commodities. The sport is increasingly in the hands of advertisers, promoters, and entrepreneurs, with television, radio, and print media feeding the national passion for the sport and its stars. (Appadurai 106)

22. Short Quotation

The citation in parentheses follows the quotation marks that close a short quotation. If the quotation ends with an exclamation point or question mark, put it inside the quotation marks. If the material you are quoting contains quotation marks, use double quotation marks to enclose the quotation as a whole and single quotation marks to enclose the interior quotation.

> According to Dubisch, "Being a 'healthfood person' involves more than simply changing one's diet or utilizing an alternative medical system" (61).

23. Visual in Text

In your discussion, refer to the visual as a figure (abbreviated *fig.*). Include citation information in the caption for the visual.

TEXT

> Satellite photos (fig. 2) indicate the flood damage caused by Hurricane Katrina.

FIGURE CAPTION

> Fig. 2. Extent of flooding on September 8, 2005 (National Aeronautics and Space Administration).

24. Email, Interview, or Personal Communication

Direct readers to the information in your works cited list (pp. 219, 230) by giving the name of the writer or the person interviewed.

> One of the director's assistants recalls that staging the first show was "an experiment in chaos and misunderstanding" (Shiels).

25. Numbered Paragraphs or Screens

If a source contains numbered paragraphs or screens, use *par(s).* or *screen(s)* to identify the location of information or a quotation.

> "Life Without Principle" challenges readers to "consider the way in which we spend our lives" (Thoreau, par. 3).

26. Work Cited More Than Once

If you refer to a source more than once in a paragraph without mentioning another source in between, you may be able to combine references.

Giddens views contemporary society as "a runaway world" in which belief in reason may be outmoded but "a world of multiple possibilities" is open (Bryant and Jary 263, 264).

Giddens views contemporary society as "a runaway world" (Bryant and Jary 263). He argues that belief in reason may be outmoded but that a "world of multiple possibilities" is open (264).

26b MLA list of works cited

Provide readers with full detail about your sources in an alphabetical list following the last page of your text.

- **Page format.** Use the heading "Works Cited" (or "Works Consulted," for all sources used) centered one inch below the top edge of a new page. Continue the page numbering from the body of the paper.
- **Indentation.** Do not indent the first line of each entry. Indent additional lines one-half inch or five spaces.
- **Spacing.** Double-space all lines within and between the entries. Leave a single space (or two spaces, if you wish) after a period within an entry. Use consistent spacing throughout all entries.
- **Alphabetizing.** Alphabetize by last names of authors (and first names for authors with the same last name); then alphabetize by title multiple works by the same author. For sources without an author, use the first word in the title (other than *A*, *An*, or *The*).

DRAFT   Fem. and Polit. Theory, by C. Sunstein. UCP, 1990.

EDITED   Sunstein, Cass R. *Feminism and Political Theory*. Chicago: U of
         Chicago P, 1990. Print.

STRATEGY   **Find and match the MLA models.**

- Take bibliographic notes as you use a source (see 21a-4).
- Figure out what type of source you've used—book, article, online document, or other form. Use the Guide on the back of Part 6 divider to find the sample entry for that type. Prepare your entry following this pattern.
- Identify how many authors or other features your source has. Find the appropriate patterns for these, and rework your entry as needed.
- Check the details in each entry for the sequence of information, capitalization, punctuation, and abbreviations.

Books and Works Treated as Books

MODEL FORMAT FOR BOOKS AND WORKS TREATED AS BOOKS

period + space period + space colon + space

Author(s). *Title of Work*. Place of Publication:

Publisher, Year Published. Medium of Publication.

indent ½" comma + space period + space period
or five spaces

- **Author.** Give the last name first, followed by a comma, and then the first name and any middle name or initial. End with a period.
- **Title.** Italicize the title (and any subtitle), and capitalize the main words (see 54b). End with a period (unless the title concludes with a question or exclamation mark).
- **Publication information.** Begin with city of publication, a colon, and a space. Give the publisher's name in shortened form (*U of Chicago P* for *University of Chicago Press* or *McGraw* for *McGraw-Hill, Inc.*) followed by a comma, the year of publication, a period, the medium of publication, and a period.

1. One Author

Hockney, David. *Secret Knowledge: Recovering the Lost Techniques of the Old Masters*. New York: Viking-Studio, 2001. Print.

2. Two or Three Authors

Begin with the first author's last name. Add other names in regular order, separated by commas with *and* before the final name.

Kress, Gunther, and Theo van Leeuwen. *Reading Images: The Grammar of Graphic Design*. London: Routledge, 1996. Print.

3. Four or More Authors

After the first name, add *et al.* ("and others"). You may give all the names; if so, list them all in the text citations too (see Entry 8 on p. 204).

Bellah, Robert N., et al. *Habits of the Heart: Individualism and Commitment in American Life*. Berkeley: U of California P, 1985. Print.

Bellah, Robert N., Richard Madsen, William M. Sullivan, Ann Swidler, and Steven M. Tipton. *Habits of the Heart: Individualism and Commitment in American Life*. Berkeley: U of California P, 1985. Print.

4. Organization or Group as Author

Alphabetize by the first main word of the group's name. If this body is also the publisher, repeat its name, abbreviated if appropriate.

Nemours Children's Clinic. *Diabetes and Me*. Wilmington: Nemours, 2001. Print.

5. No Author Given

Alphabetize by the first main word of the title.

Guide for Authors. Oxford: Blackwell, 1985. Print.

6. More Than One Work by the Same Author

List multiple works by an author alphabetically by the first main word of each title. For the first entry, include the name of the author. For additional entries, use three hyphens instead of the name, ending with a period. If the author or authors are not *exactly* the same, include the names in full.

Tannen, Deborah. *The Argument Culture: Moving from Debate to Dialogue*.

New York: Random, 1998. Print.

---. *You're Wearing That? Understanding Mothers and Daughters in*

Conversation. New York: Random, 2006. Print.

7. One or More Editors

Begin with the editor's name followed by *ed.* (or *eds.*).

Achebe, Chinua, and C. L. Innes, eds. *African Short Stories*. London:

Heinemann, 1985. Print.

8. Author and Editor

Begin with either the author's or the editor's name depending on whether you are using the text itself or the editor's contributions.

Wardlow, Gayle Dean. *Chasin' That Devil Music: Searching for the Blues*. Ed.

Edward Komara. San Francisco: Miller, 1998. Print.

9. Translator

Begin with the author unless you emphasize the translator's work.

Baudrillard, Jean. *Cool Memories II: 1978-1990*. Trans. Chris Turner.

Durham: Duke UP, 1996. Print.

10. Edition Following the First

> Coe, Michael D. *The Maya*. 7th ed. New York: Thames, 2005. Print.

11. Reprint

> Kerouac, Jack. *On the Road*. 1957. New York: Viking, 1997. Print.

12. Multivolume Work

Indicate the total number of volumes after the title (or after the editor's or translator's name).

> Tsao, Hsueh-chin. *The Story of the Stone*. Trans. David Hawkes.
>
>   5 vols. Harmondsworth: Penguin, 1983-86. Print.

For a specific volume, supply its number and publication information. For more than one volume, give the total number of volumes or the full range of dates.

> Tsao, Hsueh-chin. *The Story of the Stone*. Trans. David Hawkes. Vol. 1.
>
>   Harmondsworth: Penguin, 1983. Print. 5 vols.

13. Work in a Series

Besides the series (*Ser.*) name, add any item number.

> Grover-Friedlander, Michael. *Vocal Apparitions: The Attraction of Cinema to*
>
>   *Opera*. Princeton: Princeton UP, 2005. Print. Princeton Stud. in Opera 2.

14. Book Pre-1900

The publisher's name is optional; when omitted, add a comma after place of publication.

> Darwin, Charles. *Descent of Man and Selection in Relation to Sex*.
>
>   New York, 1896. Print.

15. Graphic Novel or Illustrated Work

> Satrapi, Marjane. *Persepolis: The Story of a Childhood*. New York: Pantheon,
>
>   2004. Print.

If focusing on the illustrator (as distinct from the author), give the illustrator's name first, followed by a comma and *illus.* (for "illustrator"), the title, a period, and the word *By* followed by the author's name.

16. Anthology or Collection of Articles

Supply the editor's name, with *ed.*, and then the title of the collection. (To cite a selection, see Entries 35 and 36 on p. 217–18.)

> Wu, Duncan, ed. *Romantic Women Poets: An Anthology*. Oxford: Blackwell,
>
> 1997. Print.

17. Conference Proceedings

Begin with the title unless an editor is named. Follow with details about the conference, including name and date.

> *Childhood Obesity: Causes and Prevention*. Symposium Proc., 27 Oct. 1998.
>
> Washington: Center for Nutrition Policy and Promotion, 1999. Print.

18. Title Within a Title

Within a book title, don't italicize another book's title, but italicize a title normally in quotation marks.

> Weick, Carl F. *Refiguring* Huckleberry Finn. Athens: U of Georgia P, 2000.
>
> Print.

> Golden, Catherine, ed. *The Captive Imagination: A Casebook on "The Yellow*
>
> *Wallpaper."* New York: Feminist, 1992. Print.

19. Pamphlet

Use the same form for a pamphlet as for a book.

> Vareika, William. *John La Farge: An American Master (1835-1910)*.
>
> Newport: Gallery of American Art, 1989. Print.

20. Dissertation Published

When published, a doctoral dissertation is treated as a book. Add *Diss.*, the school, and the date of the degree.

> Said, Edward W. *Joseph Conrad and the Fiction of Autobiography*.
>
> Diss. Harvard U, 1964. Cambridge: Harvard UP, 1966. Print.

21. Dissertation Unpublished

Use quotation marks for the title; add *Diss.*, the school, and the date.

> Swope, Catherine Theodora. "Redesigning Downtown: The Fabrication of
>
> German-Themed Villages in Small-Town America." Diss. U of
>
> Washington, 2003. Print.

22. Government Document

Begin with the name of the government agency, the independent agency, or the author, if any. Start with *United States* for a report from a federal agency or for congressional documents, adding *Cong.* (*Congress*), the branch (*Senate* or *House*), and the number and session (*110th Cong., 1st sess.*). Include the titles of both the document and any book in which it is printed. Use *GPO* for the federal Government Printing Office.

> Sheppard, David I., and Shay Bilchick, comps. *Promising Strategies to*
>
> *Reduce Gun Violence Report*. US Dept. of Justice. Office of Juvenile
>
> Justice and Delinquency Prevention. Washington: GPO, 1999. Print.
>
> United States. Cong. House. *Anti-Spamming Act of 2001*. 107th Cong., 1st
>
> sess. Washington: GPO, 2001. Print.

23. Sacred Text

Identify the version, any editor or translator, and the publication information.

> *Zondervan NIV Study Bible*. Grand Rapids: Zondervan, 2006. Print.

Articles from Periodicals and Selections from Books

MODEL FORMAT FOR ARTICLES AND SELECTIONS

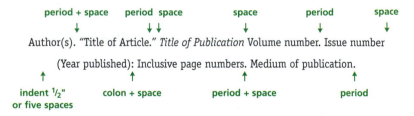

period + space   period space   space   period   space

Author(s). "Title of Article." *Title of Publication* Volume number. Issue number

(Year published): Inclusive page numbers. Medium of publication.

indent ½"   colon + space   period + space   period
or five spaces

- **Author.** Give the last name first, followed by a comma. Add the first name and any middle name or initial. End with a period.
- **Article title.** Give the full title in quotation marks, with the main words capitalized. Conclude with a period inside the quotation marks (unless the title ends in a question mark or an exclamation point).
- **Publication information.** Italicize the publication title. Supply volume number and issue number (if known), year of publication, inclusive page numbers, and medium of publication. The volume number appears on the publication's title page or cover; use Arabic numerals even if the periodical uses Roman numerals. Introduce page

numbers with a colon except for selections from books and in a few
other situations shown in entries that follow. For page ranges, limit
the second number to its two final numerals (14–21, 162–79) unless
unclear (1498–1524).

Article in Print Journal

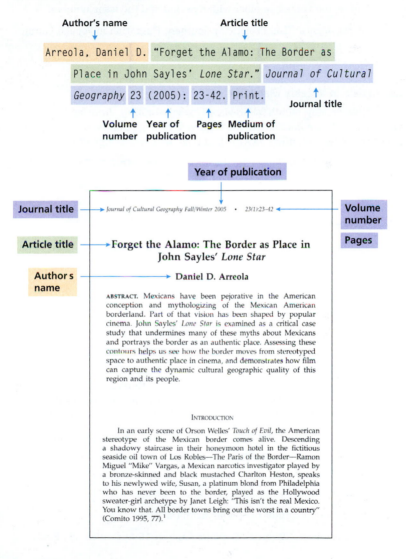

Author's name

Article title

Arreola, Daniel D. "Forget the Alamo: The Border as
Place in John Sayles' *Lone Star*." *Journal of Cultural
Geography* 23 (2005): 23-42. Print.

Journal title

Volume number — Year of publication — Pages — Medium of publication

Year of publication

Journal title → *Journal of Cultural Geography Fall/Winter 2005* • *23(1):23–42* ← **Volume number**

Pages

Article title → Forget the Alamo: The Border as Place in
John Sayles' *Lone Star*

Author s name → Daniel D. Arreola

ABSTRACT. Mexicans have been pejorative in the American
conception and mythologizing of the Mexican American
borderland. Part of that vision has been shaped by popular
cinema. John Sayles' *Lone Star* is examined as a critical case
study that undermines many of these myths about Mexicans
and portrays the border as an authentic place. Assessing these
contours helps us see how the border moves from stereotyped
space to authentic place in cinema, and demonstrates how film
can capture the dynamic cultural geographic quality of this
region and its people.

INTRODUCTION

In an early scene of Orson Welles' *Touch of Evil*, the American
stereotype of the Mexican border comes alive. Descending
a shadowy staircase in their honeymoon hotel in the fictitious
seaside oil town of Los Robles—The Paris of the Border—Ramon
Miguel "Mike" Vargas, a Mexican narcotics investigator played by
a bronze-skinned and black mustached Charlton Heston, speaks
to his newlywed wife, Susan, a platinum blond from Philadelphia
who has never been to the border, played as the Hollywood
sweater-girl archetype by Janet Leigh: "This isn't the real Mexico.
You know that. All border towns bring out the worst in a country"
(Comito 1995, 77).[1]

24. Article in Journal with Volume Number Only

Eagleton, Terry. "Political Beckett?" *New Left Review* 40 (2006): 67-74.

Print.

25. Article in Journal with Volume and Issue Numbers

Follow the volume number with a period and the issue number.

Adams, Jessica. "Local Color: The Southern Plantation in Popular Culture."

Cultural Critique 42.1 (1999): 171-87. Print.

26. Article in Weekly Magazine

Note the day, month (abbreviated except for *May*, *June*, and *July*), and year followed by a colon. Give the sequence of page numbers (27-38). If the pages are not consecutive, give the first page with a plus sign (23+).

Conlin, Michelle. "Unmarried America." *Business Week* 20 Oct. 2003: 106+.

Print.

27. Article in Monthly Magazine

Jacobson, Doranne. "Doing Lunch." *Natural History* Mar. 2000: 66-69. Print.

28. Article with No Author Given

Alphabetize by title, excluding *A*, *An*, and *The*.

"The Obesity Industry." *Economist* 27 Sept. 2003: 64+. Print.

29. Article in Newspaper

Cite pages as you would for a magazine (see Entry 26), but add any section number or letter. Omit *The*, *A*, or *An* beginning a newspaper's name. For a local paper, add the city in brackets after the title unless it's named there.

Willis, Ellen. "Steal This Myth: Why We Still Try to Re-create the Rush of

the 60's." *New York Times* 20 Aug. 2000, late ed., sec. 2: AR1+. Print.

30. Editorial

Start with the author or, if none, with the title.

"A False Choice." Editorial. *Charlotte Observer* 16 Aug. 1998: 2C. Print.

31. Letter to the Editor

Hogner, Lindon. Letter. "Mandate Time Off for Fatigued Doctors."

USA Today 18 Dec. 2006: 20A. Print.

32. Interview Published

Identify the person interviewed, not the interviewer, first. For untitled interviews, supply *Interview* (without underlining or quotation marks) in place of a title.

Stewart, Martha. "'I Do Have a Brain.'" Interview with Kevin Kelly. *Wired*

Aug. 1998: 114. Print.

33. Review

Begin with the name of the reviewer or the title for an unsigned review. For an untitled review, follow the reviewer's name with *Rev. of* ("Review of"), the work's title, *by*, and the work's author.

Muñoz, José Esteban. "Citizens and Superheroes." Rev. of *The Queen of*

America Goes to Washington City, by Lauren Berlant. *American*

Quarterly 52.1 (2000): 397-404. Print.

Hadjor, Kofi Buenor. Rev. of *The Silent War: Imperialism and the Changing*

Perception of Race, by Frank Furendi. *Journal of Black Studies* 30.2

(1999): 133-35. Print.

34. Article in Encyclopedia or Reference Work

Begin with the author's name or an unsigned article's title. For multivolume reference works arranged alphabetically, include a volume number.

Oliver, Paul, and Barry Kernfeld. "Blues." *The New Grove Dictionary of Jazz*.

Ed. Barry Kernfeld. New York: St. Martin's, 1994. Print.

"The History of Western Theatre." *The New Encyclopaedia Britannica:*

Macropaedia. 15th ed. Vol. 12. 1987. Print.

35. Chapter in Edited Book or Selection in Anthology

List the author of the selection or chapter, then its title (in quotation marks, but italicize titles of novels, plays, and so on; see 51b, 55a). Next, provide the underlined title of the book containing the selection or chapter. If the book is edited, follow with *Ed.* and the names of the editors. Add publication information, page numbers for the selection, and medium of publication.

> Atwood, Margaret. "Bluebeard's Egg." *"Bluebeard's Egg" and Other Stories*.
>
> New York: Fawcett-Random, 1987. 131-64. Print.

For a reprinted selection, you may add the original source. Use *Rpt. in* ("Reprinted in") to introduce a subsequent reprint.

> Atwood, Margaret. "Bluebeard's Egg." *"Bluebeard's Egg" and Other*
>
> *Stories*. New York: Fawcett-Random, 1987. 131-64. Rpt. in *Don't Bet on*
>
> *the Prince: Contemporary Feminist Fairy Tales in North America and*
>
> *England*. Ed. Jack Zipes. New York: Methuen, 1989. 160-82. Print.

36. More Than One Selection from Anthology or Collection

Include an entry for the collection. Use its author's name for cross-references from individual selections.

> Hooper, Glenn, and Colin Graham, eds. *Irish and Postcolonial Writing:*
>
> *History, Theory, Practice*. London: Palgrave-Macmillan, 2002. Print.
>
> Mustafa, Shakir. "Demythologizing Ireland: Revisionism and the Irish
>
> Colonial Experience." Hooper and Graham 66-86.

37. Preface, Foreword, Introduction, or Afterword

Identify the section as a *Preface*, *Foreword*, *Introduction*, or *Afterword*. Add the title of the work and its author, following *By*.

> Tomlin, Janice. Foreword. *The Complete Guide to Foreign Adoption*.
>
> By Barbara Brooke Bascom and Carole A. McKelvey. New York: Pocket,
>
> 1997. Print.

38. Letter Published

Name the letter writer as the author. Include the letter's date or any collection number.

> Garland, Hamlin. "To Fred Lewis Pattee." 30 Dec. 1914. Letter 206 of
>
> *Selected Letters of Hamlin Garland*. Ed. Keith Newlin and Joseph B.
>
> McCullough. Lincoln: U of Nebraska P, 1998. Print.

39. Dissertation Abstract

For an abstract in *Dissertation Abstracts International (DAI)* or *Dissertation Abstracts (DA)*, include *Diss.* ("Dissertation"), the institution's name, and the date of the degree. Add publication information for that volume of abstracts, as well as the medium of publication.

> Hawkins, Joanne Berning. "Horror Cinema and the Avant-Garde." Diss. U
>
> of California, Berkeley, 1993. *DAI* 55.1 (1995): 1712A. Print.

40. Unpublished Essay

Give the author's name, the title, the date the essay was written, and the letters MS (manuscript) or TS (typescript).

> Taylor, Charisse. "Writers in Transition: School to Work and Back Again."
>
> 2007 TS.

Field and Media Resources

41. Interview Unpublished

First identify the person interviewed and the type of interview: *Personal interview* (you conducted it in person), *Telephone interview* (you talked to the person over the telephone), or *Interview* (someone else conducted the interview, perhaps on radio or television). If the interview has a title, use it to replace *Interview*.

> Schutt, Robin. "Re: Interview." 7 May 2007. E-mail.

> Coppola, Francis Ford. Interview with James Lipton. *Inside the Actors*
>
> *Studio*. Bravo, New York. 10 July 2001. Television.

42. Survey or Questionnaire

MLA does not specify a form for these field resources. When citing your own research, you may wish to use this format.

> Figliozzi, Jennifer Emily, and Summer J. Arrigo-Nelson. Questionnaire on
>
> Student Alcohol Use and Parental Values. U of Rhode Island,
>
> Kingston. 15-20 Apr. 2004.

43. Observation

Because MLA does not specify a form, you may wish to cite your field notes in this way.

> Ba, Ed. Ski Run Observation. Vail, CO. 26 Jan. 2007.

44. Letter or Memo Unpublished

Give the author's name, a brief description (*Memo to Jane Cote* or *Letter to the author*), the date, and the form (see Entry 40). For letters between other people, identify any library holding the letter in its collection.

Hall, Donald. Letter to the author. 24 Jan. 1990. MS.

45. Oral Presentation

Phillips, Maureen. "Women Veterans: Degendering Patriotism." Conf. on

Coll. Composition and Communication. Hilton New York, New York.

23 Mar. 2007. Address.

46. Performance

Following the title of the play, opera, dance, or other performance, note the composer, director, writer, theater or location, city, date, and the word *Performance*. (Include actors when relevant.)

Cabaret. By Joe Masteroff. Dir. Sam Mendes. Studio 54, New York. 2 July 2001.

Performance.

47. Video or Film

Alphabetize by title, and generally name the director. Name others important for identifying the work or for your discussion. Identify the distributor, date, and other relevant information.

Rosencrantz and Guildenstern Are Dead. Dir. Tom Stoppard. Perf. Gary

Oldman, Tim Roth, and Richard Dreyfuss. Buena Vista Home Video,

1990. Videocassette.

Super Size Me. Prod. Morgan Spurlock. Perf. Morgan Spurlock. Samuel

Goldwyn Films, 2004. DVD.

48. Television or Radio Program

"The Tour." *I Love Lucy*. Dir. William Asher. Nickelodeon. 2 July 2001.

Television.

49. Recording

The Goo-Goo Dolls. *Dizzy Up the Girl*. Warner, 1998. CD.

Mozart, Wolfgang Amadeus. Symphony no. 40 in G minor. Vienna

    Philharmonic. Cond. Leonard Bernstein. Deutsche Grammophon,

    1984. LP.

50. Artwork or Photograph

Leonardo da Vinci. *Mona Lisa*. 1506. Oil on canvas. Louvre, Paris.

Larimer Street, Denver. 5 May 2007. Personal photograph by author.

51. Map or Chart

Arkansas. Map. Comfort: Gousha, 1996. Print.

52. Comic Strip or Cartoon

Provide the cartoonist's name, any title, and *Cartoon* or *Comic strip*.

Cochran, Tony. "Agnes." Comic strip. *Denver Post* 18 Apr. 2007: 13F. Print.

53. Advertisement

First, name the product or organization advertised.

Toyota. Advertisement. *GQ* July 2001: 8. Print.

Online and Electronic Resources

MODEL FORMAT FOR ONLINE BOOK OR DOCUMENT

     period + space   period space period + space   colon + space
        ↓   ↓↓   ↓   ↓
Author(s). "Title of Page or Document." *Book*. Place of Publication:

         comma + space   period + space
            ↓   ↓
Publisher, Year Published. [for print book, if available]

        period + space   comma + space
          ↓   ↓   ↓
Site Name. Sponsoring Organization, Institution,

            period + space   period
              ↓ ↓   ↓
Date posted or updated. Web. Your access date.

↑
indent ¹/₂" or five spaces

Article in Online Journal

Author's   Article
name   title
↓   ↓

Brown, Stuart. "Student Affairs and Podcasting: The New

Frontier?" *Student Affairs On-line* 7.2 (2006). Web.

14 Mar. 2007
↑   ↑   ↑   ↑
Date of   Journal   Volume   Medium of
access*   title   and issue   publication
                                  numbers

                                         ↑
                                      Year of
                                      publication

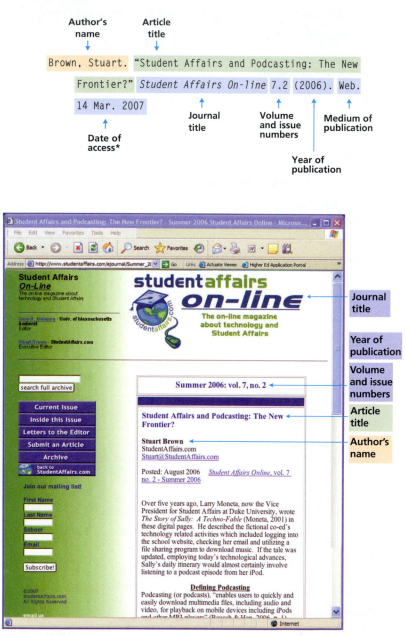

Journal title

Year of publication

Volume and issue numbers

Article title

Author's name

MODEL FORMAT FOR ONLINE ARTICLE

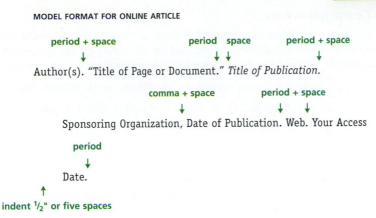

period + space   period space   period + space

Author(s). "Title of Page or Document." *Title of Publication.*

comma + space   period + space

Sponsoring Organization, Date of Publication. Web. Your Access

period

Date.

indent ½" or five spaces

- **Author, title, and publication information.** Supply available information like that for a print source so a reader could find the item.
- **Dates.** Give the date the material was posted, revised, or updated; the medium (Web); and the date you accessed the source.
- **Uniform resource locator (URL).** Provide the complete URL (beginning with *http, gopher, telnet,* or *ftp*) in angle brackets (< >) only if your instructor requires it or searches would not otherwise lead to it. Split the URL following a slash; do not add a hyphen.

54. Web Site

Cartoon America. Lib. of Congress. 21 Nov. 2006. Web. 18 Apr. 2007.

55. Academic or Professional Home Page

Note the creator, title or description such as *Home page,* any date, and sponsor.

Baron, Dennis. Home page. Dept. of English, U of Illinois, Urbana-

Champaign. 18 Apr. 2007. Web. 16 Jan. 2009.

56. Course Home Page

Give the instructor's name and the course or site title. Provide inclusive dates of the course and the department and school names. (If the site has no name, use the course name and number from the institution's course catalog.)

Brown, Rebecca M. Course home page. Introduction to Art History. Dept.

of Art and Art History, St. Mary's College of Maryland. 21 Jan.-8

May 2003. Web. 20 Feb. 2007.

57. Blog

Adapt a similar format for a new type of source, such as a blog. Name the author, the blog, the sponsor (or *N.p.* if none is given), date of posting, the medium, and date of access.

Ramsey, Doug. "Zoot, Red, Lorraine." *Rifftides*. 5 Mar. 2007. Web. 10 Mar.

2007.

58. Book: Online

Add any available information about print publication.

London, Jack. *The Iron Heel.* New York: Macmillan, 1908. *The Jack London*

Online Collection. 25 July 2006. Web. 18 Apr. 2007.

59. Selection from Online Book

Muir, John. "The City of the Saints." *Steep Trails*. 1918. Web. 17 Apr.

2007.

60. Journal Article: Online

Dugdale, Timothy. "The Fan and (Auto)Biography: Writing the Self in the

Stars." *Journal of Mundane Behavior* 1.2 (2000): n. pag. Web. 19 Apr.

2007.

61. Magazine Article: Online

Wright, Laura. "My, What Big Eyes. . . ." *Discover*. Discover, 27 Oct. 2003.

Web. 11 Nov. 2006.

62. Newspaper Article: Online

Mulvihill, Kim. "Childhood Obesity." *San Francisco Chronicle*. San Francisco
Chronicle, 12 July 2001. Web. 15 Oct. 2006.

63. Government Document: Online

United States. Dept. of Commerce. *Census Brief: Disabilities Affect One-
Fifth of All Americans*. Bureau of the Census, Dec. 1997. Web. 18
July 2006.

64. Editorial: Online

"Mall Mania/A Measure of India's Success." Editorial. *StarTribune.com
Minneapolis-St. Paul*. Star Tribune, 31 Oct. 2003. Web. 14 Nov.
2006.

65. Letter to the Editor: Online

Hadjiargyrou, Michael. Letter. "Stem Cells and Delicate Questions."
New York Times on the Web. New York Times, 17 July 2001. Web.
18 Jan. 2007.

66. Interview: Online

Payan, Victor. Interview by David Rikker. *San Diego Latino Film Festival*.
May 1999. Web. 20 Jan. 2007.

67. Review: Online

Chaudhury, Parama. Rev. of *Kandahar*, dir. Mohsen Makhmalbaf. *Film
Monthly* 3.4 (2002): n. pag. Web. 19 Jan. 2007.

68. Abstract: Online

Prelow, Hazel, and Charles A. Guarnaccia. "Ethnic and Racial Differences
in Life Stress among High School Adolescents." *Journal of
Counseling & Development* 75.6 (1997): n. pag. *Project Muse*. Web.
6 Apr. 2007.

69. General Entry: Online Database

For entries from online databases to which libraries subscribe (through services such as EBSCOhost or LexisNexis), begin with the details of print publication, if any. Name the database, the medium Web, and note your date of access. Give the URL of the search page for the site only if required by your instructor.

> Kallis, Giorgos, and Henri L. F. De Groot. "Shifting Perspectives
>
> on Urban Water Policy in Europe." *European Planning Studies*
>
> 11.1 (2003): 223-28. *Academic Search Premier*. Web. 8 Apr.
>
> 2007.

70. Journal Article: Online Database

> Stillman, Todd. "McDonald's in Question: The Limits of the Mass Market."
>
> *American Behavioral Scientist* 47.1 (2003): 107-18. *Academic Search*
>
> *Premier*. Web. 15 Nov. 2006.

71. Article Abstract: Online Database

> Lewis, David A., and Roger P. Rose. "The President, the Press, and
>
> the War-Making Power: An Analysis of Media Coverage Prior to
>
> the Persian Gulf War." *Presidential Studies Quarterly* 32.1 (2002):
>
> 559-71. Abstract. *America: History and Life*. Web. 1 Nov.
>
> 2006.

72. Magazine Article: Online Database

> Barrett, Jennifer. "Fast Food Need Not Be Fat Food." *Newsweek* 13 Oct.
>
> 2003: 73-74. *Academic Search Premier*. Web. 31 Oct. 2006.

73. Newspaper Article: Online Database

> Lee, R. "Class with the 'Ph.D. Diva.'" *New York Times* 18 Oct. 2003: B7.
>
> *InfoTrac OneFile*. Web. 31 Oct. 2006.

Journal Article from a Subscription Database (HTML Format)

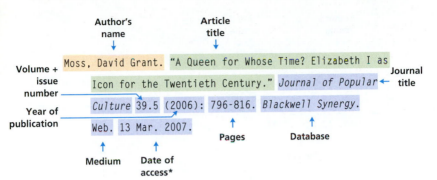

Author's name

Article title

Volume + issue number

Moss, David Grant. "A Queen for Whose Time? Elizabeth I as Icon for the Twentieth Century." *Journal of Popular Culture* 39.5 (2006): 796-816. *Blackwell Synergy.* Web. 13 Mar. 2007.

Journal title

Year of publication

Medium

Date of access*

Pages

Database

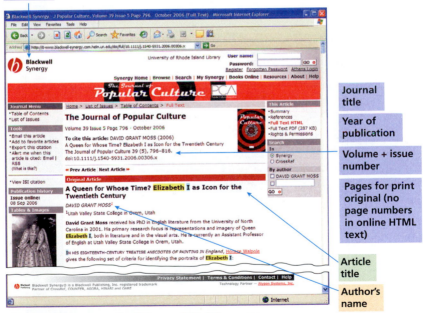

Database

Journal title

Year of publication

Volume + issue number

Pages for print original (no page numbers in online HTML text)

Article title

Author's name

*****For date of access, use the date you visited the source.**

Journal Article from a Subscription Database (PDF Format)

Author's name — **Moss, David Grant.**

Article title — **"A Queen for Whose Time? Elizabeth I as**

Volume + issue number — **Icon for the Twentieth Century."** *Journal of Popular* — Journal title

Year of publication — *Culture* **39.5 (2006): 796-816.** *Blackwell Synergy.* ← Database*

Web. 13 Mar. 2007

Pages

Medium   Date of access

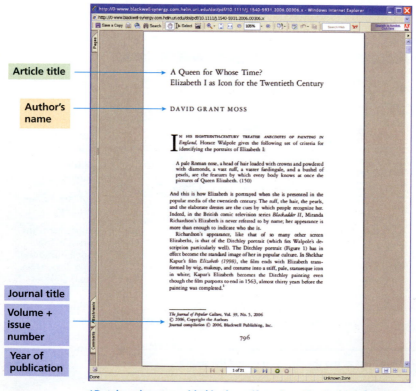

Article title → A Queen for Whose Time?
Elizabeth I as Icon for the Twentieth Century

Author's name → DAVID GRANT MOSS

IN HIS EIGHTEENTH-CENTURY TREATISE *ANECDOTES OF PAINTING IN England*, Horace Walpole gives the following set of criteria for identifying the portraits of Elizabeth I:

A pale Roman nose, a head of hair loaded with crowns and powdered with diamonds, a vast ruff, a vaster fardingale, and a bushel of pearls, are the features by which every body knows at once the pictures of Queen Elizabeth. (150)

And this is how Elizabeth is portrayed when she is presented in the popular media of the twentieth century. The ruff, the hair, the pearls, and the elaborate dresses are the cues by which people recognize her. Indeed, in the British comic television series *Blackadder II*, Miranda Richardson's Elizabeth is never referred to by name; her appearance is more than enough to indicate who she is.

Richardson's appearance, like that of so many other screen Elizabeths, is that of the Ditchley portrait (which fits Walpole's description particularly well). The Ditchley portrait (Figure 1) has in effect become the standard image of her in popular culture. In Shekhar Kapur's *Elizabeth (1998)*, the film ends with Elizabeth transformed by wig, makeup, and costume into a stiff, pale, statuesque icon in white; Kapur's Elizabeth becomes the Ditchley painting even though the film purports to end in 1563, almost thirty years before the painting was completed.[1]

Journal title
Volume + issue number
Year of publication

The Journal of Popular Culture, Vol. 39, No. 5, 2006
© 2006, Copyright the Authors
Journal compilation © 2006, Blackwell Publishing, Inc.

796

***Database is not provided in the .pdf version. Obtain this information from the database screen shown on page 227.**

74. Summary of Research: Online Database

Holub, Tamara. "Early-Decision Programs." ED470540. 2002. *ERIC Digests*.
Web. 7 Nov. 2006.

75. Collection of Documents: Online Database

"Combating Plagiarism." *CQ Researcher*. CQ P, 9 Sept. 2003. Web. 12 Nov.
2006.

76. Video or Film: Online

Apocalypse Now. Dir. Francis Ford Coppola. 1979. *Film.com*. Web. 17 July
2006.

77. Television or Radio Program: Online

Edwards, Bob. "Adoption: Redefining Family." *Morning Edition*. Natl.
Public Radio, 28-29 June 2001. Web. 17 July 2006.

78. Recording: Online

Malcolm X. "The Definition of Black Power." 8 Mar. 1964. *Great Speeches*,
2000. Web. 18 July 2006.

79. Artwork: Online

Elamite Goddess. 2100 BC (?). Louvre, Paris. Web. 8 Apr. 2007.

80. Map or Chart: Online

> "Beirut [Beyrout] 1912." Map. *Perry-Castañeda Library Map Collection.*
>
> Web. 16 July 2000.

81. Comic Strip or Cartoon: Online

> Auth, Tony. "Spending Goals." Cartoon. *Slate.* Washington Post Newsweek
>
> Interactive, 7 Sept. 2001. Web. 16 Oct. 2006.

82. Advertisement: Online

> Mazda Miata. Advertisement. *New York Magazine* 16 July 2001. Web.
>
> 18 July 2001.

83. Other Online Sources

When citing a source not shown here (such as a photo, painting, or recording), adapt the nonelectronic MLA model.

> NASA/JPL. "Martian Meteorite." *Views of the Solar System: Meteoroids and*
>
> *Meteorites.* Ed. Calvin J. Hamilton. 1999. Web. 13 June 2005.

84. FTP, Telnet, or Gopher Site

Treat a source obtained through FTP (file transfer protocol), telnet, or gopher as you would a similar Web source, and provide the complete address.

> Clinton, William Jefferson. "Radio Address of the President to the
>
> Nation." 10 May 1997. Web. 29 June 2003.
>
> <ftp://OMA.EOP.GOV.US/1997/5/10/1.TEXT.1>.

85. Email

Give the writer's name, message title or type, and date. Be sure to hyphenate *e-mail* in MLA style.

> Pell, John. "City Board." Message to the author. 17 Sept. 2006. E-mail.

86. Online Posting

Aid readers (if you can) by citing an archived version.

Brock, Stephen E. "School Crisis." Online posting. 27 Apr. 2001. *Special
Events Chat Transcripts*. Lycos Communities. Web. 18 July 2006.

87. Podcast

Loh, Sandra Tsing. "You Are Getting Sleepy. . . ." *The Loh Down on Science*.
KPCC, Natl. Public Radio, 12 Mar. 2007. Web. 10 Apr. 2007.

88. CD-ROM, Diskette, or Magnetic Tape

Note the medium (*CD-ROM, Diskette, Magnetic tape*), the name of the
vendor, and the publication date.

Shakespeare, William. *All's Well That Ends Well*. Abingdon: Andromeda
Interactive, 1994. CD-ROM.

89. CD-ROM Abstract

Add information for any parallel printed source. Identify the database
and medium (*CD-ROM, Diskette*), vendor, and publication date.

Straus, Stephen. Interview with Claudia Dreifus. "Separating Remedies
from Snake Oil." *New York Times* 3 Apr. 2001: D5+. Abstract.
CD-ROM. *InfoTrac*. 19 July 2006.

26c Sample MLA paper

The *MLA Handbook* recommends beginning a research paper with text on the first page, using the format shown on the following pages. Refer to the features of Jenny Latimer's paper, noted in the margins, as you prepare your paper.

1" from top of page

1/2" from top

Latimer 1

Jenny Latimer

Professor Schwegler

Writing 101

7 November 2006

Heading format without title page

Double-spaced heading and paper

1" margin on each side

No, Thanks, I'll Pass on That

1   One night at work my friend Kate turned down my offer
of a red licorice stick after quickly checking the ingredients
on the bag. I asked her to explain why, and she replied that
they contained hydrogenated oils, which are, according to
research articles she had read, "silent killers." She went on
briefly to describe the horrors they do to your body, the
various foods that contain them, as well as the effort she makes
to avoid hydrogenated oils. I was shocked and intrigued by
this news and decided to explore the reality of what
she'd said.

2   A day or two later, while browsing through the shelves at
the supermarket, I started checking ingredients. To my
astonishment I couldn't seem to find a snack without these words
on the back. Whether followed by the word "coconut,"
"cottonseed," or "soybean," there it was lurking amidst the other
ingredients--hydrogenated oil. I was horrified! Thinking these
scary oils couldn't be everywhere, I continued my search. A box of
toaster tarts, again yes. A can of soup, there it was. I picked up a
bag of pretzels, tossed it back on the shelf, and left the store in
frustration, needless to say without buying a snack. Returning
home I realized I needed to know the truth; I set out to find the
answers to my questions.

¶ indented 5 spaces or ½"

Anecdote introduces purpose of research

Field research confirms anecdote

1" margin at bottom

Latimer 2

3   My first question was this: what exactly does it mean to
hydrogenate an oil? This is where things get a little technical: to
hydrogenate is to add hydrogen. During the hydrogenation process,
the hydrogen atoms of a fatty acid are moved to the opposite side of
the double bond of its molecular structure (Roberts). According to
Lewis Harrison, author of *The Complete Fats and Oils Book*, this
changed fatty acid molecule can actually be toxic to the body. It can
cause oxidative stress and damage the body in the same way as
cigarette smoke and chemical toxins. It can alter the normal transport
of minerals and nutrients across cell membranes. As a result, foreign
invaders may pass the cell membrane unchallenged; also, supplies and
information important to the cell may not be allowed in. Good fats
that the body uses for many functions are not allowed to pass
through the membrane while these fatty acids build up unused
outside the cell, making us fat (Armstrong; Rudin and Felix 21).

4   To formulate hydrogenated oils, gas is fused into the oils
using a metal catalyst (such as aluminum, cobalt, and nickel).
These metals are needed to fuse the hydrogen into the oils. After
hydrogenation these fatty acids are called trans fatty acids or
hydrogenated oils (Harrison 93). As a result, my licorice snacks
were making me fat—which was a given—but not only that. They
were actually disrupting the normal functions of my cells. What
was this doing to me in the long run?

5   After production companies started using hydrogenated oils,
which were first introduced in 1914 and fully part of the food
production market by the mid-fifties, substantial increases in
several diseases occurred rapidly within the span of a few years.
According to information available from the National Institutes of

First research question

No page number given for general reference

Paragraph synthesizes several sources

Citation from book includes page number

Process summarized

Second research question

Historical background supplied

Latimer 3

Health, during 1973 to 1994 there was a 22% increase from 364 cancers of assorted types to 462 cancers for every 100,000 people. And from 1973 to 1992, those 364 cancers rose to 530 for every 100,000 people. This 31% increase was "an additional 9% increase from the previous years" (Dewey).

6   Dr. Andrew Weil, one of the nation's leading advocates of holistic medicine, claims that hydrogenated oils are "one of the most toxic substances Americans consume" (qtd. in Alter). Another article compared hydrogenated oils to inhaling cigarette smoke: "They will kill you--slowly over time, but surely as you breathe" (Armstrong). The US Food and Drug Administration and the American Heart Association agree that trans fatty acids raise LDL ("bad") cholesterol levels and lower HDL ("good") cholesterol levels, therefore increasing the risk of coronary disease--a leading cause of death in the United States. The Institute of Medicine reported this year that trans fats may raise levels of lipoprotein, higher levels of which have been associated with a greater risk of heart and blood vessel disease (Roberts). Trans fats also have artery-clogging qualities (McCord and McVeigh).

7   Hydrogenated oils have also been shown to increase the risks of breast cancer. According to research by the Cancer Research Foundation of America, women with the highest levels of trans fatty acids were 40% more likely to develop breast cancer than those with lower levels (Cancer Research Foundation; CancerWEB Project). Some have speculated that hydrogenated oils are the cause of what is called non-insulin-dependent diabetes type II, wherein a person produces enough insulin, but it does not reduce the sugar levels in the blood. It is unknown what causes the body to be insulin resistant (Dewey).

Discussion of risk continues

Indirect source (with quotation from someone else) identified

Group authors cited in sentence

Specific risks identified

Latimer 4

8   On the other hand, according to James R. Marshall in an article for *Nutrition Reviews*, there is no conclusive evidence that trans fatty acids specifically are a cause of cancer; fats in general are known to cause cancer, but trans fatty acids are not directly responsible. Marshall maintains, "Any effort to lower the risks of heart diseases should be focused on decreasing total fat intake, and not on consuming less trans fat or saturated fat." Bruce Watkins, in an article for *Food Technology*, says that foods "should be evaluated based on their impact on overall health. For instance, total fat and not trans fat or saturated fat alone, is correlated with obesity and cancer."

Opposing views acknowledged

9   So in today's health-conscious America, why do over 90% of our foods still contain hydrogenated oils? The answer is money. The process of hydrogenation increases the volume of the oil, thus making more oil available to sell. Hydrogenating creates a product that can exist at room temperature as either a solid or a liquid; therefore, any desired consistency is possible (Byers). Hydrogenated oils also give food products a rich flavor and texture at cheaper costs.

Cause of situation discussed

10   But most importantly for manufacturers, hydrogenated oils act as a preservative, which means a longer shelf life for products and fewer returns of spoiled products (Dewey). By using hydrogenated oils rather than other less health-threatening oils, food companies are saving money (Dewey). Juan Menjivar, vice president of global research and development at Rich Products, estimates that it will cost a few pennies more per pound of ingredients to eliminate trans fats (Haarlander). Research alone for a replacement for trans fats will cost companies tens of millions of dollars (Dwyer). Up until now, companies have relied on the ignorance or lack of concern of the public, along with keeping their prices lower than those of healthier foods, to stay in business.

11   This situation, however, is changing. As of January 1, 2006, the US Food and Drug Administration required that the amount of trans fatty acids in the product be listed on the label directly under the line for saturated fats. This requirement has encouraged companies to use healthier oils so as not to scare away consumers (Haarlander). The entire food industry is researching options for different oils and for ways of preparing new products, said Stephanie Childs of the Grocery Manufacturers of America (Dwyer).

Future situation identified

12   The FDA gave food companies three years because this is such a large change, and companies need time to adjust. Because there will be a need for new products, these products need time to grow. Food doesn't grow overnight. Many countries have recognized the health issues of hydrogenated oils for some time. In Denmark, the country with the lowest diagnosed rates of heart disease, cancers, and diabetes, hydrogenated oils have been banned for over forty years. Many other countries have limitations on the amounts of hydrogenated oils in foods (Dewey).

13   So, for now, how can one avoid trans fats? Although trans fats do occur naturally in tiny amounts in some dairy products and meats, the majority of trans fats come from processed foods. In addition to the many health-food stores full of hydrogenated-free foods, most supermarkets stock them in special sections. Although the greater part of what you will find in your snack food, frozen food, and ready-bake aisles will contain hydrogenated oils, some

Advice for readers

Latimer 6

producers have already made the switch from trans fats: Frito-Lay
Doritos, Jolly Time Pop Corn, Tostitos and Cheetos, Take Control
Spread, I Can't Believe It's Not Butter products, some Kraft food
products, and products from Jaret International, which makes Sour
Patch Kids and Swedish Fish (Dwyer).

14   There are also ways to find the amount of trans fatty acids
that are in a food. Where the words "hydrogenated oil" appear on
the list of ingredients is a clue; the higher up on the list, the
greater the content in the product. Take the amount of total fat
listed on the label, and subtract all the other fats listed; chances
are the remaining amount is trans fat. The highest levels of trans
fats are found in the foods that you might expect: French fries,
doughnuts, cookies, cakes, margarine, single-serving soups such as
ramen noodles, grilled foods, pizza, waffles, breaded fish sticks,
pot pies, and many frozen convenience items ("Think"). As an

Article
without
author
cited by
title

alternative, try making things from scratch, using canned veggies
and soups, having butter instead of margarine, going for broiled or
baked over grilled or fried, and if you're craving a snack, choosing
jelly beans or gummy bears over chocolate and cookies.

15   So I return to the supermarket, and as I walk in, I am
surrounded by processed hydrogenated food, rows upon rows of
cookies and candies, boxes and bags of tantalizing treats. But now
that I've found the answers to my questions and know what is in
the things I have been eating, I find it easy to resist temptation.
Instead I walk to the small health-food section toward the back.

Anecdote
concludes
with
outcomes
of research

It's more expensive—but worth it. Actually, I feel great. If giving
up licorice sticks is what it takes to keep my body in good health,
then that's a price I'm willing to pay.

Latimer 7

Works Cited

Alter, Alexandra. "Alarms Raised over Partially Hydrogenated Oil."
    Columbia News Service 21 May 2006. Web. 26 Oct. 2006.

American Heart Association. "Hydrogenated Fats." 2002. Web.
    26 Oct. 2006.

Armstrong, Eric. "What's Wrong with Partially Hydrogenated Oils?"
    Treelight Health.com. 2001. Web. 30 Sept. 2006.

Byers, Tim. "Hardened Fats, Hardened Arteries?" Abstract. *New
    England Journal of Medicine* 337.21 (1997): 1554. *Academic
    Search Premier*. Web. 26 Oct. 2006.

Cancer Research Foundation of America. "Trans Fatty Acids Linked
    to Breast Cancer Risk." Cancer Research Foundation of
    America, Aug. 1998. Web. 10 Sept. 2006.

CancerWEB Project. "Hydrogenation." *On-Line Medical Dictionary*.
    Dept. of Medical Oncology, U of Newcastle upon Tyne, 9 Oct.
    1977. Web. 10 Sept. 2006.

Dewey, David Lawrence. "Food for Thought: Hydrogenated Oils
    Are Silent Killers." 18 Sept. 1998. Web. 30 Sept. 2006.

Dwyer, Kelly Pate. "Frito-Lay Removes Trans Fats from Chips."
    Knight Ridder/Tribune Business News 28 Sept. 2003.
    InfoTrac OneFile. Web. 26 Oct. 2006.

Haarlander, Lisa. "Nutrition: Getting the Fat Out." *News Business
    Reporter* 1 Sept. 2003. Web. 24 Oct. 2006.

Harrison, Lewis. *The Complete Fats and Oils Book*. New York: Avery-
    Penguin, 1996. Print.

Marshall, James R. "Trans Fatty Acids in Cancer." Abstract.
    Nutrition Reviews May 1996: n. pag. *Health & Wellness
    Resource Center*. Web. 26 Oct. 2006.

Latimer 8

McCord, Holly, and Gloria McVeigh. "Smart Bites." *Prevention* Dec.
2001. *Academic Search Premier*. Web. 26 Oct. 2006.

Roberts, Shauna S. "IOM Takes Aim at Trans Fats." *Diabetes Forecast*
56.1 (2003): 17-18. *Academic Search Premier*. Web. 26 Oct.
2006.

Rudin, Donald, and Clara Felix. *The Omega-3 Phenomenon*. New York:
Rawson, 1987. Print.

"Think Before You Eat: Trans Fats Lurking in Many Popular Foods."
Knight Ridder/Tribune News Service 8 Sept. 2003. *InfoTrac
OneFile*. Web. 26 Oct. 2006.

United States. Food and Drug Administration. "What Every
Consumer Should Know about Trans Fatty Acids." 9 July
2003. Web. 23 Oct. 2006. <http://www.fda.gov/oc/
initiatives/transfat/q_a.html>.

Watkins, Bruce A. "Trans Fatty Acids: A Health Paradox?" *Food
Technology* 52.3 (1998): 120. Abstract. *Health & Wellness
Resource Center*. Web. 26 Oct. 2006.

Documenting Sources: APA Style

▼ TAKING IT ONLINE

APA STYLE.ORG
http://www.apastyle.org

Visit this official Web site of the American Psychological Association for current, accurate information about APA style. For special issues, click on topics such as electronic references, style tips, or FAQs (frequently asked questions).

For further advice on using APA style, check the home page of your library or tutoring center or other academic sites such as those below. Be certain that any site you use has been revised and updated to reflect the most current APA style.

APA FORMATTING AND STYLE GUIDE
http://owl.english.purdue.edu/owl/resource/560/01

Sponsored by the Purdue University Online Writing Lab, this page explains how to lay out a paper and supplies links to sample in-text citations and entries for a reference list following APA style.

APA CITATION STYLE
http://www.liu.edu/cwis/cwp/library/workshop/citapa.htm

This color-coded guide makes it easy to see what's needed for entries in an APA reference list.

CITING YOUR SOURCES
http://www.libraries.wright.edu/find/references/citing.html

This page offers links to help you find advice on style guides for several fields, including the *WSU Writing Center Mini-Manual for Using APA Style in Research Papers*.

PART 7

Documenting Sources: APA Style

Guide to APA Formats for In-Text (Parenthetical) Citations

Guide to APA Formats for References

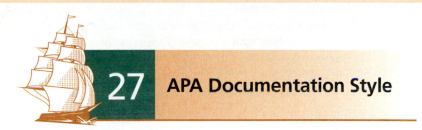

27 APA Documentation Style

APA (American Psychological Association) documentation style is a name-and-date format. It identifies a source in the text by naming its author and a date of publication (often in parentheses), as (Kitwana, 2002) illustrates, and guides readers to a corresponding entry in a concluding reference list.

Kitwana, B. (2002). *The hip hop generation: Young blacks and the crisis in*

African American culture. New York: Basic Civitas.

STRATEGY **Decide when to use APA style.**

ACADEMIC SETTINGS
When readers expect APA or a name-and-date style

WORK AND PUBLIC SETTINGS
When business or professional readers prefer a name-and-date system or want to see at once how current your sources are
When you need a simple way to identify sources and dates
When other writers or publications in your setting use APA style, modified APA style, or a similar informal system

For more on this documentation style, consult the *Publication Manual of the American Psychological Association* (5th ed., Washington, DC: APA, 2001). Updates are posted on the APA Web site at <http://www.apastyle.org>.

27a APA in-text citation examples

The APA system provides in-text parenthetical citations for quotations, paraphrases, summaries, and other specific information from a source. (For advice on what to document, see 24c–d.) APA style makes the year of publication part of an in-text citation that refers to a reference list.

DRAFT   The current argumentative climate impedes exchanges among those with differing ideas (Tannen).

EDITED   The current argumentative climate impedes exchanges among those with differing ideas (Tannen, 1998).

1. Author's Name in Parentheses

When you include both the author's name and the year of publication in parentheses, separate them with a comma. To specify the location of a quotation, paraphrase, summary, or other information, add a comma, *p.* or *pp.*, and the page number(s) on which the material appears in the source.

One recent study examines the emotional intensity of "the fan's link to the star" (Gitlin, 2001, p. 129).

2. Author's Name in Discussion

When you include an author's name in your discussion, give the date of the source in parentheses after the name. Provide the page number in the source following any quotation or paraphrase.

For Gitlin (2001), emotion is the basis of "the fan's link to the star" (p. 129).

3. Specific Reference

When you document information from a particular place in a source, indicate what you are citing: p. ("page"), chap. ("chapter"), figure, para. or ¶ ("paragraph") in electronic sources. Spell potentially confusing words. For classical works always indicate the part (chap. 5), not the page.

Teenagers who survive suicide attempts experience distinct stages of recovery (Mauk & Weber, 1991, Table 1).

4. One Author

You can vary your in-text citations as you present both the name and date in parentheses, both in the text, or the name in the text.

Dell's 2002 study of charter schools confirmed issues identified earlier
(James, 1996) and also updated Rau's (1998) school classification.

5. Two Authors

In parenthetical citations (and the reference list), separate the names
with an ampersand (&); in your text, use the word *and*.

Given evidence that married men earn more than unmarried men (Chun &
Lee, 2001), Nakosteen and Zimmer (2001) investigated how earnings
affect spousal selection.

6. Three to Five Authors

Include all the names, separated by commas, in the first citation. In parenthetical citations (and the reference list), use an ampersand (&), not *and*.

Sadeh, Raviv, and Gruber (2000) related "sleep problems and
neuropsychological functioning in children" (p. 292).

In any following references, give only the first author's name and *et al.* ("and
others"): Sadeh et al. (2000) reported their findings.

7. Six or More Authors

In all text citations, follow the first author with *et al.*: (Berg et al.,
2007). For your reference list, see Entry 2 on page 247.

8. Organization or Group as Author

Spell out the name of the organization, corporation, or agency in the
first citation. Follow any cumbersome name with an abbreviation in brackets, and use the shorter form in later citations.

FIRST CITATION   Besides instilling fear, hate crimes limit where women live and
work (National Organization of Women [NOW], 2001).

LATER CITATION   Pending legislation would strengthen the statutes on bias-
motivated crimes (NOW, 2001).

9. No Author Given

Give the title or the first few words of a long title.

The photographs capture people from all walks of life (*Friendship*, 2001).

Full title: *Friendship: Celebration of humanity.*

10. Work Cited More Than Once

When you cite the same source more than once in a paragraph, repeat the source as necessary to clarify a page reference or specify one of several sources. If a second reference is clear, don't repeat the date.

> Much of the increase in personal debt can be linked to unrestrained use of
>
> credit cards (Schor, 1998, p. 73). In fact, according to Schor, roughly a
>
> third of consumers "describe themselves as either heavily or moderately
>
> in financial debt" (p. 72).

11. Authors with the Same Name

When your references include works by two authors who share the same last name, provide the author's initials for each in-text citation.

> Scholars have examined the development of African American culture
>
> during slavery and reconstruction (E. Foner, 1988), including the role of
>
> Frederick Douglass in this process (P. Foner, 1950).

12. Personal Communications, Including Interviews and Email

In your text, cite letters, interviews, memos, telephone calls, email (hyphenated as e-mail in APA style), and so on using the name of the person, the expression *personal communication*, and the full date. Readers have no access to such sources, so you omit them from your reference list.

> According to J. M. Hostos, the state no longer funds services duplicated
>
> by county agencies (personal communication, October 7, 2006).

13. Two or More Sources in a Citation

If you sum up information from several sources, include them all in your citation. Separate the authors and years with commas; separate the sources with semicolons. List the sources alphabetically, then oldest to most recent for several by the same author, in the same order used in the reference list.

> Several studies have related job satisfaction with performance (Faire,
>
> 2002; Hall, 1996, 1999).

14. Two or More Works by the Same Author in the Same Year

If you use works published in the same year by the same author or author team, alphabetize the works, and add letters after the year to distinguish them.

> Gould (1987a, p. 73) makes a similar point.

15. Work Cited in Another Source

Include the phrase *as cited in* as part of a parenthetical citation for a source you did not use directly but drew from another source.

> Writing in the late 1800s about Halloween customs, William Shepard Walsh lamented that "gangs of hoodlums throng the streets, ringing the door-bells or wrenching the handles from their sockets, and taking gates from off their hinges" (as cited in Skal, 2002, pp. 33–34).

16. Electronic Source

To identify the location of specific information, use what the document provides: page numbers, paragraph numbers (para. or ¶), or the section name and paragraph under it, counted to identify a number.

> Bodybuilders sometimes suffer from muscle dysmorphia, an obsessive-compulsive disorder similar to anorexia (Lee, 2006, What is dysmorphia? section, para. 4).

17. Sacred or Classical Text

Give the number or name of the chapter, section, or part along with the date or name of the version or translation you are citing, especially if no original date is available. Cite a standard source in your text only.

> Aristotle argues in *Politics* (trans. 1999) that liberty is a fundamental element of democracy (6.1.6).

18. Content Footnote

You may use a content footnote to expand material in the text. Place a superscript number above the related line of text; number the notes consecutively. On a separate page at the end, below the centered heading "Footnotes," present the notes in numerical order. Begin each with its superscript number. Indent five to seven spaces for the first line only of each note, and double-space all notes.

TEXT   I tape-recorded and transcribed all interviews.[1]

NOTE   [1]Although background noise obscured some parts of the tapes, these gaps did not substantially affect the material studied.

27b APA reference list

On a separate page at the end of your text (before notes or appendixes), provide a list of references to the sources you've cited.

- **Page format.** Allow a one-inch margin, and center the heading "References" without underlining or quotation marks.
- **Alphabetizing.** List the works alphabetically by author or by the first main word of the title if there is no author. Arrange two or more works by the same author from oldest to most recent, by year of publication.
- **Spacing.** Double-space within and between all entries.
- **Indentation.** Do not indent the first line, but indent all additional lines like paragraphs, consistently a half inch or five to seven spaces.

DRAFT   Carlson, NR., and Buskist, Wm. (1997), *Psychology: The Science of*

         Behavior. Boston, Allyn & Bacon.

EDITED   Carlson, N. R., & Buskist, W. (1997). *Psychology: The science of behavior*

         (5th ed.). Boston: Allyn & Bacon.

Books and Works Treated as Books

MODEL FORMAT FOR BOOKS AND WORKS TREATED AS BOOKS

period   period +   period +
+ space   space   space

↓   ↓   ↓

Author(s). (Date). *Title of work*. Place of

Publication: Publisher.

↑   ↑   ↑

indent ½" or   colon + space   period
5–7 spaces

- **Author.** Give the author's last name followed by a comma and the *initials only* of the first and middle names. Use the same inverted order for all the names of coauthors. Separate the names of coauthors with commas, and use an ampersand (&) before the name of the last author.
- **Date.** Put the year of publication in parentheses followed by a period.
- **Title.** Italicize the title, but capitalize only proper names and the first word of the main title and any subtitle.
- **Publication information.** Name the city (and the country or the state's postal abbreviation except for major cities) followed by a colon and a space. Supply the publisher's name without words such as *Inc.* or *Publishers*.

1. One Author

     Ortner, S. B. (2003). *New Jersey dreaming: Capital, culture, and the class of*

         '58. Durham, NC: Duke University Press.

2. Two or More Authors

List up to six authors; add *et al.* to indicate any others.

Biber, D., Conrad, S., & Reppen, R. (1998). *Corpus linguistics:*

Investigating language structure and use. Cambridge, England:

Cambridge University Press.

3. Organization or Group as Author

Treat the group as an author. When author and publisher are the same, give the word *Author* after the place instead of repeating the name.

Amnesty International. (2001). *Annual report 2001* [Brochure]. London:

Author.

4. No Author Given

Boas anniversary volume: Anthropological papers written in honor of Franz

Boas. (1906). New York: Stechert.

5. More Than One Work by the Same Author

List works chronologically with the author's name in each entry.

Aronowitz, S. (1993). *Roll over Beethoven: The return of cultural strife.*

Hanover, NH: Wesleyan University Press.

Aronowitz, S. (2000). *From the ashes of the old: American labor and*

America's future. New York: Basic Books.

6. More Than One Work by the Same Author in the Same Year

If works by the same author appear in the same year, list them alphabetically based on the first main word in the title. Add lowercase letters after the dates to distinguish them in text citations: (Gould, 1987b).

Gould, S. J. (1987a). *Time's arrow, time's cycle: Myth and metaphor in the*

discovery of geological time. Cambridge, MA: Harvard University Press.

Gould, S. J. (1987b). *An urchin in the storm: Essays about books and*

ideas. New York: Norton.

7. One or More Editors

Include (*Ed.*) or (*Eds.*) after the names of the editor or editors.

Bowe, J., Bowe, M., & Streeter, S. C. (Eds.). (2001). *Gig: Americans talk*

about their jobs. New York: Three Rivers Press.

8. Translator

> Bourdieu, P. (1990). *In other words: Essays towards a reflexive sociology*
>
> (M. Adamson, Trans.). Stanford, CA: Stanford University Press.

9. Edition Following the First

Identify the edition in parentheses after the title (for example, *3rd ed.* or *Rev. ed.* for "revised edition").

> Groth-Marnat, G. (2003). *Handbook of psychological assessment* (4th ed.).
>
> New York: Wiley.

10. Reprint

> Butler, J. (1999). *Gender trouble*. New York: Routledge. (Original work
>
> published 1990)

11. Multivolume Work

> Strachey, J., Freud, A., Strachey, A., & Tyson, A. (Eds.). (1966-1974). *The*
>
> *standard edition of the complete psychological works of Sigmund*
>
> *Freud* (J. Strachey et al., Trans.) (Vols. 3-5). London: Hogarth Press
>
> and the Institute of Psycho-Analysis.

12. Anthology or Collection of Articles

> Appadurai, A. (Ed.). (2001). *Globalization*. Durham, NC: Duke University
>
> Press.

13. Encyclopedia or Reference Work

> Winn, P. (Ed.). (2001). *Dictionary of biological psychology*. London:
>
> Routledge.

14. *Diagnostic and Statistical Manual of Mental Disorders*

After an initial full in-text citation, you may use standard abbreviations: *DSM–III* (1980), *DSM–III–R* (1987), *DSM–IV* (1994), or *DSM–IV–TR* (2000).

> American Psychiatric Association. (1994). *Diagnostic and statistical*
>
> *manual of mental disorders* (4th ed.). Washington, DC: Author.

15. Dissertation Unpublished

> Gomes, C. S. (2001). *Selection and treatment effects in managed care.*
>
> Unpublished doctoral dissertation, Boston University.

16. Government Document

> Select Committee on Aging, Subcommittee on Human Services, House
>
> of Representatives. (1991). *Grandparents' rights: Preserving*
>
> *generational bonds* (Com. Rep. No. 102-833). Washington, DC:
>
> U.S. Government Printing Office.

17. Report

Begin with the individual, group, or agency that has written the report. If the same body publishes the report, use *Author* in the publication information. If the report has a number, put it in parentheses after the title but before the period.

> Dossey, J. A. (1988). *Mathematics: Are we measuring up?* (Report No. 17-M-02).
>
> Princeton, NJ: Educational Testing Service. (ERIC Document
>
> Reproduction Service No. ED300207)

Articles from Periodicals and Selections from Books

MODEL FORMAT FOR ARTICLES

period +   period +   period +   comma +
   space   space   space   space

↓   ↓   ↓   ↓

Author(s). (Date). Title of article. *Title of Periodical,*

Volume Number, Page numbers.

↑   ↑   ↑   ↑

indent ½" or   number   comma   period
5–7 spaces   italicized   italicized

- **Author.** Follow the author's last name and initials with a period.
- **Date.** Supply the date in parentheses followed by a period.
- **Title of article.** Capitalize only proper names and the first word of the title and any subtitle. Do not use quotation marks or italics. End with a period.
- **Title of journal, periodical, or book.** Italicize the journal title, with all main words capitalized, and the volume number. Follow with page numbers. Capitalize a book title like an article title, but italicize it.

Article in Print Journal

Authors' names   Date of publication

Riddle, K., Eyal, K., Mahood, C., & Potter, W. J. (2006).

Article title → Judging the degree of violence in media portrayals:

A cross-genre comparison. *Journal of Broadcasting &*

Electronic Media, 50(2), 270-286.   Journal title

Volume and issue numbers Pages

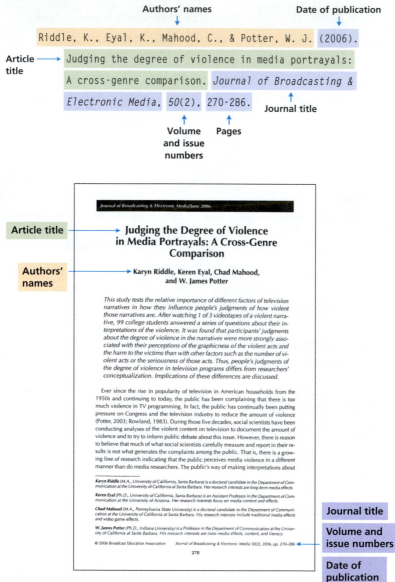

Article title →

Judging the Degree of Violence in Media Portrayals: A Cross-Genre Comparison

Authors' names →

Karyn Riddle, Keren Eyal, Chad Mahood, and W. James Potter

This study tests the relative importance of different factors of television narratives in how they influence people's judgments of how violent those narratives are. After watching 1 of 3 videotapes of a violent narrative, 99 college students answered a series of questions about their interpretations of the violence. It was found that participants' judgments about the degree of violence in the narratives were more strongly associated with their perceptions of the graphicness of the violent acts and the harm to the victims than with other factors such as the number of violent acts or the seriousness of those acts. Thus, people's judgments of the degree of violence in television programs differs from researchers' conceptualization. Implications of these differences are discussed.

Ever since the rise in popularity of television in American households from the 1950s and continuing to today, the public has been complaining that there is too much violence in TV programming. In fact, the public has continually been putting pressure on Congress and the television industry to reduce the amount of violence (Potter, 2003; Rowland, 1983). During those five decades, social scientists have been conducting analyses of the violent content on television to document the amount of violence and to try to inform public debate about this issue. However, there is reason to believe that much of what social scientists carefully measure and report in their results is not what generates the complaints among the public. That is, there is a growing line of research indicating that the public perceives media violence in a different manner than do media researchers. The public's way of making interpretations about

Karyn Riddle (M.A., University of California, Santa Barbara) is a doctoral candidate in the Department of Communication at the University of California at Santa Barbara. Her research interests are long-term media effects.

Keren Eyal (Ph.D., University of California, Santa Barbara) is an Assistant Professor in the Department of Communication at the University of Arizona. Her research interests focus on media content and effects.

Chad Mahood (M.A., Pennsylvania State University) is a doctoral candidate in the Department of Communication at the University of California at Santa Barbara. His research interests include traditional media effects and video game effects.

W. James Potter (Ph.D., Indiana University) is a Professor in the Department of Communication at the University of California at Santa Barbara. His research interests are mass media effects, content, and literacy.

© 2006 Broadcast Education Association Journal of Broadcasting & Electronic Media 50(2), 2006, pp. 270-286

270

Journal title

Volume and issue numbers

Date of publication

Pages

18. Article in Journal Paginated by Volume

Omit the issue number when the page numbers run continuously throughout the different issues making up a volume.

Klein, R. D. (2003). Audience reactions to local TV news. *American*

Behavioral Scientist, 46, 1661-1672.

19. Article in Journal Paginated by Issue

When page 1 begins each issue, include the issue number in parentheses, but not italicized, directly after the volume number.

Sadeh, A., Raviv, A., & Gruber, R. (2000). Sleep patterns and sleep

disruptions in school-age children. *Developmental Psychology, 36*(3),

291-301.

20. Special Issue of Journal

Begin with the special issue's editor (if other than the regular editor). If no editor is indicated, begin with the title.

Balk, D. E. (Ed.). (1991). Death and adolescent bereavement [Special

issue]. *Journal of Adolescent Research, 6*(1).

21. Article in Weekly Magazine

Adler, J. (1995, July 31). The rise of the overclass. *Newsweek, 126*, 33-34,

39-40, 43, 45-46.

22. Article in Monthly Magazine

Dold, C. (1998, September). Needles and nerves. *Discover, 19*, 59-62.

23. Article with No Author Given

True tales of false memories. (1993, July/August). *Psychology Today, 26*,

11-12.

24. Article in Newspaper

Use *p.* or *pp.* to introduce the article's page numbers.

Murtaugh, P. (1998, August 10). Finding a brand's real essence.

Advertising Age, p. 12.

25. Editorial or Letter to the Editor

Ellis, S. (2001, September 7). Adults are problem with youth sports
[Letter to the editor]. *USA Today,* p. A14.

26. Interview Published

Although APA does not specify a form for published interviews, you
may wish to employ the following form.

Dess, N. K. (2001). The new body-mind connection (John T. Cacioppo)
[Interview]. *Psychology Today, 34*(4), 30-31.

27. Review with Title

Following the title of the review, describe in brackets the kind of work
(book, film, television program), and give the work's title.

McMahon, R. J. (2000). The Pentagon's war, the media's war [Review of
the book *Reporting Vietnam: Media and military at war*]. *Reviews in
American History, 28,* 303-308.

28. Review Without Title

Verdery, K. (2002). [Review of the book *The politics of gender after
socialism*]. *American Anthropologist, 104,* 354-355.

29. Article in Encyclopedia or Reference Work

Chernoff, H. (1978). Decision theory. In *International encyclopedia of
statistics* (Vol. 1, pp. 131-135). New York: Free Press.

30. Chapter in Edited Book or Selection in Anthology

Chisholm, J. S. (1999). Steps to an evolutionary ecology of mind. In A. L.
Hinton (Ed.), *Biocultural approaches to the emotions* (pp. 117-150).
Cambridge, England: Cambridge University Press.

31. Dissertation Abstract

Yamada, H. (1989). American and Japanese topic management strategies in
business conversations. (Doctoral dissertation, City University of Hong
Kong, 1989). *Dissertation Abstracts International, 50* (09), 2982B.

If you consult the dissertation on microfilm, end with the University Microfilms
number in parentheses: (UMI No. AAC–9004751).

Field and Media Resources

32. Unpublished Raw Data

When you use data from field research, briefly describe its topic within brackets, and end with *Unpublished raw data.*

Hernandez, J. (2003). [Survey of attitudes on unemployment benefits]. Unpublished raw data.

33. Interview Unpublished

If you have conducted an interview, cite it only in the text: (R. Gelles, personal communication, November 20, 2006).

34. Personal Communications Including Email

Cite letters, email, phone calls, and other communications unavailable to readers only in your text (see Entry 12 on p. 244).

35. Paper Presented at a Meeting

Johnson, S. (2000, April). *Test fairness: An oxymoron? The challenge of measuring well in a high stakes climate.* Paper presented at the annual meeting of the American Educational Research Association, New Orleans, LA.

36. Video or Film

Musen, K. (Producer/Writer), & Zimbardo, P. (Writer). (1990). *Quiet rage: The Stanford prison study* [DVD]. (Available from Insight Media, 2162 Broadway, New York, NY 10024-0621)

37. Television or Radio Program

Siceloff, J. L. (Executive Producer). (2002). *Now with Bill Moyers* [Television series]. New York: WNET.

38. Recording

Begin with the name of the writer and the copyright date.

Freeman, R. (1994). Porscha [Recorded by R. Freeman & The Rippingtons]. On *Sahara* [CD]. New York: GRP Records.

Online and Electronic Resources

Article in Online Journal

Author's name   Date of publication   Article title

Starkman, N. (2007, March). What students want : : Leave me alone . . . I'm socializing. *THE Journal.* ← Journal title
Retrieved* from http://www.thejournal.com/articles/20336

URL**

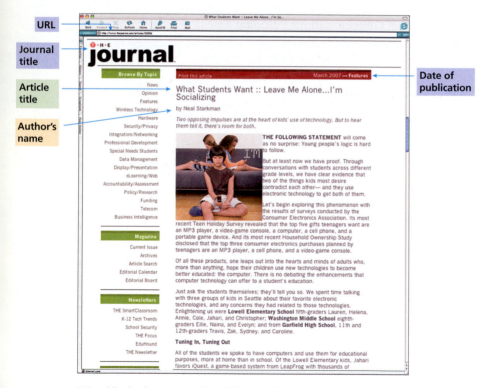

URL

Journal title

Article title

Author's name

Date of publication

* Provide the date you retrieved the item (the date of access) only if the source is (1) undated or has no volume and issue number, or (2) is likely to be revised.

** If you need to continue a URL on a second line, do not insert a hyphen. Break the URL *before* a punctuation mark, but *after* http://. Do not put a period at the end of the URL.

39. Web Site

Brown, D. K. (1998, April 1). *The children's literature Web guide*. Retrieved from http://www.acs.UCalgary.ca/~dkbrown

40. Book or Document: Online

If you can't pinpoint a date of publication, use *n.d.* ("no date").

Frary, R. B. (n.d.). *A brief guide to questionnaire development*. Retrieved November 14, 2005, from http://ericae.net/ft/tamu/upiques3.htm

41. Selection from Online Book or Document

Lasswell, H. D. (1971). Professional training. In *A pre-view of policy sciences* (chap. 8). Retrieved from http://www.policysciences.org/apreviewpolsci/pps_chapter8.pdf

42. Article in Online Journal Without DOI

Sheridan, J., & McAuley, J. D. (1998). Rhythm as a cognitive skill: Temporal processing deficits in autism. *Noetica, 3*(8). Retrieved from http://www.cs.indiana.edu/Noetica/OpenForumIssue8/McAuley.html

43. Article in Online Journal with DOI

Some scholarly publishers provide a DOI (Digital Object Identifier) with documents, creating permanent identification of and access to the material. When a source provides a DOI, cite the DOI instead of the URL.

Abrahms, M. (2006). Why terrorism does not work. *International Security, 31*(2), 42–78. doi: 10.1162/isec.2006.31.2.42

44. Newsletter Article: Online

Cashel, J. (2007, January 23). Community metrics. *Online Community Report*. Retrieved from http://www.onlinecommunityreport.com/archives/134-Community-Metrics.html

45. Newspaper Article: Online

Phillips, D. (1999, June 13). 21 days, 18 flights. *Washington Post Online*. Retrieved from http://www.washingtonpost.com/wp-srv/business/daily/june99/odyssey13.htm

46. Organization or Agency Document: Online

Arizona Public Health Association. (n.d.). *Indigenous health section.*
Retrieved September 6, 2005, from http://www.geocities.com
/native_health_az/AzPHA.htm

47. Government Document: Online

U.S. Department of Labor, Women's Bureau. (2001). *Women's jobs
1964-1999: More than 30 years of progress.* Retrieved from
http://www.dol.gov/dol/wb/public/jobs6497.htm

48. Document from Academic Site: Online

Cultural Studies Program. (n.d.). Retrieved September 9, 2005, from Drake
University, Cultural Studies Web site: http://www.multimedia
.drake.edu/cs/

49. Report: Online

Amnesty International. (1998). *The death penalty in Texas: Lethal
injustice.* Retrieved from http://www.web.amnesty.org/ai.nsf
/index/AMR510101998

50. Report from Academic Site: Online

Use "Available from" rather than "Retrieved from" if the URL will take
your reader to access information rather than the source itself.

Vandell, D. L., & Wolfe, B. (2000). *Child care quality: Does it matter and
does it need to be improved?* (Special Report No. 78). Available from
University of Wisconsin, Institute for Research on Poverty Web site:
http://www.ssc.wisc.edu/irp/sr/sr78.pdf

51. Abstract: Online

Include the source of the original work.

National Bureau of Economic Research. (1998). Tax incentives for
higher education. *Tax Policy and the Economy, 12,* 49-81. Abstract
retrieved from http://www-mitpress.mit.edu/journal-editor
.tcl?ISSN=08928649

Journal Article from a Subscription Database (HTML Format)

Authors' names
↓

Buboltz, W. C., Jr., Soper, B., Brown, F., & Jenkins, S. ← Article title

Date of publication → (2002). Treatment approaches for sleep difficulties in — Volume and issue numbers

college students. *Counselling Psychology Quarterly, 15(2),* — Journal title

Pages* → 229-237. Retrieved from Academic Search Premier database. — Journal title

↑
Database**

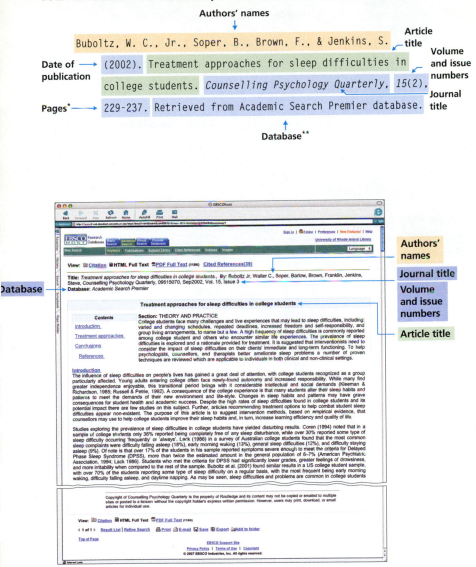

Database

Authors' names

Journal title

Volume and issue numbers

Article title

* Pages are for print original. No page numbers are provided in online HTML text.

** For materials retrieved from electronic databases, you do not need to include the database's name. If you decide to include the name, do not include the URL.

Journal Article from a Subscription Database (PDF Format, DOI)

Authors' names

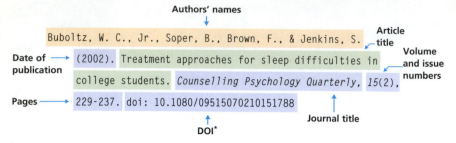

Buboltz, W. C., Jr., Soper, B., Brown, F., & Jenkins, S.

Date of publication → (2002). Treatment approaches for sleep difficulties in

college students. *Counselling Psychology Quarterly,* 15(2),

Pages → 229-237. doi: 10.1080/09515070210151788

Article title

Volume and issue numbers

Journal title

DOI*

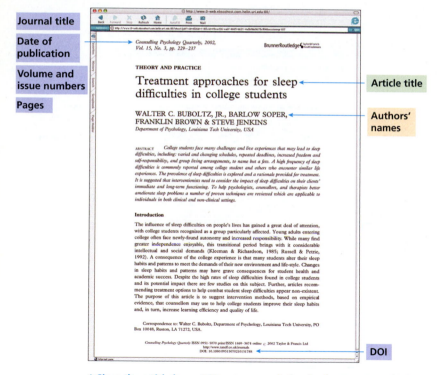

Journal title

Date of publication

Volume and issue numbers

Pages

Counselling Psychology Quarterly, 2002,
Vol. 15, No. 3, pp. 229–237

BrunnerRoutledge

THEORY AND PRACTICE

Treatment approaches for sleep difficulties in college students

Article title

WALTER C. BUBOLTZ, JR., BARLOW SOPER, FRANKLIN BROWN & STEVE JENKINS
Department of Psychology, Louisiana Tech University, USA

Authors' names

ABSTRACT   *College students face many challenges and live experiences that may lead to sleep difficulties, including: varied and changing schedules, repeated deadlines, increased freedom and self-responsibility, and group living arrangements, to name but a few. A high frequency of sleep difficulties is commonly reported among college student and others who encounter similar life experiences. The prevalence of sleep difficulties is explored and a rationale provided for treatment. It is suggested that interventionists need to consider the impact of sleep difficulties on their clients' immediate and long-term functioning. To help psychologists, counsellors, and therapists better ameliorate sleep problems a number of proven techniques are reviewed which are applicable to individuals in both clinical and non-clinical settings.*

Introduction

The influence of sleep difficulties on people's lives has gained a great deal of attention, with college students recognized as a group particularly affected. Young adults entering college often face newly-found autonomy and increased responsibility. While many find greater independence enjoyable, this transitional period brings with it considerable intellectual and social demands (Kleeman & Richardson, 1985; Russell & Petrie, 1992). A consequence of the college experience is that many students alter their sleep habits and patterns to meet the demands of their new environment and life-style. Changes in sleep habits and patterns may have grave consequences for student health and academic success. Despite the high rates of sleep difficulties found in college students and its potential impact there are few studies on this subject. Further, articles recommending treatment options to help combat student sleep difficulties appear non-existent. The purpose of this article is to suggest intervention methods, based on empirical evidence, that counsellors may use to help college students improve their sleep habits and, in turn, increase learning efficiency and quality of life.

Correspondence to: Walter C. Buboltz, Department of Psychology, Louisiana Tech University, PO Box 10048, Ruston, LA 71272, USA.

Counselling Psychology Quarterly ISSN 0951-5070 print/ISSN 1469-3674 online © 2002 Taylor & Francis Ltd
http://www.tandf.co.uk/journals
DOI: 10.1080/09515070210151788

DOI

* Since the article has a DOI, you can omit the database name and URL.

52. Journal Article: Online Database

Piko, B. (2001). Gender differences and similarities in adolescents' ways of coping. *Psychological Record, 51*(2), 223-236. Retrieved from InfoTrac Expanded Academic database.

53. Newspaper Article: Online Database

Sappenfield, M. (2002, June 24). New laws curb teen sports drugs. *The Christian Science Monitor*. Retrieved from America Online: News Publications database.

54. Presentation from Virtual Conference

Brown, D. J., Stewart, D. S., & Wilson, J. R. (1995). *Ethical pathways to virtual learning*. Paper presented at the Center on Disabilities 1995 virtual conference. Retrieved from http://www.csun.edu/cod /95virt/0010.html

55. Email

Cite email only in your text. (See Entry 12, p. 244.)

56. Online Posting

Treat online postings as personal communications (see Entry 12, p. 244) unless they are archived and accessible.

Lanbehn, K. (2001, May 9). Effective rural outreach. Message posted to State Independent Living Council Discussion Newsgroup, archived at http://www.acils.com/silc

57. Blog

Baron, D. (2006, October 26). I found it on Wikipedia, the eBay for facts. *The Web of language*. Message posted to http://webtools.uiuc.edu /blog/view?blogld=25&topicId= 298&count=&ACTION=TOPIC _DIALOGS&skinId=286

58. Podcast

Malakoff, D. (Producer). (2007, April 30). Your questions: Carbon power.

National Public Radio and National Geographic Society. Podcast

retrieved from http://www.npr.org/rss/podcast_directory.php

59. Computer Program

Begin with the name of an author who owns rights to a program or with its title (without italics).

Family Tree Maker (Version 16.0) [Software]. (2006). Fremont, CA:

Learning Company.

60. CD-ROM Database

Hall, Edward T. (1998). In *Current biography: 1940-1997*. Retrieved from

Wilson database.

27c Sample APA paper

The APA manual recommends beginning a paper with a separate title page, as illustrated on the following pages. The student also included an abstract before the paper and her questionnaire in the appendix following it.

Number title page and all others using short title

Body Esteem   1

Abbreviate title (50 characters maximum) for heading
Running head: BODY ESTEEM

Center title and all other lines
Body Esteem in Women and Men

Sharon Salamone

The University of Rhode Island

Supply name and institution

Professor Robert Schwegler

Writing 233

Section 2

April 30, 2003

Supply course information and date if requested by your instructor

Center heading

Begin on new page

Do not indent

Abstract

Undergraduate students, male and female, were asked to complete a Body Esteem Survey to report attitudes toward their bodies (body images). Responses to the survey provided an answer to the question of whether the men or the women had higher body esteem. The mean responses for women and men indicated a higher level of body esteem among men with a statistically significant difference in the means. Because the sample was limited to college undergraduates and displayed little variety in ethnicity (predominantly White), the findings of the study are limited. Prior research on ethnicity and body image suggests that a more ethnically varied sample might produce different results.

Summarize paper in one ¶, no more than 120 words

Double-space abstract and paper

[Besides the abstract, typical sections in an APA paper are Introduction, Method, Results, and Discussion.]

Body Esteem in Men and Women

1   The concept of beauty has changed over the years in
Western society, especially for women. In past centuries the
ideal was a voluptuous and curved body; now it is a more
angular and thin shape (Monteath & McCabe, 1997). Lean,
muscular bodies are currently held up as ideals for men, too.
Ideals of physical appearance and attractiveness play an
important role in the lives of people. Often, people considered
attractive are preferred as working partners, as dating partners,
or as job candidates (Lennon, Lillethun, & Buckland, 1999).
Media images endorse particular body ideals as well; for
example, "media in Western countries have portrayed a
steadily thinning female body ideal" (Monteath & McCabe,
1997, p. 711).

2   Most of us assume that women are quite concerned about
their weight and appearance--their body images--and that they
often lack positive body esteem, perhaps as a result of media
images and other cultural influences (Polivy & Herman, 1987;
Rodin, Silberstein, & Striegel-Moore, 1984; Wilcox & Laird, 2000).
But what about men? Are they concerned as well? Is their level
of body esteem higher or lower than women's or about the
same? In this paper I report on a study I undertook with a
group of college undergraduates to compare the attitudes of men
and women toward their bodies. In particular, I wanted to
determine whether or not the men had a higher body esteem
than the women had.

1" margin on each side

Indent ¶s and reference list consistently, 1/2" or 5–7 spaces

Problem and background introduced

Citation includes more than one source

Research questions identified

1" margin at bottom

Body Esteem   4

Center subheading   Introduction

Background including prior studies

3   Thinness is prized in contemporary society, especially for women. In our culture, thinness, a statistical deviation, has become the norm, leading millions of women to believe their bodies are abnormal. Therefore, it is reasonable for women to be concerned about their appearance and compare themselves to others on the basis of what they believe to be the norm (Lennon et al., 1999). As Lennon et al. point out, "Comparison with such images may be related to negative outcomes such

Citations from passage included in quotation, but only actual source listed with references

as low self-esteem (Freedman, 1984), dissatisfaction with appearance (Richens, 1991), eating disorders (Peterson, 1987; Stice et al., 1994), and negative body image (Freedman, 1984)" (p. 380).

Body image and women introduced

4   Body image is basically made up of two important components: one's perception and one's attitude toward body image. Social factors can play a large role in determining both components (Monteath & McCabe, 1997). Given the cultural pressures on women to be thin, we might expect many women to have somewhat negative body images. As Wilcox and Laird (2000) put it, "To many observers, the media appear to be unwittingly engaged in a campaign to make women feel badly about themselves" (p. 279).

Body image and men introduced

5   On the other hand, some researchers suggest that "men seem less obsessed with and disturbed by being or becoming fat: thus, the occurrence of pathogenic values related to eating and body size is extremely low among men" (Demarest & Allen, 2000, p. 465). Although there is some research, "the literature on body image

perception in men is far more limited" than that on women
(Pope et al., 2000, p. 1297). Possible reasons to suspect that
men also suffer from distorted perceptions of body image
have been evident in two recent studies. First, men with eating
disorders believe that they are fatter than men of normal
weight believe. Also, recent studies have shown that athletes
perceive themselves to be small and frail when they are, in
fact, large and muscular (Pope et al., 2000). Moreover, in one
study, men indicated that they would prefer to have a body
with 27 pounds more muscle than they actually have
(Pope et al., 2000). Thus it seems reasonable to ask
whether men and women have clearly different levels of body
esteem.

Method

6   To measure differences between men's and women's levels of
body esteem, I administered a Body Esteem Scale (BES) (Franzoi &   **Procedure for study explained**
Sheilds, 1984). Participants in my study were 174 undergraduate
college students from a state university. I approached them and
asked them to complete the BES. I asked each willing participant to
read and sign an informed consent form before participating. This
form states that the participant may stop at any point if he or she
feels uncomfortable answering a particular question or group of
questions and reassures each person that he or she will remain
anonymous.

7   The majority of the participants, between the ages of 18 and
59, were White, making up 81% of the sample. Blacks and African   **Participants described**
Americans made up 6.3%; Asian/Pacific Islanders made up 3.4%;

Body Esteem   6

Latino/Latina, mixed race, and all others made up 2.9% each; and
Native Americans made up 0.6% of the sample. The sample was
equally divided between men and women.

8   The Body Esteem Scale (BES) consists of general questions
(see Appendix) followed by three components (BES 1, BES 2, and
BES 3). BES 1 makes up the Physical/Sexual Attractiveness part
of the scale, focusing primarily on elements of the body; BES 3
consists of the Physical Condition component of the scale,
covering such matters as stamina, physical condition, and strength.
BES 1 and BES 3 have different forms and questions for women
and men. For BES 2, the women's questionnaire constitutes the
Weight Concern component of the scale while the men's
questionnaire constitutes the Upper Body Strength component
of the scale.

Questionnaire described with cross-reference to appendix

Results

9   I recorded the results from the questionnaires in an Excel
spreadsheet. In order to determine whether women or men had
higher levels of body esteem as measured by the BES, I calculated
the average score for each group (statistical mean). The mean
for women was lower than for men: for women, $M = 3.2304$; for
men, $M = 3.6514$. From this I arrived at my preliminary conclusion
that for this particular sample of college students, the men had
clearly higher body esteem than did the women, by 0.4211, or
approximately 0.4 on a scale of 1-5.

Findings explained

10   I realized, however, that results can occur by chance and
that there are statistical procedures for determining the likelihood
that chance was responsible for the difference between the two

groups. To determine whether the results were statistically significant (not occurring by chance), I had the spreadsheet program calculate an ANOVA (univariate analysis of variance) to compare the two body esteem indexes. The results indicated that the differences were significant, $F(1.172) = 28.05$, $p < .05$.

11   I conducted this study in order to determine whether men had higher, lower, or similar levels of body esteem compared with the levels women had, at least for the group of people (university undergraduates) I was studying. For this group, it is clear that men had higher levels of body esteem.

Main conclusion stated

Discussion

12   Comparing men's and women's body esteem is not as simple as this study might seem to suggest, however. The body esteem scales for men and women are certainly comparable, but they do not measure exactly the same things. According to Franzoi and Shields (1984), body esteem for women appears to consist of three primary components: sexual attractiveness, weight concern, and physical condition. The sexual attractiveness subscale consists of physical attributes that cannot generally be changed through exercise, but only through cosmetics. The physical appearance subscale includes body parts that can be altered through exercise or the control of food intake. The third subscale pertains to qualities such as stamina, agility, and strength. For men, the first subscale measures facial features and some aspects of the physique. The second subscale is composed of upper body parts and functions that can be altered through exercising. The third subscale is similar to the woman's physical subscale, consisting of stamina, agility, and strength.

Findings qualified

APA Documentation Style

13   As social attitudes and values change, perhaps men's and women's versions of the BES may need to change too. As sports and physical strength become more important to women, parts of the BES may possibly need to be revised to be more parallel to the men's. Right now, however, the BES seems to provide some understanding of the different levels of bodily self-esteem held by women and men.

Possibilities for future research suggested

14   The great pressure on women in our society to be thin and physically attractive according to standards that do not represent a normal range of body types and sizes probably accounts for the difference between the women's and men's results. Franzoi and Shields (1984) made a comment that helps explain the higher body esteem of the males: "It appears that men associate these body parts and functions, not with how they and others assess them as static objects, but with how they will help or hinder physical activity" (p. 178).

Findings analyzed

15   My results are consistent with other research. For example, "in studies of body-shape perception, men typically have more positive body images than women do, regardless of their weight" (Demarest & Langer, 1996, p. 569). Overall, men are generally satisfied with their body sizes, although they misjudge what women think to be attractive (Demarest & Allen, 2000).

16   Gender is not the only factor that influences body image. Ethnicity is also very important, especially among women. In interviews conducted by Lopez, Blix, and Blix (1995) and by Rosen and Gross (1987), Black women seem to have more positive body images and less desire to be thin than White or Hispanic women

(Demarest & Allen, 2000). When compared to Black women, White women showed greater body dissatisfaction at lower body weights (Demarest & Allen). It has also been found that Black men were less likely than White men to refuse a date with a woman because she was overweight. According to Demarest and Allen, among the female participants, Black women have a more accurate view of the perception of men, whereas White women have a more distorted perception.

17   In my study, the majority of the sample consisted of White participants. This may have affected my results and my conclusions. Because ethnicity is important in a study such as this, a more varied sample would lead to stronger conclusions.

References

**Begin on
new page**

Demarest, J., & Allen, R. (2000). Body image: Gender, ethnic, and
        age differences. *Journal of Social Psychology, 140,* 465-471.

Demarest, J., & Langer, E. (1996). Perception of body shape by
        underweight, average-weight, and overweight men and
        women. *Perceptual and Motor Skills, 83,* 569-570.

Franzoi, S. L., & Shields, S. A. (1984). The body esteem scale:
        Multidimensional structure and sex differences in a college
        population. *Journal of Personality Assessment, 407,* 173-178.

Lennon, S. J., Lillethun, A., & Buckland, S. S. (1999). Attitudes
        toward social comparison as a function of self-esteem:
        Idealized appearance and body image. *Family & Consumer
        Sciences Research Journal, 27,* 379-405.

Lopez, E., Blix, G., & Blix, A. G. (1995). Body image of Latinas
        compared to body image of non-Latina white women. *Health
        Values, 19,* 3-10.

Monteath, S. A., & McCabe, M. P. (1997). The influence of societal
        factors on female body image. *Journal of Social Psychology,
        137,* 708-727.

Polivy, J., & Herman, C. P. (1987). The diagnosis and treatment of
        abnormal eating. *Journal of Consulting and Clinical
        Psychology, 55,* 635-644.

Pope, H. G., Bureau, B., DeCol, C., Gruber, A. J., Hudson, J. I.,
        Jouvent, R., et al. (2000). Body image perception among men
        in three countries. *American Journal of Psychiatry, 157,*
        1297-1301.

Rodin, J., Silberstein, L., & Striegel-Moore, R. (1984). Women and
        weight: A normative discontent. In T. B. Sonderegger (Ed.),

Nebraska symposium on motivation: Psychology and gender (pp. 267-307). Lincoln: University of Nebraska Press.

Rosen, J. C., & Gross, J. (1987). Prevalence of weight reducing and weight gaining in adolescent boys and girls. *Health Psychology, 6,* 131-147.

Wilcox, K., & Laird, J. D. (2000). The impact of media images of super-slender women on women's self-esteem: Identification, social comparison, and self-perception. *Journal of Research in Personality, 34,* 278-286.

Body Esteem   12

Appendix

Body Esteem Scale for Adolescents and Adults:

General Questions

Instructions: Indicate how often you agree with the following statements, ranging from "never" (0) to "always" (4). Circle the appropriate number beside each statement.

Never = 0   Seldom = 1   Sometimes = 2   Often = 3   Always = 4

1. I like what I look like in pictures.   0 1 2 3 4

2. Other people consider me good looking.   0 1 2 3 4

3. I'm proud of my body.   0 1 2 3 4

4. I am preoccupied with trying to change my
   body weight.   0 1 2 3 4

5. I think my appearance would help me get
   a job.   0 1 2 3 4

6. I like what I see when I look in the mirror.   0 1 2 3 4

7. There are lots of things I'd change about
   my looks if I could.   0 1 2 3 4

8. I am satisfied with my weight.   0 1 2 3 4

9. I wish I looked better.   0 1 2 3 4

10. I really like what I weigh.   0 1 2 3 4

11. I wish I looked like someone else.   0 1 2 3 4

12. People my own age like my looks.   0 1 2 3 4

13. My looks upset me.   0 1 2 3 4

14. I'm as nice looking as most people.   0 1 2 3 4

15. I'm pretty happy about the way I look.   0 1 2 3 4

16. I feel I weigh the right amount for my height. 0 1 2 3 4

17. I feel ashamed of how I look.   0 1 2 3 4

18. Weighing myself depresses me.   0 1 2 3 4

Begin on new page

Body Esteem   13

19. My weight makes me unhappy.   0 1 2 3 4

20. My looks help me to get dates.   0 1 2 3 4

21. I worry about the way I look.   0 1 2 3 4

22. I think I have a good body.   0 1 2 3 4

23. I'm looking as nice as I'd like to.   0 1 2 3 4

PART 8

Documenting Sources: CMS and CSE Styles

▼ *TAKING IT ONLINE*

THE CHICAGO MANUAL OF STYLE ONLINE

http://www.chicagomanualofstyle.org/CMS_FAQ/new/new_questions01.html

This official Web site for *The Chicago Manual of Style* answers detailed questions from students, writers, and editors on topics such as commas, compounds, numbers, quotations, URLs, and usage.

COUNCIL OF SCIENCE EDITORS WEB SITE

http://www.councilscienceeditors.org

Formerly the Council of Biology Editors (CBE) and now the Council of Science Editors (CSE), this group sponsors *Scientific Style and Format*, the guide to CSE style. This official Web site supplies updates on the style and access to the latest electronic formats of the National Library of Medicine, which CSE generally follows.

For more advice on using the CMS and CSE styles, check the home page for your library or tutoring center, or refer to other reliable academic sites. Check the revision date for any site you use; rely on sites that reflect the most current editions of these style guides. Visit the following sites for information on many academic or professional style guides.

RESOURCES FOR DOCUMENTING SOURCES

http://owl.english.purdue.edu/handouts/research/r_docsources.html

This site lists style guides for about twenty fields, noting both the official sites of the organizations sponsoring the style guides and helpful academic and other sites with explanations useful to students.

CITATION STYLE GUIDES

http://www.libraries.wright.edu/find/reference/citing.html

Sponsored by the Wright State University Libraries, this page offers links to style guides and aids for citing sources in a variety of fields.

PART 8

Documenting Sources: CMS and CSE Styles

Guide to CMS Formats for Endnotes and Footnotes

Guide to CMS Formats for Bibliography Entries

Guide to CSE Formats for References

Books and Works Treated as Books
1. One Author 299
2. Two or More Authors 299
3. Organization or Group as Author 299
4. Editor 299
5. Translator 299
6. Conference Proceedings 299
7. Report 300

Articles from Periodicals and Selections from Books
8. Article in Journal Paginated by Volume 300
9. Article in Journal Paginated by Issue 300

10. Article with Organization or Group as Author 301
11. Entire Issue of Journal 301
12. Chapter in Edited Book or Selection in Anthology 301
13. Figure from Article 301

Online and Electronic Resources
14. Patent from Database or Information Service 301
15. Article: Online 301
16. Abstract: Online 302
17. Book: Online 302
18. CD-ROM Abstract 302

28 CMS Documentation Style

The CMS (*Chicago Manual of Style*) outlines a system for references using endnotes or footnotes. These notes are less compact than parenthetical references and may distract a reader, but they allow detailed citations.

STRATEGY Use CMS style in the arts and sciences to place citations in notes.

ACADEMIC SETTINGS
When readers expect "Turabian," "Chicago," or footnotes or endnotes

PUBLIC AND WORK SETTINGS
When your readers expect footnotes or endnotes
When readers won't need to consult each note as they read and might be distracted by names, page numbers, or dates in parentheses
When other writers or publications addressing your readers use CMS

The CMS style is one of two systems of documentation outlined in a reliable guide, *The Chicago Manual of Style* (15th edition, Chicago: University of Chicago Press, 2003). Its Web site at <http://www.chicagomanualofstyle.org/cmosfaq.html> answers many questions for writers and editors who routinely use CMS. This style is detailed for students in *A Manual for Writers of Research Papers, Theses, and Dissertations: Chicago Style for Students and Researchers,* by Kate L. Turabian and others (7th ed., Chicago: University of Chicago Press, 2007). CMS style is often called simply "Chicago" or "Turabian."

28a   CMS endnotes and footnotes

To indicate a reference in your text, add a superscript number above the line; number the references consecutively. Provide the details about the source at the end of the paper (in an endnote) or at the bottom of the page (in a footnote). (For advice on what to document, see 24c–f.)

TEXT   Wideman describes his impoverished childhood neighborhood as being not simply on "the wrong side of the tracks" but actually *"under* the tracks."[1]

NOTE   1. John Edgar Wideman, *Brothers and Keepers* (New York: Penguin Books, 1984), 39.

Most word-processing programs will position footnotes between the text and the bottom margin. Otherwise, you'll probably prefer endnotes. Most readers mark the endnote page for easy reference, but you should put all necessary information in the text, not the notes, in case a reader skips a note.

Place endnotes following your paper, after any appendix but before the bibliography, which alphabetically orders your sources. Supply the notes on a separate page with the centered heading "Notes." Indent the first line of each note like a paragraph; type its number on the line, followed by a period and a space. Do not indent any following lines. CMS suggests double-spacing all of your text, but Turabian suggests single-spaced notes. Although both alternatives appear in this chapter, we advise double-spacing for ease of reading.

Notes can also supply material of interest to only a few readers, but avoid excessive detail that may obscure a source reference.

TEXT   Another potential source of workplace misunderstanding comes from differences in the ways orders are given by men (directly) and women (indirectly, often as requests or questions).[2]

NOTE   2. Deborah Tannen, "How to Give Orders Like a Man," *New York Times Magazine,* August 18, 1994, 46. Tannen provides a detailed and balanced discussion of the ways men and women use language in *Talking from 9 to 5* (New York: William Morrow, 1994).

28b CMS note examples

A typical note provides the author's name in regular order, the title, publication information, and the page reference.

Books and Works Treated as Books

MODEL FORMAT FOR BOOKS AND WORKS TREATED AS BOOKS

note	comma		colon
number space	+ space space		+ space

↓ ↓　　　↓　　↓　　　　　↓

1. Author(s), *Title* (Place of Publication: Publisher, Year), Page number(s).

↑

comma + space

1. One Author

1. Bobby Bridger, *Buffalo Bill and Sitting Bull: Inventing the Wild West* (Austin: University of Texas Press, 2002), 297.

2. Two Authors

2. William H. Gerdts and Will South, *California Impressionism* (New York: Abbeville Press, 1998), 214.

3. Three Authors

3. Michael Wood, Bruce Cole, and Adelheid Gealt, *Art of the Western World* (New York: Summit Books, 1989), 206-10.

4. Four or More Authors

Follow the name of the first author with *et al.* (meaning *and others*). (Generally supply all the names, up to ten, in the bibliography entry.)

4. Anthony Slide *et al.*, *The American Film Industry: A Historical Dictionary* (New York: Greenwood Press, 1986), 124.

5. No Author Given

5. *The Great Utopia* (New York: Guggenheim Museum, 1992), 661.

6. One Editor

To emphasize the editor, translator, or compiler, begin with that name.

6. Robert H. Ferrell, ed., *Dear Bess: The Letters from Harry to Bess Truman 1910-1959* (New York: W. W. Norton, 1983), 71-72.

The word *by* with the author's name may follow the title but isn't needed if the name appears in the title.

7. Two or More Editors

7. Cris Mazza, Jeffrey DeShell, and Elisabeth Sheffield, eds., *Chick-Lit 2: No Chick Vics* (Normal, IL: Black Ice Books, 1996), 173-86.

8. Author and Editor

Name any editor (ed.), translator (trans.), compiler (comp.), or some combination of these after the title.

8. Francis Bacon, *The New Organon*, ed. Lisa Jardine, trans. Michael Silverthorne (Cambridge: Cambridge University Press, 2000), 45.

9. Edition Following the First

After the title, abbreviate the edition: *3rd ed.* ("third edition") or *rev. ed.* ("revised edition").

9. Thomas E. Skidmore and Peter H. Smith, *Modern Latin America*, 6th ed. (New York: Oxford University Press, 2004), 243.

10. Reprint

Note original publication of a reprint or paperback edition.

10. Henri Frankfort *et al.*, *The Intellectual Adventure of Ancient Man* (1946; repr., Chicago: University of Chicago Press, 1977), 202-4.

11. Multivolume Work

If you cite the whole work, include the total number of volumes after the title. Separate volume and page numbers for a specific volume with a colon. For a separately titled volume, give the volume number and name after the main title and only a page reference at the end.

11. Sigmund Freud, *The Standard Edition of the Complete Psychological Works of Sigmund Freud*, trans. James Strachey (London: Hogarth Press, 1953), 11:180.

Articles from Periodicals and Selections from Books

MODEL FORMAT FOR ARTICLES

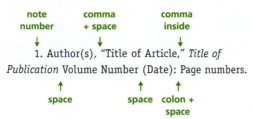

1. Author(s), "Title of Article," *Title of Publication* Volume Number (Date): Page numbers.

12. Article in Journal Paginated by Volume

When page numbers run continuously through the issues in a volume, give only the volume number. Supply specific page numbers for part or inclusive numbers for all of an article, such as 98–114.

12. Lily Zubaidah Rahim, "The Road Less Traveled: Islamic Militancy in Southeast Asia," *Critical Asian Studies* 35 (2003): 224.

13. Article in Journal Paginated by Issue

If each issue of a journal begins with page 1, give the volume number and *no.* ("number") with the issue number. If the issue is identified by month or season, include this inside the parentheses with the year: (Winter 1994) or (February 1996).

13. Jose Pinera, "A Chilean Model for Russia," *Foreign Affairs* 79, no. 5 (2000): 62-73.

14. Article in Magazine

Follow the magazine title with the date, for example, *November 25, 2006.*

14. Joan W. Gandy, "Portrait of Natchez," *American Legacy*, Fall 2000, 51-52.

15. Article in Newspaper

Identify newspapers by date: February 4, 2002. Omit the section (*sec.*) number or letter and the page, which may change in different editions. Add the city, state, or country, as needed: *Westerly (R.I.) Sun*, *Times* (London).

15. Janny Scott, "A Bull Market for Grant, A Bear Market for Lee," *New York Times*, September 30, 2000.

16. Chapter in Edited Book

Follow the title with *ed.* and the editor's name.

16. John Matviko, "Television Satire and the Presidency: The Case of *Saturday Night Live*," in *Hollywood's White House: The American*

Presidency in Film and History, ed. Peter C. Rollins and John E. O'Connor (Lexington: University of Kentucky Press, 2003), 341.

17. Selection in Anthology

17. W. E. B. Du Bois, "The Call of Kansas," in *W. E. B. Du Bois: A Reader*, ed. David Levering Lewis (New York: Henry Holt, 1995), 113.

Field and Media Resources

18. Interview Unpublished

For unpublished interviews by someone else, supply the name of the person interviewed, *interview by*, the name of the interviewer, the date, and the place where the interview is stored as well as any file number (*Erie County Historical Society, Buffalo, NY*). Identify interviews you conduct as *interview by author*; include the place and date of the interview.

18. LeJon Will, interview by author, May 22, 2007, transcript, Tempe, AZ.

19. Audio or Video Recording

Start with the title unless the recording features a particular individual. Give names and roles (if appropriate) of performers or others. Add any recording number (audio) after the company.

19. *James Baldwin*, VHS, directed by Karen Thorsen (San Francisco: California Newsreel, 1990).

Online and Electronic Resources

20. Book: Online

20. Sharon Marcus, *Apartment Stories: City and Home in Nineteenth-Century Paris and London* (Berkeley: University of California Press, 1999), http://ark.cdlib.org/ark:13030/ft0d5n99jz/ (accessed October 15, 2004).

21. Older Book: Online

For a book previously in print, include all standard information, the URL, and your access date if expected in the field.

21. Charles Darwin, *On the Origin of Species by Means of Natural Selection, or the Preservation of Favoured Races in the Struggle for Lif*e (1859; Project Gutenberg, 1998), http://www.gutenberg.org/etext/1228 (accessed November 1, 2006).

22. Journal Article: Online

> 22. Alfred Willis, "A Survey of Surviving Buildings of the Krotona Colony in Hollywood," *Architronic* 8, no. 1 (1999), http://architronic.saed.kent.edu/ (accessed September 29, 2002).

23. Magazine Article: Online

> 23. Alexander Barnes Dryer, "Our Liberian Legacy," *The Atlantic Online*, July 30, 2003, http://www.theatlantic.com/unbound/flashbks/liberia.htm (accessed October 24, 2005).

24. Newspaper Article: Online

> 24. Joshua Klein, "Scaring Up a Good Movie," *Chicago Tribune Online Edition*, October 28, 2003, http://www.chicagotribune.com/ (accessed December 28, 2005).

25. Web Site

> 25. Smithsonian Center for Folklife and Cultural Heritage, "2002 Smithsonian Folklife Festival: The Silk Road," Smithsonian Institution, http://www.folklife.si.edu/CFCH/festival2002.htm (accessed October 27, 2005).

26. Online Posting

> 26. Justin M. Sanders, e-mail to alt.war.civil.usa, February 15, 2002, http://groups.google.com/groups?q=civil+war&hl= en&lr=&ie=UTF-8&selm=civil-war-usa/faq/part2_1013770939%40rtfm.mit.edu&rnum=1 (accessed October 21, 2004).

27. CD-ROM

Add the medium, *CD-ROM*.

> 27. Mark Rose, ed., "Elements of Theater," *The Norton Shakespeare Workshop CD-ROM*, CD-ROM, version 1.1. (New York: Norton Publishing, 1997).

Multiple Sources and Sources Cited in Prior Notes

28. Multiple Sources

Separate several references with semicolons. Give the entries in the order in which they are cited in the text.

> 28. See Greil Marcus, *Mystery Train: Images of America in Rock 'n Roll Music* (New York: E. P. Dutton, 1975), 119; Susan Orlean, "All Mixed Up," *New Yorker*, June 22, 1992, 90; and Cornel West, "Learning to Talk of Race," *New York Times Magazine*, August 2, 1992, 24.

29. Work Cited More Than Once

In your first reference, provide full information. Later, provide only the author's last name, a short title, and the page.

> 29. Pinera, "Chilean," 63.

> 30. Wood, Cole, and Gealt, *Art*, 207.

If two notes in a row refer to the same source, you can use the traditional *ibid.* (from Latin *ibidem*, "in the same place") for the second note. Add a new page reference if the specific page is different.

> 31. Tarr, "'A Man,'" 183.

> 32. Ibid.

> 33. Ibid., 186.

28c CMS bibliography

In addition to your notes, provide an alphabetical list of sources, titled "Selected Bibliography," "Works Cited," "References," or something similar. Place this list on a separate page at the end of your paper; center the title two inches from the top. Continue the page numbering used for the text. Although we show single-spaced entries below to conserve space, we recommend double-spacing throughout for ease of reading. (Check with your instructor.) Do not indent the first line, but indent any subsequent lines five spaces. Alphabetize by authors' last names or by the first word of the title, excluding *A*, *An*, and *The*, if the author is unknown.

Books and Works Treated as Books

MODEL FORMAT FOR BOOKS AND WORKS TREATED AS BOOKS

period +   period +   colon +
space   space   space
  ↓   ↓   ↓
Author(s). *Title*. Place of Publication:

  Publisher, Date.
  ↑   ↑
indent   comma + space
5 spaces

1. One Author

Bridger, Bobby. *Buffalo Bill and Sitting Bull: Inventing the Wild West.*
  Austin: University of Texas Press, 2002.

2. Two Authors

> Gerdts, William H., and Will South. *California Impressionism*. New York: Abbeville Press, 1998.

3. Three Authors

> Wood, Michael, Bruce Cole, and Adelheid Gealt. *Art of the Western World*. New York: Summit Books, 1989.

4. Four or More Authors

> Slide, Anthony, Val Almen Darez, Robert Gitt, and Susan Perez Prichard. *The American Film Industry: A Historical Dictionary*. New York: Greenwood Press, 1986.

5. No Author Given

> *The Great Utopia*. New York: Guggenheim Museum, 1992.

6. One Editor

> Ferrell, Robert H., ed. *Dear Bess: The Letters from Harry to Bess Truman 1910-1959*. New York: W. W. Norton, 1983.

7. Two or More Editors

> Mazza, Cris, Jeffrey DeShell, and Elisabeth Sheffield, eds. *Chick-Lit 2: No Chick Vics*. Normal, IL: Black Ice Books, 1996.

8. Author and Editor

> Bacon, Francis. *The New Organon*. Edited by Lisa Jardine. Translated by Michael Silverthorne. Cambridge: Cambridge University Press, 2000.

9. Edition Following the First

> Skidmore, Thomas E., and Peter H. Smith. *Modern Latin America*. 6th ed. New York: Oxford University Press, 2004.

10. Reprint

> Frankfort, Henri, H. A. Frankfort, John A. Wilson, Thorkild Jacobsen, and William A. Irving. *The Intellectual Adventure of Ancient Man*. 1946. Reprint, Chicago: University of Chicago Press, 1977.

11. Multivolume Work

> Freud, Sigmund. *The Standard Edition of the Complete Psychological Works of Sigmund Freud*. Translated by James Strachey. Vol. 11. London: Hogarth Press, 1953.

Articles from Periodicals and Selections from Books

MODEL FORMAT FOR ARTICLES AND SELECTIONS

period +
space   period   space   space
↓   ↓   ↓   ↓
Author(s). "Title." *Name of Publication* Volume (Date): Pages.
                                                    ↑
                                          colon + space

12. Article in Journal Paginated by Volume

> Rahim, Lily Zubaidah. "The Road Less Traveled: Islamic Militancy in Southeast Asia." *Critical Asian Studies* 35 (2003): 209-32.

13. Article in Journal Paginated by Issue

> Pinera, Jose. "A Chilean Model for Russia." *Foreign Affairs* 79, no. 5 (2000): 62-73.

14. Article in Magazine

> Gandy, Joan W. "Portrait of Natchez." *American Legacy*, Fall 2000, 51-52.

15. Article in Newspaper

Do not include a newspaper article in your bibliography unless it is particularly important to your discussion.

> Scott, Janny. "A Bull Market for Grant, A Bear Market for Lee." *New York Times*, September 30, 2000, sec. A.

16. Chapter in Edited Book

> Matviko, John. "Television Satire and the Presidency: The Case of *Saturday Night Live*." In *Hollywood's White House: The American Presidency in Film and History*, edited by Peter C. Rollins and John E. O'Connor, 341–60. Lexington: University of Kentucky Press, 2003.

17. Selection in Anthology

Du Bois, W. E. B. "The Call of Kansas." In *W. E. B. Du Bois: A Reader*,
edited by David Levering Lewis, 101-21. New York: Henry Holt,
1995.

Field and Media Resources

18. Interview Unpublished

Generally treat an unpublished interview as a personal or informal
communication, cited only in your notes. (See Entry 18, p. 280.)

19. Audio or Video Recording

James Baldwin. VHS. Directed by Karen Thorsen. San Francisco: California
Newsreel, 1990.

Online and Electronic Resources

20. Book: Online

Marcus, Sharon. *Apartment Stories: City and Home in Nineteenth-Century
Paris and London*. Berkeley: University of California Press, 1999.
http://ark.cdlib.org/ark:13030/ft0d5n99jz/ (accessed October 15,
2004).

21. Older Book: Online

Darwin, Charles. *On the Origin of Species by Means of Natural Selection, or
the Preservation of Favoured Races in the Struggle for Life*. 1859.
Project Gutenberg, 1998. http://www.gutenberg.org/etext/1228
(accessed November 1, 2006).

22. Journal Article: Online

Willis, Alfred. "A Survey of Surviving Buildings of the Krotona Colony in
Hollywood." *Architronic* 8, no. 1 (1999). http://architronic.saed.kent.
edu./ (accessed September 29, 2002).

23. Magazine Article: Online

Dryer, Alexander Barnes. "Our Liberian Legacy." *The Atlantic Online*, July
30, 2003. http://www.theatlantic.com/unbound/flashbks/liberia.htm
(accessed October 24, 2005).

24. Newspaper Article: Online

Do not include a newspaper article in your bibliography unless it is particularly important to your discussion.

> Klein, Joshua. "Scaring Up a Good Movie." *Chicago Tribune Online Edition*, October 28, 2003. http://www.chicagotribune.com/ (accessed December 28, 2005).

25. Web Site

> Smithsonian Center for Folklife and Cultural Heritage. "2002 Smithsonian Folklife Festival: The Silk Road." Smithsonian Institution. http://www.folklife.si.edu/CFCH/festival2002.htm (accessed October 27, 2005).

26. Online Posting

Treat an online posting as a personal or informal communication, cited only in your notes. (See Entry 26, p. 281.)

27. CD-ROM

> Rose, Mark, ed. "Elements of Theater." *The Norton Shakespeare Workshop CD-ROM*. CD-ROM, Version 1.1. New York: Norton Publishing, 1997.

Multiple Sources

28. Multiple Sources

When a note mentions more than one source, list each one separately in your bibliography.

28d Sample CMS Paper

The following paper contains a title page in CMS style and includes CMS footnotes and bibliography.

Center title

STUDY DRUGS: THE NEW DRUG CRAZE AMONG COLLEGE STUDENTS

**Begin
one-third
of the way
down the
page**

Jenna Ianucilli

Dr. Schwegler

Wrt 106

March 2, 2007

**Center and
double-
space all
lines**

Indent ½"

1"   ½"
1

Doublespace

1   Have you ever had to stay up all night to cram for a bio exam? Have you ever had to write three papers in one night because you put them all off until the last night? Ever felt like you could use something that could make you focus on your work during an all-night study session? Many people think they have

Introduces topic

found an effective strategy in the newest drug craze to sweep college campuses: drugs to increase academic performance.

2   The drugs they use are normally prescribed for attention deficit hyperactivity disorder (ADHD), with the most common drugs being Ritalin and Adderall. The

1"   1"

drugs are usually prescribed to people suffering from ADHD to allow them to reach normal functioning level by stimulating the frontal lobes of the brain,

Superscript numbers refer to endnotes

areas that monitor task performance;[1] college students, however, often use the drugs as study aids. Dr. Eric Heiligenstein, a psychiatrist at the University of Wisconsin who studies substance abuse,

Two ¶s provide background and explain the problem

points out that when taken by people with normal brain function, "The drugs can give healthy people an almost superhuman ability to focus for long periods."[2]

3   The drugs are stimulants, in the class of cocaine, caffeine, amphetamines, and methamphetamines, so the result in normal people is to feel like they are on "speed." They will have huge amounts of energy and will require less sleep. That can be a useful feeling

1"

2

when it is almost midnight and one has to cram
in lots of studying for an organic chemistry exam
at eight o'clock the next morning, yet side effects
can include emotional and physical strains and
anxiety and, in some cases, addiction or
dependence.

4   In a survey of 13,500 college students conducted
by the American College Health Association, 94
percent of respondents reported feeling overwhelmed
by everything they had to do at school.[3] College life
creates increased stress. Extracurricular activities
that build résumés for graduate schools create
strain. Students sleep less than normal. They worry
more than ever about financial, social, and academic
pressures.

5   In a survey I conducted, all the students believed
that the competitiveness of college life might cause
someone to choose to take drugs to improve academic
performance.[4] The students also agreed that parents,
peers, relatives, and teachers were other sources of
pressure. Jobs are yet another cause of stress. Some
college students work a substantial number of hours
every week, not just for extra spending money but also
to lighten some of the heavy debt load of student
loans they will have once they graduate. For many, it
is easier to pop a pill to aid concentration than to
have to struggle to fit more sleep time into a full
schedule of classes, extracurricular activities, parties,

**Focus on
danger**

**Writer
draws on
own field
research**

**CMS does
not re-
quire
note, but
instruc-
tor did**

3

and work. Such students are at risk for misusing or abusing study drugs.

Article cited
in footnote
summarizes
studies at
Johns Hop-
kins and
Wisconsin

6   According to a 2002 Johns Hopkins University study, up to 20 percent of college-age students have regularly used drugs to enhance academic performance, and another study at the University of Wisconsin confirmed this.[5] Dr. Tim Wilens of Massachusetts General Hospital reports that a quarter of college-age students have tried stimulants such as Ritalin or Adderall without prescriptions.[6] These are staggering

Problem is
widespread

figures, which show the great lengths to which students will go to gain an edge.

7   Where do the drugs come from, and how do they work? The drugs were developed to treat attention deficit hyperactivity disorder (ADHD), a condition that begins appearing in children in their preschool years. Between 30 and 70 percent of children with the disorder will continue to exhibit symptoms in their adult years. The principal characteristics of ADHD are inattention, hyperactivity, and impulsivity.[7]

8   Medications are one of the main treatments for ADHD. The most effective medications are stimulants such as Adderall and Ritalin. For many people afflicted with ADHD, the stimulants dramatically

How the
drugs work

reduce hyperactivity and impulsivity and improve the ability to focus, work, and learn.[8]

9   They have similar effects for college students, allowing them to work more efficiently while

4

requiring less sleep. Adderall stimulates the central

nervous system (the brain and nerves) by increasing

the amount of certain chemicals, such as dopamine and

norepinephrine, in the brain. These chemicals or

neurotransmitters help the brain send signals between

nerve cells. Adderall helps restore the balance of

these neurotransmitters to the parts of the brain

that control the ability to focus and pay attention.[9]

"Think of a staticky radio signal," says Anthony

Rostain, Professor of Psychiatry and Pediatrics at

the University of Pennsylvania School of Medicine.

"You turn the dial, and you get a better signal--the

focusing and concentration are better."[10]

10 Ritalin is a mild stimulant to the central nervous

system. The exact way that it works is unknown. The

U.S. Drug Enforcement Administration states that the

medication produces the same effects as cocaine and

amphetamines.[11] Adderall prescriptions have grown

greatly, overtaking the once-popular medication

Ritalin as the leader in treating ADHD. Adderall is

the most common study drug as well.[12]

11 These seemingly innocuous academic-enhancing drugs

can have serious and long-lasting side effects. For

normal, healthy people who take them, the drugs can

cause emotional and physical strain.[13] Side effects

of Ritalin include insomnia, nervousness, drowsiness,

dizziness, headache, blurred vision, tics, abdominal

pain, nausea, vomiting, decreased appetite or

Discussion of Adderall

Discussion of Ritalin

Negative effects of the drugs

5

weight loss, and slower weight gain. More serious side effects include irregular or fast heartbeat, confusion, and liver damage.[14] Side effects of Adderall include irregular heartbeat, very high blood pressure, hallucinations, abnormal behavior, and confusion. Other side effects include restlessness or tremor, anxiety or nervousness, headache, dizziness, insomnia, dryness of the mouth or unpleasant taste, diarrhea or constipation, and impotence or changes in sex drive.[15] Dr. John D. Hall, an addiction psychiatrist working in student mental health services at the University of Florida, says, "If you don't have ADHD, Adderall or Ritalin can cause significant anxiety."[16]

More negative effects

12   Users of study drugs are also at risk for dependence or addiction; users may become addicted to the energy the drug gives them.[17] With continued use of Adderall, a person can develop a tolerance and need for a higher dose to achieve the same effects. Physical and psychological dependence can also occur. Ritalin can produce physical dependence as well.[18] There is also a risk of overdose, especially when the drug is obtained through a friend's prescription. Adderall or Ritalin dosage is carefully determined by height, weight, and symptoms. Another person's dosage can be dangerous, particularly if the person is bigger.[19]

13   In a society where the notion of popping a pill to solve problems is encouraged by advertisements

6

suggesting that you "ask your doctor if Drug X is right for you," it seems logical for students to look for something that will help them stay alert longer and concentrate harder, especially if there are no obvious side effects. These seemingly innocuous and academically beneficial drugs can have serious side effects, however.

14   Though there have been no reported overdoses of study drugs, their use is still a serious problem, on a par with the use of performance-enhancing drugs in sports. The side effects of the drugs outweigh any academic advantage, and their use raises ethical questions as well in that it gives some students an unfair advantage. Dr. Hall, the addiction psychiatrist, offers simple advice: "Don't depend on a pill to get you through the pressures of exam week. The long-term solution is to plan ahead, do as well as you can in your exams, and take life as it comes."[20]

**Final
warning**

2"   7

Center → NOTES

Double-space   1. Deborah Chun, "Abuse of Drugs for ADHD Up for Finals," *GainesvilleSun.com,* April 29, 2004, http://www.psychiatry.ufl.edu/Gainesvillesun_com2.htm (accessed January 20, 2007).

Indent ½"   2. William Campbell Douglass, "College-Age Students Use ADHD Drugs to Make the Grade," *Real Health Breakthroughs,* January 14, 2005, http://www.healthiernews.com/dailydose/dd200501/dd20050114.html (accessed February 12, 2007).

Endnotes listed in order in which they appear in the paper

3. Richard Kadison, "Getting an Edge--Use of Stimulants and Antidepressants in College," *The New England Journal of Medicine* 353 (2005): 1089.

4. Jenna Ianucilli, Survey of students' attitudes on academic-enhancing drugs, unpublished raw data, University of Rhode Island, 2007.

Subsequent references to the same source include author's last name, shortened title, and page numbers

5. Kadison, "Getting an Edge," 1090.

6. New York University Health Center, "Health Promotion and Wellness--Study Drugs," New York University, http://www.nyu.edu/nyuhc/studydrugs (accessed January 31, 2007).

7. National Institute of Mental Health, *Attention Deficit Hyperactivity Disorder* (Baltimore: National Institute of Mental Health, 2003), 5.

8. Michael I. Reiff, *ADHD: A Complete and Authoritative Guide* (Chicago: American Academy of Pediatrics, 2004), 23.

***Ibid.* is used for a subsequent reference to the same source when there are no intervening references**

9. Ibid., 15.

10. Ibid., 24.

11. New York University Health Center, "Health Promotion and Wellness."

12. National Institute of Mental Health, *Attention Deficit Hyperactivity Disorder,* 7.

8

13. Kadison, "Getting an Edge," 1090.

14. New York University Health Center, "Health Promotion and Wellness."

15. Ibid.

16. Chun, "Abuse of Drugs."

17. Kadison, "Getting an Edge," 1091.

18. New York University Health Center, "Health Promotion and Wellness."

19. Chun, "Abuse of Drugs."

20. Ibid.

2"   9

Center ────────────▶   BIBLIOGRAPHY

Double-space Chun, Deborah. "Abuse of Drugs for ADHD Up for

First line of
each entry is   Finals." *GainesvilleSun.com*, April 29, 2004.
flush with
the left-hand   http://www.psychiatry.ufl.edu/Gainesvillesun_
margin;
subsequent   com2.htm (accessed January 20, 2007).
lines are
indented ½" Douglass, William Campbell. "College-Age Students Use

                       ADHD Drugs to Make the Grade." *Real Health*

                       Breakthroughs, January 14, 2005.

        1"   http://www.healthiernews.com/dailydose/   1"
     ◀──────▶   dd200501/dd20050114.html (accessed February 12,

                       2007).

CMS does   Ianucilli, Jenna. Survey of Students' Attitudes on
not provide
a form for   Academic-Enhancing Drugs. Unpublished raw data,
this kind of
entry; writer   University of Rhode Island, 2007.
provides
key infor- Kadison, Richard. "Getting an Edge--Use of Stimulants
mation
                       and Antidepressants in College." *The New England*

                       Journal of Medicine 353 (2005): 1089-91.

Entries are National Institute of Mental Health. *Attention Deficit*
listed alpha-
betically   *Hyperactivity Disorder.* Baltimore: National
according to
the author's   Institute of Mental Health, 2003.
last name
             New York University Health Center. "Health Promotion

                       and Wellness--Study Drugs." New York University.

                       http://www.nyu.edu/nyuhc/studydrugs (accessed

                       January 31, 2007).

             Reiff, Michael I. *ADHD: A Complete and Authoritative*

                       Guide. Chicago: American Academy of Pediatrics,

                       2004.

29 CSE Documentation Style

One widely used form of documentation in the sciences is the CSE (Council of Science Editors) style. CSE advocates a simplified international scientific style and presents three options for documentation: a name-and-year, a number, and a name system. This handbook focuses on the first two systems.

STRATEGY Use CSE style in physical, life, and technical sciences.

ACADEMIC SETTINGS
When readers expect CSE or "scientific documentation"

PUBLIC AND WORK SETTINGS
When a professional group or company division expects you to use CSE or some type of scientific documentation
When readers prefer a name-and-year or number system
When other writers or publications addressing audiences like yours use CSE, modified CSE, or a similar style

---

CSE style tends to vary more than the other styles, mainly because different scientific and engineering fields have different requirements. Check expectations with your instructor or your readers. If you are advised to follow the style of a specific journal, find its guidelines for authors, or compare examples from it with general CSE advice. For more information, see *Scientific Style and Format: The CSE Manual for Authors, Editors, and Publishers* (7th ed., Reston, VA: Council of Science Editors, 2006) or the CSE Web site at <http://www.councilscienceeditors.org>.

29a CSE in-text citation examples

You can use one of two methods for CSE in-text references.

1 Use the name-and-year method

With this method, include the name of the author and the publication date in parentheses unless you mention the name in the text.

PARENTHETICAL   Decreases in the use of lead, cadmium, and zinc have resulted in a "very large decrease in the large-scale pollution of the troposphere" (Boutron 1991).

NAMED IN TEXT   Boutron (1991) found that decreases in the use of lead, cadmium, and zinc have resulted in a "very large decrease in the large-scale pollution of the troposphere."

Distinguish several works by the same author, all dated in a single year, by letters (*a, b*, and so forth) after the date.

2 Use the number method

With this method, use numbers instead of names of authors. The numbers can be placed in parentheses in the text or raised above the line; they correspond to numbered works in your reference list.

Decreases in the use of lead, cadmium, and zinc have reduced pollution in the troposphere (1).

Your first option is to number your in-text citations consecutively as they appear and to arrange them accordingly on the references page. Your second is to alphabetize your references first, number them, and then use the corresponding number in your paper. Because only the number appears in your text, you should mention the author's name in the discussion if it is important.

29b CSE reference list

You may use "References" to head your list. The samples below follow the number method. If you use the consecutive number (citation-sequence) method, arrange your references according to which work comes first in your paper, which second, and so on. The sample paper in 29c uses this method. If you use the alphabetized number method, arrange your list alphabetically, and then number the entries. If you use the name-and-year method instead, alphabetize the references by the last name of the main author, and then order works by the same author by date of publication. Place the date after the author's name, followed by a period.

Books and Works Treated as Books

MODEL FORMAT FOR BOOKS AND WORKS TREATED AS BOOKS

NAME-AND-YEAR METHOD

period +   period +   period +
space   space   space
↓   ↓   ↓
Author(s). Date. Title of work. Place of
Publication: Publisher. Total pages.
↑   ↑
colon   period
+ space   + space

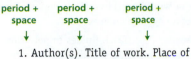

period + space   period + space   period + space

1. Author(s). Title of work. Place of
   Publication: Publisher; Date. Total pages.

colon + space   semicolon + space   period + space

1. One Author

Include the total number of pages at the end of the entry for a book.

1. Bishop RH. Modern control systems analysis and design using MATLAB and SIMULINK. Menlo Park (CA): Addison Wesley; 1997. 251 p.

2. Two or More Authors

2. Freeman JM, Kelly MT, Freeman JB. The epilepsy diet treatment: an introduction to the ketogenic diet. New York (NY): Demo; 1994. 180 p.

3. Organization or Group as Author

If an organization is also the publisher, include the name in both places. You can replace the name with a well-known acronym.

3. Intergovernmental Panel on Climate Change. Climate change 1995: the science of climate change. Cambridge (England): Cambridge University Press; 1996. 572 p.

4. Editor

4. Dolphin D, editor. Biomimetic chemistry. Washington (DC): American Chemical Society; 1980. 437 p.

5. Translator

If the work has an editor as well as a translator, place a semicolon after *translator*, name the editor, and add *editor*.

5. Jacob F. The logic of life: a history of heredity. Spillmann BE, translator. New York (NY): Pantheon Books; 1982. 348 p.

6. Conference Proceedings

6. Witt I, editor. Protein C: biochemical and medical aspects. Proceedings of the International Workshop; 1984 Jul 9-11; Titisee, Germany. Berlin (DE): De Gruyter; 1985. 195 p.

7. Report

Include the information a reader would need to order a report. Bracket a widely accepted acronym following an agency's name.

> 7. Environmental Protection Agency (US) [EPA]. Guides to pollution prevention: the automotive repair industry. Washington (DC): US EPA; 1991. 46 p. Available from: EPA Office of Research and Development, Washington, DC; EPA/625/7-91/013.

Articles from Periodicals and Selections from Books

MODEL FORMAT FOR ARTICLES

NAME-AND-YEAR METHOD

period + space   period + space   period + space

Author(s). Year. Title of article. Title of Journal. Volume Number:Pages.

period + space   colon + no space

NUMBER METHOD

period + space   period + space   period + space

1. Author(s). Title of article. Title of Journal. Date;Volume Number:Pages.

period + space   semicolon + no space   colon + no space

8. Article in Journal Paginated by Volume

> 8. Yousef YA, Yu LL. Potential contamination of groundwater from Cu, Pb, and Zn in wet detention ponds receiving highway runoff. J Environ Sci Hlth. 1992;27:1033-1044.

9. Article in Journal Paginated by Issue

Give the issue number in parentheses with no space after the volume number.

> 9. Boutron CF. Decrease in anthropogenic lead, cadmium and zinc in Greenland snows since the late 1960's. Nature. 1991;353(6340):153-155, 160.

10. Article with Organization or Group as Author

> 10. Derek Sims Associates. Why and how of acoustic testing. Environ Eng. 1991;4(1):10-12.

11. Entire Issue of Journal

> 11. Savage A, editor. Proceedings of the workshop on the zoo-university connection: collaborative efforts in the conservation of endangered primates. Zoo Biol. 1989; (1 Suppl).

12. Chapter in Edited Book or Selection in Anthology

The first name and title refer to the selection and the second to the book in which it appears.

> 12. Moro M. Supply and conservation efforts for nonhuman primates. In: Gengozian N, Deinhardt F, editors. Marmosets in experimental medicine. Basel (Switzerland): S. Karger AG; 1978. p. 37-40.

13. Figure from Article

Identify a figure (or graphic) by name, number, and page.

> 13. Kanaori Y, Kawakami SI, Yairi K. Space-time distribution patterns of destructive earthquakes in the inner belt of central Japan. Eng Geol. 1991;31(3-4):209-230. (Table 1, p. 216).

Online and Electronic Resources
CSE recommends following the National Library of Medicine formats for Internet sources, reflected here and available through the CSE Web site.

14. Patent from Database or Information Service

> 14. Collins FS, Drumm ML, Dawson DC, Wilkinson DJ, inventors; Method of testing potential cystic fibrosis treating compounds using cells in culture. United States patent US 5,434,086. 1995 Jul 18. Available from: Lexis/Nexis/Lexpatlibrary/ALLfile.

15. Article: Online

> 15. Grolmusz V. On the weak mod m representation of Boolean functions. Chi J Theor Comp Sci [Internet]. 1995 [cited 1996 May 3]; 100-105. Available from: http://www.csuchicago.edu/publication/cjtcs/articles/1995/2/contents.html

16. Abstract: Online

16. Smithies O, Maeda N. Gene targeting approaches to complex genetic diseases: atherosclerosis and essential hypertension [abstract]. Proceedings of the Natl Acad Sci USA [Internet]. 1995 [cited 1996 Jan 21]; 92(12):5266–5272. [1 screen]. Available from: Lexis/Medline/ABST.

17. Book: Online

17. Darwin C. On the origin of species by means of natural selection, or the preservation of favoured races in the struggle for life [Internet]. London (England): Down, Bromley, Kent; 1859 [cited 2007 Feb 12]. Available from: http://www.gutenberg.org./etext/1228

18. CD-ROM Abstract

18. MacDonald R, Fleming MF, Barry KL. Risk factors associated with alcohol abuse in college students [abstract]. Am J Drug and Alc Abuse [CD-ROM]. 2001;17:439-449. Available from: SilverPlatter File: PsycLIT Item: 79-13172.

29c Sample CSE paper

The paper that follows contains a title page and abstract in CSE style. It also includes in-text references following the number format and a "References" list in the same format.

Center title

Predator Occurrence at Piping Plover Nesting Sites
in Rhode Island

Begin one-third of the way down the page

Title indicates that paper will report on a scientific research project

Anne S. Bloomfield
University of Rhode Island

Center and double-space all lines

WRT 333
Professor Robert A. Schwegler
17 April 2006

Abstract

Abstract provides concise summary of content

During the spring of 2006, I recorded predator occurrence based only on animal tracks on two beaches in Rhode Island. The main objective of the study was to predict the occurrence of potential predator species on piping plover (*Charadrius melodus*) nesting grounds in the area. I quantified the spatial distribution of predators at both beaches. Predators showed a preference for an area that was easily accessible to a salt pond from the barrier beach ($P < 0.05$ Table 1). Predator species present included gulls (*Laridae*), striped skunk (*Mephitis mephitis*), muskrat (*Ondatra zibethicus*) and red fox (*Vulpes vulpes*). This method was simple and low cost, but I found flaws in the experimental design that should be addressed in future studies.

Table 1. Chi-squared analysis showing preference of predators for a given area on a piping plover nesting site at Moonstone Beach, Rhode Island, spring 2006

Actual Segment	Sign	No Sign
0–500	1	9
501–1000	1	9
1001–1500	1	9
1501–2000	11	7

Expected Segment	Sign	No Sign
0–500	2.917	1.458
501–1000	2.917	1.458
1001–1500	2.917	1.458
1501–2000	5.250	12.750

$P < 0.001$

Bloomfield 1

1   In Rhode Island, the threatened piping plover
(*Charadrius melodus*) prefers to breed on open beaches and
sandflats.[1] Habitat destruction due to development of
beaches and predation are contributing factors to the
birds' decline.[2] For most ground-nesting bird species, the
primary cause of nesting mortality is due to egg
predation.[3] I investigated the spatial distribution and
abundance of potential predators. This information,
coupled with information on plover nesting success, could
be used to better manage the species.

2   The main objectives of my research were to discover
what types of predators occur at potential breeding sites
and their spatial distribution along the beach. I was
also interested in which species occurred most often. My
data were collected solely based on mammalian and avian
tracks on sites at the breeding grounds. Information on
such studies has not been easily located in peer-reviewed
literature. This approach was low cost, as the researcher
only needs to visually search the beach for tracks. No
restraint techniques or cameras were used to capture live
predators physically or on film. A pen and paper were the
only materials needed to collect data on site.

3   The results of my study will help wildlife
biologists to implement the proper management strategies
for predator control on the beaches. If the species
predating the nests are better understood, then
management strategies can be tailored to a specific
species or a specific area.

Focuses on specific topic and problem

Specific phenomenon being studied

Potential usefulness of research

States two closely related research questions

Literature review— little prior work on the subject

29c
CSE

**Center headings
if used**

Study Area

**Describes
location
for the
study**

4   I conducted fieldwork at Moonstone Beach at Trustom
Pond National Wildlife Refuge (NWR) and East Beach at
Ninigret NWR. The study was focused at Moonstone Beach,
but additional data were collected at Ninigret. These
areas are important seasonal nesting areas for the piping
plover. Both areas are barrier beaches with grassy dunes,
bordering large coastal salt ponds. Moonstone Beach had a
particular section which measured about 62 m that was
free of vegetation and dunes. This area of the beach
supplied a direct path from Trustom Pond to the beach
area and coastal waters. This type of habitat was not
present at my study site at Ninigret. These areas are
managed by the U.S. Fish and Wildlife Service (USFWS) for
piping plovers. Moonstone Beach is annually closed to the
public, for this reason, beginning on April 1. After
April 1, I conducted fieldwork only at Ninigret NWR.

Methods

**Describes
specific
time,
place, and
technique
(method)
of study**

5   During my research, I based the occurrence of
predators on the presence of their tracks in the sand. At
Moonstone Beach a 610 m stretch of beach was searched.
This area was searched on 24 March and 29 March for two
hours each day. The beach was marked in 30.5 m (100 ft)
sections by PVC pole markers on the foredune.

6   During each study period I recorded any factors on
the beach that would disrupt or bias data collection. This
mainly included human and domestic dog (*Canis familiaris*)

Bloomfield 3

tracks on the beach. I searched for tracks in each 30.5
meter section. When a track was located, the species was
recorded. In addition to the species, I recorded the
quality of the track on a 1-3 scale (1 being poorest). I
also noted whether the track was found in wet or dry sand.
To limit identification error, I always carried a tracking
text with me which included photographs, diagrams, and
measurements. The same method was used at Ninigret, with
the exception of the 30.5 m markers.

7   I used a chi-squared test to assess the spatial
distribution of predator tracks on the beach. This test
was only done for Moonstone Beach because the tracks and
beach quality at Ninigret were very poor during the study
period. Also, figures were constructed to show the
frequency of track occurrence, number of species per
section, and number of tracks per section at Moonstone
Beach. The data from Ninigret could only be used
qualitatively to indicate which species were present.

**Describes
method
used to
understand
the data**

**Notes a
limitation**

Results

8   The only predatory species present at Ninigret NWR
was gulls (*Laridae*). At Moonstone Beach, the spatial
distribution of predators was not uniform ($P < 0.001$),
with more tracks present on the section of beach extending
from pole 15 to pole 20 (Table 1). The numbers of species
per section and number of tracks recorded were greatest
in this area as well (Figures 1 and 2). This was
particularly true in section 17, which was located in the

**Summarizes
data**

Conclusions

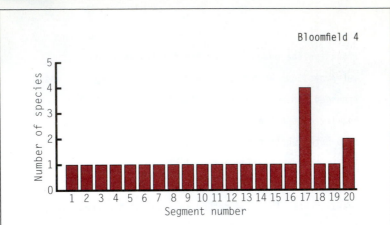

Figure 1. Number of species present at Moonstone Beach
is highest in segment 17, Rhode Island, spring 2006

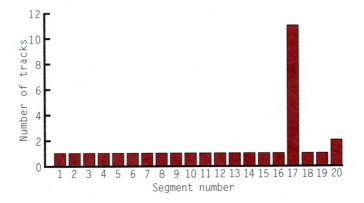

Figure 2. Sets of tracks counted at Moonstone Beach,
Rhode Island, spring 2006, and section 17 showed the
greatest number of total tracks overall

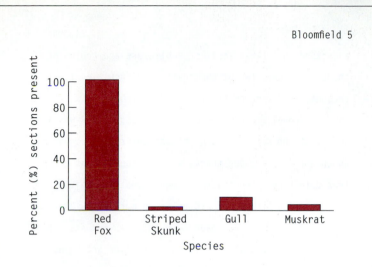

Bloomfield 5

Figure 3. Occurrence of species across entire beach shows the red fox is present all along the shore of Moonstone Beach, Rhode Island, spring 2006

area with immediate access to the pond from the beach. Red fox (*Vulpes vulpes*) covered the largest distance over the study area, occurring in all 20 sections during both study periods (Figure 3). The tracks always ran in a straight path parallel to the shore all the way across the study site and beyond.

Discussion

9   Using tracks to determine the presence of predators on the beach is a low-cost method which has the potential to yield promising results. Although this method was low-cost and a simple way to collect data, I found that there were many flaws in the experimental design that should be

Bloomfield 6

addressed in further studies. Public use and roping of
the beaches were two of the greatest difficulties I
encountered during my study.

10   The condition of East Beach at Ninigret NWR was so
poor that the data had to be almost entirely discredited.
Human and domestic dog tracks were so abundant at the site
that detecting other tracks seemed almost impossible.
Ninigret also lacked the PVC poles to mark every 30.5 m.
The quality of the data made them unusable for statistical
and quantitative analysis. It is also important to note
that one study suggested that in areas of beach open to
domestic dogs, nests not protected by exclosures were all
lost to dogs.[4] Keeping dogs off the beach or leashed is
very important to the birds' survival.

11   The areas at Ninigret that were not overrun with
human and dog tracks were roped off for the piping
plovers. I tried to view tracks over the ropes with
binoculars but decided this was not a very accurate
technique. In the future, observers should be uniformed
volunteers with USFWS so they can go behind roped areas.

Suggestions for future studies Letting the public know about the study would cut back on
the amount of "clutter" to sort through on the beach.

12   Although ghost crabs (*Ocypode quadrata*) are more of
a problem in southern areas, it is relatively unknown how
large an impact they have on piping plover nest
failure rates. Crab predation in Rhode Island is
something my study did not address. Their tracks in the

Bloomfield 7

sand would have been impossible to find with all of the human disturbance. One study documented a ghost crab predating a piping plover chick. The research indicates that more studies must be done to determine if it was an isolated incident or if ghost crabs really are frequent predators of the piping plover.[5] Another study examined a beach with high piping plover mortality rates and abundant ghost crabs. The results showed a correlation, not necessarily a causation. Their data, at the same time, seemed to suggest that adult plovers would avoid bringing their chicks to forage in areas of abundant ghost crabs. They indicated that this could possibly indirectly lead to higher mortality rates of the chicks.[6]

13 My research neglected to account for small mammal predation. Maier and DeGraff discovered, in 2000, that captive wild-caught white-footed mice (*Peromyscus leucopus*) were capable of consuming house sparrow eggs (*Passer domesticus*) in laboratory trials. They also noted that the effectiveness of the white-footed mouse as a significant predator of ground-nesting birds appears to be questionable.[7] While my study did not address crab or small mammal predation, it appears that the relevant literature does not show strong evidence for these animals as important nest predators.

14 Based on the results (Table 1, Figures 1-3), I would expect the highest predation levels to be in segment 17 near the salt pond. More research must be done though,

Bloomfield 8

because according to Golden and Regosin, plover broods
with access to a salt pond habitat experienced higher
fledgling success than broods limited to an ocean
beachfront habitat.[1] Further research must be done to
figure out how the birds can have higher fledgling success
rates near salt ponds if predator occurrence also appears
to be higher near salt ponds.

15   Predator exclosures are one way to reduce predation
rates. A previous study[8] found that daily survival rates
of pectoral sandpiper (*Calidris melanotos*) nests,
behavioral responses to exclosures, and the fact that no
protected nests were predated suggested that exclosure
was effective at deterring predators. The authors suggest
that this method may be used for other shorebirds as
well. In addition, 9 out of 13 nests had attempted
predation by Arctic fox (*Alopex lagopus*), but all of
these nests remained successful. The exclosures had an
effective anchoring system and mesh wire.

16   Some exclosures can actually cause the plovers to
abandon their nests. Research was done to determine what
conditions and types of exclosures resulted in nest
abandonment. The data suggested that exclosure
construction, size, shape, mesh size, and fence height
were not significantly related to nest abandonment, but
covered exclosures were.[9]

17   My data could be useful to people interested in nest
exclosures because if a biologist can predict what
predators are in the area, an exclosure can be tailored

Cites first reference again

Possible applications

Bloomfield 9

to meet specific needs. Different designs could be
implemented based on whether the predators are mainly
diggers or mostly avian. My data could also be used to
reduce nest abandonment related to exclosures. If
biologists know where the predators are distributed
along the beach, they can predict exactly where an
exclosure is needed. If there is a low occurrence of
predators in an area, then there is little or no need
for an exclosure. In addition, knowing where predators
occur could make it easier for biologists to trap
predators in the area.

18   In summary, exclosures are a good way to protect
nests if done correctly. Predator occurrence by tracking
needs to be further researched to improve accuracy but
appears to be a cost-effective way to sample for
predators on beaches. This technique is only useful if
the volunteer trackers are very skilled at tracking in
sand. In addition, it was only efficient to collect data
under ideal conditions when there was little or no human
disturbance on the beaches. If the techniques are
further developed and the problems addressed, this
method has great potential to be a low-budget and easy
way to determine presence of predators on piping plover
nest sites.

Applications set

References

1. Goldin MR, Regosin JV. Chick behavior, habitat use, and reproductive success of piping plovers at Goosewing Beach, Rhode Island. J Field Ornith. 1998;69:228-234.

2. Haig SM. Piping plover. In: Poole A, Stettenheim PS, and Gill F, editors. The birds of North America. Washington (DC): American Ornithologists' Union; 1992. p. 1-18.

3. Skutch AF. A breeding bird census and nesting success in Central America. Ibis. 1996;108:1-16.

4. Nol E, Brooks RJ. Effects of predator exclosures on nesting success of killdeer. J Field Ornith. 1982;53:263-268.

5. Loegering JP, Fraser JD, Loegering LL. Ghost crab preys on piping plover chick. Wilson Bulletin. 1995;107:768-769.

6. Wolcott DL, Wolcott TG. High mortality of piping plovers on beaches with abundant ghost crabs: correlation, not causation. Wilson Bulletin. 1999;111:321-329.

7. Maier TJ, DeGraaf RM. Predation on Japanese quail vs. house sparrow eggs in artificial nests: small eggs reveal small predators. Condor. 2000;102:325-332.

8. Estelle VB, Mabee TJ, Farmer AH. Effectiveness of predator exclosures for pectoral sandpiper nests in Alaska. J Field Ornith. 1996;67:447-452.

Center heading

Indent references from number; no other indentation needed (number system)

Number sources (number method) or list references alphabetically (name & year system)

Bloomfield 11

9. Vaske JJ, Rimmer DW, Deblinger RD. The impact of different predator exclosures on piping plover nest abandonment. J Field Ornith. 1994;65:201-209.

Grammar

▼ TAKING IT ONLINE

PURDUE ONLINE WRITING LAB (OWL)
http://owl.english.purdue.edu/
Visit this site for the most complete list of resources, handouts, and
exercises about grammar and editing collected by any American university.
The site also offers grammar advice for ESL writers.

THE GOOD GRAMMAR, GOOD STYLE ARCHIVE
http://www.protrainco.com/info/grammar.htm
Do you have a grammar question? Check this site's searchable database,
the *Good Grammar, Good Style Archive.*

INTERACTIVE QUIZZES
http://grammar.ccc.commnet.edu/grammar
This page will lead you to nearly two hundred grammar quizzes, some
written by students, to help you brush up on the topics of your choice.

GRAMMAR MOMENT: THE TOP EIGHT PET GRAMMAR MISTAKES
http://itsfiveoclocksomewhere.blogspot.com/2007/01/
grammar-moment-top-eight-pet-grammar.html
This blog entry will help you spot some of the most irritating and serious
errors in your own writing.

DAVE'S ESL CAFÉ HINT OF THE DAY
http://eslcafe.com/webhints/hints.cgi
Read the hint of the day, and search the archive for past hints, too.

PART 9

Grammar

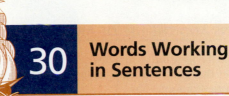

30 Words Working in Sentences

To edit effectively, you need to recognize sentence components and their working relationships. At the simplest level, sentences consist of different types of words, often called *parts of speech.*

30a Nouns and articles

To identify a **noun**, look for a word that names a person, a place, an idea, or a thing. Most nouns form the **plural** (two or more) by adding -*s* or -*es* to the **singular** (one): *cow* + -*s* = *cows*; *gas* + -*es* = *gases*. Some are irregular: *child, children; deer, deer*. A noun's **possessive** form expresses ownership.

SINGULAR	SINGULAR POSSESSIVE ('S)	PLURAL	PLURAL POSSESSIVE (')
student	student's	students	students'

A noun often requires an **article**: *the, a* (before a consonant sound), or *an* (before a vowel sound).

An **intern** prepared a **report** for the **doctor** at **Hope Hospital**.

TYPES OF NOUNS

Count noun Names individual items that can be counted: *four* cups, *a hundred* beans

Noncount noun (mass noun) Names material or abstractions that cannot be counted: *flour, water, steel*

Collective noun Names a unit composed of more than one individual or thing (see 34b-2 on agreement): *group, board of directors, flock*

Proper noun Names specific people, places, titles, or things (see 54b on capitalizing): *Miss America; Tuscaloosa, Alabama; Microsoft Corporation*

Common noun Names nonspecific people, places, or things (see 54b on capitalizing): *children, winner, town, mountain, company, bike*

ESL ADVICE: NOUNS AND THE USE OF ARTICLES

Notice how to use the **indefinite articles** (*a* or *an*) and the **definite article** (*the*). Remember that you'll still communicate your meaning even if you choose the wrong article or forget one.

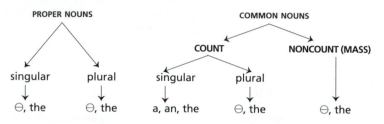

$\ominus$ = no article

- **Singular proper nouns** generally use no article, and **plural proper nouns** usually use *the*.

  SINGULAR   Rosa Parks helped initiate the civil rights movement.

  PLURAL   The Everglades have abundant wildlife and plants.

- **Singular count nouns** use *a*, *an*, or *the* and cannot stand alone.

  SINGULAR   The pig is an intelligent animal.

- **Plural count nouns** use either no article (to show a generalization) or *the* (to refer to something specific).

  GENERAL   Books are the best teachers. [books in general]

  SPECIFIC   The books on his desk are due Monday. [specific books]

- **Noncount (mass) nouns** use either no article or *the*, never *a* or *an*. **General noncount nouns** sometimes stand alone. **Specific noncount nouns**, which have been limited in some way, use *the*.

  DRAFT   A laughter is good medicine.

  GENERAL   Laughter is good medicine. [laughter in general]

  SPECIFIC   The laughter of children is good medicine. [specific type of laughter]

Follow these guidelines when you select *a*, *an*, or *the*.

- Use *a* or *an* when you are not referring to any specific person or thing (using a nonspecific, singular count noun). Use *a* before a consonant sound and *an* before a vowel sound.

  I need **a** car to go to work. [unknown, nonspecific car or any car]

- Use *the* when you are referring to an exact, known person or thing (using a specific, singular noun).

  I need **the** car to go to work. [specific, known car]

  The car that she bought is metallic gray. [specific, known car]

- Generally use no articles with plural count and noncount nouns.

  COUNT   Airline tickets to Chicago are at half price.

  NONCOUNT   Information about flights to Chicago is available.

- Use *the* when a plural count noun or a noncount noun is followed by a modifier, such as an adjective clause (see 31c-1) or prepositional phrase (see 31b-1), that makes the noun specific.

  COUNT   **The** airline tickets that you bought are at half price.

  NONCOUNT   **The** information on the flight board has changed.

30b Pronouns

To identify a **pronoun**, look for a word like *them, she, his,* or *it* that takes the place of a noun and can play the same roles in a sentence. You can use a pronoun to avoid repeating a noun, but the pronoun's meaning depends on a clear relationship to the noun to which it refers—its **antecedent** or **headword**. (See 34d on agreement and 38a on pronoun reference.)

antecedent   pronoun
Jean presented **her** proposal to the committee.

You can also use a pronoun to modify a noun or another pronoun.

This part has been on order for a month, and **that** one for a week.

A pronoun changes form to show number (singular or plural), gender (masculine, feminine, or neuter), and role in a sentence—subject, object, or possessive (see 31a on sentence structure and 33a on pronoun form).

30c Verbs

To identify **verbs**, look for words that express actions (*jump, build*), occurrences (*become, happen*), and states of being (*be, seem*). Change a verb's form to reflect person and number (see 34a on agreement) and to signal relationships in time (see 32a–g on **tense**).

PERSON	She **restores** furniture.	They **restore** furniture.
NUMBER	The copier **makes** noise.	The copiers **make** noise.
TENSE	They **prepare** the invoices.	They **prepared** the invoices.

Other forms show voice (see 32i and 7b-3) and mood (see 32h).

ACTIVE VOICE   The pump **cleans** the water.

PASSIVE VOICE   The water **is cleaned** by the pump.

INDICATIVE MOOD   The report **was** on the desk.

SUBJUNCTIVE MOOD   If the report **were** on the desk, I would have found it.

PRONOUNS AND THEIR FUNCTIONS

Personal pronouns	Designate persons or things using a form reflecting the pronoun's role in the sentence (see 33a)
SINGULAR	*I, me, you, he, him, she, her, it*
PLURAL	*we, us, you, they, them*
Possessive pronouns	Show ownership (see 33a on pronouns and 50a on apostrophes)
SINGULAR	*my, mine, your, yours, her, hers, his, its*
PLURAL	*our, ours, your, yours, their, theirs*
Relative pronouns	Introduce clauses that modify or add information to a main clause (see 31c and 43b on subordination)
	who, whom, whose, which, that
Interrogative pronouns	Introduce questions
	who, which
Reflexive and intensive pronouns	End in *-self* or *-selves*; enable the subject or doer also to be the receiver of an action (reflexive); add emphasis (intensive)
SINGULAR	*myself, yourself, herself, himself, itself*
PLURAL	*ourselves, yourselves, themselves*
Indefinite pronouns	Refer to people, things, and ideas in general rather than a specific antecedent (see 34c-5)
SINGULAR	*anybody, each, every, neither, none, something*
PLURAL	*both, few, fewer, many, others, several*
VARIABLE	*all, any, enough, more, most, some*
Demonstrative pronouns	Point out or highlight an antecedent; can refer to a noun or pronoun or sum up a phrase or clause
	this, that, these, those
Reciprocal pronouns	Refer to individual parts of a plural antecedent *one another, each other*

Use a main verb alone or with **helping** (**auxiliary**) **verbs** (forms of *be*, *do*, and *have*). A helping verb and a main verb form a **verb phrase**. You can use **modal auxiliary verbs** as helping verbs but not as main verbs. They include *will/would*, *can/could*, *shall/should*, *may/might*, *must*, and *ought*. (See 32d.)

MAIN VERB   The city **welcomes** tourists all year round.

HELPING + MAIN   The tourist agency **is planning** a video.

MODAL + MAIN   They **might decide** to include the Old Courthouse.

Use **action verbs** to show action or activity: *swim, analyze, dig, turn*. Use **linking verbs** (or **state-of-being verbs**) to express a state of being or an occurrence: *is, seems, becomes, grows*. These verbs link a subject with a **complement** that renames or describes it.

ACTION   The company and the union **negotiated** a contract.

LINKING   The flowers **smelled** musky.

A **phrasal verb** includes a verb plus a closely associated word that seems like a preposition but is known as a **particle**, as in *throw up* ("regurgitate"). The meaning of a phrasal verb differs from that of the separate words. For example, *clear out* means "depart" and *run by* means "consult." In contrast, a verb *plus* a preposition is the sum of its parts: *run* (action) + *by* (direction).

phrasal verb   verb + preposition
I **ran** the idea **by** the committee.   I **ran by** the house.

30d Adjectives

To identify **adjectives**, look for words that modify nouns, pronouns, or word groups acting as nouns. Adjectives come in three degrees of comparison: *high, higher, highest; crooked, more crooked, most crooked*. Adjectives answer questions like "How many?" "Which one?" or "What kind?" (See also Chapter 35.)

HOW MANY?   The **two** reports reached different conclusions.

WHICH ONE?   Our report is the **last** one.

WHAT KIND?   Their proposal was **unrealistic**.

ESL ADVICE: ADJECTIVE FORMS

Adjectives in English never use a plural form.

DRAFT   Santo Domingo is renowned for beautifuls beaches.

EDITED   Santo Domingo is renowned for beautiful beaches.

30e Adverbs

To identify **adverbs**, look for words that modify verbs, adjectives, other adverbs, or entire sentences. They answer questions such as "When?" "Where?" "Why?" "How often?" "Which direction?" "What conditions?" and "What degree?"

WHEN?	Our committee met **yesterday**. [modifies verb *met*]
WHAT DEGREE?	We had a **very** long meeting. [modifies adjective *long*]
HOW OFTEN?	I attend board meetings **quite** frequently. [modifies adverb *frequently*, which modifies verb *attend*]

Adverbs may consist of an adjective plus *-ly* (*quickly, blindly, frequently*) although some adjectives also end in *-ly* (*neighborly, lovely*). Other common adverbs include *very, too, tomorrow, not, never, sometimes,* and *well.* Adverbs come in three degrees of comparison: *frequently, more* (or *less*) *frequently, most* (or *least*) *frequently* (see 35a).

You can use **conjunctive adverbs** such as *however, moreover, thus,* and *therefore* to indicate logical relationships. (See 43a for a list.)

They opposed the policy; **nevertheless**, they implemented it.

30f Prepositions

To recognize a **preposition**, look for a word like *in* or *at* followed by a noun or pronoun, forming a **prepositional phrase** (see 31b-1). The phrase adds precise, detailed information to a sentence.

The office <u>in **this region**</u> sells homes priced <u>above **$150,000**</u>.

COMMON PREPOSITIONS				
about	at	despite	near	to
above	before	down	of	toward
across	behind	during	off	under
after	below	except	on	until
against	beneath	for	out	up
along	between	from	outside	upon
among	beyond	in	over	with
around	by	into	past	within
as	concerning	like	through	without

ESL ADVICE: PREPOSITIONS

In general, use prepositional phrases in this order: place, then time.

place + time
The runners will start **in the park** <u>on Saturday</u>.

PREPOSITIONS OF PLACE: *AT, ON, IN,* AND NO PREPOSITION

AT	*ON*	*IN*	NO PREPOSITION
the mall*	the bed*	(the) bed*	downstairs
home	the ceiling	the kitchen	downtown
the library*	the floor	the car	inside
the office	the horse	(the) class*	outside
school*	the plane	the library*	upstairs
work	the train	school*	uptown

*You may sometimes use different prepositions for these locations.

PREPOSITIONS OF PLACE: *AT, ON,* AND *IN*

Use *at* for specific addresses; use *on* for names of streets, avenues, and boulevards; use *in* for names of areas of land—states, countries, continents.

She works **at** 99 Tinker Street **in** Dayton.

TO OR NO PREPOSITION TO EXPRESS GOING TO A PLACE

When you express the idea of going to a place, use the preposition *to.*

I am going **to** work.   I am going **to** the office.

In the following cases, use no preposition.

I am going home.   I am going downstairs (downtown, inside).

PREPOSITIONS OF TIME: *AT, ON,* AND *IN*

Use *at* for a specific time; use *on* for days and dates; use *in* for nonspecific times during a day, month, season, or year.

Brandon was born **at** 11:11 a.m. **on** a Monday **in** 1991.

FOR AND *SINCE* IN TIME EXPRESSIONS

Use *for* with an amount of time (minutes, hours, days, months, years) and *since* with a specific date or time.

The housing program has operated **for** many years.

The housing program has operated **since** 1971.

PREPOSITIONS WITH NOUNS, VERBS, AND ADJECTIVES

NOUN + PREPOSITION   He has an <u>understanding</u> **of** global politics.

VERB + PREPOSITION   Managers <u>worry</u> **about** many things.

ADJECTIVE + PREPOSITION   Life in your country is <u>similar</u> **to** life in mine.

NOUN + PREPOSITION COMBINATIONS

approval of	confusion about	hope for	participation in
awareness of	desire for	interest in	reason for
belief in	grasp of	love of	respect for
concern for	hatred of	need for	understanding of

VERB + PREPOSITION COMBINATIONS

ask about	differ from	pay for	study for
ask for	grow into	prepare for	think about
belong to	look at	refer to	trust in
care for	participate in	step into	work for

ADJECTIVE + PREPOSITION COMBINATIONS

afraid of	careless about	interested in	similar to
angry at	familiar with	made of	sorry for
aware of	fond of	married to	sure of
capable of	happy about	proud of	tired of

30g Conjunctions

To identify **conjunctions**, look for words that join other words or word groups, signaling their relationships.

Coordinating conjunctions. Use *and, but, or, nor, for, yet*, and *so* to link grammatically equal elements (see 43a).

WORDS	analyze **and** discuss, compare **or** contrast
PHRASES	over past sales **yet** under current goals
CLAUSES	They petitioned the board, **but** they lost their appeal.

Subordinating conjunctions. Use words such as *because* or *if* to create a **subordinate** (or **dependent**) **clause**. Such a clause cannot stand on its own as a sentence; you need to attach it to a **main** (or **independent**) **clause** that it qualifies or limits. (See 43b for a list of conjunctions.)

          main clause   subordinate clause
Li spoke persuasively, **though** the crowd favored her opponent.

Correlative conjunctions. These pairs include *not only . . . but also, either . . . or, both . . . and*, and similar combinations. They join sentence elements that are grammatically equal. (See 42b on parallelism.)

30h Interjections

To identify **interjections**, look for expressions that convey a strong reaction or emotion, such as surprise (*Hey!*) or disappointment (*Oh, no!*). They may stand alone or be loosely related to the rest of a sentence.

31 Sentence Parts and Patterns

Careful editing depends on your ability to recognize the different parts of sentences so that you can choose among alternative patterns. See also Chapter 30, which reviews the functions of the words in sentences.

31a Subjects and predicates

A **subject** names the topic or doer of a sentence. A **predicate** indicates an action or a relationship expressed in a sentence. It may specify consequences or conditions.

1 Look for sentence subjects

To identify a simple subject, look for one or more nouns (or pronouns) naming the doer or the topic. To identify a **complete subject**, find the simple subject *plus* all its modifying words.

SIMPLE SUBJECT   **Email** has changed business communication.

COMPLETE SUBJECT   **All the sales staff on this floor** left early.

A subject may be singular, plural, or compound (linked by *and* or *or*).

SINGULAR SUBJECT   **She** put the monitor on the desk.

PLURAL SUBJECT   **These pills** are difficult to swallow.

COMPOUND SUBJECT   **John and Chifume** are medical students.

In most sentences, the subject comes before the verb. There are exceptions to this pattern. An **expletive construction** (*there is/are* or *here is/are*) allows you to delay the subject until after the verb (see 7b-2).

USUAL ORDER   **Homeless people** <u>camped</u> here.

EXPLETIVE   There <u>were</u> **homeless people** camping here.

For emphasis, you can reverse (invert) the subject and verb.

INVERTED   In this tiny house <u>was born</u> **a leader**.

Questions often place the subject between helping and main verbs.

QUESTION   <u>Did</u> **the board** <u>approve</u> the light-rail proposal?

325

In an **imperative** sentence expressing a request or command, the subject *you* generally is implied, not stated (see 31d).

IMPERATIVE   [**You**] <u>Put</u> the insulation around the door frame.

2 Look for sentence predicates

A **simple predicate** includes only a verb (see 30c) or verb phrase (see 32d).

VERB   The bus **stopped**.   VERB PHRASE   The bus **might stop**.

The verb may be single or compound (linked by *and* or *or*).

SINGLE   The client **slipped**.   COMPOUND   The client **slipped and fell**.

To recognize a **complete predicate**, look for a verb or verb phrase *plus* modifiers and other words that receive the action or complete the verb.

COMPLETE PREDICATE   The lab tech **gave me the printout**.

FIVE BASIC PREDICATE PATTERNS

Most sentences employ one of these predicate structures, often in expanded or combined form.

1. Subject + intransitive verb

Our team **lost**.   Last week, the ferryboat **sank**.

An **intransitive verb** doesn't take an object or a complement (see below); neither is needed to complete the meaning.

OBJECT PATTERNS

2. Subject + transitive verb + direct object

The bank officer **approved** <u>the loan</u>.

A sentence with a **transitive verb** can include a **direct object** in the predicate, telling *who* or *what* receives the action.

3. Subject + transitive verb + indirect object + direct object

The Marine Corps reserve **gives** <u>needy children</u> toys.

A sentence with a transitive verb can also include an **indirect object**, a noun or pronoun telling readers *to whom* or *for whom* the action is undertaken.

(Continued)

FIVE BASIC PREDICATE PATTERNS (*continued*)

4. Subject + transitive verb + direct object + object complement

NOUN   His coworkers elected <u>Jim</u> <u>project leader</u>.

ADJECTIVE   Critics judged **the movie** <u>inferior</u>.

An **object complement**, a noun or adjective that renames or describes the direct object, adds information to a sentence predicate.

SUBJECT COMPLEMENT PATTERNS

5. Subject + linking verb + subject complement

The grant proposal **is** <u>too complicated</u>.

A sentence with a **linking verb**, such as *is*, *seems*, or *feels* (see 30c), can include a **subject complement**, "completing" the subject by describing or renaming it.

31b Phrases

A **sentence** is a word group with a subject and a predicate that can stand alone (see 31d). In contrast, a **phrase** is a word group that lacks a subject, a predicate, or both. A phrase cannot stand alone and must be integrated within a freestanding sentence. If you capitalize and punctuate a phrase as if it were a sentence, you create a fragment (see 36a).

1 Look for prepositional phrases

To recognize a **prepositional phrase**, look first for a **preposition**—a word like *at*, *for*, *under*, or *except* (see the list in 30f). Then identify the **object of the preposition**—the noun, pronoun, or word group that follows the preposition.

to <u>the beach</u>   **near** <u>her</u>   **after** <u>a falling out</u>   **inside** <u>the case</u>

A prepositional phrase can act as an adjective or as an adverb.

AS ADJECTIVE   The coupons **in the newspaper** offer savings **on groceries**.

AS ADVERB   Her watch started beeping **during the meeting**.

During the meeting, her watch started beeping.

2 Look for absolute phrases

An **absolute phrase** modifies a sentence as a whole. It includes a noun (or a pronoun or word group acting as a noun) plus a present or past participle and any modifiers.

> They fought the fire, **the dense smoke slowing their efforts**.

3 Look for appositive phrases

An **appositive** adds information by renaming a noun or pronoun. An appositive plus its modifiers is an **appositive phrase**. (see also 48c).

> Ken Choi, **my classmate**, won an award for his design.

> He uses natural materials, **berry dyes**, for example.

4 Look for verbal phrases

Verb parts, known as **verbals**, are participles, gerunds, or infinitives. These can function as nouns, adjectives, or adverbs—but never stand alone as verbs. A **verbal phrase** is a verbal plus its modifiers, object, or complements.

Participial phrases. Use the *-ing* (present participle) or *-ed/-en* (past participle) forms of a verbal in a **participial phrase** acting as an adjective to modify a noun or pronoun.

> Few neighbors **attending the meeting** owned dogs.

> They signed a petition **addressed to the health department**.

Gerund phrases. Use the *-ing* form of a verbal (present participle) in a **gerund phrase** acting as a noun in a subject, object, or subject complement.

> sentence subject   object of preposition
> **Closing the landfill** may keep it from **polluting the bay**.

Infinitive phrases. Use the *to* form of a verbal in an **infinitive phrase** acting as an adjective, adverb, or noun.

ADVERB   He used organic methods **to raise his garden**.

NOUN (SUBJECT)   **To live in the mountains** was his goal.

ESL ADVICE: VERBALS

GERUNDS

Use a gerund, not an infinitive, after some verbs, as in this sentence: Children **enjoy** reading fairy tales.

COMMON VERBS TAKING GERUNDS

admit	consider	finish	postpone
anticipate	delay	imagine	practice
appreciate	deny	keep	quit
avoid	discuss	mind	recommend
can't help	enjoy	miss	suggest

GERUNDS WITH IDIOMATIC EXPRESSIONS

- After *go* (any tense): I **go** swimming.   I **went** kayaking.
- After *spend time*: Volunteers **spend** a lot of **time** helping others.
- After *have* + noun: Pilots **have difficulty** flying in bad weather.
- After a preposition: Midwives are trained **in** assisting at childbirth.

GERUNDS WITH *TO* ACTING AS A PREPOSITION

In each of the following examples, *to* is not part of an infinitive. *To* acts like a preposition and must be followed by a gerund ending in *-ing*.

I look **forward** to working at the museum.

He is **accustomed** to designing exhibits.

Patrons are **used** to viewing complex displays.

INFINITIVES

Some verbs take only an infinitive, not a gerund, as in this sentence: Some students **need** to work part time.

COMMON VERBS TAKING AN INFINITIVE

agree	expect	need	refuse
ask	fail	offer	seem
choose	hope	plan	venture
claim	intend	pretend	want
decide	manage	promise	wish

COMMON VERBS TAKING AN OBJECT + INFINITIVE

Other verbs take an object and an infinitive.

Doctors often **advise** <u>their patients</u> to eat well.

advise	encourage	need	teach
allow	expect	permit	tell
ask	force	persuade	urge
convince	help	require	want

When *make, let,* and *have* suggest "caused" or "forced," they use the infinitive without *to* (the base form).

She	**made/let/had** me	clean my room.

Certain adjectives are also followed by infinitives.

I	**am**	<u>delighted</u>	<u>to meet</u> you.
The report	**is**	<u>easy</u>	<u>to understand.</u>
The volunteers	**are**	<u>pleased</u>	<u>to help.</u>

GERUNDS OR INFINITIVES

The meaning stays the same when you use most verbs that can be followed by either a gerund or an infinitive.

GERUND   Developers prefer **working** with local contractors.

INFINITIVE   Developers prefer **to work** with local contractors.

COMMON VERBS TAKING EITHER GERUNDS OR INFINITIVES

begin	hate	like	start
can't stand	intend	love	stop
continue	learn	prefer	try

Remember, forget, regret, and *stop* change meaning with a gerund or an infinitive.

GERUND   I **remembered** <u>meeting</u> Mark. [I recall an event in the past.]

INFINITIVE   I **remembered** <u>to meet</u> Mark. [I did not forget to do this in the past.]

GERUND   I will never **forget** <u>visiting</u> Texas. [I recall a past event.]

INFINITIVE   I never **forget** <u>to study</u> for exams. [I remember to do something.]

GERUND   I **regret** <u>telling</u> you about her. [I'm sorry I told you in the past.]

INFINITIVE   I **regret** <u>to tell</u> you that you were not hired. [I'm sorry to tell you now.]

GERUND   I **stopped** <u>smoking</u>. [I do not smoke anymore.]

INFINITIVE   I **stopped** <u>to smoke</u>. [I paused to smoke.]

31c Subordinate clauses

A **main clause** is a word group that includes a subject and a verb and can stand alone as a complete sentence. (A main clause is sometimes called an **independent clause**.)

MAIN CLAUSE   I had many appointments last Friday.

In contrast, a **subordinate** (or **dependent**) **clause** contains both a subject and a predicate yet cannot stand on its own as a sentence. It begins with a subordinating word such as *if, that,* or *although* that prevents the clause from standing on its own. (See the list of subordinating words in 43b.) A subordinate clause must be attached to a main clause.

SUBORDINATE CLAUSE   **because** I was busy

CONNECTED TO SENTENCE   **Because I was busy**, I didn't call.

Don't punctuate a subordinate clause as a sentence. If you do, you create a fragment (see 36a).

1 Look for subordinate clauses as adjectives

If you begin a subordinate clause with a word like *who, which, that, whom,* or *whose* (**relative pronouns**) or with *when* or *where* (**relative adverbs**), you can use the clause as an adjective to modify a noun or pronoun. Generally, you put the modifying clause right after the noun or pronoun it modifies.

Many people **who live in Erie** came to the meeting.

They opposed the road **that the county plans to approve**.

Who, whom, whose, and *that* modify people. *Which, whose,* and *that* modify animals, places, and things. In spoken English *whom* generally is optional, but it is used in formal writing, especially in the academic community.

STRATEGY   **Use adjective clauses to combine short sentences.**

CHOPPY   I have an aunt. Her book is on the best-seller list.

COMBINED   I have an aunt **whose** book is on the best-seller list.

2 Look for subordinate clauses as adverbs

If you begin a clause with a subordinating conjunction such as *because, although, since,* or *while* (see list in 43b), you can use the subordinating clause as an adverb (modifying verbs, adjectives, or adverbs).

| WHY? | She volunteered **because she supports the zoo**. |
| WHEN? | **As the rally continued**, Jean joined the picket line. |

3 Look for subordinate clauses as nouns

Noun clauses begin with *who, whom, whose, whoever, whomever, what, whatever, when, where, why, whether,* or *how.* Look for them in the roles of nouns: subject, object, object of a preposition, or complement.

| SENTENCE SUBJECT | **What she said** is interesting. |
| DIRECT OBJECT | You should pack **what you need for the trip**. |

ESL ADVICE: ADJECTIVE, ADVERB, AND NOUN CLAUSES

ADJECTIVE CLAUSES

You may include or drop a relative pronoun if it is not the subject of the clause. Either way is correct.

| INCLUDED | The Web site **that** we designed was very popular. |
| OMITTED | The Web site we designed was very popular. |

When a relative pronoun is the subject of an adjective clause, the clause can be changed to an **adjective phrase**. In a clause with a *be* verb, omit the relative pronoun and the *be* verb.

X   X

| CLAUSE (WITH *BE*) | He is the man **who is studying German**. |
| PHRASE | He is the man **studying German**. |

With another verb, omit the relative pronoun, and change the verb to a present participle. (See 31b-4 on participial phrases.)

X

| CLAUSE (NOT *BE*) | He is the man **who wants to study German**. |
| PHRASE | He is the man **wanting to study German**. |

ADVERB CLAUSES

TIME	**When** the weather changes, the malls stock winter clothes.
REASON	It is difficult to buy shorts **because** winter has started.
CONTRAST	**Although** some shoppers turn to catalogs, others do not.
CONDITION	Our online customers may do the same **unless** we expand our inventory.

SOME WORDS TO INTRODUCE ADVERB CLAUSES

TIME	REASON	CONTRAST	CONDITION
after	as	although	as long as
as, while	because	even though	even if
before	now that	though	if
once	since	while	only if
since	whereas		provided that
until			unless
when			

NOUN CLAUSES

When you form a complex sentence by combining a noun clause with other sentence parts, the clause acts like a noun in the sentence.

THAT CLAUSE   I believe **that** life exists in other solar systems.

YES/NO QUESTION CLAUSE   I wonder **if** life exists in other solar systems.

        I wonder **whether** life exists in other solar systems.

WH- QUESTION CLAUSE   I wonder **where** signs of other life may be found.

When the noun clause follows an introductory clause, the noun clause uses question word order.

QUESTION   Who discovered the fire?

NOUN CLAUSE   Do you know **who discovered the fire**? [question word order]

Change to statement order when the question includes a form of *be* and a subject complement, a modal, or the auxiliary *do, does, did, have, has,* or *had.* Also use statement word order with *if* and *whether* clauses.

QUESTION   Who **are** your friends?

NOUN CLAUSE   I wonder who your friends **are**. [statement word order]

QUESTION   How **can** I meet them?

NOUN CLAUSE   Please tell me how I **can** meet them. [statement word order]

31d Different types of sentences

Sentences vary according to the kind and number of clauses they contain (sentence structure) and the relationships they establish with readers (purpose).

1 Look for sentence structures

A sentence with one main (independent) clause and no subordinate (dependent) clauses is a **simple sentence**.

The mayor proposed an expansion of city hall.

A sentence with two or more main (independent) clauses and no subordinate (dependent) clauses is a **compound sentence**. (See 43a on coordination.)

main clause   main clause
Most people praised the plans, yet **some found them dull**.

A sentence with one main (independent) clause and one or more subordinate (dependent) clauses is a **complex sentence**. (See 43b on subordination.)

subordinate clause   main clause
Because people objected, **the architect revised the plans**.

A sentence with two or more main (independent) clauses and one or more subordinate (dependent) clauses is a **compound-complex sentence**.

subordinate clause   subordinate clause
Because he wanted to make sure that the expansion did not damage
main clause
the existing building, **the architect examined the frame of the older**
main clause
structure, and **he asked the contractor to test the soil stability**.

2 Look for sentence purposes

A **declarative sentence** makes a statement. An **interrogative sentence** poses a question. An **imperative sentence** requests or commands. An **exclamatory sentence** exclaims.

DECLARATIVE   The motor is making a rattling noise.

INTERROGATIVE   Have you checked it for overheating?

IMPERATIVE   Check it again.

EXCLAMATORY   It's on fire!

32 Using Verbs

In casual speech, many different verb forms may be acceptable to listeners, especially those within your own dialect community.

CASUAL SPEECH   My daddy **be pushin'** me to do good in school.

Jimmy **should'a went** with them.

We **were fixin'** to eat dinner.

You **might could carpool** to work with Don.

LISTENER'S REACTION: **What sounds fine when we talk might not be correct in a paper.**

In your writing, however, nonstandard verb forms may distract readers who expect you to write fluently in standard English. Some readers may even assume that you are uneducated or careless if you don't edit the verb forms in your final drafts. Adjust to the expectations of your readers. After all, the formal language of the academic community is as inappropriate on the street corner as casual language is in a history paper or marketing report.

32a Simple present and past tense verbs

When you use a simple verb in a sentence, you put that verb into the **present tense** for action occurring *now* or the **past tense** for action that has *already occurred*. Most verbs form the past tense by adding *-ed* to the present tense form, also called the **base form**. Depending on the verb, this addition may be pronounced as *-t* (*baked*), *-d* (*called*), or *-ed* (*defended*).

ESL ADVICE: SIMPLE PRESENT AND SIMPLE PAST

Only these two tenses stand alone with no helping verbs. (See 32d.)

SIMPLE PRESENT   They **live** in the new dormitory.

SIMPLE PAST   They **lived** in an apartment last semester.

32b Present tense verbs

You need no special ending to mark the present tense *except* in the third person singular form (with *he, she,* or *it* or a singular noun). Use *-s* or *-es* for the third person singular.

The cafeteria **opens** at eight o'clock.

For plurals in the third person (*I, you, we, they* or a plural noun), you do not use -*s* or -*es*. This can be confusing because plural nouns often end in -*s* or -*es* but the verb should not (*customers + wait*).

The customers **wait** in line until the cafeteria **opens**.

PRESENT TENSE IN ACADEMIC SETTINGS

In the academic community, readers may expect special uses of the present tense. When writing for your humanities courses, use the present tense to discuss a piece of literature, a film, an essay, a painting, or a similar creative production. Treat events, ideas, characters, or statements from such works as if they exist in an ongoing present tense.

In Erdrich's *Love Medicine*, Albertine **returns** to the reservation.

In the social sciences and sciences, use the present tense to discuss the results and implications of a current study or experiment, but use the past tense to review the findings of earlier researchers.

Although Maxwell (2004) **identified** three crucial classroom interactions, the current survey **suggests** two others as well.

ESL ADVICE: THE THIRD PERSON -*S* OR -*ES* ENDING

Be sure to add an -*s* or -*es* to verbs that are third person singular.

SUBJECT	VERB	SUBJECT	VERB + -*S*
I/you/we/they	**write**	he/she/it (animal, thing, concept)	**writes**

32c Past tense verbs

When you write the past tense of a regular verb, you usually add -*ed* to its base form. Sometimes you may leave off the -*ed* if you don't "hear" it, especially when a word beginning in *d* or *t* follows the verb.

DRAFT   The company **use** to provide dental benefits.

EDITED   The company **used** to provide dental benefits.

About sixty **irregular verbs** are exceptions to the "add -*ed*" rule; most change an internal vowel in the simple past tense (*run, ran*).

DRAFT   The characters in the movie **sweared** constantly.

EDITED   The characters in the movie **swore** constantly.

COMMON IRREGULAR VERBS

PRESENT	PAST	PAST PARTICIPLE
arise	arose	arisen
am/is/are	was/were	been
bear	bore	borne
begin	began	begun
bite	bit	bitten/bit
blow	blew	blown
break	broke	broken
bring	brought	brought
buy	bought	bought
catch	caught	caught
choose	chose	chosen
come	came	come
creep	crept	crept
dive	dived/dove	dived
do	did	done
draw	drew	drawn
dream	dreamed/dreamt	dreamt
drink	drank	drunk
drive	drove	driven
eat	ate	eaten
fall	fell	fallen
fight	fought	fought
fly	flew	flown
forget	forgot	forgotten
forgive	forgave	forgiven
get	got	got/gotten
give	gave	given
go	went	gone
grow	grew	grown
hang (person)	hanged/hung	hanged/hung
hang (object)	hung	hung
hide	hid	hidden
know	knew	known
lay	laid	laid
lead	led	led
lie	lay	lain
light	lit/lighted	lit
lose	lost	lost
prove	proved	proved/proven
ride	rode	ridden
ring	rang	rung

(Continued)

COMMON IRREGULAR VERBS (*continued*)

PRESENT	PAST	PAST PARTICIPLE
rise	rose	risen
run	ran	run
see	saw	seen
seek	sought	sought
set	set	set
shake	shook	shaken
sing	sang/sung	sung
sink	sank/sunk	sunk
sit	sat	sat
speak	spoke	spoken
spring	sprang	sprung
steal	stole	stolen
strike	struck	struck
swear	swore	sworn
swim	swam	swum
take	took	taken
tear	tore	torn
throw	threw	thrown
wake	woke/waked	woken/waked/woke
wear	wore	worn
write	wrote	written

32d Complex tenses and helping verbs

To recognize complex tenses, look for a **helping** or **auxiliary verb** (such as *is* or *has*) with a main verb in the form of the **past participle** (the *-ed/-en* form) or the **present participle** (the *-ing* form).

The **present participle** is formed by adding *-ing* to the base form of the verb (the form with no endings or markers).

	helping verb	**main verb (present participle)**
He	was/will be/had been	**loading** the truck.

The **past participle** of most verbs is just like the simple past tense (base form + *-ed*). Because this form can be irregular, check the chart on irregular verbs (see 32c) or the dictionary if you are uncertain of the form.

		helping verb	**main verb (past participle)**
REGULAR VERB	Mike has/had	**rented** the truck.
IRREGULAR VERB	The copier has/had	**broken** down.

ESL ADVICE: PRINCIPAL PARTS OF VERBS AND HELPING VERBS

PRINCIPAL PARTS OF VERBS

BASE FORM	PAST	PRESENT PARTICIPLE	PAST PARTICIPLE
REGULAR VERBS			
live	lived	living	lived
want	wanted	wanting	wanted
IRREGULAR VERBS			
eat	ate	eating	eaten
run	ran	running	run

HELPING VERBS AND VERB PHRASES

Most verbs combine one or more helping verbs (also called auxiliary verbs) with a main verb to form a **verb phrase**.

HELPING VERB I **was walking** to school during the snowstorm.

HELPING VERBS I **have been walking** to school for many years.

Helping verbs include *am, is, are, will, would, can, could, have, has, had, was, were, should, might, may, must, do, does,* and *did.* These words may be combined, as in *have been, has been, had been, will be, will have,* and *will have been.*

VERB AND HELPING VERB FORMS FOR *BE* AND *HAVE*

PROGRESSIVE FORMS OF *BE*

PAST subject + *was/were* + present participle
I **was** working in my studio yesterday.

PRESENT subject + *am/is/are* + present participle
I **am** working in my studio right now.

FUTURE subject + *will* (modal) + *be* + present participle
I **will be** working in my studio tomorrow.

PERFECT FORMS OF *HAVE*

PAST subject + *had* + past participle
I **had** tried to call you all day yesterday.

PRESENT subject + *have/has* + past participle
I **have** tried to call you all day today.

FUTURE subject + *will* (modal) + *have* + past participle
I **will have** called you by midnight tonight.

32e Progressive and perfect tenses

When you use the **present**, **past**, and **future progressive** tenses, you can show an action in progress at some point in time.

PRESENT PROGRESSIVE	The carousel **is turning** quickly.
PAST PROGRESSIVE	The horses **were bobbing** up and down.
FUTURE PROGRESSIVE	The children **will be laughing** from the thrill.

In progressive tenses, the main verb must take the *-ing* ending. In the future progressive tense, the verb must also include *be*.

Indicating the order of events. Turn to the three **perfect tenses** to show the order in which events take place.

Use the **past perfect tense** for the first event to indicate that it had already happened before something else took place.

The fire **had burned** for an hour before the brigade arrived.

Avoid substituting simple past tense for the past participle.

| MISTAKEN PAST | The band **had forgot** the first tour. |
| EDITED | The band **had forgotten** the first tour. |

Use the **present perfect tense** much like the past perfect, showing action that has happened before without a specific time marker or that you insist has already occurred.

I **have reported** the burglary already.

The present perfect also shows action begun in the past and continuing into the present. It differs from the simple past, which indicates an action already completed or specified in time.

| PRESENT PERFECT | I **have lived** in St. Louis for three weeks. |
| SIMPLE PAST | I **lived** in St. Louis in 1998. |

Select the **future perfect tense** to show that something will have happened by the time something else will be taking place.

The chef **will have baked** all the cakes before noon.

ESL ADVICE: SIMPLE PRESENT AND PRESENT PROGRESSIVE TENSES

PRESENT TENSE HABITUAL ACTIVITIES

Use the **simple present** tense to describe factual or habitual activities. These occur in the present but are not necessarily in progress.

| SHOWS FACT | The planets **revolve** around the sun. |
| SHOWS HABIT | The bus usually **arrives** late. |

These common time expressions indicate present tense habitual activities.

all the time	every holiday	every year	rarely
always	every month	frequently	sometimes
every class	every semester	most of the time	usually
every day	every week	often	never

ACTIVITIES IN PROGRESS

Use the **present progressive** tense to describe activities in progress. If you wish, you can add expressions to pinpoint the time of the activity.

am/is/are + present participle

DeVaugh **is testing** the process.

DeVaugh **is testing** the process **this month**.

These common time expressions indicate activities in progress.

at the moment	this afternoon	this month	this year
right now	this evening	this morning	today

When you choose between the simple present and present progressive tenses, think about the time of the activity. Is it happening only at the moment (present progressive) or all the time as a fact or habit (simple present)?

PRESENT (FACT)	All people communicate in some language.
PRESENT (HABIT)	The students speak their own languages at home.
PRESENT PROGRESSIVE (AT THE MOMENT)	Kim is studying Spanish this term.

VERBS THAT ARE TROUBLESOME IN PROGRESSIVE TENSES

	EXAMPLE	OTHER USAGES AND MEANINGS
SENSES		
see	I **see** the beauty.	I **am seeing** that doctor. (meeting with, visiting, dating)
hear	I **hear** the birds.	I **have been hearing** about the problem for a while. (receiving information)
smell	The flowers **smell** strong.	I **am smelling** the flowers. (action in progress)
taste	The food **tastes** good.	The cook **is tasting** the soup. (action in progress)
POSSESSION		
have	We **have** many friends.	We **are having** a lot of fun. (experiencing)

own	They **own** many cars.
possess	She **possesses** wealth.
belong	The book **belongs** to me.

STATES OF MIND

be	I **am** tired.	
know	I **know** the city well.	
believe	She **believes** in God.	
think	I **think** it is true.	I **am thinking** about moving.
	(know, believe)	(having thoughts about)
recognize	She **recognizes** him.	
	(knows)	
understand	The professor **understands**	
	the equation.	
mean	I **don't mean** to pry.	I **have been meaning** to visit.
	(don't want)	(planning, intending)

WISH OR ATTITUDE

| want | We **want** peace. |
| desire | He **desires** freedom. |

WISH OR ATTITUDE

need	We **need** rain.	
love	Children **love** snow.	I **have been loving** this book.
		(enjoying)
hate	Dan **hates** mowing.	
like	Lee **likes** skiing.	
dislike	She **dislikes** tests.	
seem	They **seem** kind.	
appear	He **appears** tired.	He **is appearing** at the
	(seems to be)	theater.
		(acting, performing)
look	He **looks** tired.	We **are looking** at the map.
	(seems to be)	(action of using eyes)

32f Troublesome verbs (*lie, lay, sit, set*)

Here are a few verbs confused even by experienced writers.

VERB	PRESENT	PAST	PARTICIPLE
lie (oneself)	lie	lay	lain
lay (an object)	lay	laid	laid
sit (oneself)	sit	sat	sat
set (an object)	set	set	set

DRAFT   I **laid** down yesterday for a nap. I **have laid** down every afternoon this week.

EDITED   I **lay** down yesterday for a nap. I **have lain** down every afternoon this week.

DRAFT   First Eric and Lisa **sat** the projector down on the table. Then they **set** down as the meeting began.

EDITED   First Eric and Lisa **set** the projector down on the table. Then they **sat** down as the meeting began.

32g Clear tense sequence

    Conversation can jump from tense to tense with little warning. In writing, however, readers expect you to stick to one tense or to follow a clear **sequence of tenses** that relates events and ideas in time (see 40b).

               present   past

LOGICAL   People **forget** that four candidates **ran** in 1948.

               future   present

LOGICAL   I **will accept** your report even if it **is** a bit late.

                        past

LOGICAL   The accountant **destroyed** crucial evidence because no one

past perfect
had asked him to save the records.

                       past perfect

LOGICAL   None of the crew **had realized** that food stored in cans sealed

present (for generally true statement)
with lead solder **is** poisonous.

32h Subjunctive mood

    Sentences can be classified by **mood**, the form of a verb that reflects the speaker's or writer's attitude. Most sentences are in the **indicative** (statements intended as truthful or factual like "The store closed at ten") or the **imperative** (commands like "Stop!"). Occasionally the **subjunctive** expresses uncertainty—supposition, prediction, possibility, desire, or wish.

SUBJUNCTIVE   **Were** the deadline today, our proposal would be late.

    The subjunctive has faded from most casual speech and some writing. It is still expected by many readers in formal writing using **conditional statements**, often beginning with *if* and expressing the improbable or hypothetical.

| DRAFT (PAST) | If fuel efficiency **was** improved, driving costs would go down. |
| EDITED (SUBJUNCTIVE) | If fuel efficiency **were** improved, driving costs would go down. |

Don't add *would* to the *had + verb* structure in the conditional clause, even if *would* appropriately appears in the **result clause** that follows the conditional.

| EXTRA *WOULD* | If fuel efficiency **would have improved**, driving costs **would have gone** down. |
| EDITED | If fuel efficiency **had improved**, driving costs **would have gone** down. |

Finally, some clauses with *that* require a subjunctive verb when they follow certain verbs that make demands or requests.

| DRAFT (PAST) | The judge asked that the witnesses **be swore** in. |
| EDITED | The judge asked that the witnesses **be sworn** in. |

Use the present tense form with *that*, even in the third person singular.

The court ordered that I/you/he/she/it/we/they appear.

For the verb *is*, the forms are *be* (present) and *were* (past).

ESL ADVICE: TYPES OF CONDITIONAL STATEMENTS

TYPE I: TRUE IN THE PRESENT

IF CLAUSE	RESULT CLAUSE

• **Generally true in the present as a habit or as a fact**

| *if* + subject + present tense | subject + present tense |
| If I drive to school every day, | I get to class on time. |

• **True in the future as a one-time event**

| *if* + subject + present tense | subject + future tense |
| If I drive to school today, | I will get to class on time. |

• **Possibly true in the future as a one-time event**

| *if* + subject + present tense | subject + modal + base form verb |
| If I drive to school today, | I may/should get to class on time. |

TYPE II: UNTRUE IN THE PRESENT

IF CLAUSE	RESULT CLAUSE
if + subject + past tense	subject + *would/could/might* + base form verb
If I drove to school,	I would arrive on time.
If I were a car owner,	I could arrive on time.

With Type II, the form of the verb *be* in the *if* clause is always *were*.

TYPE III: UNTRUE IN THE PAST

IF CLAUSE	RESULT CLAUSE
if + subject + past perfect tense	subject + *would/could/might* + *have* + past participle
If I had driven to school,	I would not have been late.

32i Active and passive voice

To recognize a verb in the **active voice**, look for a sentence in which the agent or doer of an action is the subject of the sentence (see 7b-3).

	AGENT (SUBJECT)	ACTION (VERB)	GOAL (OBJECT)
ACTIVE	The car	**hit**	the lamppost.
ACTIVE	Dana	**distributed**	the flyers.

In contrast, when a verb is in the **passive voice**, the goal of the sentence appears in the subject position, and the doer may appear in the object position, after the word *by* (in an optional prepositional phrase). The verb itself adds a form of *be* as a helping verb to the participle form.

	GOAL (SUBJECT)	ACTION (*BE* FORM + VERB)	[AGENT: PREPOSITIONAL PHRASE]
PASSIVE	The lamppost	**was hit**	[by the car].
PASSIVE	The flyers	**were distributed**	[by Dana].

The active and passive versions of a sentence create different kinds of emphasis because they use different words as sentence subjects.

ACTIVE	The city council **banned** smoking in restaurants.
PASSIVE	Smoking in restaurants **was banned** by the city council.
AGENT OMITTED	Smoking in restaurants **was banned**.

ESL ADVICE: PASSIVE VOICE

All tenses can appear in the passive voice *except* these progressive forms: present perfect, past perfect, future, future perfect. In the following sentences, the agent or doer of the action is not the subject *food*, but rather *chef*.

TENSES	SUBJECT + *BE* FORM + PAST PARTICIPLE
PRESENT	The food **is prepared** by the chef.
PRESENT PROGRESSIVE	The food **is being prepared** by the chef.
PAST	The food **was prepared** by the chef.
PAST PROGRESSIVE	The food **was being prepared** by the chef.

PRESENT PERFECT	The food **has been prepared** by the chef.
PAST PERFECT	The food **had been prepared** by the chef.
FUTURE	The food **will be prepared** by the chef.
FUTURE PERFECT	The food **will have been prepared** by the chef.

Each passive verb must have a form of *be* and a past participle (ending in *-ed* for regular verbs). Sometimes the *-ed* ending is hard to hear when spoken, so edit carefully for it.

| MISSING *-ED* | The young man was **call** to the conference room. |
| EDITED | The young man was **called** to the conference room. |

33 Using Pronouns

Readers count on you to use different forms of pronouns to guide them through your sentences. The wrong choices can mislead or irritate them.

DRAFT	**Him** and *me* will make a strong management team.
	READER'S REACTION: *Him* and *me* makes the writer sound careless and uneducated.
EDITED	**He** and **I** will make a strong management team.

Although most pronouns won't give you trouble, at times you may struggle with choices between *we* or *us*, *her* or *she*, and *who* or *whom*.

33a Pronoun forms

A pronoun changes form according to its role in a sentence: subject, object, or possessive, showing possession or ownership. (See also 30b.)

subjective possessive   objective
He and **his** design team created the furniture for **us**.

1 Choosing subjective forms

Choose a subjective form if a pronoun acts as the subject of all or part of a sentence or if it renames or restates a subject.

She wants to know why the orders have not been filled.

Because **they** were unable to get a loan, the business failed.

Atco will be hiring people **who** are willing to work the night shift.

I attend class more regularly than **he** [does].

When you use a pronoun to rename the subject following a form of the verb *be* (*is, am, are, was, were*) you create a **subject complement** (see 31a-2). Choose the subjective form because you are restating the subject.

SUBJECTIVE FORM   **The last art majors** to get jobs were Becky and **I.**

In conversation, people may use the objective form. In writing, however, use the correct form. If it sounds stilted or unnatural, rewrite the sentence.

CONVERSATION   The new traffic reporter is **him.**

STILTED   The new traffic reporter is **he.**

REWRITTEN   **He** is the new traffic reporter.

FORMS OF PRONOUNS

PERSONAL PRONOUNS

	SUBJECTIVE		OBJECTIVE		POSSESSIVE	
	SINGULAR	PLURAL	SINGULAR	PLURAL	SINGULAR	PLURAL
First person	I	we	me	us	my	our
					mine	ours
Second person	you	you	you	you	your	your
					yours	yours
Third person	he		him		his	
	she	they	her	them	her	their
					hers	theirs
	it		it		its	

RELATIVE AND INTERROGATIVE PRONOUNS

SUBJECTIVE	OBJECTIVE	POSSESSIVE
who	whom	whose
whoever	whomever	
which	which	
that	that	
what	what	

INDEFINITE PRONOUNS

SUBJECTIVE	OBJECTIVE	POSSESSIVE
anybody	anybody	anybody's
everyone	everyone	everyone's

2 Choosing objective forms

When you make a pronoun the direct (or indirect) object of an entire sentence, use the objective form. Also use it for pronouns playing other object roles in a sentence.

indirect object   direct object
The company bought **her** **an antivirus program**.

STRATEGY   Choosing objective forms.

As you edit, check whether a pronoun is acting as an object within some part of a sentence. Check also whether it renames or restates an object. If it plays either role, choose the word's objective form.

object of preposition
The rest of **them** had to wait several months for the software.

object in relative clause
An accountant **whom** the firm hired helped her out.

object in gerund phrase
Mr. Pederson's research for the report included interviewing **them**.

object in participial phrase
Having interviewed **us**, too, Mr. Pederson had a lot of material to summarize.

The report contained interviews with the two dissatisfied workers,
appositive renames object
her and him.

You may find pronouns used with infinitives (*to* + a verb) tricky so keep the following example in mind.

OBJECTIVE FORM   Mr. Pederson asked **us** to review the minutes.

Us might seem the subject of the phrase *to review the minutes.* It is the direct object of the sentence, however (*Mr. Pederson asked* **us**). The objective form is correct.

3 Choosing possessive forms

When you use a pronoun to show possession, choose the possessive form. The particular form you use depends on whether the pronoun appears *before a noun* or *in place of a noun*.

BEFORE NOUN   The Topeka office requested a copy of **her** report.

REPLACING NOUN   **Hers** was the most up-to-date study available.

You should also use the possessive form before gerunds (*-ing* verb forms that act as nouns). Because this use of the possessive is often ignored in speech, you may need to practice writing it until it begins to "sound right" to you.

CONVERSATION   Them requesting the report pleased our supervisor.

EDITED   **Their** requesting the report pleased our supervisor.

English nouns also vary in form to show possession, signaled by an apostrophe ('*s* or '): *the study/the study's conclusions.* (See Chapter 50.) Don't confuse nouns and pronouns by adding an apostrophe to a possessive pronoun.

STRATEGY   Choosing between *its* and *it's*.

Its, not *it's*, is the form of the possessive pronoun. Test which you need by replacing the pronoun with *it is* (the expansion of *it's*). If *it is* fits, keep the apostrophe. If *it is* doesn't fit, omit the apostrophe.

DRAFT   The food pantry gave away (*its/it's*) last can of tuna.

REPLACEMENT TEST   The food pantry gave away **it is** last can of tuna.
It is **doesn't make sense.**

USE POSSESSIVE   The food pantry gave away **its** last can of tuna.

33b Editing common pronoun forms

Many problems with pronoun forms occur at predictable places. Pay attention to the following troublesome constructions.

1 Compound subjects and objects

When you use a compound subject such as *the committee and I* or *Jim and me*, the rule is simple: Use the same case for the pronoun in the compound that you would use for a single pronoun in the same role.

COMPOUND SUBJECT   Denise or (*he? him?*) should check the inventory.

SUBJECTIVE FORM   Denise or **he** should check the inventory.

COMPOUND OBJECT   The coach selected (*she? her? and he? him?*) as captains.

OBJECTIVE FORM   The coach selected **her and him** as captains.

STRATEGY Focus-imagine-choose.

- **Focus** on the pronoun whose form you need to choose.

  DRAFT Anne-Marie and **me** will develop the videotape.
  FOCUS: *I or me?*

- **Imagine** each choice for the pronoun as the subject (or object).

  #1 (INCORRECT) **Me** will develop the videotape.

  #2 (CORRECT) **I** will develop the videotape.

- **Choose** the correct form for the compound subject (or object).

  EDITED Anne-Marie and **I** will develop the videotape.

If the appropriate form is not immediately clear to you, see the chart in 33a. Choosing what "sounds right" may not work with compounds.

2 Pronouns that rename or are paired with nouns

When you rename a preceding noun or pronoun in an **appositive**, match the form of the word being renamed. If you pair pronouns like *we* or *us* with nouns, identify the role of the noun and match the pronoun form with it—*we, they* (subjective) or *us, them* (objective).

STRATEGY Test alternatives.

- For appositives, imagine alternative versions of the sentence without the noun (or pronoun) that was renamed.

  SENTENCE The two book illustrators on the panel, (*she? her?*) and (*I? me?*), discussed questions from the audience.

  #1 (INCORRECT) **Her** and **me** discussed questions from the audience.

  #2 (CORRECT) **She** and **I** discussed questions from the audience.

  EDITED The two book illustrators on the panel, **she** and **I**, discussed questions from the audience.

- For pronoun-noun pairs, imagine alternatives without the noun.

  SENTENCE The teaching evaluation should be conducted by (*us? we?*) students, not by the faculty or administration.

  #1 (INCORRECT) The teaching evaluation should be conducted by **we**. . . .

  #2 (CORRECT) The teaching evaluation should be conducted by **us**. . . .

  EDITED The teaching evaluation should be conducted by **us** students, not by the faculty or administration.

3 Comparisons with *than* or *as*

When creating a comparison with *than* or *as* followed by a pronoun, make sure the pronoun form you choose accurately signals the information left out. A pronoun in the subjective case acts as the subject of the implied statement; a pronoun in the objective case acts as the object.

SUBJECTIVE   I gave her sister more help than **she** [did].

OBJECTIVE   I gave her sister more help than [I gave] **her**.

If readers may miss the grammatical signals, rewrite the sentence.

MAY BE
AMBIGUOUS   I like working with Aisha better than she.

               READER'S REACTION: **Does this mean that you prefer to work with Aisha? Or that you like to work with Aisha better than someone else does?**

REWRITTEN   She doesn't like working with Aisha as much as I do.

4 *Who* and *whom*

You often use the pronouns *who* and *whom*, *whoever* and *whomever* to begin subordinate clauses known as **relative clauses** or **adjective clauses** (see 31c). Choose *who* and *whoever* when you use the pronouns as subjects; choose *whom* and *whomever* when you use them as objects.

SUBJECT   The boy **who wins the race** should get the prize.

OBJECT   Give this delicate assignment to **whomever you trust**.

Choose between *who* and *whom* according to the role the pronoun plays *within the relative clause*. Ignore the role the clause plays *within the sentence*.

DRAFT   The fine must be paid by **whomever** holds the deed.

           Although the whole clause is the object of the preposition *by*, within the clause the pronoun acts as a subject, not an object.

EDITED   The fine must be paid by **whoever** holds the deed.

At the beginning of a question, you should use *who* when the pronoun is the subject of the sentence and *whom* when the pronoun is an object.

SUBJECT   **Who** is most likely to get the reader's sympathy at this point in the novel, Huck or Jim?

OBJECT   **Whom** can Cordelia trust at the end of the scene?

34 Making Sentence Parts Agree

Readers get mixed signals when sentence parts are not coordinated.

INCONSISTENT The city council and the mayor is known for her skillful responses to civic debate.

> **READER'S REACTION: I thought the sentence was about two things— the city council and the mayor—but when I read *is* and *her*, it seemed to be about only one, the mayor.**

EDITED The city council and the mayor **are** known for **their** skillful responses to civic debate.

Readers expect you to help them understand how the ideas in a sentence relate by making the parts of a sentence work together grammatically—by showing **agreement** in number, person, and gender.

34a Agreement

Within a sentence, a subject and verb should agree in **number** (singular or plural) and **person** (first, second, or third).

You **know** our client. She **wants** to see the design next week.

In addition, each pronoun should agree with its **antecedent**, the noun or other pronoun to which it refers, in **number** (singular, plural), **person** (first, second, third), and **gender** (masculine, feminine, neuter).

The **crews** riding their snowplows left early; the **airport** needed its runways cleared.

AGREEMENT: NUMBER, PERSON, AND GENDER

- *Number* shows whether words are singular (one person, animal, idea, or thing) or plural (two or more) in meaning.

  SINGULAR This **community** needs its own recreation center.

  PLURAL Local **communities** need to share their facilities.

- *Person* indicates the speaker or subject being spoken to or about.

(Continued)

AGREEMENT: NUMBER, PERSON, AND GENDER (*continued*)

First person (speaker): *I, we*

> I <u>operate</u> the compressor.   We <u>operate</u> the compressor.

Second person (spoken to): *you*

> You <u>operate</u> the forklift.

Third person (spoken about): *he, she, it, they*; nouns naming things, people, animals, ideas

> He/she/it <u>operates</u> the drill.   They <u>operate</u> the drill.

- *Gender* refers to masculine (*he, him*), feminine (*she, her*), or neuter (*it*) qualities attributed to a noun or pronoun.

  MASCULINE/FEMININE
  The future <u>father</u> rushed for **his** car keys, while his <u>wife</u> packed **her** bag.

  NEUTER
  Despite **its** recent tune-up, the <u>car</u> stalled near the hospital.

34b Creating simple subject-verb agreement

To make subjects and verbs agree, make sure they are aligned in two ways: **number** (singular or plural) and **person** (first, second, or third). Keeping them aligned helps your sentences convey consistent, clear meaning.

1 Check subjects, then verbs

First look for the subject. Identify its number (singular or plural) and person (first, second, or third). Then edit the verb so that it agrees.

DRAFT   The clients is waiting.

BOTH PLURAL   The **clients** <u>are</u> waiting.

BOTH SINGULAR The **client** <u>is</u> waiting.

2 Watch out for plurals

Most plural nouns end in *-s* or *-es*, yet exactly the opposite is the case for present tense verbs.

- **Look for a plural subject:** nouns ending in *-s* or *-es*; plural pronouns such as *they* and *we*.

  EXCEPTIONS
- Nouns with irregular plurals (*person/people* or *child/children*)
- Nouns with the same form for singular and plural (*moose/moose*)

SINGULAR   The dam prevent**s** flooding.

PLURAL   The dam**s** prevent flooding.

- **Check for a plural verb:** -s or -es in present tense.

  EXCEPTIONS
  - Verbs with irregular forms, including *be* and *have* (see 32c).
  - **Check the verb again.** If you find a main verb *plus* a helping verb, remember this: the helping verb *sometimes* changes form for singular and plural, but the main verb remains the same (see 32d).

	HELPING VERB CHANGES FORM	HELPING VERB DOES NOT CHANGE
SINGULAR	The **park** does seem safer.	The **park** might seem safer.
PLURAL	The **parks** do seem safer.	The **parks** might seem safer.

ESL ADVICE: SUBJECT-VERB AGREEMENT WITH *BE, HAVE,* AND *DO*

Some troublesome verbs change form according to person or tense.

SERIOUS ERROR

- *Be* verbs (present and past)

  I **am/was**.   He/She/It **is/was**. You/We/They **are/were**.

- **Helping verb *be*** (present progressive and past progressive tenses)

  I   **am** talking.   I/He/She/It   **was talking**.
  You/We/They   **are** talking.   We/You/They   **were talking**.
  He/She/It   **is** talking.

- *Have* verbs (present)

  I/You/We/They   **have** a new home.   He/She/It   **has** a new home.

- **Helping verb *have*** (present perfect and present perfect progressive tenses)

  I/You/We/They   **have** lived here   **have** been living
                            for years.   here since May.
  He/She/It   **has** lived here   **has** been living
                            for years.   here since May.

- *Do* or *does* to show emphasis

  I/You/We/They   **do** want the job.   He/She/It   **does** want it.

- *Doesn't* or *don't* to show the negative

  I/You/We/They   **don't** exercise   He/She/It   **doesn't** exercise
                            enough.   enough.

SERIOUS ERROR

34c Creating complex subject-verb agreement

Checking for subject-verb agreement sometimes becomes complicated. Try to remember the words and structures that cause problems, and be ready to look up the editing strategies that follow.

1 Watch for collective nouns or plural nouns with singular meanings

A **collective noun** is singular in form yet identifies a group of individuals (*audience, mob, crew, troop, tribe,* or *herd*). When the group acts as a single unit, choose a singular verb. When group members act individually, choose a plural verb.

ONE SINGLE UNIT   The **staff** is hardworking and well trained.

INDIVIDUAL
MEMBERS   The **staff** have earned the respect of our clients.

Nouns with plural forms and singular meanings. Nouns like *politics, physics, statistics, mumps,* and *athletics* have -*s* endings but are singular.

Mathematics is an increasingly popular field of study.

Titles and names. When your sentence subject is a book title or company name, choose a singular verb even if the name or title is plural. Think to yourself, "The *company* pays . . ." or "The *book* is. . . ."

Home Helpers **pays** high wages and **has** excellent benefits.

The White Roses **is** second on the best-seller list this month.

Numbers. A measurement or figure (even one ending in -*s*) may still be singular if it names a quantity or unit as a whole. When it refers to individual elements, treat it as a whole.

Four years is the amount of time she spent studying stress.

STRATEGY   Use the pronoun test.

Decide which pronoun accurately represents a complicated subject: *he, she,* or *it* (singular) or *they* (plural). Read your sentence aloud using this replacement pronoun; edit the verb to agree.

DRAFT   The **news** about the job market _____ surprisingly good.
PRONOUN TEST: I could replace "The news" with "It" and say "It is."

EDITED   The **news** about the job market **is** surprisingly good.

---

2 Check subjects linked by *and, or,* and *nor*

And creates a compound subject; *or* and *nor* create alternative subjects.

Compound subjects. Because *and* or *both . . . and* make the subject plural (even if its parts are singular), you generally need to choose a plural verb.

PLURAL   **Ham and eggs** <u>are</u> ingredients in this casserole.

TWO PEOPLE   **My friend and my coworker** <u>have</u> paintings in the show.

If the parts should be taken as a unit or if the parts designate a single person, thing, or idea, you need to choose a singular verb.

UNIT (SINGULAR)   **Ham and eggs** <u>is</u> still my favorite breakfast.

ONE PERSON   **My friend and coworker** <u>has</u> paintings in the show.

Both . . . and always needs a plural verb, whether the elements joined are singular or plural.

Both the president **and** her advisor <u>are</u> in Tokyo this week.

Both the president **and** her advisors <u>are</u> in Tokyo this week.

Alternative subjects. When you use *or* or *nor* (*either . . . or, neither . . . nor*) to connect alternative parts of the subject, the verb agrees with the closer part. Putting the plural element closer to the verb often is less awkward.

PLURAL CLOSE   The auditor or **the accountants** <u>review</u> each report.
TO VERB

SINGULAR CLOSE   False records or **late reporting** <u>weakens</u> the review process.
TO VERB

Either . . . or, neither . . . nor, and *not only . . . but also* may take either a singular or a plural verb, depending on the subject closer to the verb.

Either the president **or** her <u>advisor</u> <u>is</u> in Tokyo.

Neither the president **nor** her <u>advisors</u> <u>are</u> in Tokyo.

3 Pay attention to separated subjects and verbs

When you insert words between the subject and verb of a sentence, you may be tempted to make the verb agree with one of the intervening words rather than the actual subject.

To find the real subject, imagine the subject without intervening words or phrases. Then check that the subject and verb agree.

DRAFT   The new trolley system, featuring expanded routes and lower
                      fares, are especially popular with senior citizens.

FAULTY   The new **trolley system** . . .
AGREEMENT   **are** especially popular with senior citizens.

EDITED   The new **trolley system**, featuring expanded routes and
                      lower fares, <u>is</u> especially popular with senior citizens.

ESL ADVICE: SEPARATED SUBJECTS AND VERBS

PHRASE SEPARATES   A person **with sensitive eyes** has to wear sunglasses.

CLAUSE SEPARATES   A person **whose eyes are sensitive** has to wear sunglasses.

When the subject is the same in both the main and subordinate clauses, the verbs must agree.

SAME SUBJECT   A **person** who **wants** to protect her eyes **wears** sunglasses.

If you mistake a phrase like *as well as, in addition to, together with,* or *along with* for *and*, you may be tempted to treat a noun following it as the subject.

     The **provost**, as well as the deans, has issued new guidelines.

If you mean *and*, use the word itself.

REWRITTEN   The provost **and** the deans have issued new guidelines.

DRAFT   A regular tune-up, along with frequent oil **changes**, prolong the life of your car.
       IMAGINE: **A regular tune-up . . . prolongs the life of your car.**

EDITED   A regular **tune-up**, along with frequent oil changes, prolongs the life of your car.

4 Recognize unusual word order

When you alter typical word order to create emphasis or ask a question, make sure the verb still agrees with the subject. The verb and subject should agree even with inverted (reversed) word order.

QUESTION   Are **popular comedy and action films** mere escapism?

EMPHASIS   After victory comes **overconfidence** for many teams.

There is, there are. Expletive constructions such as *there are* and *it is* invert (reverse) the usual subject-verb sentence order, allowing you to put the subject *after* the verb (see 7b-2). Then the verb agrees with the subject that follows it.

SINGULAR   There is **opportunity** for people starting service industries.

PLURAL   There are many **opportunities** for service industries.

***Is, appears, feels,* and other linking verbs.** When you build a sentence around *is, appears, feels* or another linking verb (see 30c), make sure the verb agrees with the subject. You may be tempted to make it agree with the noun or pronoun renaming the subject (the complement, see 30c), but edit carefully to avoid this problem.

                         subject   verb   complement
DRAFT   The chief **obstacle** to change are the **mayor and her allies**.

EDITED   The chief **obstacle** to change is the mayor and her allies.

ESL ADVICE: SUBJECT-VERB AGREEMENT

- Check for agreement with compound verbs (more than one verb) in a simple sentence.

  The clerk **collects**, **sorts**, and **files** reports.

- Check for subject-verb agreement in a complex sentence (see 31d).

  ADVERB CLAUSE When the snow **falls**, we enjoy the scenery.

  ADJECTIVE CLAUSE The young man that I work with **lives** in town.

  The young man that **works** with me **lives** in town.

- Check for correct selection of helping verbs.

  THIRD PERSON *DOES* That restaurant **does** give special dinner discounts.

  MODAL The president **might** give a speech this evening.

5 Pay attention to troublesome words

Watch for words such as *all, everybody, who, that,* and *each.*

All, everybody, none. *All, everybody,* and *none* (and other indefinite pronouns) do not refer to specific ideas, people, or things. Most have clearly singular meanings and require singular verbs.

Someone is mailing campaign flyers.

Everybody has the duty to vote.

You can treat a few pronouns, such as *all, any, most, none,* and *some,* as either singular or plural according to meaning.

SOME INDEFINITE AND RELATIVE PRONOUNS

GENERALLY SINGULAR		PLURAL	EITHER SINGULAR OR PLURAL
another	neither	both	all
anybody	nobody	few	any
anyone	none	many	enough
anything	no one	others	more
each	nothing	several	most
either	one		some
every	other		that
everybody	somebody		which
everyone	someone		who
everything	something		whose
much			

STRATEGY Ask "Can it be counted?"

Does the pronoun refer to something that *cannot be counted*? Choose singular.

> SINGULAR **All** of the <u>food</u> **is** for the camping trip next week.
> *food* = food in general (not countable); *all* = singular

Does the pronoun refer to two or more elements of something that *can be counted*? Choose plural.

> PLURAL **All** of the <u>supplies</u> **are** for the camping trip next week.
> *supplies* = many kinds of supplies (countable), such as baking mixes, bottled water, and dried fruit; *all* = plural

Who, which, and that. *Who, which,* and *that* (relative pronouns, see 30b) do not have singular and plural forms, yet the words to which they refer (antecedents) generally do. Choose a singular or plural verb according to the number of the antecedent.

> SINGULAR   He likes **a film** that **focuses** on the characters.

> PLURAL   I prefer **films** that **combine** action and romance.

Make a habit of noticing the phrases *one of* and *the only one of*. They can create agreement problems when they come before *who, which,* or *that.*

> Dr. Tazu is **one** of the engineers who design storage systems.

Who refers to the plural *engineers*; the verb, *design*, is plural. There are other engineers like Dr. Tazu.

Dr. Tazu is **the only one** of the engineers who designs storage systems.

Who refers to the singular *Dr. Tazu*; the verb, *designs*, is singular. Dr. Tazu is the only one who designs storage systems.

Each **and** *every.* Your placement of *each* or *every* can create a singular (*each one*) or plural (*they each*) meaning.

> *Each* before compound subject + singular verb
> **Each** supervisor and manager checks the logs daily.

> *Each* after compound subject + plural verb
> The supervisors and managers **each** check the logs daily.

ESL ADVICE: QUANTIFIERS

A **quantifier**—a word like *each, one,* or *many*—indicates the amount or quantity of a subject.

EXPRESSIONS FOLLOWED BY A PLURAL NOUN + A SINGULAR VERB
Each of/Every one of/One of/None of the **students** lives on campus.

EXPRESSIONS FOLLOWED BY A PLURAL NOUN + A PLURAL VERB
Several of/Many of/Both of the **students** live off campus.

In some cases, the noun after the expression determines the verb form.

EXPRESSIONS FOLLOWED BY EITHER A SINGULAR OR A PLURAL VERB
  noncount noun + singular verb
Some of/Most of/All of/A lot of the **produce** is fresh.

  plural noun + plural verb
Some of/Most of/All of/A lot of the **vegetables** are fresh.

MUCH AND MOST (NOT MUCH OF OR MOST OF) WITH NONCOUNT AND PLURAL NOUNS

NONCOUNT NOUN **Much traffic** occurs during rush hour.

PLURAL NOUN **Most Americans** live in the cities or suburbs.

OTHER, OTHERS, AND ANOTHER AS PRONOUNS OR ADJECTIVES
PRONOUNS
Others + **plural verb:** adds points about a topic; there may be more points.

I enjoy Paris for many reasons. Some reasons are the architecture and gardens; **others are** the wonderful people, culture, and language.

The others (plural) + plural verb; *the other* (singular) + singular verb: adds the last point or points about the topic; there are no more.

Some hikers favor Craig's plan; **the others want** to follow Tina's.

ADJECTIVES
Another + singular noun: adds an idea; there may be more ideas.
Other + plural noun: adds more ideas; there may be more ideas.

One strength of our engineering team is our knowledge of the problem. **Another strength** is our experience. **Other strengths** include our communication skills, teamwork, and energy.

The other + singular or plural noun: adds the final point or points to be discussed.

Of the two very important sights to see in Paris, one is the Louvre Museum, and **the other one** is the Cathedral of Notre Dame.

One of the major sights in Paris is the Louvre Museum. **The other sights** are the Eiffel Tower, the Champs-Élysées, the Cathedral of Notre Dame, and the Arc de Triomphe.

34d Creating pronoun-antecedent agreement

Agreement between a pronoun and its antecedent (in **number**, **person**, and **gender**—see 34a) helps readers recognize the link between them.

plural antecedent   pronoun
Campers should treat **their** tents with a mildew-preventing spray.

STRATEGY Find the specific word to which a pronoun refers.

If you are uncertain about which pronoun form to use, circle or mark the specific word (or words) to which it refers. Then edit either the pronoun or the antecedent so that the two elements match.

INCONSISTENT   Proposals should address its audience.

CLEAR   **Proposals** should address **their audiences**.

CLEAR   **A proposal** should address **its audience**.

A **collective noun** such as *team*, *group*, *clan*, *audience*, *army*, or *tribe* can act as a singular or plural antecedent, depending on whether it refers to the group as a whole or to the members acting separately.

SINGULAR   The **subcommittee** submitted **its** revised report.

PLURAL   The **subcommittee** discussed **their** concerns.

1 Check antecedents linked by *and, or,* and *nor*

When a pronoun refers to several things (Luis *and* Jennifer, for example), the pronoun form you choose usually depends on the word that links the elements of the antecedent.

Antecedents joined by *and*. When you form a **compound antecedent** by joining two or more antecedents with *and*, refer to them with a plural pronoun (such as *they*), even if one or more are singular.

> **Luis and Jenni** said that the lab tests they ran were conclusive.

> **The other students and I** admit that the tests we ran were not.

This guideline has two exceptions.

- If a compound antecedent refers to a single person, thing, or idea, use a singular pronoun.

  > **My colleague and coauthor** is someone skilled at lab analysis.

- If you place *each* or *every* before a compound antecedent to single out the individual members of the compound, use a singular pronoun.

  > **Each** of the soil and water samples arrives in its own container.

Antecedents joined by *or* or *nor*. When you join the parts of an antecedent with *or* or *nor* (or *either . . . or, neither . . . nor*), make sure the pronoun agrees with the part closer to it.

> **Neither** the manager **nor** the **engineers** wrote their reports on time.

If one part is singular and the other plural, try putting the plural element second or rewriting to avoid an awkward or confusing sentence.

CONFUSING   Either Jim and Al or Dalhat will include the projections in his report.

> READER'S REACTION: **Will Jim and Al add to Dalhat's report? Or will the projections go into one of two reports, Dalhat's or Jim and Al's?**

EDITED	Either Dalhat or **Jim** and **Al** will include the projections in their report.
REWRITTEN	Either Dalhat will include the projections in his report, or Jim and Al will include them in theirs.
REWRITTEN	Either Dalhat or Jim and Al will include the projections in the team's report.

2 Watch for pronouns that refer to other pronouns

Many words like *somebody* and *each* (indefinite pronouns; see 34c-4) are singular. The pronouns that refer to them should also be singular.

Somebody on the team left her racket on the court.

Each of the men has his own equipment.

To avoid either sexist language (see 46b) or inconsistency, use *both* a plural pronoun and a plural antecedent, especially when writing for the academic community.

SEXIST	**Everybody** included charts in **his** sales **talk**.
INFORMAL (SPOKEN)	**Everybody** included charts in **their** sales **talks**.
WRITTEN	**All presenters** included charts in **their** sales **talks**.

ESL ADVICE: DEMONSTRATIVE ADJECTIVES OR PRONOUNS

Demonstrative adjectives or **pronouns** are either singular (*this*, *that*) or plural (*these*, *those*), depending on the noun being modified. (See 30b.)

INCONSISTENT	This crystals of water make snowflakes.
BOTH PLURAL	**These crystals** of water make snowflakes.
INCONSISTENT	Those snowflake crystal is made of frozen water.
BOTH SINGULAR	**That snowflake crystal** is made of frozen water.

35 Using Adjectives and Adverbs

If you confuse adjectives and adverbs or use them improperly, many readers will notice these errors.

DRAFT   The new medication acts **quick**.

> **READER'S REACTION:** *Quick* doesn't fit here. Maybe the writer is careless or doesn't know what to use.

EDITED   The new medication acts **quickly**.

Academic readers may be especially alert to these differences, but use modifiers carefully in formal contexts, whatever the community.

35a What adjectives and adverbs do

Adjectives and adverbs modify—add to, qualify, focus, limit, or extend the meaning of—other words and thus are called **modifiers**.

FEATURES OF ADJECTIVES AND ADVERBS

ADJECTIVES

- Modify nouns and pronouns
- Answer "How many?" "What kind?" "Which one (or ones)?" "What size, color, or shape?"
- Include words like *blue*, *complicated*, *good*, and *frightening*
- Include words created by adding endings like *-able*, *-ical*, *-less*, *-ful*, and *-ous* to nouns or verbs (such as *controllable*, *sociological*, *seamless*, *careful*, *nervous*)

ADVERBS

- Modify verbs, adjectives, and other adverbs
- Modify phrases (*almost* beyond the building), clauses (*soon after* I added the last ingredients), and sentences (*Remarkably*, the mechanism was not damaged.)
- Answer "When?" "Where?" "How?" "How often?" "Which direction?" "What degree?"
- Consist mostly of words ending in *-ly*, like *quickly* and *carefully*
- Include some common words that do not end in *-ly*, such as *fast*, *very*, *well*, *quite*, and *late*

You can use most modifiers in three forms, depending on how many things you compare—no other things, two things, or three or more.

POSITIVE	The cab drove **quickly** on the **smooth** road.
COMPARATIVE (2)	The cab drove **more quickly** on the **smoother** road.
SUPERLATIVE (3+)	The cab drove **most quickly** on the **smoothest** road.

ESL ADVICE: ADJECTIVES IN A SERIES

When you use two or more adjectives in a series, you need to place them in the appropriate order before the main noun.

DETERMINER	QUALITY	PHYSICAL DESCRIPTION	NATIONALITY	MATERIAL	QUALIFYING NOUN	MAIN NOUN
that	expensive	smooth black	German	fiberglass	racing	car
four	little	round white		plastic	Ping-Pong	balls
several	beautiful	young red	Japanese		maple	trees

COMPARATIVE AND SUPERLATIVE FORMS

ADJECTIVES

ONE SYLLABLE

Most add -er and -est (*pink, pinker, pinkest*).

TWO SYLLABLES

Many add -er and -est (*happy, happier, happiest*).

Some add either -er and -est or more and most (*foggy, foggier, foggiest; foggy, more foggy, most foggy*).

THREE (OR MORE) SYLLABLES

Add more and most (*plentiful, more plentiful, most plentiful*).

ADVERBS

ONE SYLLABLE

Most add -er and -est (*quick, quicker, quickest*).

TWO (OR MORE) SYLLABLES

Most add more and most (*carefully, more carefully, most carefully*).

NEGATIVE COMPARISONS

ADJECTIVES AND ADVERBS

Use *less* and *least* (*less agile, least agile; less clearly, least clearly*).

(Continued)

IRREGULAR COMPARATIVES AND SUPERLATIVES (*continued*)

ADJECTIVE	COMPARATIVE	SUPERLATIVE
bad	worse	worst
good	better	best
ill (harsh, unlucky)	worse	worst
a little	less	least
many	more	most
much	more	most
some	more	most
well (healthy)	better	best
ADVERB		
badly	worse	worst
ill (badly)	worse	worst
well (satisfactorily)	better	best

35b Editing adjectives and adverbs

Because not all adverbs end in *-ly* and some adjectives do (*friendly, lonely*), you can't always rely on *-ly* to help you choose a modifier.

1 Figure out what a modifier does in a sentence

First try to analyze what the modifier will do in your sentence.

- Do you need an adjective? Adjectives answer the questions "How many?" "What kind?" "Which one (or ones)?" or "What size, color, or shape?"
- Or do you need an adverb? Adverbs answer the questions "When?" "Where?" "How?" "How often?" "Which direction?" or "What degree?"

DRAFT   Write **careful** so that the directions are clear.

QUESTION: Write *how*? This word answers an adverb question.

EDITED   Write **carefully** so that the directions are clear.

The word modified also can tell you whether to use an adverb or adjective.

STRATEGY   **Draw an arrow.**

Point to the word that is modified. If this word acts as a noun or pronoun, modify it with an adjective; if it acts as a verb, adjective, or adverb, modify it with an adverb.

DRAFT   The insulation underwent **remarkable** quick deterioration.

CONNECTION: *Remarkable* modifies *quick* (and answers the adverb question "How quick?"). *Quick* in turn modifies *deterioration* (and answers the adjective question "What kind of deterioration?"). Replace *remarkable* with an adverb.

EDITED   The insulation underwent **remarkably** quick deterioration.

2 Check the sentence pattern

Verbs such as *look*, *feel*, and *prove* can show both states of being (**linking verbs**) and activities (**action verbs**). The verb *is* always acts as a linking verb. Choose an adjective for a state of being; choose an adverb for an action or activity.

subject	linking verb	complement (adjective)
The room	smelled	musty.
The procedure	proved	unreliable.

ADJECTIVE (BEING)	The metal cover over the motor turned **hot**.
ADVERB (ACTION)	The large wheel turned **quickly**.
ADJECTIVE	The movement grew **rapid**. [The motion became quick.]
ADVERB	The movement grew **rapidly**. [The group spread its ideas.]

3 Pay special attention to *real/really, sure/surely, bad/badly, and good/well*

Common uses of *real/really*, *sure/surely*, *bad/badly*, and *good/well* may be acceptable in speech but not in other settings.

INFORMAL SPEECH   I feel **badly** that our group argues so much.

READER'S REACTION: Someone who *feels badly* has a poor sense of touch.

BAD/BADLY; GOOD/WELL

- Use *bad* (adjective) with linking verbs such as *is*, *seems*, or *appears* (see 30c, 31a-2).

I feel **bad** that our group argues so much. [not *badly*]

- Use *badly* (adverb) with action verbs.

  The new breathing apparatus <u>works</u> **badly**. [not *bad*]

- Use *good* (adjective) with linking verbs.

  The chef's new garlic dressing <u>tastes</u> **good**. [not *well*]

- Use *well* (adverb) with action verbs unless it refers to health.

  The new pump <u>works</u> **well**. [not *good*]

REAL/REALLY; SURE/SURELY

- Use *really* (adverb) to modify an adjective like *fast, efficient,* or *hot.*

  Lu Ming is **really** <u>efficient</u>. [not *real*]

  Lu Ming works **really** <u>efficiently</u>. [not *real*]

- Use *surely* (adverb) to modify adjectives like *misleading, outdated,* or *courageous.*

  This diagram is **surely** <u>misleading</u>. [not *sure*]

4 Pay attention to comparisons and double negatives

Someone with only two children may say, "She's my oldest." In writing, however, you need to be more precise.

To compare two things, use the **comparative form** (*-er* or *more*); to compare three or more, use the **superlative form** (*-est* or *most*).

INACCURATE   The survey covered four age groups: 20–29, 30–44, 45–59, and 60+. Those in the older group smoked least.

READER'S REACTION: **Does this mean that the people in the older *groups* smoked least or that the people in the *oldest* group smoked least?**

PRECISE   The survey covered four age groups: 20–29, 30–44, 45–59, and 60+. Those in the **oldest group** smoked least.

Double comparatives. Most readers will not accept a double comparative (combining the *-er* form and *more*) or a double superlative (combining the *-est* form and *most*).

DRAFT   Jorge is the **most agilest** athlete in the squadron.

EDITED   Jorge is the **most agile** athlete in the squadron.

Illogical comparatives. Some adjectives and adverbs such as *unique, impossible, pregnant, dead, gone, perfectly,* and *entirely* cannot logically take comparative or superlative form.

ILLOGICAL	Gottlieb's "Nightscape" is a **most unique** painting.
	READER'S REACTION: How can a thing be *more* or *most* if it is unique— the only one?
LOGICAL	Gottlieb's "Nightscape" is a **unique** painting.

SERIOUS ERROR

Double negatives. Informal speech and dialects may combine negatives such as *no, none, not, never, hardly, scarcely,* and *haven't* and *don't* (formed with *n't,* abbreviating *not*). In writing, however, readers are likely to feel that two negatives used together—a **double negative**—cancel each other out.

DRAFT	The nurses **can't hardly** manage routine care, much less emergencies.
	READER'S REACTION: This sounds more like a conversation than a staffing report.
EDITED	The nurses **can hardly** manage routine care, much less emergencies.

PART 10

Sentence Problems

▼ TAKING IT ONLINE

WHAT IS A SENTENCE FRAGMENT?

http://www.harpercollege.edu/writ_ctr/fragmnt.htm

This Web site includes examples, suggestions, and links to two simple tests for detecting fragments. Its conversational tone makes this site easy to understand and use.

HOW TO FIX 50% OF YOUR GRAMMAR PROBLEMS

http://www.uark.edu/campus-resources/qwrtcntr/resources/handouts/fix50.htm

This site offers advice for dealing with common problems.

THE MISPLACED MODIFIER, A.K.A. THE SENTENCE DANGLER

http://ace.acadiau.ca/english/grammar/mmodifier.htm

This page identifies one of the "ten most wanted" grammar outlaws and includes quizzes to help you rehabilitate this outlaw.

SEQUENCE OF VERB TENSES

http://grammar.ccc.commnet.edu/grammar/

Search for the handy charts on the sequence of tenses in the "Word and Sentence Level" section.

PARALLELISM

http://www.english.uiuc.edu/cws/wworkshop

Visit "Parallelism" in both the "Grammar Handbook" and "Writing Tips" for advice on what parallel structure is and how to use it effectively.

COORDINATION/SUBORDINATION

http://www.calstatela.edu/centers/write_cn/e100effsent.htm

This site can help you use coordination and subordination effectively.

PART 10

Sentence Problems

36 Sentence Fragments

If you punctuate a group of words as a sentence when they do not actually form a complete sentence, you are likely to irritate readers and undermine your authority as a writer.

PARTS MISSING   The insurance company processing the claim.
> **READER'S REACTION: Something is missing. What did the company do?**

EDITED   **The insurance company** processing the claim <u>sent</u> a check.

Despite having a capital letter at the beginning and a period at the end, a **sentence fragment** is only part of a sentence, not a complete sentence.

A fragment is considered the most serious sentence-level error by many college instructors as well as workplace and public readers. On occasion, an **intentional fragment** may create emphasis or a change of pace, especially in imaginative writing (see 36c). An unintentional fragment, however, forces readers to do the writer's job, mentally reattaching a word group to a nearby sentence or supplying missing information. If you make readers do your work, they may be too distracted to attend to your ideas and may harshly judge your writing (and you as a writer).

SERIOUS ERROR   **36a**   **Sentence fragments**

Before you can edit fragments effectively, you need to be able to distinguish complete sentences from word groups missing a subject or a verb (see 31a) and from clauses detached from sentences to which they belong.

1 Look for a subject and a verb

A **complete sentence** contains both a subject and a complete verb, expressed or implied. If a word group lacks either, it's a fragment.

STRATEGY   **Ask questions.**

Sentence Test 1: Ask *Who* (or *what*) *does*? Or *Who* (or *what*) *is*?

- Does a word group answer "Who?" or "What?" If not, it *lacks a subject* and is a fragment.

  FRAGMENT   Also needs a family counselor.
  > **READER'S REACTION: I can't tell *who* (or *what*) needs a counselor.**

  EDITED   **Hope Clinic** also needs a family counselor.

In an imperative sentence (see 31 d-2), the subject *you* is understood and needn't be stated.

IMPERATIVE	[**You**] Use the spectrometer to test for the unknown chemical.

- Does a word group answer "Does?" or "Is?" If not, it *lacks a verb* and is a fragment.

FRAGMENT	The new policy to provide health care coverage on the basis of hours worked each week.
	READER'S REACTION: I can't tell what the new policy *does* or *is*.
EDITED	The new policy **provides** health care coverage on the basis of hours worked each week.

Sentence Test 2: See if you can turn a word group into a question that can be answered *yes* or *no*. If you can, the word group is a sentence.

WORD GROUP	They bought a van to carry the equipment.
QUESTION	Did they buy a van to carry the equipment?
CONCLUSION	The word group is a sentence.

WORD GROUP	Bought the building for a warehouse.
QUESTION	Did _____ buy the building for a warehouse?
CONCLUSION	The question doesn't have a subject, so the word group is a fragment.
EDITED	**Johnson Plumbing** bought the building for a warehouse.

WORD GROUP	The company providing repairs for our computers.
QUESTION	Does the company **providing** repairs for our computers?
	CAUTION: Do not begin the question with *is, are, has,* or *have*, or you may unintentionally provide a verb for the word group being tested.
CONCLUSION	*Providing* can't act as the verb in its current form, so this is a fragment.
EDITED	The company **is** providing repairs for our computers.

Confusing verbs and verbals. In checking for fragments, be careful not to mistake a **verbal** for a verb. Verbals include participles (*testing, tested*), infinitives (*to test*), and gerunds (*testing*) (see 31b-4). A verbal alone can never act as the verb in a sentence. If you add words like *is, has, can, or should* (helping verbs, see 32d), you can turn verbals into verbs (*was testing, should test*).

RECOGNIZING A SENTENCE

A **sentence**—also called a **main** (or **independent**) **clause**—is a word group with a subject and verb that can stand alone.

SENTENCE   **The hungry bears** <u>were hunting</u> food.

SENTENCE   Because spring snows had damaged many plants, **the hungry bears** <u>were hunting</u> food in urban areas.

A **subordinate** (or **dependent**) **clause** has a subject and a predicate, yet it cannot stand on its own as a sentence because it begins with a subordinating word like *because*, *although*, *which*, or *that* (see 43b).

FRAGMENT   Because **spring snows** <u>had damaged</u> many plants.

A **phrase** is a word group that lacks a subject, a predicate, or both. It cannot stand alone.

FRAGMENTS were hunting in urban areas the hungry bears

---

2 Look for words like *although, because, that,* and *since*

  Pay attention to word groups containing a subject and a verb but beginning with subordinators such as *although, if, because,* or *that* (see the list in 43b). These words tell readers to regard the clause that follows as part of a larger statement.

  Once you have identified a word group beginning with a subordinator or with a relative pronoun (*that, what, which,* or *who*; see 33a), check whether it is attached to a main clause—a cluster of words that can stand on its own as a sentence (see the box above). If the word group is unattached, it is a fragment.

FRAGMENT   Residents love the mild climate. <u>Which</u> **has encouraged outdoor events**.

EDITED   Residents love the mild climate, **which** has encouraged outdoor events.

3 Pay attention to *for example* and verbal fragments

  Word groups beginning with phrases like *for example, such as,* or *for instance* are sometimes disconnected from sentences and mistakenly made to stand on their own. Often, too, verbal phrases (verbal plus object and modifiers, 31b-4) are detached from related sentences and asked, inappropriately, to stand on their own.

SERIOUS ERROR **36b** Editing sentence fragments

You can correct sentence fragments in four ways.

1 Supply the missing element

FRAGMENT   The judge allowing adopted children to meet their natural parents.

EDITED
(VERB ADDED)   The judge **favors** allowing adopted children to meet their natural parents.

2 Attach the fragment to a nearby main clause. Rewrite if necessary

FRAGMENT   Trauma centers give prompt care to heart attack victims. Because **rapid treatment can minimize heart damage**.

ATTACHED   Trauma centers give prompt care to heart attack victims **because** rapid treatment can minimize heart damage.

FRAGMENT   **Introducing competing varieties of crabs into the same tank.** He did this in order to study aggression.

REWRITTEN   He **introduced** competing varieties of crabs into the same tank in order to study aggression.

3 Drop a subordinating word, turning a fragment into a sentence

FRAGMENT   **Although** several people argued against the motion. It still passed by a majority.

EDITED   Several people argued against the motion. It still passed by a majority.

4 Rewrite a passage to eliminate a fragment

FRAGMENT   Some sports attract many participants in their fifties, sixties, and even seventies. **For example, tennis and bowling.**

EDITED
(ATTACHED)   Some sports, **such as tennis and bowling**, attract many participants in their fifties, sixties, and even seventies.

REWRITTEN
(EMPHASIZED)   Some sports attract many participants in their fifties, sixties, and even seventies. For example, **tennis and bowling appeal to older adults year-round**.

36c Using partial sentences

In magazines, campaign literature, advertisements, and even well-written essays, you may encounter **partial sentences**—sentence fragments used intentionally, effectively, but sparingly. Partial sentences can call attention to details ("Deep rose, not red."), emphasize ideas ("Wilson. For the future."), heighten contrasts ("And in the last lane, my brother."), or add transition ("Next, the results."). Other uses include informal questions and answers ("Where?" "On my desk.") and exclamations ("Too bad!").

- Use partial sentences only when readers are likely to accept them.
- When in doubt, seek a reader's advice, or look at comparable writing.
- Have a clear purpose—describing, emphasizing, or contrasting.
- Be sure readers can supply missing elements or connect word groups.
- Make sure readers won't mistake your partial sentence for a fragment.

37 Comma Splices and Fused Sentences

You can easily confuse and annoy readers if you inappropriately join two or more sentences using either a comma only (**comma splice**) or no punctuation at all (**fused sentence**). If you don't clearly mark the parts and boundaries of a sentence, readers may have to puzzle over its meaning.

COMMA SPLICE
CBS was founded in 1928 by William S. Paley, his uncle and his father sold him a struggling radio network.

READER'S REACTION: At first I thought CBS had three founders: Paley, his uncle, and his father. Then I realized that Paley probably bought the network from his relatives.

EDITED
CBS was founded in 1928 by William S. Paley ; his uncle and his father sold him a struggling radio network.

FUSED SENTENCE
The city had only one swimming pool without an admission fee the pool was poorly maintained.

READER'S REACTION: I can't decide whether the single pool in town is poorly maintained or the only free pool is in bad shape.

EDITED
The city had only one swimming pool , but without an admission fee, the pool was poorly maintained.

A **comma splice** links what could be two sentences (two main or independent clauses) by a comma alone. A **fused sentence** (or **run-on sentence**) joins what could be two sentences without any punctuation mark or connecting word to establish clear sentence boundaries. These errors are likely to occur when you draft quickly or when you write sentences with the same subject, with related or contrasting ideas, or with one illustrating the other.

37a Comma splices

To find comma splices, look for commas scattered between word groups that could stand on their own as sentences. Join these word groups by more than a comma alone.

COMMA SPLICE   The typical Navajo husband serves as a trustee, the wife and her children own the family's property.

EDITED   The typical Navajo husband serves as a trustee **,** **but** the wife and her children own the family's property.

READER'S REACTION: **Until you added** *but,* **I missed your point about the woman playing a more important role than the man.**

37b Fused sentences

SERIOUS ERROR

Fused sentences may be any length, but look especially for long sentences with little or no internal punctuation. If your sentence seems to contain more than one statement, check for appropriate punctuation and connecting words.

FUSED SENTENCE   The scientists had trouble identifying the fossil skeleton it resembled that of both a bird and a lizard.

WRITER'S REACTION: **I've made two statements here.**

EDITED   The scientists had trouble identifying the fossil skeleton **because** it resembled that of both a bird and a lizard.

READER'S REACTION: **Adding** *because* **separates the two main points and makes the ideas easier to understand.**

37c Editing comma splices and fused sentences

SERIOUS ERROR

Here are six strategies for correcting comma splices and fused sentences. Choose a strategy that highlights your ideas and creates emphasis.

1 Create separate sentences. (_____. _____.)

COMMA SPLICE   The sport calls for a total of fourteen people (or twelve people and two dogs) divided into two teams, they throw a disk called a Frisbee up and down a field.

EDITED	The sport calls for a total of fourteen people (or twelve people and two dogs) divided into two teams. **T**hey throw a disk called a Frisbee up and down a field.
FUSED SENTENCE	Football does not cause the most injuries among student athletes gymnastics is the most dangerous sport.
EDITED	Football does not cause the most injuries among student athletes. **G**ymnastics is the most dangerous sport.

2 Use a comma plus *and, but, or, for, nor, so,* or *yet.* (____ , and ____.)

When main clauses convey equally important ideas, try linking them with a comma plus a coordinating conjunction telling how they relate.

COMMA SPLICE	The finance department has reviewed the plan, the operations department is still analyzing it.
EDITED	The finance department has reviewed the plan, **but** the operations department is still analyzing it.
FUSED SENTENCE	The emergency room is understaffed it still performs well.
EDITED	The emergency room is understaffed, **yet** it still performs well.

Three or more closely related clauses can be punctuated as a series to emphasize their connection. Especially for the academic community, include both a comma and a coordinating conjunction before the last item (see 48d).

SERIES OF CLAUSES	We collected the specimens, we cleaned them, **and** we measured them.

3 Make one clause subordinate. (*Because* ____, ____.)

Subordinators such as *although, when, because, until, where,* and *unless* (see 43b) can specify a range of relationships between clauses, as can relative pronouns such as *who, which,* or *that* (see 33a). A **subordinate clause** includes the subordinator plus a subject and a verb; it cannot stand alone as a sentence.

COMMA SPLICE	Automobiles are increasingly complex, skilled mechanics may spend several weeks a year in training.
EDITED	**Because** automobiles are increasingly complex, skilled mechanics may spend several weeks a year in training.
FUSED SENTENCE	Margaret Atwood is best known for her novels her essays and poems are also worth reading.
EDITED	**Although** Margaret Atwood is best known for her novels, her essays and poems are also worth reading.

4 Use a semicolon. (____; ____.)

Use a semicolon to join two main clauses and emphasize their similar importance. (See 49a.)

COMMA SPLICE

An autopilot is a device that corrects drift, the system senses and reacts to changes in the aircraft's motion.

EDITED

An autopilot is a device that corrects drift; the system senses and reacts to changes in the aircraft's motion.

FUSED SENTENCE

Most colleges offer alternatives to four years on campus study abroad, exchange programs with other schools, and cooperative programs are common.

EDITED

Most colleges offer alternatives to four years on campus; study abroad, exchange programs with other schools, and cooperative programs are common.

5 Use wording like *however, moreover, for example,* and *in contrast* plus a semicolon. (____; however, ____.)

However, consequently, moreover, and other **conjunctive adverbs** (see 43a–b) specify relationships between clauses. You can use transitional expressions such as *in contrast* and *in addition* for similar purposes.

COMMA SPLICE

To draw the human body, you must understand it, therefore, art students sometimes dissect cadavers.

EDITED

To draw the human body, you must understand it; **therefore,** art students sometimes dissect cadavers.

FUSED SENTENCE

Chickens reach market size within months the lobster takes six to eight years.

EDITED

Chickens reach market size within months; **in contrast,** the lobster takes six to eight years.

Conjunctive adverbs and transitional expressions can begin the second main clause or appear within it. Set them off with a comma or commas; join the clauses with a semicolon (see 49a-2).

BEGINNING OF CLAUSE

The Great Lakes were once heavily polluted; **however,** recently fish and other wildlife have returned.

MIDDLE OF CLAUSE

The Great Lakes were once heavily polluted; recently, **however,** fish and other wildlife have returned.

END OF CLAUSE

The Great Lakes were once heavily polluted; recently fish and other wildlife have returned, **however.**

6 Use a colon. (___: ___.)

When a clause summarizes, illustrates, or restates a preceding clause, you can join the two with a colon. (See 49b-3.)

COMMA SPLICE — Foreign study calls for extensive language preparation, vaccinations and a passport are not enough.

EDITED — Foreign study calls for extensive language preparation**:** vaccinations and a passport are not enough.

ESL ADVICE: *BECAUSE* AND *BECAUSE OF*

The subordinator *because* introduces a clause with a subject and verb; the preposition *because of* introduces a phrase with its object.

DRAFT — Because of the pay is low, José must look for another job.

EDITED — **Because** the pay is low, José must look for another job.

EDITED — **Because of** the low pay, José must look for another job.

ESL ADVICE: CONNECTING WORDS WITH THE SAME MEANING

Connecting words may have the same meaning but need different punctuation.

COORDINATOR — José likes his job**,** **but** it doesn't pay enough.

CONJUNCTIVE ADVERB — José likes his job**;** **however,** it doesn't pay enough.

38 Pronoun Reference

Readers expect pronouns to make a sentence less repetitive and easier to understand by taking the place of nouns (or other pronouns). For this substitution to work effectively, your readers must recognize the word to which a pronoun refers so they can tell exactly what the sentence means.

AMBIGUOUS
REFERENCE
    Much of my life with the circus consisted of leading the elephants from the cages and hosing **them** down.

      READER'S REACTION: **What got hosed down? elephants? cages? both?**

EDITED
    Much of my life with the circus consisted of hosing the elephants down after leading **them** from **their** cages.

The word to which the pronoun refers is known as its **antecedent** (or **headword**). When **pronoun reference**—the connection between pronoun and antecedent—isn't clear and specific, readers may be confused. By creating clear pronoun reference, you tie ideas and sentences together, clarify their relationships, and focus readers' attention.

SERIOUS
ERROR

38a   Unclear pronoun reference

If readers say they "get lost" reading your work or "can't figure out what you are saying," make sure each pronoun refers *clearly* to one specific antecedent, either one word or several words acting as a unit.

1 Watch for ambiguous or distant pronoun reference

A pronoun may seem to refer to more than one possible antecedent (**ambiguous reference**) or may be too distant from its antecedent (**remote reference**) for a reader to recognize the connection.

AMBIGUOUS
REFERENCE
    Robespierre and Danton disagreed over the path the French Revolution should take. **He** believed that the Revolution was endangered by internal enemies.

      READER'S REACTION: **I'm lost. Who's *he*? Robespierre or Danton?**

EDITED
    Robespierre and Danton disagreed over the path the French Revolution should take. **Robespierre** believed that the Revolution was endangered by internal enemies.

2 Look for vague or implied pronoun reference

If readers have to guess what a pronoun refers to, you may have referred to the entire idea of an earlier passage (**vague** or **broad pronoun reference**) or to an **implied antecedent**, suggested but not stated.

IMPLIED
ANTECEDENT
    A hard frost damaged most of the local citrus groves, but **it** has not yet been determined.

      READER'S REACTION: **I'm not sure what *it* means, though I guess it's related to the frost damage.**

STATED
    A hard frost damaged most of the local citrus groves, but **the extent of the loss** has not yet been determined.

Certain words—*it, they, you, which, this,* or *that*—are especially likely to refer to vague, implied, or indefinite antecedents. To spot imprecise references, search for these pronouns. In each case, see if you can find an antecedent stated in the passage.

38b Editing for clear pronoun reference

Your choices for editing pronoun reference will depend on the particular problem you are trying to correct.

1 Correcting ambiguous or distant reference

When a pronoun threatens to confuse readers because it refers to two or more possible antecedents (ambiguous reference), you can correct the problem in two ways.

1. **Replace** the troublesome pronoun with a noun.
2. **Reword** the sentence.

AMBIGUOUS
REFERENCE
> Detaching the measuring probe from the glass cylinder is a delicate job because **it** breaks easily.
>
> READER'S REACTION: **Which is so fragile, the probe or the cylinder?**

REPLACED WITH
NOUN
> Detaching the measuring probe from the glass cylinder is a delicate job because **the probe** breaks easily.

REWORDED
> Because the measuring probe breaks easily, detaching it from the glass cylinder is a delicate job.

If a pronoun is too far away from its antecedent to refer to it clearly, either move the pronoun closer or replace it with a noun.

2 Editing vague or implied reference

Keeping pronouns and antecedents together is especially important for word groups beginning with *who, which,* and *that* (relative pronouns). Avoid confusion by placing the pronoun right after its antecedent.

CONFUSING
> In my old bedroom, I saw a stale piece of the bubble gum under **the dresser that I loved to chew as a boy**.

EDITED
> In my old bedroom, I saw under the dresser a stale piece of **the bubble gum that I loved to chew as a boy**.

Sometimes you need to follow *which, this,* or *that* with an explanation of the pronoun's referent.

VAGUE REFERENCE | Redfish have suffered from oil pollution and the destruction of their mangrove swamp habitat. **This** has led to a rapid decline in the redfish population.

READER'S REACTION: Does *this* refer to the destruction of habitat, to oil pollution, or to both?

SPECIFIED | Redfish have suffered from oil pollution and the destruction of their mangrove swamp habitat. **This combination** has led to a rapid decline in the redfish population.

EXPLAINED | Redfish have suffered from oil pollution and the destruction of their mangrove swamp habitat. **That increasingly serious pair of challenges** has led to a rapid decline in the redfish population.

You is commonly accepted in letters, emails, and other kinds of writing where it means, "you, the reader" (see 40a). When *you* refers to people and situations in general, however, it may lead to imprecise sentences.

INDEFINITE ANTECEDENT | In Brazil, **you** pay less for an alcohol-powered car than for a gasoline-powered one.

READER'S REACTION: Who is *you*? I'm not likely to buy a car in Brazil.

REPLACED WITH NOUN | In Brazil, **consumers** pay less for an alcohol-powered car than for a gasoline-powered one.

REWRITTEN | In Brazil, alcohol-powered cars cost less than gasoline-powered ones.

3 Clarifying the antecedent to which the pronoun refers

Many academic readers will consider a possessive noun used as an antecedent an error, although the pattern is common in informal writing. Pair a possessive noun with a possessive pronoun (*Kristen's . . . hers*), or rewrite to eliminate the possessive noun.

UNCLEAR | The **company's** success with a well-known jazz fusion artist led **it** to contracts with other musicians.

EDITED (POSSESSIVE PAIR) | The **company's** success with a well-known jazz fusion artist led to **its** contracts with other musicians.

EDITED (NO POSSESSIVE) | Success with a well-known jazz fusion artist led the company to other contracts.

INAPPROPRIATE | In William Faulkner's *The Sound and the Fury*, he begins the story from the point of view of a mentally retarded person.

EDITED | In *The Sound and the Fury*, **William Faulkner** begins the story from the point of view of a mentally retarded person.

4 Reworking a passage to create a reference chain

You can guide readers through a passage using a chain of pronouns to connect sentences. A **reference chain** begins with a statement of your topic, which is then linked to pronouns (or nouns) later in the passage.

UNCLEAR

Sand paintings were a remarkable form of Pueblo art. An artist would sprinkle dried sand of different colors, ground flower petals, corn pollen, and similar materials onto the floor to create **them**. The sun, moon, and stars as well as animals and objects linked to the spirits were represented in the figures **they** contained. Encouraging the spirits to send good fortune to humans was **their** purpose.

Because *them* and *they* are buried at the ends of sentences in the middle of the paragraph, readers may lose sight of the topic, sand paintings.

EDITED TO CREATE A REFERENCE CHAIN

Sand paintings were a remarkable form of Pueblo art. To create **them**, an artist would sprinkle dried sand of different colors, ground flower petals, corn pollen, and similar materials onto the floor. **They** contained figures representing the sun, moon, and stars as well as animals and objects linked to the spirits. **Their** purpose was to encourage the spirits to send good fortune to humans.

STRATEGY   Techniques for developing a reference chain.

- State the antecedent clearly in the opening sentence.
- Link the antecedent to pronouns in sentences that follow.
- Be sure no other possible antecedents interrupt the links in the chain.
- Don't interrupt the chain and then try to return to it later.
- Call attention to the links by giving the pronouns prominent positions (usually beginning sentences); vary their positions only slightly.

39 Misplaced, Dangling, and Disruptive Modifiers

Readers sometimes see a sentence like a string of beads. If the silver bead is designed to reflect the red one, they expect to find those beads placed next to each other just as they expect to find related parts of a sentence together.

MISPLACED
MODIFIER
The wife believes she sees a living figure behind the wallpaper in the story by Charlotte Perkins Gilman, which adds to her sense of entrapment.

READER'S REACTION: **How could a story add to a feeling of entrapment?**

MODIFIER
MOVED
The wife **in the story by Charlotte Perkins Gilman** believes she sees a living figure behind the wallpaper, which adds to her sense of entrapment.

MODIFIER
MOVED
In the story by Charlotte Perkins Gilman, the wife believes she sees a living figure behind the wallpaper, which adds to her sense of entrapment.

In the draft, the modifier is not positioned to relate clearly to the word it modifies. Once the sentence is rearranged, the wife is "in the story," and the wallpaper "adds to her sense of entrapment." If the relationship between a modifier and the word(s) it modifies is unclear, the result will be unanswered questions and confusion.

SERIOUS
ERROR

39a Misplaced, dangling, and disruptive modifiers

When a modifier is poorly positioned or illogically related to the word(s) it is supposed to modify (its **headword**), readers are likely to find a sentence vague, illogical, or unintentionally humorous.

1 Look for misplaced modifiers

A word or word group that is not close enough to its headword is a **misplaced modifier**. It appears to modify some other word or to modify *both* the word before and the word after.

CONFUSING
The caterer served food to the directors standing around the room on flimsy paper plates.

READER'S REACTION: **Surely the directors weren't standing on the plates!**

MODIFIER
MOVED
The caterer served food **on flimsy paper plates** to the directors standing around the room.

2 Look for dangling modifiers

To find a **dangling modifier**, look for a sentence that begins with a modifier but doesn't name the person, idea, or thing modified. Readers will assume that this modifier refers to the subject of the main clause immediately following. If it doesn't, the modifier dangles.

DANGLING
Looking for a way to reduce complaints from nonsmokers, a new ventilation fan was installed.

READER'S REACTION: **How could a fan look for anything? The sentence never tells me *who* wants to reduce complaints.**

SUBJECT ADDED   Looking for a way to reduce complaints from nonsmokers, **the company installed** a new ventilation fan.

3 Look for disruptive modifiers

Readers generally expect subjects and verbs to stand close to each other. The same is true for other sentence elements—verbs and their objects or complements, for example. Modifiers that come between such elements may be **disruptive modifiers** if they create long and distracting interruptions.

DISRUPTIVE   The researcher, **because he had not worked with chimpanzees before and was unaware of their intelligence**, was surprised when they undermined his experiment.

However, a brief, relevant interruption can add variety and suspense.

CLEAR   The researcher, **unfamiliar with chimpanzees**, was surprised when they undermined his experiment.

How can you tell whether modifiers placed between subject and verb are disruptive? Modifiers that provide information related to both subject and verb are likely to be disruptive because a reader can't tell which they relate to. Modifiers related to the subject alone generally aren't disruptive.

                         subject   modifier
DISRUPTIVE   Work on the building, **due to problems with the construction**
                         verb
permits, was completed three months late.

                 subject   modifier   verb
NOT DISRUPTIVE   The youth center **that opened last month** has drawn crowds.

ESL ADVICE: POSITION OF MODIFIERS

Some languages clarify the relationship between a modifier and its headword through the form or ending of the words. Because modifiers in English tend to change location, not form, to show which words they describe, the position of a modifier can drastically change its meaning.

SERIOUS ERROR

39b Editing misplaced, dangling, and disruptive modifiers

Each kind of modifier problem calls for a slightly different correction strategy.

1 Editing misplaced modifiers

Try these two techniques for editing misplaced modifiers.

- **Move** the modifier closer to the words it should modify.
- **Rewrite** or **modify** a sentence so that the connection between modifier and words to be modified is clear.

Who, which,* or *that. For a clear connection, try to put *who, which,* or *that* immediately after its headword to avoid modifying the wrong word.

MISPLACED

The environmental engineers discovered another tank behind the building that was leaking toxic wastes.

READER'S REACTION: I know a building can leak, but I'll bet the writer meant that the tank was the culprit.

MOVED AFTER
HEADWORD

Behind the building, the environmental engineers discovered another tank **that** was leaking toxic wastes.

***Only, hardly, merely,* and similar words.** In most cases, move a word like *only, almost, hardly, just, merely, simply,* and *even* (**limiting modifiers**) directly before the word to which it applies.

Only charities for children are maintaining their support.
They are the sole charities able to maintain support.

Charities for **only** children are maintaining their support.
The charities are for children from families with one child.

Charities for children are **only** maintaining their support.
They are not increasing the levels of support.

Squinting modifiers. If a modifier appears to modify the wording both before and after it, move this **squinting modifier** to eliminate the ambiguity, or rewrite.

SQUINTING

People who abuse alcohol **often** have other problems.

READER'S REACTION: Do they abuse alcohol *often* or *often* have other problems?

EDITED

People who **often abuse alcohol** tend to have other problems.

REWRITTEN

People who abuse alcohol tend to have other problems **as well**.

2 Editing dangling modifiers

When the subject being modified does not appear in the sentence, you have a dangling modifier. You can correct the problem in three ways.

- **Add a subject** to the modifier.

DANGLING   While shopping, the stuffed alligator caught my eye.

SUBJECT ADDED   While **I was** shopping, the stuffed alligator caught my eye.

- **Change the subject** of the main clause.

DANGLING   Jumping into the water to save the drowning swimmer, the crowd
applauded the lifeguard.

SUBJECT
CHANGED   Jumping into the water to save the drowning swimmer, **the
lifeguard** was applauded by the crowd.

- **Rewrite** the entire sentence.

DANGLING   Having debated changes in the regulations for months, the
present standards were allowed to continue.
READER'S REACTION: *Who* is debating? Not the standards!

REWRITTEN   The commission debated changes in the regulations for months
but decided to continue the present standards.

3 Editing disruptive modifiers

To correct problems caused by disruptive modifiers, move them so that
sentence elements are near each other just as readers expect.

Readers expect a subject and verb to stand together and an object or
complement to come right after the verb.

CLUMSY   Joanne began collecting, **using her survey form**, data for
her study of dating preferences.

EDITED   **Using her survey form**, Joanne began collecting data for her
study of dating preferences.

If a modifier splits the parts of an infinitive (*to* plus a verb, as in *to enjoy*),
readers may have trouble relating the parts. Some readers will find any **split
infinitive** irritating, clear or not.

IRRITATING   The dancers moved **to** very rapidly **align** themselves.

EDITED   The dancers moved very rapidly **to align** themselves.

At times, however, a split infinitive may be the most concise alternative.

Our goal is **to** more than **halve** our manufacturing errors.

40 Making Shifts Consistent

Although readers are willing to shift attention many times, they expect you to make shifts logically consistent and to signal them clearly.

SHIFTED   If **parents** would call the school board, **you** could explain why **we** oppose the proposal.

READER'S REACTION: **I'm confused. Who's who? Who should do what?**

EDITED   If **parents** would call the school board, **they** could explain why **they** oppose the proposal.

EDITED   If **you** would call the school board, **you** could explain why **you** oppose the proposal.

EDITED   If **all of us meeting tonight** would call the school board, **we** could explain why **we** oppose the proposal.

SERIOUS ERROR 40a Shifts in person and number

Watch for unexpected shifts in person and number (see 34c). **Person** refers to the ways you use nouns and pronouns (*I, you, she, they*) to shape the relationship involving you, your readers, and your subject. Switching from one person to another as you refer to the same subject can be illogical. **Number** shows whether words are singular (one) or plural (two or more). Look for confusing shifts between words like *person* and *people* that identify groups or their members.

FIRST, SECOND, AND THIRD PERSON

FIRST PERSON (*I, WE*)

- Use *I* to refer to yourself as the writer or as the subject of an essay.
- Use *we* in a collaborative project when more than one person is author or subject.
- Use *we* for both yourself and your readers when discussing shared experiences or understandings.
- Use *we* in some academic fields such as the study of literature ("In this part of the poem we begin to see . . .") but not in others (for example, chemistry or engineering).
- Use *we* to represent an organization or workgroup.

(Continued)

388

FIRST, SECOND, AND THIRD PERSON (*continued*)

SECOND PERSON (*YOU*)
- Use *you* to refer directly to the reader.
- Do not use *you* in most kinds of academic and professional writing unless called for by the situation, as in a set of instructions.
- Use *you* in a political, civic, or activist appeal urging readers to action.

THIRD PERSON (*HE*, *SHE*, *IT*, *THEY*; *ONE*, *SOMEONE*, *EACH*, AND OTHER INDEFINITE PRONOUNS)
- Use third person for the ideas, things, and people you are writing about.
- *People* and *person* are third person nouns, as are names of groups of things, ideas, and people (for example, *students*, *teachers*, *doctors*).

INCONSISTENT   When **a business executive is** looking for a new job, **they** often consult a placement service.

READER'S REACTION: **Does *they* mean business executives as a group? The sentence mentions only one executive.**

EDITED   When **business executives are** looking for **new jobs**, **they** often consult a placement service.

Check for illogical shifts between singular and plural forms, between first and second person, or between second and third person. Then edit to make the relationships consistent.

INCONSISTENT NUMBER   If **a person has** some money to invest, **they** should seek advice from a financial consultant.

EDITED   If **a person has** some money to invest, **he or she** should seek advice from a financial consultant.

EDITED   If **people have** some money to invest, **they** should seek advice from a financial consultant.

INCONSISTENT PERSON   If a **person** is looking for a higher return on investments, **you** might consider mutual funds.

EDITED   If **you** are looking for a higher return on investments, **you** might consider mutual funds.

40b Shifts in tense and mood

When you change verb tense within a passage, you signal a change in time and the relationship of events in time. Illogical shifts can mislead your readers and contradict your meaning.

ILLOGICAL SHIFT Scientists digging in Montana **discovered** nests that **indicated** how some dinosaurs **take care** of their young.

LOGICAL Scientists digging in Montana **discovered** nests that **indicate** how some dinosaurs **took care** of their young.

Although the actions of both the dinosaurs and the scientists clearly occurred in the past, *indicate* (present tense) is appropriate because researchers interpret the evidence in the present.

Make sure you keep verb tenses consistent and logical within a passage. If you begin narrating events in the past tense, avoid shifting suddenly to the present to try to make events more vivid.

INCONSISTENT TENSE We **had been searching** for a new site for the festival when Tonia **starts yelling**, "I've found the place!"

EDITED We **had been searching** for a new site for the festival when Tonia **started yelling**, "I've found the place!"

ESL ADVICE: VERB TENSE AND EXPRESSIONS OF TIME

Use both verb tense and expressions of time (*yesterday, today, soon*) to indicate changes in time. Make sure the two are consistent.

INCONSISTENT I **study** English last year, and now I **worked** for an American company.

EDITED I **studied** English last year, and now I **work** for an American company.

The **mood** of a verb shows the writer's aim or attitude (see 31d-2): to command or request (**imperative**), to state or question (**indicative**), or to offer a conditional or hypothetical statement (**subjunctive**; see 32h). If you shift mood inappropriately, your sentences may be hard to follow.

INCONSISTENT (IMPERATIVE AND INDICATIVE)
To reduce costs, **distribute** fewer copies of drafts, and **you should encourage** employees to replace paper memos with email messages.

CONSISTENT (IMPERATIVE)
To reduce costs, **distribute** fewer copies of drafts, and **encourage** employees to replace paper memos with email messages.

40c Shifts in active or passive voice

When a verb is in the **active voice**, the agent or doer of the action functions as the subject of the sentence. When a verb is in the **passive**

voice, the goal of the action functions as the sentence's subject. (See 32i and 47b-3.)

	subject	verb	object
ACTIVE	The lava flow **destroyed**	twelve houses.	
	agent	action	goal

	subject	verb	
PASSIVE	Twelve houses **were destroyed**	[by the lava flow].	
	goal	action	[agent]

Try to focus on either active or passive voice within a sentence, rewriting if necessary, to use either active or passive voice consistently.

INCONSISTENT Among the active volcanoes, Kilauea **erupts** most frequently, and over 180 houses **have been destroyed** since 1983.

READER'S REACTION: **The first part mentions Kilauea, but the second part doesn't. Did Kilauea alone destroy the houses, or were some other volcanoes also responsible?**

EDITED Among the active volcanoes, Kilauea **has erupted** most frequently in recent years, and it has destroyed over 180 houses since 1983.

Sometimes you may shift voice to emphasize or highlight a subject.

active   active
UNEMPHATIC Volcanic activity **built** Hawaii, and the island still **has** active volcanoes.

passive   active
EDITED Hawaii **was built** by volcanic activity, and the island still **has** active volcanoes.

The first sentence shifts subjects from *volcanic activity* to *the island*; the second shifts between passive and active to keep Hawaii as the focus.

40d Shifts between direct and indirect quotations

Through **direct quotation** you present someone's ideas and feelings in that person's exact words, set off with quotation marks. Through **indirect quotation** you report the substance of those words but in your own words without quotation marks. Credit your sources with either form of quotation (see Chapter 24).

DIRECT QUOTATION According to Aguilar, beachfront property "has wreaked havoc on sea turtle nesting patterns" (16).

INDIRECT QUOTATION Aguilar explained how beachfront property interferes with the breeding habits of sea turtles (16).

STRATEGY   **Rewrite awkward shifts between quotations.**

AWKWARD
(INDIRECT +
DIRECT)
Writing about the Teenage Mutant Ninja Turtles, Phil Patton **names** cartoonists Peter Laird and Kevin Eastman as their creators and **said**, "They were born quietly in 1983, in the kitchen of a New England farmhouse" (101).

EDITED
Phil Patton **credits** cartoonists Peter Laird and Kevin Eastman with creating the Teenage Mutant Ninja Turtles, who "were born quietly in 1983, in the kitchen of a New England farmhouse" (101).

For indirect quotation, use past tense to report what someone has said.

DIRECT
QUOTATION
As Lan **notes**, "The region **is expected** to forfeit one of every three jobs" (4).

INDIRECT
QUOTATION
Lan **projected that** the area **would lose** one-third of its jobs during the next ten years (4).

Follow convention, however, and use present tense when you analyze events in a creative work, such as a novel, film, or television show. (See 32b.)

INCONSISTENT
As the novel begins, Ishmael **comes** to New Bedford to ship out on a whaler, which he soon **did**.

CONVENTIONAL
As the novel begins, Ishmael **comes** to New Bedford to ship out on a whaler, which he soon **does**.

41   Mixed and Incomplete Sentences

When someone switches topics or jumbles a sentence during a conversation, you can ask for clarification. When you are reading, however, you can't stop in the middle of a sentence to ask the writer to explain.

TOPIC SHIFT
One **skill** I envy is **a person** who can meet deadlines.
READER'S REACTION: **How can a *skill* be a *person*?**

EDITED
One **skill** I envy is **the ability** to meet deadlines.

Sentences with confusing shifts (called **mixed sentences**) mislead readers by undermining the patterns they rely on as they read. An **incomplete sentence** does the same because it omits wording necessary to make a logical and consistent statement.

41a   Mixed sentences

Mixed sentences switch topics or sentence structures without warning, for no clear reason. They throw readers off track by undermining patterns that readers rely on.

1 Look for topic shifts

In most sentences, the subject announces a topic, and the predicate comments on or renames the topic. In a sentence with a **topic shift** (**faulty predication**), the second part of the sentence comments on or names a topic *different* from the one first announced. As a result, readers may have trouble figuring out the true focus of the sentence.

| STRATEGY | Ask "Who does what?" or "What is it?" |

If the answer to "Who does what?" or "What is it?" is illogical, edit the sentence to make its meaning clear.

TOPIC SHIFT
In this factory, **flaws** in the product noticed by any worker **can stop** the assembly line with the flip of a switch.
QUESTION: **Who does what? Flaws can't stop the line or flip a switch.**

EDITED
In this factory, **any worker** who notices flaws in the product **can stop** the assembly line with the flip of a switch.

2 Pay attention to mixed patterns

If you begin one grammatical pattern but shift to another, your sentence may confuse readers because it doesn't follow the pattern they expect.

| STRATEGY | Check who does what to whom. |

- Read your sentences aloud. Pay attention to the *meaning*, especially how the subject and predicate relate.
- Ask, "What is the topic? How does the rest of the sentence comment on it or rename it?"

MIXED PATTERN
By wearing bell-bottom pants and tie-dyed T-shirts was how many young people challenged mainstream values in the 1960s.
CHECK: *Who did what to whom* **is not clear.**

EDITED
By wearing bell-bottom pants and tie-dyed T-shirts, many young people challenged mainstream values in the 1960s.

41b Editing mixed sentences

In general, you can eliminate problems with topic shifts by making sure the topic in both parts of a sentence is the same.

1 Rename the subject

When you use the verb *be* (*is, are, was, were*), you may use the sentence predicate to rename or define the subject. Balance the topics on each side of the verb; for example, pair a noun with a noun.

If the topics on each side of *be* are not roughly equivalent, edit the second part of the sentence to rename the topic in the first part.

TOPIC SHIFT   **Irradiation** is **food** that is preserved by radiation.

EDITED   **Irradiation** is a **process** that can be used to preserve food.

2 Cut *is when* or *is where*

Is when and *is where* make a balance on both sides of *be* impossible.

NOT BALANCED   **Blocking** is **when** a television network schedules a less popular program between two popular ones.

EDITED   **Blocking** is the **practice** of scheduling a less popular television program between two popular ones.

3 Omit *the reason . . . is because*

Readers find *the reason . . . is because* illogical because they expect the subject (topic) to be renamed after *is*. When *because* appears there instead, it cannot logically rename the subject.

- Drop *the reason . . . is*.

  DRAFT   The **reason** he took up skating **is because** he wanted winter exercise.

  EDITED   He took up skating **because** he wanted winter exercise.

- Change *because* to *that*.

  EDITED   The **reason** he took up skating **is that** he wanted winter exercise.

4 Stick to a consistent sentence pattern

If you mistake words between the subject and verb for the sentence topic, you may mix up different sentence patterns.

TOPIC SHIFT	Programming **decisions** by television executives generally <u>think about</u> gaining audience share.
	READER'S REACTION: **How can decisions think about viewers?**
EDITED	**Television executives** making programming decisions generally <u>think about</u> gaining audience share.
EDITED	When **they are making** programming decisions, **television executives** generally <u>think about</u> gaining audience share.

5 Be alert for sentences that begin twice

Watch for sentences in which you repeat a topic more often than the sentence structure allows or mistakenly start the sentence over again.

MIXED	**The new procedures for testing cosmetics**, **we** designed them to avoid cruelty to laboratory animals.
EDITED	**We** designed **the new procedures for testing cosmetics** to avoid cruelty to laboratory animals.
EDITED	**The new procedures for testing cosmetics** were designed to avoid cruelty to laboratory animals.

41c Incomplete sentences

Incomplete sentences lack either grammatical (see 36a) or logical completeness. They leave out words necessary to meaning or logic, or they don't complete an expected pattern, such as a comparison. For example, if you begin a comparison with "*X* is larger," you should complete it: "*X* is larger *than Y*." Read sentences aloud to identify missing words. Listen for omissions such as needed articles, prepositions, pronouns, parts of verbs, or parts of a comparison.

INCOMPLETE	The new parking plan is much better.
	READER'S REACTION: **Better than what? another plan? no plan?**
EDITED	The new parking plan is much better **than the last plan**.

You create an **incomplete comparison** when you omit an item being compared or the wording needed for a clear, complete comparison. To edit, supply the words that complete a comparison.

INCOMPLETE	The senior members of the staff respect the new supervisor more than their coworkers.
	READER'S REACTION: **Do the senior staff members respect the supervisor more than they respect their coworkers? Or do they respect the supervisor more than their coworkers do?**

CLEAR   The senior members of the staff respect the new supervisor more **than do** their coworkers.

CLEAR   The senior members of the staff respect the new supervisor more **than they respect** their coworkers.

You create an **illogical comparison** when you seem to compare things that cannot be reasonably compared. To edit, add missing words or a possessive to make a comparison logical.

ILLOGICAL   The amount of fat in even a small hamburger is greater than a skinless chicken breast.

READER'S REACTION: **I'm confused. Why is the writer comparing the** *amount of fat* **in one food to another** *kind* **of food (chicken breast)?**

EDITED
(WORDS ADDED)   The amount of fat in even a small hamburger is greater than **that in** a skinless chicken breast.

EDITED
(POSSESSIVE USED)   Even a small **hamburger's** fat content is greater than a skinless chicken **breast's**.

42   Parallelism

When you use consistent patterns, readers can easily follow and understand your ideas. They can concentrate on what you mean because they know just what to expect and how your ideas relate.

WEAK   I furnished my apartment with what I purchased at discount stores, buying items from the want ads, and gifts from my relatives.

READER'S REACTION: **This list seems wordy and jumbled.**

PARALLEL   I furnished my apartment with **purchases from discount stores**, **items from the want ads**, and **gifts from my relatives**.

Parallelism is the expression of similar or related ideas in similar grammatical form. Besides emphasizing the relationships of ideas, parallelism can create intriguing sentence rhythms and highlights.

42a Faulty parallelism

Once you begin a parallel pattern, you need to complete it. If you mix structures, creating incomplete or **faulty parallelism**, your sentences may disappoint readers' expectations and be hard to read.

MIXED	Consider swimming if you want an exercise that **aids** cardiovascular fitness, **develops** overall muscle strength, and **probably without causing** injuries.
PARALLEL	Consider swimming if you want an exercise that **aids** cardiovascular fitness, **develops** overall muscle strength, and **causes** few injuries.

42b Editing for parallelism

Whether you create parallelism with words, phrases, or clauses, all the elements need to follow the same grammatical patterns.

1 Rework a series, pair, or list using parallel forms

When you place items in a series, pair, or list, make sure they have the same structure even if they differ in length and wording. Mixed grammatical forms can make a series clumsy and distracting.

WORDS MIXED	To get along with their neighbors, residents need to be patient, tactful, and to display tolerance.
WORDS PARALLEL	To get along with their neighbors, residents need to be patient, tactful, and **tolerant**.
PHRASES MIXED	The singer Jim Morrison is remembered for his innovative style, his flamboyant performances, and for behavior that was self-destructive.
PHRASES PARALLEL	The singer Jim Morrison is remembered for his innovative style, his flamboyant performances, and **his self-destructive behavior**.
CLAUSES MIXED	In assembling the research team, Cryo-Com looked for engineers whose work was creative, with broad interests, and who had boundless energy.
CLAUSES PARALLEL	In assembling the research team, Cryo-Com looked for engineers whose work was creative, **whose interests were broad, and whose energy was boundless**.

And, but, or. When you join sentence elements with *and, but, or, for, nor, so,* and *yet* (**coordinating conjunctions**), presenting the paired elements in parallel form can direct readers' attention to similarities or differences.

WORDS MIXED	A well-trained scientist keeps a detailed lab notebook and the entries made accurately.
WORDS PARALLEL	A well-trained scientist keeps a **detailed and accurate** lab notebook.
PHRASES MIXED	First-year chemistry teaches students how to take notes on an experiment and the ways of writing a lab report.
PHRASES PARALLEL	First-year chemistry teaches students **how to take notes on an experiment** and **how to write a lab report**.

Both . . . and . . . . When you wish to call special attention to a relationship or contrast, you may choose pairs of connectors such as *both . . . and, not only . . . but also, either . . . or, neither . . . nor,* or *whether . . . or* (**correlative conjunctions**). Make the joined elements parallel.

DRAFT	Americans claim to marry "for love," yet their pairings follow clear social patterns. They choose partners from the same social class and economic level. Most marriages bring together people with similar educational and cultural backgrounds. Similarities in race and ethnic background are important as well.
EDITED	Americans claim to marry "for love," yet their pairings follow clear social patterns. They choose partners not only **with the same class and economic background** but also **with the same educational, cultural, racial, and ethnic background**.

Lists. Use parallel form for items in a list. Suppose, for example, you were listing social changes of the early 1960s.

UNEDITED (CONFUSING)
1. A growing civil rights movement
2. Emphasis increased on youth in culture and politics.
3. Taste in music and the visual arts was changing.

EDITED FOR PARALLELISM (CLEAR)
1. **A growing** civil rights movement
2. **An increasing** emphasis on youth in culture and politics
3. **A changing** taste in music and the visual arts

2 Build clear parallel patterns

INCOMPLETE	The main character from the novel *Tarzan of the Apes* has appeared on television, films, and comic books.
	READER'S REACTION: I doubt he was *on* films or *on* comic books.
EDITED	The main character from the novel *Tarzan of the Apes* has appeared **on** television, **in** films, and **in** comic books.

Repeat or state words that complete grammatical or idiomatic patterns. You needn't repeat the same lead-in word for all items in a series.

Mosquitoes can breed **in** puddles, ~~in~~ ponds, and ~~in~~ swimming pools.

3 Use parallelism to organize sentence clusters

You can use parallelism to strengthen **sentence clusters**, groups of sentences that develop related ideas or information. The parallel elements can clarify difficult information, highlight the overall pattern of argument or explanation, link examples, or guide readers through steps or stages.

> Each of us probably belongs to groups whose values conflict. **You may belong to** a religious organization that **endorses restraint in** alcohol use or **in** relations between the sexes while **you also belong to** a social group with activities that **support contrasting values. You may belong to** a sports team **that supports** competing and winning and a club **that promotes** understanding among people.

You can also use parallelism, as simple as brief opening phrases, to reinforce the overall pattern of a cluster of paragraphs.

PARALLEL PARAGRAPH OPENERS
One reason for approving this proposal now is . . .
A second reason for action is . . .
The most important reason for taking immediate steps is . . .

43 Coordination and Subordination

Suppose you were asked to rewrite the following passage, filled with short, choppy sentences that fail to emphasize connections among ideas.

> California's farmers ship fresh lettuce, avocados, and other produce to supermarkets. They never send fresh olives. Fresh olives contain a substance that makes them bitter. They are very unpleasant tasting. Farmers soak fresh olives in a solution that removes oleuropein, the bitter-tasting substance. They leave just enough behind to produce the tangy "olive" taste.

You might **coordinate** the sentences, giving equal emphasis to each statement.

> California's farmers ship fresh lettuce, avocados, and other produce to supermarkets, **but** they never send fresh olives. Fresh olives contain a substance that makes them bitter, **so** they are very unpleasant tasting. Farmers soak fresh olives in a solution that removes oleuropein, the bitter-tasting substance; **however**, they leave just enough behind to produce the tangy "olive" taste.

Or you might show the relative importance of ideas by **subordination**, making some of the sentences modify others through the use of subordinating words like *because* and *though*.

> California's farmers ship fresh lettuce, avocados, and other produce to supermarkets, **though** they never send fresh olives. **Because** fresh olives contain a substance that makes them bitter, they are very unpleasant tasting. **When** farmers soak fresh olives in a solution that removes oleuropein, the bitter-tasting substance, they leave just enough behind to produce the tangy "olive" taste.

43a Creating coordination

When you want to link words, clauses, or phrases and emphasize their equal weight, use coordination. When you coordinate main (independent) clauses, you create a single **compound sentence** (see 31d-1).

RELATIONSHIPS   Cats have no fear of water. They do not like wet and matted fur.
NOT SPECIFIED   Cats like to feel well groomed.

CLEAR   Cats have no fear of water, **but** they do not like wet and
RELATIONSHIPS   matted fur, **for** they like to feel well groomed.

CREATING AND PUNCTUATING COORDINATION

JOINING WORDS AND CLUSTERS OF WORDS (PHRASES)

1. **Use *and, but, or, nor,* or *yet* (coordinating conjunctions).**

   cut **and** hemmed   smooth **or** textured   intrigued **yet** suspicious

2. **Use pairs like *either . . . or, neither . . . nor,* and *not only . . . but also.***

   either music therapy **or** pet therapy
   not only a nursing care plan **but also** a home care program

JOINING MAIN (INDEPENDENT) CLAUSES

1. **Use *and, but, or, for, nor, so,* or *yet* (coordinating conjunctions) preceded by a comma.**

   The students observed the responses of shoppers to long lines, **and** they interviewed people waiting in line. Most people in the study were irritated by the checkout lines, **yet** a considerable minority enjoyed the wait.

   (Continued)

CREATING AND PUNCTUATING COORDINATION (*continued*)

2. **Use a semicolon** (see 49a-1).

    The wait provoked physical reactions in some people **;** they fidgeted, grimaced, and stared at the ceiling.

3. **Use words like *however, moreover, nonetheless, thus,* and *consequently* (conjunctive adverbs) preceded by a semicolon** (see 49a-2).

    Store managers can take simple steps to speed up checkout lines **;** however **,** they seldom pay much attention to the problem.

4. **Use a colon** (see 49b-3).

    Tabloids and magazines in racks by the checkout counters serve a useful purpose **:** they give customers something to read while waiting.

EXPRESSING RELATIONSHIPS THROUGH COORDINATION

RELATIONSHIP	COORDINATING CONJUNCTION	CONJUNCTIVE ADVERB	
addition	, and	; in addition,	; furthermore,
opposition	, but	; in contrast,	
or contrast	, yet	; however,	; nonetheless,
result	, so	; therefore,	; consequently, ; thus,
cause	, for		
choice	, or	; otherwise,	
negation	, nor		

43b Creating subordination

Use subordination to create a sentence with unequal elements: one **main or independent clause** that presents the central idea and at least one **subordinate or dependent clause** that modifies, qualifies, or comments on the main clause. You signal readers about this unequal relationship by beginning the subordinate clause with a word like *although* or *that* and by attaching it to the main clause in a **complex sentence** (see 31d-1).

MAIN CLAUSES — Malcolm uses a computer to track clinic expenses. He knows how much we pay each year for lab tests.

SUBORDINATED — **Because** Malcolm uses a computer to track clinic expenses, he knows how much we pay each year for lab tests.

READER'S REACTION: Now I know how the ideas relate—one is a cause and the other an effect.

EXPRESSING RELATIONSHIPS THROUGH SUBORDINATION

Time	before, while, until, since, once, whenever, whereupon, after, when
Cause	because, since
Result	in order that, so that, that, so
Concession or contrast	although, though, even though, as if, while, even if
Place	where, wherever
Condition	if, whether, provided, unless, rather than
Comparison	as
Identification	that, which, who

CREATING AND PUNCTUATING SUBORDINATION

USING SUBORDINATING CONJUNCTIONS

You can use a subordinating conjunction such as *although*, *because*, or *since* (see the list in the box above) to create a subordinate clause at the beginning or end of a sentence (see 30g and 31c–d).

PUNCTUATING WITH SUBORDINATING CONJUNCTIONS

Use a comma *after* an introductory clause that begins with a subordinating conjunction. At the end of a sentence, do not use commas if the clause is *essential* to the meaning of the main clause (restrictive); use commas if the clause is *not essential* (nonrestrictive). (See 37c.)

BEGINNING   **Once she understood the problem**, she had no trouble solving it.

END   Radar tracking of flights began **after several commercial airliners collided in midair**. [Essential]

END   The present air traffic control system works reasonably well, **although accidents still occur**. [Nonessential]

USING RELATIVE PRONOUNS

You can use a relative pronoun (*who*, *which*, *that*) to create a relative clause (also called an adjective clause) at the end or in the middle of a sentence (see 31c).

(Continued)

CREATING AND PUNCTUATING SUBORDINATION *(continued)*

PUNCTUATING WITH RELATIVE PRONOUNS

If the modifying clause contains information that is *not essential* to the meaning of the main clause, the modifying clause is nonrestrictive and you should set it off with commas. If the information is *essential*, the modifying clause is restrictive and you should not set it off with commas. (See 37c.)

RESTRICTIVE (ESSENTIAL)	The anthropologists discovered the site of a building **that early settlers used as a meetinghouse**.
NONRESTRICTIVE (NONESSENTIAL)	At one end of the site they found remains of a smaller building**,** **which may have been a storage shed**.
RESTRICTIVE (ESSENTIAL)	The people **who organized the project** work for the archaeology department.
NONRESTRICTIVE (NONESSENTIAL)	Graduate student Lu-Ming Mao**,** **who was leading a dig nearby,** first discovered signs of the meetinghouse.

43c Editing coordination and subordination

How can you tell if you're using too much or too little coordination or subordination? Read your writing aloud. Watch for short, choppy sentences or long, dense passages.

1 Be alert for too much coordination or subordination

If you use words like *and*, *so*, or *but* merely to string together loosely related sentences, you risk boring readers with excessive coordination.

DRAFT   Ripe fruit spoils quickly, **and** fresh grapefruit in markets is picked before it matures to avoid spoilage, **and** it can taste bitter, **but** grapefruit in cans is picked later, **and** it tastes sweeter.

EDITED   Ripe fruit spoils quickly. Fresh grapefruit in markets is picked before it matures**,** **so** it may taste bitter. Grapefruit in cans is picked later**;** **consequently,** it tastes sweeter.

Excessive subordination can overload readers. Divide sentences to simplify.

CONFUSING   The election for mayor will be interesting **because** the incumbent has decided to run as an independent **while** his former challenger for the Democratic nomination has decided to accept the party's endorsement **even though** the Republican nominee is her former campaign manager.

EDITED   The election for mayor will be interesting● The incumbent has decided to run as an independent● His former challenger for the Democratic nomination has decided to accept the party's endorsement **even though** she will have to run against her former campaign manager.

2 Watch for illogical or unclear relationships

Sometimes the subordinating word you choose may not specify a clear relationship, or it may indicate an illogical relationship.

STRATEGY   Use questions to identify problems in logic or meaning.

To identify illogical or unclear relationships, state a sentence's meaning to yourself with a slightly different wording.

- Ask, "Does the original sentence convey my intended meaning?"
- Ask, "Can the subordinating word I have chosen convey several different meanings?"

UNCLEAR EMPHASIS   Since she taught middle school, Jean developed keen insight into the behavior of twelve- and thirteen-year-olds.

> READER'S REACTION: **Does** *since* **mean that she developed insight** *because* **she was a teacher or** *after* **she quit teaching?**

EDITED   **Because** she taught middle school, Jean developed keen insight into the behavior of twelve- and thirteen-year-olds.

3 Highlight important information

Subordination enables you to put some information in the foreground (in a main clause) and other information in the background (in a subordinate clause). In general, move your most important point to the main clause.

DRAFT   His training and equipment were inferior, although Jim still set a school record throwing the discus.

> READER'S REACTION: **Isn't Jim's achievement the key point?**

EDITED   **Although** his training and equipment were inferior, Jim still set a school record throwing the discus.

ESL ADVICE: GRAMMATICAL STRUCTURES FOR COORDINATION AND SUBORDINATION

The following sentence has both a subordinator, *although*, and a coordinator, *but*. Use one pattern, not both at once.

MIXED

Although frogs can live both on land and in water, **but** they need to breathe oxygen.

CONSISTENT COORDINATION

main clause   main clause
Frogs can live both on land and in water, **but** they need to breathe oxygen.

CONSISTENT SUBORDINATION

subordinate clause   main clause
Although frogs can live both on land and in water, they need to breathe oxygen.

PART 11

Words and Style

▼ TAKING IT ONLINE

MERRIAM-WEBSTER ONLINE

http://www.m-w.com

THE AMERICAN HERITAGE DICTIONARY OF THE ENGLISH LANGUAGE

http://www.bartleby.com/61/

Each dictionary site encourages you to type in a word and find its definition, history, and pronunciation.

THESAURUS.COM

http://www.thesaurus.reference.com/

Simply enter a word on the site, hit "Enter" to see a list of synonyms, and then click on each of those for dozens more.

GENDER FAIR LANGUAGE

http://www.rpi.edu/web/writingcenter/genderfair.html

Use the suggestions on this page to avoid sexist slips.

IDIOMS AND SLANG

http://www.iteslj.org/links/ESL/Idioms_and_Slang

This Web site can help ESL students and native speakers alike learn some of the most common English idioms. More than fifty links to short quizzes are sorted by category.

WORLD WIDE WORDS

http://www.quinion.com/words/

This engaging site encourages you to think about word choice and precise meaning. Visit the "Topical Words" and "Weird Words" sections to see how new and strange words come into use.

A.WORD.A.DAY

http://www.wordsmith.org/awad/

Do you want to build your vocabulary? This site archives one of the Internet's most popular mailing lists, sending out a word each day.

PART 11

Words and Style

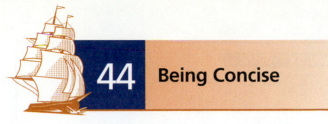

44 Being Concise

Leaving extra words in your writing wastes valuable space—and your readers' time.

WORDY **There is evidence that the use of** pay **as an** incentive **can be a contributing or causal factor in** improvement **of the** quality **of** work.
READER'S REACTION: Why is this so long-winded? What's the point?

TRIMMED Incentive pay improves work quality.
READER'S REACTION: That's short and direct—but maybe too abrupt.

RESHAPED Incentive pay **often encourages** work **of higher** quality.
READER'S REACTION: Now I'm gaining a fuller, more subtle perspective.

Conciseness means using only the words you need—not the fewest words possible, but those appropriate for your purpose, meaning, and readers. (See 45a.)

44a Common types of wordiness

Imagine an ideal reader—a respected teacher, a savvy coworker, or a wise civic leader. If a passage seems wordy, ask, "What would I need to tell X here?" Or think of X asking, "What's your point?"

Look for **wordy phrases** you can shrink to a word or two.

WORDY Carbon 14 can be used to date a site only **in the event that** organic material has survived. **In a situation in which** rocks need dating, potassium-argon testing is used.

CUT Carbon 14 can be used to date a site only **if** organic material has survived. **When** rocks need dating, potassium-argon testing is used.

Watch for **intensifying phrases** (*for all intents and purposes, in my opinion*), intended to add force but often carrying little meaning.

WORDY **As a matter of fact**, most archaeological discoveries can be dated accurately.

CUT Most archaeological discoveries can be dated accurately.

Target clutter such as **all-purpose words** (*factor, aspect, situation, type, field, range, thing, kind, nature*) and **all-purpose modifiers** (*very, totally, major, central, great, really, definitely, absolutely*).

<table>
<tr><td colspan="3">COMMON WORDY PHRASES</td></tr>
<tr><td>PHRASE</td><td></td><td>REPLACEMENT</td></tr>
<tr><td>due to the fact that</td><td>=</td><td>because</td></tr>
<tr><td>at the present moment</td><td>=</td><td>now</td></tr>
<tr><td>a considerable proportion of</td><td>=</td><td>many, most</td></tr>
<tr><td>has the capability to</td><td>=</td><td>can</td></tr>
<tr><td>regardless of the fact that</td><td>=</td><td>although</td></tr>
<tr><td>concerning the matter of</td><td>=</td><td>about</td></tr>
</table>

WORDY   In the short story, Young Goodman Brown is so **totally** overwhelmed by **his own** guilt that he becomes **extremely** suspicious of the people around him. [25 words]

CUT   In the short story, Young Goodman Brown is so overwhelmed by guilt that he becomes suspicious of the people around him. [21 words]

REWRITTEN   In the short story, Young Goodman Brown's **overwhelming** guilt makes him **suspect everyone**. [13 words]

Simplify pairs that say the same thing twice (*each and every*) and **redundant phrases** in which adjectives repeat nouns (*final outcomes*), adverbs repeat verbs (*completely finished*), or specific words imply general (*small in size*).

WORDY   Because it was **sophisticated in nature** and **tolerant in style**, Kublai Khan's administration aided China's development in the 1200s.

CUT   Because it was **sophisticated and tolerant**, Kublai Khan's administration aided China's development in the 1200s.

REWRITTEN   Kublai Khan's **adept and tolerant administration** aided China's development in the 1200s.

44b Editing for conciseness

Edit both wordy expressions and wordy sentence patterns.

Trim ideas already stated or implied.   Cut, but retain useful repetition that helps readers follow an explanation or argument.

REPETITIVE   **Our proposal** outlines a **three-step** program for **converting the building** into a **research center** for the study of film and culture. Each of the **three steps** discussed in **our proposal** should be completed in six months. We expect that **the building** will be **converted** to a **research center** eighteen months from the time work is begun.

CUT

We propose **three steps** for **converting the building** into a center for the study of film and culture. Allowing six months for each **step**, we expect **the building** to be **converted** in eighteen months.

Trim *which, who, or that* clauses and *of* phrases. Convert clauses to phrases, phrases to words.

CLAUSES

Chavez Park, **which is an extensive facility in the center of town**, was named after Cesar Chavez, **who fought for migrant farmers' rights**.

CUT TO PHRASES

Chavez Park, **an extensive facility in the center of town**, was named after Cesar Chavez, **an advocate for migrant farmers**.

CUT TO WORDS

Chavez Park, **an extensive downtown facility**, was named after **migrant advocate** Cesar Chavez.

Replace generalities with connections and details. First, highlight the key words in a passage. Then, combine sentences to eliminate vague or repetitive wording, and add specific, concrete detail to support your main points.

WORDY

Glaciers were of central importance in the **shaping** of **the North American landscape**. They were responsible for many familiar geological features. Among the many remnants of glacial activity are **deeply carved valleys** and **immense piles of sand and rock**.

SENTENCES COMBINED

Glaciers carved deep valleys and left behind immense piles of sand and rock, shaping much of the North American landscape in the process.

DETAILS ADDED

Glaciers carved deep valleys and left behind immense piles of sand and rock, shaping much of the North American landscape in the process. **Cape Cod and Long Island are piles of gravel deposited by glaciers. The Mississippi River and the Great Lakes remained when the ice melted.**

Reduce unnecessary writer's commentary. Make sure your comments guide readers, but don't overdo the commentary and end up talking about yourself rather than your subject.

IRRITATING

In my paper, I intend to show that the benefits of placebos (pills with no physical effect) include improvements and cures, **as mentioned above**.

EDITED

The benefits of placebos (pills with no physical eff include improvements and cures.

45 Choosing Appropriate Words

Edit your words so that you express what you mean correctly and appropriately for your readers.

DRAFT Dr. Parsippani **assassinated** Mr. Rollet.

READER'S REACTION: **Was Mr. Rollet a political figure? Or is this wording imprecise?**

Here, *assassinated* might fit if Rollet were a political figure. If the writer didn't intend this meaning, *killed* might be the most precise choice. Audience expectations also affect **diction**, the choice of words and phrases. For instance, the criminal justice system defines *murder* by degree and distinguishes *homicide* from *manslaughter*.

Besides being *correct*, words need to be *appropriate*. For example, referring in an academic paper to "this guy's theories" technically isn't *incorrect* since *guy* does refer to a person. But it violates expectations and therefore is *inappropriate*. Attending to community sensitivities of this kind reassures a teacher, supervisor, or member of the public of your credibility.

45a Demands of context and purpose

When you choose specific words as you draft and revise, bear in mind the demands of your specific context and audience as well as your purpose and your persona (the image of yourself that you project in your writing).

1 Adjust your diction to your context and your readers

A particular context—an academic discipline or workplace, for example—may call for specialized and precise language choices.

TOO GENERAL [*in an analysis of a painting for an art history course*] Tiepolo's *Apotheosis of the Pisani Family* (1761) is a lively painting typical of the period when it was painted with lots of action going on and nice colors.

READER'S REACTION: **This wording seems too general for an analysis in my field of art history.**

ЭITED Tiepolo's *Apotheosis of the Pisani Family* (1761) shows affinities with typical rococo frescoes of the period, including bright colors with characters in highlighted actions set against dark border accents.

When you write for readers in academic or workplace settings, they will generally expect a high level of formality. Avoid **colloquialisms**, informal expressions typical of a region or group.

TOO INFORMAL   The stock market crash didn't seem to **faze** many of the investors with **megabucks stashed** in property assets.

> READER'S REACTION: **This seems so informal that I'm not sure I trust the writer's authority.**

EDITED   The stock market crash did not profoundly affect investors with extensive property assets.

Exceptions to the need for formality are deliberately informal notes, responses, journal entries, and quoted speech.

2 Adjust your diction to your purpose

In many academic, public, or work settings, readers may favor balanced reasoning over highly emotional language.

BIASED   Most proponents of rock-music censorship grew up listening to pablum, thinking wimpy bands like the Beach Boys were a bunch of perverts.

> READER'S REACTION: **This writer seems too biased and emotional to weigh all sides of the debate.**

EDITED   Proponents of rock-music censorship may unfairly stereotype all of rock-and-roll culture as degenerate or evil.

3 Adjust your diction to your persona

Word choice that creates an objective, detached image of you as a writer (a **persona**) in a clinical report assures readers of accuracy, but this same persona might seem cold and impersonal in the adoption column of an animal shelter newsletter. (See also 3c.)

TOO CLINICAL FOR CONTEXT   Three domestic canines, *Canis familiaris*, type Shetland sheepdog; age: 8 weeks; coloring: burnt umber with variegated blond diameters; behaviorally modified for urination and defecation; inoculated.

> READER'S REACTION: **Why would someone at the shelter talk so uncaringly about puppies, as if they were laboratory specimens?**

EDITED   Three healthy sheltie puppies 8 weeks old, brown with light spots, housebroken, all shots.

45b Editing for precise diction

When you choose among **synonyms**, words identical or nearly so meaning, consider their **connotations**—"shades" of meaning or associati acquired over time. Use concrete, direct wording unless the context ca specialized language or more abstraction.

STRATEGY **Choose precise, concrete, and direct words.**

- Replace an inexact word with an appropriate synonym.

  IMPRECISE   The senator **retreated** from the gathering.

  READER'S REACTION: **Did the senator feel attacked, bewildered, or overcome? Or did she just leave?**

  EDITED   The senator **left** the gathering.

- Replace vague words with specific ones.

  VAGUE   [*in a do-it-yourself brochure on bathroom remodeling*] Do not place flooring over uneven floor or damaged area.

  READER'S REACTION: **What's this about a damaged area?**

  EDITED   Do not **install** flooring over **existing** floors that are **uneven or show signs of wood rot**. **Replace** any damaged **flooring material before installing new flooring**.

- Stick mostly to simple, familiar words.

  STUFFY   The reflections upon premarital cohabitation promulgated by the courts eventuated in the orientation of the population in the direction of moral relaxation on this issue.

  READER'S REACTION: **How dull! Say it more plainly, please.**

  EDITED   Court decisions about living together before marriage led to greater public acceptance of this practice.

Idioms are expressions, often with "forgotten histories," whose meanings differ from their literal definitions, as in *wipe the slate clean* for "start over." Overused idioms can lose their freshness, becoming trite or clichéd; replace them with precise words.

IDIOMATIC   The losers complained of **dog-eat-dog** politics.

EDITED   The losers consoled themselves after their defeat.

ESL ADVICE: IDIOMS IN AMERICAN ENGLISH

Whether an expression is an **idiom** or a **phrasal verb** (see 30c), the meanings of its separate words will not reveal its meaning as a whole. Although memorizing idioms will enrich your spoken English, these expressions may be too informal in many writing situations. In class or at work, note how many and which idioms appear in well-written papers by native ers; adjust your usage accordingly.

46 Using Respectful Language

To represent others fairly, writers and editors eliminate sexist and discriminatory language from their work.

DRAFT   Early in his career, Lasswell published his **seminal** work on propaganda.

> **READER 1: Why do you have to use this word? It's offensive to associate originality and creativity with being male.**
>
> **READER 2: You could replace *seminal* with *important* or *influential*.**
>
> **READER 3: Aren't you overreacting? You wouldn't throw out *matrimony* just because it's related to the Latin word for *mother* or *patriot* because it comes from the word for *father*.**

As these reactions show, not everyone agrees on what language might be sexist or discriminatory. But no matter how you feel about diversity, as a writer you *must* consider how readers react to your representation of men, women, and members of minority groups. You don't want to alienate readers, prejudice people against your ideas, or perpetuate unhealthy attitudes.

46a Home and community language varieties

How do you talk at school, at work, at home, or in your neighborhood? Do you use language to represent yourself differently with friends, teachers, or bosses? Every speaker of English uses a particular variety of the language shaped by region, culture, exposure to other languages, and home community. Where they're used, these varieties seem natural. In most academic, business, and broad public settings, however, variations aren't seen as acceptable but as "errors" or sloppiness.

HOME VARIETY   Unless **if** RayCorp ordered the resistors, the shipment was sent out **on** accident.

> **READER'S REACTION: Who made all these mistakes in a company memo?**

EDITED   **Unless** RayCorp ordered the resistors, the shipment was sent out **by** accident.

Except in casual, personal situations, writers substitute more general standards for their regional, cultural, and home language varieties. Readers, ev in a local area, expect most writing to conform to general standards, pa because it can readily move to other settings. Becoming a flexible means developing awareness of differences between the habits of your own community and the expectations of more general communities of readers and writers.

1 Learn to see dialect variations as "rules"

Every major language is spoken in a variety of ways called **dialects**. English has dozens of dialects that vary between countries (like England and the United States) and between regions or specific places (like Tuscaloosa, Alabama, and Bar Harbor, Maine). Dialects can also vary by culture, ethnicity, and ancestry. Cuban and Puerto Rican Americans in New York City not only speak different dialects, but their dialects may vary between the Bronx and Brooklyn.

What counts for a "rule" in one dialect may break a rule in another. This is how all language works—the rules are simply structures and conventions that people within a group agree, unconsciously, to use in their speech. Pronouncing *pen* to rhyme with *hen* is a rule of Northern speech, but much of the South rhymes it with *tin*. Each group follows the *rules* of its own community. To break them is to be an outsider.

2 Understand "standard" English as a function of power and prestige

If every community has its own language rules, then who's to say why the so-called standard language should be "better"? Why *should* it be any more correct to say "There isn't anyone who can tell me anything" than to say "Ain't no body gon' tell me nuffin'"?

Around the world, languages have a prestige dialect considered more "correct" or "proper" than other dialects. How this dialect came to be preferred is almost always a matter of historical, political, and social forces. If your home dialect differs from this standard, you may be unfairly stereotyped or discriminated against by those in positions of power. Even unbiased people may not listen to you because they can't: they aren't part of your dialect group. Whether or not society ever accepts more language varieties, people without power will stay powerless if they can't communicate in the language of the powerful. But if they can gain positions of power, maybe they can help change public views of language.

3 Distinguish accents from written variations

While Americans don't usually mind differences in leaders' *accents*, people ~~~ght balk at a president who said, "Them senators ain't ready for this-here veto." ~~~riting, the most glaring (and least forgiven) variations are *grammatical*, followed by *lexical* differences (word choice, slang, jargon). Readers may unfairly see these as signs of ignorance or laziness.

46b   Gender stereotypes

The most common form of sexist language uses *mankind* or *men* for humankind; *he, his,* or *him* for all people; and words implying men in occupations (*fireman*). When editing the generic *he,* try first to make the construction plural (for example, use *their* for *his* or for the clumsy *his or her*).

SEXIST	Every trainee should bring **his** laptop with **him**.
AWKWARD	Every trainee should bring **his or her** laptop with **him or her**.
BETTER	All trainees should bring **their** laptops with **them**.

Some guides suggest that a plural pronoun is better than the generic *he,* even if the pronoun does not agree in number with the subject (see 34b). Some readers, however, object more strenuously to the agreement error than to the sexist language. Reword to avoid both problems.

ORIGINAL	**Everyone** has at some time squandered **his** money.
PROBLEMATIC	**Everyone** has at some time squandered **their** money.
BETTER	**Most people have** at some time squandered **their** money.
BETTER	**Everyone** has at some time squandered money.

Your readers are likely to object to negative stereotypes based on gender, such as assumptions that men are stronger or women are worse at math.

STEREOTYPED	The OnCall Pager is **smaller than most doctors' wallets and easier to answer than phone calls from their wives**.
	READER'S REACTION: I'm a woman and a doctor. I'm insulted by the assumption that all doctors are male and by the negative reference to "wives." OnCall will never sell a pager in my office!
EDITED	The OnCall Pager **will appeal to doctors because it is small and easy to operate**.

46c   Racial, ethnic, and cultural stereotypes

Most readers won't tolerate racism and will stop reading material with discriminatory language. Don't rely on your intent; think about how your reader *might* construe your words.

DEMEANING — My paper focuses on the **weird** courtship rituals of a **barbaric** Aboriginal tribe in southwestern Australia.

READER'S REACTION: **Your paper sounds biased. How can you treat this topic fairly if you don't respect the tribe?**

EDITED — My paper focuses on the unique courtship rituals of an Aboriginal tribe in southwestern Australia.

Some racial and cultural stereotypes are so ingrained that you may not notice them at first. You may be used to hearing derogatory terms in others' speech, or you may not even know that a term is derogatory. Trusted readers can circle stereotypes and derogatory wording for you, and you can do the same for them.

RACIST — The economic problems in border states are compounded by an increased number of **wetbacks** from Mexico.

READER'S REACTION: **This derogatory name is offensive. I object to characterizing a group of people this way.**

EDITED — The economic problems in border states are compounded by an increased number of illegal immigrants from Mexico.

HOMOPHOBIC — The talk show included a panel of **fags** who spoke about what it's like to be a **homo**.

READER'S REACTION: **Emotionally loaded names for people don't encourage reasonable discussion. You'll have to be more objective if you want me to pay attention to your ideas.**

EDITED — The talk show included a panel of gay guests who shared their thoughts about homosexuality.

DEROGATORY — In typical **white-male** fashion, the principal argued against the teachers' referendum.

READER'S REACTION: **The fact that white men are in the majority doesn't give you permission to stereotype them negatively.**

EDITED — The principal argued against the teachers' referendum.

DISCRIMINATORY — The Johnsons **welshed** on their promise.

READER'S REACTION: **What made you think that you could say this without offending people of Welsh descent? Casual stereotyping is just as offensive as deliberate insults.**

EDITED — The Johnsons broke their promise.

Deciding how to identify groups may be difficult. The term *American Indian* is still widely accepted, but *Native American* is preferred. In the 1960s, *Negro* gradually gave way to *black*, but *African American* has gained popularity in its place. *Colored* has been out of use for some time, but *people of color* is now preferred for members of any "nonwhite" group (although some object to *nonwhite*). Terms for those of Hispanic descent include *Chicano* (and its feminine form, *Chicana*) for Mexicans and *Latino* and *Latina* for people from South and Central America in general.

- Whenever possible, use the term preferred by the group itself.
- When there is disagreement within the group, choose the *most widely accepted term* or one favored by a majority of the members.

47 Style, Vocabulary, and Dictionaries

The richer your vocabulary, the more effectively you will write and read.

CIVIC
NEWSLETTER
Despite our efforts to lobby for a compromise, the Senate engaged in an **internecine** feud over the bill.

READER'S REACTION: I like *internecine* here to suggest the Senate's destructive internal conflict.

WORK MEMO
Thanks to the marketing team for its **stellar** effort.

READER'S REACTION: What a nice way to say "job well done"!

A varied vocabulary is essential to effective writing and easy reading in academic, work, and public communities. The more extensive your language options, the more varied, accurate, and metaphoric your prose can be. And readers will appreciate your efforts to find just the right word.

47a Style and community

Academic, public, and workplace audiences have stylistic preferences you can identify with questions like the following.

Values. Are writers expected to address values, preferences, and emotions directly or leave them in the background?

Language. What **diction**—word choices—will readers expect?

Formality. Will readers expect writing that is formal, complicated, and somewhat technical or relaxed, direct, and everyday?

Writer's stance. What pronouns, if any, do writers use to identify themselves, readers, and subject matter: *I, we, you, he, she, it, they*?

Style in Academic, Public, and Work Communities			
	Academic	**Public**	**Work**
APPROACH	Complex, formal, or detailed analysis	Emotional, value-laden, but reasoned argument	Clear, everyday, or informal explanation
VALUES	From the discipline's knowledge base or methods	From the cause, issue, or group's area of interest	From organizational goals such as service and efficiency
LANGUAGE	Technical terms and methods of the field	Lively and emotional with few technical terms and little slang	Plain or technical terms but little vivid, figurative wording
FORMALITY	Formality supports analytical approach and values of the field	Informality reveals personal involvement with serious issues	Informality reflects or builds sense of team-work or closeness
STANCE	Observer (*he, she, it*) or participant (*I, we*)	Involved individual (*I, you*) or representative (*we, you*)	Team member (*we*) with personal concern (*I, you*)
DISTANCE	Objective and dispassionate, not personal or emotional	Personal and passionate about cause, issue, or group	Supportive, committed closeness with mutual respect

Distance. Is a writer typically distant from or personally involved with the issue, problem, or topic?

Although specific written or spoken texts may have their own variations, each major community of writers and readers has a typical approach to style.

47b Language expectations

To avoid stereotypes and get others to listen to your ideas, you'll need to edit home or community language variations that are not widely shared.

1 Learn how to code-shift

One way speakers and writers adjust to differing expectations is by **code-shifting**. Many people use a home or community language with friends but shift into formal language in a college essay, letter to the mayor, or company report. There they adopt a variety that works across many communities, often ed standard edited American English.

To learn to shift to more formal language, consult someone from me language community who also has good facility with standard edited American English. Ask for advice about how to edit one of your papers for readers who expect this form of English. As you work together, try to figure out this person's techniques for using several language varieties successfully.

2 Focus on grammatical variations

Grammatical variations in your home dialect can be tricky to notice; after all, they may not look the least bit problematic—to you. But someone who isn't a member of your dialect community will see them right away.

HOME VARIETY Miss Brill **know** that the lovers **making** fun of her, but she **act like** she **don't** care.

EDITED Miss Brill **knows** that the lovers **are making** fun of her, but she **acts as if** she **doesn't** care.

STRATEGY Look for the "rules" of your home language.

On the left side of a notebook page, record examples of patterns in your home language; on the right side, note corresponding examples in standard English. Explain the differences in your own terms.

Rule in KY: The lawn needs mowed.

Rule elsewhere: The lawn needs to be mowed.

3 Resist hypercorrection

Worrying about language habits that aren't seen as the norm can lead you to **hypercorrection**—unconsciously creating new errors by guessing that a construction is wrong and ironically substituting an error.

HYPERCORRECTED Stuart gave the petitions to Mary and **I**.

EDITED Stuart gave the petitions to Mary and **me**.

Similarly, if you try too hard to be formal and sophisticated, you may end up writing tangled prose that frustrates readers.

CONVOLUTED That the girl walks away, and the showing of the parrot to the restaurant owner who, having closed shop, will not let her inside, is indicative of that which characterizes the novel, i.e., denial and deception.

EDITED The central theme of denial and deception is illustrated wh the girl tries to show the parrot to the restaurant owner is turned away.

STRATEGY | **Mark possible errors—then check.**

When you feel unsure about your writing, circle the words or put a star in the margin. Then check the rule, or ask for advice. List any cases of hyper-correction you (or a reader) note; explain them in your own words.

47c Language resources for writers

The writer can rework this sentence for a grant proposal *because she has options*—words like *beneficence* or *sustenance*.

> Without **help**, the food-shelf program may be **ineffective**.

> Without the **aid** of the Talbot Foundation, the food-shelf program may become **obsolete**.

> Without the **beneficence** of the Talbot Foundation, the food-shelf program may **die**.

> Without the **financial** beneficence of the Talbot Foundation, the food-shelf program in Seattle may die **of starvation**.

> Without the financial **sustenance** of the Talbot Foundation, Seattle's food-shelf program may **slowly** die of starvation.

STRATEGY | **Build a personal vocabulary list.**

Use your **journal** (a record of your observations and insights) or any notebook to list unfamiliar words. Look them up, review them, incorporate them as you write, and cross them out when you can use them comfortably. Gather these words from whatever you read—public opinion pieces in the newspaper, textbooks for school, or technical materials at work.

47d The dictionary and the thesaurus

Hundreds of times you've flipped the dictionary open and checked a word's spelling or meaning. Look carefully to find much more. (See Figure 47.1, an example from *Merriam-Webster's Collegiate Dictionary*.) Like the printed versions, software dictionaries may also supply definitions, usage notes, word histories, and spelling correctors that can be personalized by adding words used *~*ten in a particular community.

A **thesaurus**, printed or electronic, is a dictionary of **synonyms** and *~*yms—words related or opposite in meaning. Under *funny*, for example,

Word Division   Pronunciation   Grammatical Function (Part of Speech)   Etymology (Origin or History)

col•lege\'kälij *n often attrib* [ME, fr. MF, fr. L *collegium* society, fr. *collega* colleague—more at COLLEAGUE] (14c) **1:** a body of clergy living together and supported by a foundation **2:** a building used for an educational or religious purpose **3a:** a self-governing constituent body of a university offering living quarters and instruction, but not granting degrees <Balliol and Magdalen *Colleges* at Oxford> called also *residential college* **b:** a preparatory or high school **c:** an independent institution of higher learning offering a course of general studies leading to a bachelor's degree; *also:* a university division offering this **d:** a part of a university offering a specialized group of courses **e:** an institution offering instruction usu. in a professional, vocational, or technical field <business~> **4:** COMPANY, GROUP *specific*: an organized body of persons engaged in a common pursuit or having common interests or duties **5a:** a group of persons considered by law to be a unit **b:** a body of electors— compare ELECTORAL COLLEGE **6:** the faculty, students, or administration of a college

Meaning →
Examples →
Example in Context →
Cross-Reference →

FIGURE 47.1 Sample dictionary entry

Source: By permission. From *Merriam-Webster's Collegiate® Dictionary, Eleventh Edition* © 2006 by Merriam-Webster, Incorporated (www.merriamwebster.com).

Webster's Collegiate Thesaurus lists synonyms such as *laughable, comical, ludicrous,* and *ridiculous.* Entries may also refer you to contrasted or compared words and related alternatives.

STRATEGY Develop your skills as a "wordsmith."

- **Use a dictionary.** Circle any words you've learned recently or rarely used; look them up to be sure you've used them correctly. Try an ESL dictionary if you're not a native speaker.

- **Turn to a thesaurus.** Consider whether a new word choice is more accurate, more flavorful, or less redundant than your original choice. If in doubt, stick with words you know.

- **Learn a new word every day.** Select a word you read or heard at school, at work, or in a public setting. Look up its definition and history. Work it into your speech or writing three times during the day, or make up sentences and repeat them to yourself.

- **Try the slash/option technique.** As you draft, note alternative words, separated with slashes. Decide later which word fits best.

- **Fight insecurity with simplicity.** Ask yourself which salesperson you would trust—one who talks in simple, honest language or one who uses fancy words for product features. Choose direct, concrete words yourself.

- **Ask a colleague or supervisor.** Someone more experienced may able to tell you whether a term fits your community or context.

Punctuation, Mechanics, and Spelling

▼ *TAKING IT ONLINE*

PUNCTUATION QUIZZES FOR ESL WRITERS

http://www.eslcafe.com/quiz/punctuation1.html
http://www.eslcafe.com/quiz/punctuation2.html

These two quizzes are aimed at helping ESL students to distinguish the comma and the semicolon and to use other marks correctly.

PUNCTUATION MADE SIMPLE

http://lilt.ilstu.edu/golson/punctuation

This Web site aims to help writers overcome their fear of punctuation, starting with a reassuring essay and covering the colon, semicolon, comma, dash, and apostrophe.

WRITE WORDS: THE ELUSIVE APOSTROPHE

http://www.rightwords.co.nz/index.shp?option=com_content&task
=view&id=21&itemid=30/view/21/30/

The brief article on this New Zealand-based Web site outlines how and when to use apostrophes.

WHEN TO USE—AND NOT TO USE—QUOTATION MARKS

http://www.wilbers.com/quotes.htm

This handy list of rules and instructions from the *Writing for Business and Pleasure* Web site also includes a helpful article: "Quotation Marks Make Reading Easy, Writing Hard."

A SPELLING TEST

http://www.sentex.net/~mmcadams/spelling.html

This interactive spelling test of fifty of the most commonly misspelled words in American English will tabulate your score automatically. The site also offers advice on ways to become a better speller.

CANDIDATE FOR A PULLET SURPRISE

http://www.jir.com/pullet.html

There are many versions of this humorous but enlightening poem published on the Internet. It reveals just how unreliable computer spelling checkers can be. Can ewe right another verse or too?

PART 12

Punctuation, Mechanics, and Spelling

48 Commas

Of all the punctuation marks in English, the comma is probably the easiest to misuse.

DRAFT   During the study interviews were used to gather responses from participants and, to supplement written artifacts.

READER'S REACTION: This sentence is hard to read. I can't tell where ideas end and begin.

EDITED   During the study, interviews were used to gather responses from participants and to supplement written artifacts.

Readers who expect commas in certain situations are likely to find inappropriate commas confusing or disruptive.

SERIOUS ERROR

48a Joining sentences

When you use *and, but, or, for, nor, so,* or *yet* (**coordinating conjunctions**) to link two word groups that could stand alone as sentences (**main clauses**), place a comma *before* the conjunction.

The election was close, **and** he couldn't tell who was winning.

He heard no cheering, **yet** he decided to return to headquarters.

Precincts were still reporting, **but** the mayor's lead had grown.

Join main clauses with a comma *plus* a coordinating conjunction. If you omit the conjunction and join the clauses with only a comma, you create a **comma splice** (see 37a). Readers will react more strongly if you omit a conjunction than a comma, but they'll see both as errors in formal writing.

COMMA SPLICE   The rain soaked the soil, the mud slide buried the road.

EDITED   The rain soaked the soil, **and** the mud slide buried the road.

STRATEGY   **Deciding whether to add a comma.**

When a coordinating conjunction links two word groups, how can you decide whether to add a comma? Analyze the word groups. If both can stand on their own as sentences (main clauses), add a comma *before* the conjunction.

(and, but, or, for,
main clause,   **nor, so, yet)**   main clause

We wanted to deliver the order **,** **but** the weather was too bad.

If one or both of the groups *cannot* stand alone as a sentence (main clause), do *not* separate the items in the pair with a comma.

PAIR SPLIT   We sanded **,** and stained the old oak table.

EDITED   We **sanded** and **stained** the old oak table.

PAIR SPLIT   I bought the wood stain because it was inexpensive **,** and easy to clean up.

EDITED   I bought the wood stain **because it was inexpensive** and **easy to clean up**.

When two main clauses are very short, a comma is always appropriate but sometimes can be omitted, especially in public and informal contexts.

The temperature dropped **and** the homeless shelters reopened.

Some academic readers, however, will expect you to use this comma in nearly every case.

48b Setting off sentence elements

A comma can help your readers distinguish potentially confusing sentence parts. The simplest sentences, consisting of a noun phrase and a verb phrase, need no comma.

noun phrase   verb phrase

Dr. Bandolo is my physician.

When you add another layer to the beginning—an **introductory word or word group**—you may need to signal the addition with a comma.

Although I am healthy , I see my doctor for a regular checkup.

For the past decade , Dr. Bandolo worked in an HMO.

Nonetheless , she may open her own practice.

The basic structure of a sentence can be interrupted with all sorts of **parenthetical expressions** that add information: words like *however* and *moreover* (**conjunctive adverbs**, see 35a); phrases like *on the other hand* or *for example* (**transitional expressions**); and **parenthetical remarks** or **interrupters** (*in fact, more importantly*). If the expression begins or ends the sentence, use one comma. If it falls in the middle, use a pair.

TRANSITIONAL	**On the other hand**, the hail caused severe damage.
INTERRUPTER	It broke, **I think**, a dozen stained glass windows.
CONJUNCTIVE ADVERB	We hope, **therefore**, that someone starts a repair fund.

Also set off tag questions, statements of contrast, and direct address.

TAG QUESTION	We should contribute, **shouldn't we**?
CONTRAST	The church's beauty touches all of us, **not just the members**.
DIRECT ADDRESS	Recall, **friends of beauty**, that every gift helps.

1 Put a comma after an introductory word or word group

Readers usually expect a comma to simplify reading by signaling where introductory wording ends and the main sentence begins. To decide whether to include a comma, consider the readability of a sentence.

CONFUSING	Forgetting to alert the media before the rally Jessica rushed to the park.
EDITED	Forgetting to alert the media before the rally, Jessica rushed to the park.

In contrast, these sentences are easy to understand without a comma.

CLEAR	By noon Jessica will be finished with her speech.
CLEAR	Suddenly it started raining, and Jessica quit speaking.

In general, put a comma at the end of a long introductory element introduced by words like *although, because,* and *when* (subordinators, see 43b–c); words like *during* and *without* (prepositions, see 30f); or words like *running, distracted,* and *to analyze* (verbals, see 31a-4). Also use a comma if a short introductory element might briefly confuse readers.

CONFUSING	By six boats began showing up.
EDITED	By six, boats began showing up.

2 Set off parenthetical expressions with commas

Use a pair of commas around a parenthetical expression or interrupter in the middle of a sentence; use a single comma with one at the beginning or end.

DRAFT	Teams should meet even spontaneously as often as needed.
EDITED	Teams should meet, even spontaneously, as often as needed.

SERIOUS ERROR

48c Setting off nonessential modifiers

Modifiers qualify or describe nouns, verbs, or other sentence elements. You change the meaning of a sentence when you decide whether to set off a modifying word or phrase with commas. You can use a **restrictive modifier** to present essential information. Add the essentials *without* commas so that readers see them as a necessary, integral part of the sentence.

RESTRICTIVE   The charts **drawn by hand** were hard to read.

> READER'S REACTION: I assume that the other charts, maybe generated on a computer, were easier to read than these.

You also can use a **nonrestrictive modifier** to add information that is interesting or useful but not necessary for the meaning. Set the nonessentials off *with* commas so that readers regard them as helpful but not necessary details.

NONRESTRICTIVE   The charts **,** **drawn by hand** **,** were hard to read.

> READER'S REACTION: All the charts were hard to read. The detail that they were hand drawn doesn't necessarily relate to readability.

STRATEGY Use the drop test for nonrestrictive and restrictive modifiers.

Drop the modifier from the sentence. If you can do so without altering the essential meaning, even if the sentence is less informative, the modifier is *nonrestrictive* (nonessential). Set it off with commas.

DRAFT   Their band **which performs primarily in small clubs** has gotten fine reviews.

DROP TEST   Their band has gotten fine reviews.

> The meaning is the same, although the sentence does not offer as much interesting information. The modifier is nonrestrictive.

COMMAS ADDED   Their band **,** **which performs primarily in small clubs** **,** has gotten fine reviews.

If dropping the modifier changes the meaning of the sentence, the modifier is *restrictive* (essential). Delete any commas with it.

DRAFT   Executives **,** **who do not know how to cope with stress** **,** are prone to stress-related illness.

DROP TEST   Executives are prone to stress-related illness.

> The intended meaning is that *some* executives are prone to stress-related problems; in contrast, the shortened sentence says they *all* are. The modifier is restrictive.

COMMAS OMITTED   Executives **who do not know how to cope with stress** are prone to stress-related illness.

Try memorizing this formula.

*non*restrictive = *non*essential = *not* integrated (separated by commas)
restrictive   = essential   = integrated (not separated by commas)

Place commas before, after, or around nonrestrictive modifiers.

                         nonrestrictive
main clause begins,   modifier,   main clause ends
The public hearing ❟ set for 7 p.m. ❟ will address cable TV rates.

nonrestrictive modifier,   main clause
Because of rising costs ❟ the companies have requested a rate hike.

       main clause,   nonrestrictive modifier
Many residents oppose the hike ❟ which is larger than last year's.

Clauses with *who, which,* and *that*. Use commas to set off nonrestrictive clauses beginning with *who, which, whom, whose, when,* or *where* (see 31c). Because *that* can specify rather than simply add information, it is used in restrictive (essential) clauses. *Which* is often used to add nonessential information but can be used both ways.

NONRESTRICTIVE   Preventive dentistry ❟ **which is receiving great emphasis** ❟ may actually reduce visits to the dentist's office.

NONRESTRICTIVE   At the heart of preventive dentistry are toothbrushing, flossing, and rinsing ❟ **which are all easily done**.

RESTRICTIVE   Dentists **who make a special effort to encourage good oral hygiene** often supply helpful pamphlets.

RESTRICTIVE   They also provide samples of toothbrushes and floss **that encourage preventive habits**.

Appositives. An **appositive** is a noun or pronoun that renames or stands for a preceding noun. Most are nonrestrictive and need commas.

NONRESTRICTIVE   Amy Nguyen ❟ **a poet from Vietnam** ❟ recently published her latest collection of verse.

RESTRICTIVE   The well-known executive **Louis Gerstner** went from heading RJR Nabisco to the top job at IBM.

SERIOUS ERROR

48d Separating items in a series

When you list items of roughly equal status in a series, separate the items with commas. Readers expect such commas because reading a series can be difficult, even confusing, without them.

The human relations office has forms for medical benefits **,** insurance options **,** **and** retirement contributions.

If an item has more than one part, put a comma after the entire unit.

The human relations office has forms for medical and dental benefits **,** disability and insurance options **,** **and** retirement contributions.

Avoid confusion by placing a comma before the *and* that introduces the last item in a series. Outside the academic community, this comma is often omitted, especially in a short, clear list. Within the academic community, however, both the MLA and APA style guides recommend this comma because it reduces ambiguity (see Chapters 26–27).

CONFUSING   New members fill out applications, interest-group surveys, mailing labels and publication request forms.
    READER'S REACTION: Does *mailing labels and publication request forms* refer to one item or two?

EDITED   New members fill out applications, interest-group surveys, mailing labels **,** and publication request forms.

Punctuate a numbered or lettered list in a sentence as a series. If items in a list contain commas, separate them with semicolons (see 49a-3).

You should (a) measure the water's salinity **,** (b) weigh any waste in the filter **,** and (c) determine the amount of dissolved oxygen.

48e Separating adjectives in a sequence

When you use a pair of **coordinate adjectives**, each modifies the noun (or pronoun) on its own. Separate these adjectives with commas to show their equal application to the noun.

COORDINATE (EQUAL)   These drawings describe a **quick , simple** solution.

When you use **noncoordinate adjectives**, one modifies the other, and it, in turn, modifies the noun (or pronoun). Do not separate these adjectives with a comma.

NONCOORDINATE (UNEQUAL)   We can use **flexible plastic** pipe to divert the water.

STRATEGY **Ask questions to identify coordinate adjectives.**

If you answer one of the following questions with *yes*, the adjectives are coordinate. Separate them with a comma.

- Can you place *and* or *but* between the adjectives?

COORDINATE	Irrigation has turned dry infertile [*dry and infertile?—yes*] land into orchards.
EDITED	Irrigation has turned dry, infertile land into orchards.
NOT COORDINATE	The funds went to new computer [*new and computer?—no*] equipment.

- Is the sense of the passage the same if you reverse the adjectives?

COORDINATE	We left our small cramped [*cramped small?—yes, the same*] office.
EDITED	We left our small, cramped office.
NOT COORDINATE	We bought a red brick [*brick red?—no, not the same*] condo.

Because *brick red* is a color, the condo could be wooden.

48f Dates, numbers, addresses, place names, people's titles, and letters

Readers will expect you to follow conventional practice.

Dates. Put a comma between the date and the year, between the day of the week and the date, and after the year when you give a full date.

I ordered a laptop on May 3, 2007, that arrived Friday, May 18.

You don't need commas when a date is inverted (5 July 1973) or contains only month and year, month and day, or season and year.

We installed the software after its June 2007 test.

Numbers. To simplify long numbers for readers, use commas to create groups of three, beginning from the right. You may choose whether to use a comma with a four-digit number, but be consistent within a text.

We counted 1,746 sheep on a ranch that is worth $1,540,000.

Omit commas in addresses and page numbers of four digits or more.

18520 South Kedzie Drive   page 2054

Addresses and place names. Separate names of cities and states with commas. For an address within a sentence, place commas between all elements *except* the state and zip code. Do not place a comma before or after the zip code unless some other sentence element requires one.

If you live in South Bend, Indiana, order locally from Frelle and Family, Seed Brokers, Box 389, Holland, MI 30127.

People's names and titles. When you give a person's last name first, separate it from the first name with a comma: *Shamoon, Linda K.* Use a comma before and after a title that *follows* a person's name.

We hired **Cris Bronkowski, A.I.A.,** to design the building.

Openings and closings of letters. Use a comma after the opening of a personal letter, but use a colon in a business or formal letter. Use a comma after the closing, just before the signature.

Dear Nan,	Dear Tennis Team,	Dear Hardware Customers:
Sincerely,	Best wishes,	With affection, Regards,

SERIOUS ERROR

48g Commas with quotations

When you introduce, interrupt, or conclude a quotation with a source or context, use commas to distinguish explanation from quotation.

At the dedication, she stated, "This event celebrates Oakdale."

"Our unity," said the mayor, "is our strength."

"Tomorrow the school can reopen," the principal reported.

If your explanation ends with *that* just before a quotation, do not include a comma. If you quote a person's words indirectly (rather than word for word in quotation marks), do not use a comma after *that*.

Lu introduced her by saying that "calamity followed Jane." Jane replied that she simply outran it.

48h Commas to make your meaning clear

Even if no rule specifies a comma, add one if necessary to clarify your meaning, to remind readers of deleted words, or to emphasize.

CONFUSING   When food is scarce, animals that can expand their grazing territory at the expense of other species.

EDITED   When food is scarce, animals that can, expand their grazing territory at the expense of other species.

48i Eliminating commas that do not belong

Avoid scattering commas throughout a paper; add them as required. Today most readers prefer a style in which commas are not used heavily. Too many commas, even correctly used, can create choppy prose.

TOO MANY COMMAS (7) Rosa, always one, like her mother, to speak her mind, protested the use of force, as she called it, by two store detectives, who had been observing her.

EDITED (2) Always one to speak her mind, like her mother, Rosa protested what she called the use of force by two store detectives.

- Omit commas after words like *although* and *because*. These subordinating conjunctions (see 43b–c) introduce a clause and should not be set off with commas. Conjunctive adverbs (like *however*; see 43a) and transitional expressions (like *for example*) should be set off with commas.

  EXTRA COMMA **Although,** Jewel lost her luggage, she had her laptop.

  EDITED **Although** Jewel lost her luggage, she had her laptop.

- Remove commas between subjects and verbs unless a modifier separates them.

  SPLIT SUBJECT AND PREDICATE Cézanne's painting *Rocks at L'Estaque,* hangs in the Museu de Arte in São Paulo, Brazil.

  EDITED Cézanne's painting *Rocks at L'Estaque* hangs in the Museu de Arte in São Paulo, Brazil.

49 Semicolons and Colons

Semicolons and colons help readers make connections.

TWO SENTENCES On April 12, 1861, one of Beauregard's batteries fired on Fort **Sumter.** **The** Civil War had begun.

READER'S REACTION: Maybe these two sentences present a dramatic moment, or maybe they simply state facts, but they don't *necessarily* connect these events.

SEMICOLON   On April 12, 1861, one of Beauregard's batteries fired on Fort
Sumter ; the Civil War had begun.

READER'S REACTION: **The semicolon encourages me to link the battery
firing to the Civil War beginning.**

COLON   On April 12, 1861, one of Beauregard's batteries fired on Fort
Sumter : the Civil War had begun.

READER'S REACTION: **Now I see the guns' firing as a dramatic moment:
the beginning of the Civil War.**

All three examples are correct, yet each encourages a different perspective.
Readers expect you to use punctuation, especially semicolons and colons, to
shape their responses and show them how your ideas relate.

49a Semicolons

A semicolon creates a brief reading pause that can dramatically highlight a close relationship or a contrast. The semicolon alone can't specify the
relationship the way words like *because* or *however* can. Be sure, therefore,
that the relationship you are signaling won't be puzzling to readers.

1 Join two sentences with a semicolon

A semicolon joins main clauses that can stand alone as complete sentences.

TWO SENTENCES   The demand for paper is at an all-time high . Businesses alone
consume millions of tons each year.

ONE SENTENCE   The demand for paper is at an all-time high ; businesses alone
consume millions of tons each year.

STRATEGY   **Test both sides of the semicolon.**

To make sure you are using the semicolon correctly, test the word
groups on both sides to make sure they can stand on their own as sentences.

DRAFT   The demand for recycled paper increased greatly ; with manufacturers rushing to contract for scrap paper.

TEST CLAUSE **1**   The demand for recycled paper increased greatly.
The first clause is a complete sentence.

TEST CLAUSE **2**   With manufacturers rushing to contract for scrap paper.
The second part is a sentence fragment.

EDITED   The demand for recycled paper increased greatly ; manufacturers rushed to contract for scrap paper.

In some cases, elements within a second clause can be omitted if they "match" elements in the first clause. Then the two can be joined with a semicolon even though the second could not stand alone.

ELEMENTS INCLUDED   In winter, **the hotel guests enjoy** the log fire ; in summer, **the hotel guests enjoy** the patio overlooking the river.

ELEMENTS OMITTED   In winter, **the hotel guests enjoy** the log fire ; in summer, the patio overlooking the river.

2 Use a semicolon with words such as *however* and *on the other hand*

When you use a semicolon alone to link main clauses, you ask readers to recognize the logical link between the clauses. When you add words like *however* or *on the other hand*, you create a different effect on readers by specifying how the clauses relate.

assertion → semicolon → transition → assertion
(*pause*) (*consider relationship*)

I like apples ; however, I hate pears.
assertion pause contrast assertion

To specify the transition between clauses, you can choose a **conjunctive adverb** such as *however, moreover, nonetheless, thus,* or *therefore* (see 43a) or a **transitional expression** like *for example, in contrast,* or *on the other hand*. Vary the punctuation depending on where you place such wording.

BETWEEN CLAUSES   Joe survived the flood ; however, Al was never found.

WITHIN CLAUSE   Joe survived the flood ; Al, however, was never found.

AT END OF CLAUSE   Joe survived the flood ; Al was never found, however.

3 Use a semicolon with a complex series

When items in a series contain commas, readers may have trouble deciding which commas separate parts of the series and which belong within items. To avoid confusion, put semicolons between elements in a series when one or more contain other punctuation.

CONFUSING   I interviewed Debbie Rios, the attorney, Rhonda Marron, the accountant, and the financial director.
READER'S REACTION: How many? Three, four, or five?

EDITED   I interviewed Debbie Rios, the attorney ; Rhonda Marron, the accountant ; and the financial director.

49b Colons

Use a colon to introduce, separate, or join elements.

1 Introducing examples, lists, and quotations

The words *before* the colon generally form a complete sentence while those after may or may not. When the words after the colon don't form a sentence, begin with a lowercase letter. When a sentence follows, begin with either a capital or lowercase letter. Stick to one style in a text.

Examples. Commonly, a colon follows a statement or generalization that the rest of the sentence illustrates, explains, or particularizes.

She has only one budget priority **:** teacher salaries.

Lists. A colon can introduce a list or series following a sentence. Following a word group other than a complete sentence, do not use a colon.

DRAFT   The symptoms are **:** sore throat, fever, and headache.

EDITED   She had three symptoms **:** sore throat, fever, and headache.

EDITED   The symptoms are sore throat, fever, and headache.

Quotations. Whether you integrate a short quotation with your own words or set off a longer one in your text (see 24h-1), a complete sentence must precede a colon. If not, use a comma.

Ms. Nguyen outlined the plan **:** "Boost sales, and cut costs."

2 Separating titles and subtitles

Colons separate main titles from subtitles.

Designing Your Web Site **:** *A Beginner's Guide*   "Diabetes **:** Are You at Risk?"

Colons also separate hours from minutes (10 **:** 32); chapters from verses, as in the Bible (John 8 **:** 21–23); the salutation from the text of a business letter (Dear Ms. Billis **:**); parts of a ratio (2 **:** 3); parts of an electronic address (http **:** //www.nytimes.com); and parts of references in some documentation styles (see Chapters 25–28).

3 Using a colon to join sentences

You may use a colon to join two word groups that can stand on their own as sentences (main clauses, see 37c). Use a colon when the second clause sharply focuses, sums up, or illustrates the first.

The blizzard swept across the prairie **:** **the Oregon Trail was closed**.

50 Apostrophes

Like the dot above the *i*, the apostrophe may seem trivial. But without it, readers would stumble over your sentences, growing irritated in the process.

DRAFT   Though its an 1854 novel, Dickens *Hard Times* remain's an ageless critique of education by fact's.

     READER'S REACTION: I can't tell possessives from plurals and contractions. This is too annoying to bother reading.

EDITED   Though **it's** an 1854 novel, **Dickens's** *Hard Times* **remains** an ageless critique of education by **facts**.

50a Apostrophes that mark possession

A noun that expresses ownership is called a **possessive noun**. Mark possessive nouns to distinguish them from plurals.

MISSING   The **cats** meow is becoming fainter.

     READER'S REACTION: I expected something like "The cats meow all night." Do you mean many cats or the meow of one cat?

EDITED   The **cat's** meow is becoming fainter.

STRATEGY   Test for possession.

If you can turn a noun into a phrase using *of*, use a possessive form. If not, use a plural.

DRAFT   The officers reports surprised the reporters.

TEST   The reports **of** the officers? [yes, a possessive]

TEST   Reports surprised **of** the reporters? [no, a plural]

EDITED   The officers' reports surprised the reporters.

1 Adding an apostrophe alone or an apostrophe plus *-s*

Use these guidelines to decide whether to add an apostrophe plus *-s* or an apostrophe alone.

- **Does the noun end in a letter other than** *-s*? When you write a singular possessive noun, usually follow it with an apostrophe plus *-s*.

435

Bill's coat   Connecticut's taxes   the dog's collar

Possessive indefinite pronouns (see 33a) follow the same pattern.

nobody's report   everybody's office   someone's lunch

A few nouns form their plurals (*mice, fish*) without ending in *-s* or *-es*.

oxen's habitat   children's toys   women's locker room

- **Does the noun end in *-s*, and is it plural?** (more than one person or item)? Most plural nouns end in *-s* or *-es*. To make one possessive, simply add an apostrophe after the *-s*.

     the Solomons' house   the roses' petals   the bus**es**' routes

- **Does the noun end in *-s*, and is it singular?** (one person or item)? Stick to one of two options in a paper. The preferred convention is to add an apostrophe and another *-s*, as with another singular noun.

     Chris's van   Elliott Ness's next move

Alternatively, simply add an apostrophe to the final *-s*.

     Chris' van   Elliott Ness' next move

- **Does the noun end in *-s* and sound awkward?** Occasionally, adding a possessive *-s* (Hodges's) to a word already ending in that sound will seem awkward to say ("Hodges-es"). If so, use only the apostrophe (Hodges') to indicate only one *-s* sound, or avoid the awkwardness (*the Adams County Schools's policy*) by rewriting (*the policy of the Adams County Schools*).

In general, treat **hyphenated** and **multiple-word nouns** as a single unit, marking possession on the last word.

HYPHENATED   **My father-in-law's** library is extensive.

MULTIPLE-WORD   The **union leaders'** negotiations collapsed.

When you use a **compound noun phrase** (two or more nouns connected by *and* or *or*) as a possessive, decide whether the nouns function as separate items or as a single unit.

Billy's and Harold's lawyers were ruthless. [separate lawyers]

Billy and Harold's lawyers were ruthless. [same legal team]

2 Avoiding unnecessary apostrophes

Even though third person singular verbs end in *-s*, these are not nouns and do not have possessive forms. They don't require an apostrophe.

DRAFT	The contractor **order'**s all material early.
EDITED	The contractor **orders** all material early.

Don't add apostrophes to personal pronouns; they're already possessive. (See 50b.)

If this car is **yours**, why did you take **hers** and dent **its** fender?

50b Apostrophes that mark contractions and omissions

You can use an apostrophe to indicate the omission of one or more letters when two words are brought together to form a **contraction**.

1 Using an apostrophe to contract a verb form

You can contract pronouns and verbs into a single unit (you'll = you + will) or splice nouns followed by *is*. If this informal style seems inappropriate in your class or workplace, always err on the side of formality.

INFORMAL	**Shoshana'**s going, but her **seat'**s in the last row.
MORE FORMAL	**Shoshana is** going, but her **seat is** in the last row.

> **STRATEGY** **Use the expansion test.**
>
> To decide whether you have used a contraction appropriately, expand it.
>
> | they're | = | they + are | there | = | an adverb |
> |---|---|---|---|---|---|
> | you're | = | you + are | your | = | a possessive pronoun |
> | who's | = | who + is | whose | = | a possessive pronoun |
> | it's | = | it + is | its | = | a possessive pronoun |

For example, test your use of the contraction *it's* by expanding the expression (*it* + *is*); if the expansion doesn't make sense, use *its*.

DRAFT	**Its** the best animal shelter in **its** area.
EXPANSION TEST	**It is** [yes, a fit] the best animal shelter in **it is** [no, not a fit] area.
EDITED	**It'**s the best animal shelter in **its** area.

2 Using an apostrophe to mark plural numbers and letters

Make letters and numbers plural by adding an apostrophe plus -*s*.

LETTERS	Mind your **p'**s and **q'**s. The **x'**s mark missing lines.
NUMBERS	I'll take two size **10'**s and two size **12'**s.

Sometimes the apostrophe is omitted if it risks making a term look like a possessive (*TAs* or *TA's*). The MLA and APA styles (see Chapters 26–27) omit it from numbers and abbreviations (*1980s* and *IQs*).

3 Using an apostrophe to abbreviate a year or show colloquial pronunciation

Informally abbreviate years by omitting the first two numbers (*the '90s* or *the class of '05*) if the century is clear to readers. Also use apostrophes to indicate omissions in colloquial speech and dialects.

DIALECT   I'm **a-goin'** out for some **o'** them shrimp **an'** oysters.

51 Marking Quotations

Quotation marks play many conventional roles.

QUOTATION NOT FULLY MARKED
"Thanks to the navigator," the pilot said, we made the landing.

READER'S REACTION: **Without quotation marks, I didn't realize at first that the pilot said the last part, too.**

EDITED
"Thanks to the navigator,**"** the pilot said, **"**we made the landing.**"**

Although conventions may vary slightly by field, readers in academic, work, and public settings expect you to use quotation marks precisely. How you use these marks tells readers who said what. (See 24h.)

SERIOUS ERROR

51a Using quotation marks

Quotation marks tell readers which words are someone else's (and which words are your own).

1 Identifying direct quotations and dialogue

Whenever you directly quote someone's exact words, spoken or written, use double quotation marks (" ") both before and after the quotation. Long quotations for research papers are an exception (see 24h).

SPOKEN QUOTATION
66The loon can stay under water for a few minutes,99 the ranger said.

WRITTEN QUOTATION
Gross argues that 66every generation scorns its offspring's culture99 (9).

Use quotation marks within a sentence to separate quoted material from the words you use to introduce or comment on it.

QUOTATION INTERRUPTED
66Every generation,99 according to Gross, 66scorns its offspring's culture99 (9).

When you are writing dialogue and a new person speaks, indent as if you're starting a new paragraph. Begin with new quotation marks.

ESL ADVICE: QUOTATION MARKS

If your native language uses other marks for quotations or if you are used to British conventions, try using your computer's search capacity to find each of the marks so you can check for American usage.

2 Setting off quotations inside quotations

Whenever one quotation contains another, use single marks (' ') for the inside quotation and double marks (" ") for the one enclosing it.

De Morga's account of the sinking of the *San Diego* described the battle that 66caused his ship to 6burst asunder999 (Goddio 37).

3 Integrating indirect quotations

Whenever you paraphrase or summarize someone else's words, do not use quotation marks. (See Chapter 24g, h.)

INDIRECT QUOTATION (PARAPHRASE)
The pilot told us that the navigator made the safe landing possible.

INDIRECT QUOTATION (SUMMARY)
Samuel Gross believes that the social consequences of a major war nearly vanish after just one generation (5).

51b Titles of short works

Use quotation marks to enclose titles of short works, parts of a larger work or series, and unpublished works. (See also 55a.)

QUOTATION MARKS WITH TITLES

ARTICLES AND STORIES

"TV Gets Blame for Poor Reading"	newspaper article
"Feminism's Identity Crisis"	magazine article
"The Idea of the Family in the Middle East"	chapter in book
"Baba Yaga and the Brave Youth"	story
"The Rise of Germism"	essay

POEMS AND SONGS

"A Woman Cutting Celery"	short poem
"Evening" (from *Pippa Passes*)	section of a long poem
"Riders on the Storm"	song

EPISODES AND PARTS OF LONGER WORKS

"Billy's Back"	episode of a TV series
"All We Like Sheep" (from Handel's *Messiah*)	section of a long musical work

UNPUBLISHED WORKS

"Renaissance Men—and Women"	unpublished lecture
"Sources of the Ballads in Bishop Percy's Folio Manuscript"	unpublished dissertation

---

Do not use quotation marks for *your* own title unless it contains the title of another work or some other element requiring quotation marks.

DRAFT "The Theme of the Life Voyage in Crane's Story 'Open Boat'"

EDITED The Theme of the Life Voyage in Crane's Story "Open Boat"

51c Highlighting words, special terms, and tone of voice

You can use quotation marks or italics (see 55b) to set off technical terms, unusual terms, or words used in a special sense. Avoid too much highlighting; it distracts readers, and most terms don't require it.

In the real estate industry, "FSBO" (sometimes pronounced "fizbo") refers to a home that is "for sale by owner."

You can—*sparingly*—use quotation marks to indicate irony or sarcasm or to show a reader that you don't "lay claim" to an expression.

52 Periods, Question Marks, and Exclamation Points

When you speak, you mark sentence boundaries with changes in pitch or pauses. When you write, you use visual symbols—a period, a question mark, or an exclamation point. Use some of these marks sparingly, however.

LESS FORMAL   And why do we need your support **?** Without you, too many lovable pups will never find new homes **!**

> READER'S REACTION: **This bouncy style is great for our volunteer brochure but not for our annual report.**

MORE FORMAL   The League's volunteers remain our most valuable asset, matching abandoned animals with suitable homes **.**

52a Periods

No matter how complicated, all sentences that are *statements* must end with periods—even if they contain clauses that appear to be something other than statements. The following sentence as a whole is a statement; it reports, but does not ask, the question in the second half.

> Naomi thanked her supporters profusely but wondered whether they felt responsible for her defeat **.**

Periods also mark decimal points in numbers (22**.**6 or 5**.**75) and punctuate abbreviations by letting readers know that something has been eliminated from the word or term.

> Dr**.**   Ms**.**   Ph**.**D**.**   C**.**P**.**A**.**   pp**.**   etc**.**   a**.**m**.**   p**.**m**.**

Some abbreviations may not require periods, especially **acronyms** whose letters form pronounceable words (*OSHA*, *NATO*), terms entirely capitalized (*GOP*), and state names such as *OH*. When in doubt, turn to a dictionary.

When an abbreviation with a period occurs at the *end* of a sentence, that period will also end the sentence. If the abbreviation occurs in the *middle* of a sentence, the period may be followed by another mark, such as a comma, dash, colon, or semicolon.

> Residents spoke until 10 **p.m.,** and we adjourned at 11 **p.m.**

52b Question marks

Always end a direct question with a question mark. In a sentence with several clauses, the main clause usually determines the punctuation.

DIRECT   When is the train leaving**?**

DIRECT: QUOTED   Laitan asked, "Why is the air rising so quickly**?**"

DIRECT: TWO CLAUSES   Considering that the tax break has been widely publicized, why have so few people filed for a refund**?**

When you present an **indirect question**—a sentence whose main clause is a statement and whose embedded clause asks a question—end with a period.

INDIRECT   José asked if we needed help preparing the bid**.**

A question mark also may signal an uncertain date or other fact.

     David Robert Styles, 1632**?**–1676   Meadville, pop. 196**?**

Unless you're writing very informally, avoid adding question marks after other people's statements, using more than one question mark for emphasis, or combining question marks and exclamation points.

52c Exclamation points

Exclamation points end emphatic statements such as commands or warnings but are rarely used in most academic or workplace writing.

Like question marks, exclamation points can be used informally. They can express dismay, outrage, shock, or strong interest. As you revise and edit, look for strong words to emphasize a point.

DRAFT   Rescuers spent hours (**!**) trying to reach the child.

EDITED   Rescuers spent **agonizing** hours trying to reach the child.

53   Other Punctuation Marks

Most punctuation symbols make up a kind of toolbox for writing. You can use the tools to change the style, sense, and effect of your prose. For example, punctuation marks help guide readers through complex sentences.

DASHES   When the boy—**clutching three weeks' allowance**—returned to the store, it had already closed.

     READER'S REACTION: Dashes emphasize how hard the boy worked to save his allowance.

PARENTHESES   When the boy **(clutching three weeks' allowance)** returned to the store, it had already closed.

> READER'S REACTION: **The parentheses de-emphasize the boy's savings, making the store hours seem more important.**

COMMAS   When the boy **, clutching three weeks' allowance ,** returned to the store, it had already closed.

> READER'S REACTION: **This straightforward account doesn't emphasize either the allowance or the store hours.**

53a Parentheses

Parentheses *enclose* a word, sentence, or clause: you can't use just one. Readers interpret whatever falls between as an aside. Omit a comma *before* a parenthetical statement in the middle of a sentence. *After* the closing parenthesis, use whatever punctuation would otherwise occur.

WITHOUT PARENTHESES   When you sign up for Telepick **,** including Internet access **,** you will receive an hour of free calls.

WITH PARENTHESES   When you sign up for Telepick **(** including Internet access **) ,** you will receive an hour of free calls.

When parentheses *inside a sentence* come at the end, place the end punctuation *after* the closing mark. When enclosing a *freestanding sentence*, place end punctuation *inside* the closing parenthesis.

INSIDE SENTENCE   People on your Telepick list also get discounts **(** once they sign up **) .**

SEPARATE SENTENCE   Try Telepick now. **(** This offer excludes international calls **.)**

You can also use parentheses to mark numbered or lettered lists or to enclose detail that is not part of the structure of a sentence.

DETAIL AND LIST   Harry's Bookstore has a fax number **(** 555-0934 **)** for **(** 1 **)** ordering books, **(** 2 **)** asking about new items, or **(** 3 **)** signing up for store events.

53b Brackets

When you add your own words to a quotation for clarity or background, enclose this **interpolation** in brackets. Also bracket the word *sic* (Latin for "so" or "thus") after an error within a quotation from a source to confirm that you've quoted accurately. If *sic* appears after the quotation, enclose it in parentheses.

INTERPOLATION   As Walters explains, "When Catholic Europe adopted the Gregorian calendar in 1582 and dropped ten days in October, Protestant England ignored the shift, still following October 4 by October 5 [Julian calendar]" (71).

Academic readers expect you to use brackets scrupulously to distinguish your words from those of a source (although nonacademic readers may find them pretentious).

If one parenthetical statement falls *within* another, use brackets for the inner statement.

Contact Rick Daggett (Municipal Lumber Council [Violations Division], Stinson County Center) to report logging violations.

53c Dashes

Dashes set off material with more emphasis or spark than parentheses supply. Too many dashes may strike academic readers as informal. In contrast, dashes add flair to public and work appeals, ads, or brochures. Use your software's dash character, or type a dash as two unspaced hyphens, without space before or after: --. In print, the dash appears as a single line: —.

Dashes can set off an idea or a series of items, especially to open or close dramatically or call attention to an assertion. Use one dash to introduce material that concludes a sentence; use a pair of dashes to highlight words in the middle.

MATERIAL IN THE MIDDLE
After hours of service to two groups—**Kids First and Food Basket**—Olivia was voted Volunteer of the Year.

OPENING LIST
Extended visitation hours, better meals, and more exercise—these were the inmates' major demands.

STRATEGY   **Convert excessive dashes to other marks.**

If your draft is full of dashes, circle those that seem truly valuable—maybe setting off a key point. Replace the others with commas, colons, parentheses, or more emphatic wording.

53d Ellipses

The **ellipsis** (from Greek *elleipsis*, "an omission") is a series of three *spaced* periods showing that something has been left out. Academic readers expect you to use ellipses to mark omissions from a quotation. Readers in other communities may prefer complete quotations to ellipses.

PLACEMENT OF ELLIPSIS MARKS

- Use three spaced periods ● ● ● for ellipses within a sentence or line of poetry. In quoting a text that already uses ellipses, bracket yours (MLA style).
- Use a period before an ellipsis that ends a sentence ● ● ● ●
- Leave a space before the first period ● ● ● and after the last unless the ellipsis is bracketed.
- Omit ellipses when you begin quotations (unless needed for clarity), or use words or phrases that are clearly incomplete.
- Retain another punctuation mark before omitted words if needed for the sentence structure; ● ● ● omit it otherwise.
- Supply a series of spaced periods (MLA style) to show an omitted line (or more) of poetry in a block quotation.

Ellipses mark material omitted from a quotation because it is irrelevant, too long, or located between two useful parts of the quotation. When you drop *part* of a sentence, keep a normal structure that readers can follow.

ORIGINAL INTERVIEW NOTES
Museum director: "We expect the Inca pottery in our special exhibit to attract art historians from as far away as Chicago, while the colorful jewelry draws the general public."

CONFUSING DRAFT
The museum director hopes "the Inca pottery ● ● ● art historians ● ● ● the colorful jewelry ● ● ● the general public."

EDITED
The museum director "expect[s] the Inca pottery ● ● ● to attract art historians ● ● ● while the colorful jewelry draws the general public."

In fictional or personal narrative, you may want to use ellipses to indicate a pause or gap showing suspense, hesitation, uncertainty, or ongoing action.

FOR SUSPENSE   Large paw prints led to the tent ● ● ● ●

53e Slashes

When indicating alternatives, the slash may translate as *or* or *and*.

Be certain that the **on/off** switch is in the vertical position.

This shorthand is common in technical documents, but some readers object to its informality or imprecision (and prefer *or* in its place).

To quote poetry *within* your text instead of using a block quotation (see 24h), separate lines of verse with a slash, with spaces before and after.

> The speaker in Sidney's sonnet hails the moon: "O Moon, thou climb'st the skies! **/** How silently, and with how wan a face!" (1–2).

53f Symbols in electronic addresses

When you note an electronic address, record its characters exactly—including slashes, @ ("*at*") signs, underscores, colons, and periods.

> j **.** bon **@** ceo **.** uc **.** edu

> http **://** www **.** access **.** gpo **.** gov **/** su__docs

53g Combining punctuation marks

- **Pair marks that enclose**: **( ) [ ] " " ' '** Pair commas and dashes to enclose midsentence elements. Type a dash as a pair **––** of hyphens.
- **Use multiple marks when each plays its own role**. If an abbreviation with a period falls in the *middle* of a sentence, the period may be followed by another mark.

  Lunch begins at **11 a . m . ,** right after the lab.

- **Eliminate multiple marks when their roles overlap**. When an abbreviation with a period concludes a sentence, that one period also ends the sentence. Omit a comma *before* parentheses; *after* the parentheses, use whatever mark would otherwise occur.
- **Avoid confusing duplications**. If items listed within a sentence include commas, separate them with semicolons, not more commas.

  ____ **,** ____ **,** and ____ **;** ____ **,** ____ **,** and ____ **;** and ____ **.**

  If one set of parentheses falls within another, use brackets to enclose the internal element.

  ____ **(____ [____] ____) .**

  Use one pair of dashes at a time, not dashes within dashes.

  ____ **––** ____ **––** ____ **.**

54 Capitalizing

Capitalization makes reading easier. Readers expect capital letters to signal where sentences start or to identify specific people, places, and things.

CAPITALS MISSING

thanks, ahmed, for attaching a copy of the 2007 plant safety guidelines. i'll review this file by tuesday.

READER'S REACTION: **Even though email may be informal, the missing capitals here distract me from the message.**

CAPITALS IN PLACE

Thanks, Ahmed, for attaching a copy of the 2007 Plant Safety Guidelines. I'll review this file by Tuesday.

If you ignore conventions for capitals, readers may assume that you are careless. Be especially alert to conventions for capitalizing titles, company divisions, and the like.

54a Capitalizing to begin sentences

Sentences begin with capital letters, whether complete sentences or fragments used appropriately as partial sentences. (See 36c.)

Two national parks, Yellowstone and Grand Teton, are in Wyoming.

1 Capitalize the opening word in a quoted sentence

Capitalization varies with the completeness of a quotation. The following examples include MLA-style page citations (see 26a). Notice that you capitalize when a quotation is a complete sentence or begins your sentence.

QUOTED SENTENCE

Galloway observes, "The novel opens with an unusual chapter" (18).

SENTENCE OPENER

"An unusual chapter" (Galloway 18) opens the novel.

Do not capitalize after you interrupt a quotation with your own words or as you integrate a quotation into the structure of your own sentence.

INTERRUPTED QUOTATION

"The novel," claims Galloway, "opens with an unusual chapter"(18).

INTEGRATED QUOTATION

Galloway notes that the book "opens with an unusual chapter" (18).

2 Capitalize a freestanding sentence in parentheses

Capitalize the first word of a sentence if it stands on its own in parentheses but not if it falls *inside* another sentence.

FREESTANDING
SENTENCE
The Union forces were split up into nineteen sections. (**N**evertheless, Grant was determined to unite them.)

ENCLOSED
SENTENCE
Saskatchewan's economy depends on farming (**o**ver half of Canada's wheat crop comes from the province).

3 Capitalize the first word of a line of poetry

Lines of poetry traditionally begin with a capital letter.

We said goodbye at the barrier,
And she slipped away. . . .

—ROBERT DASELER, "At the Barrier," *Levering Avenue*

If a poem ignores this or other conventions, follow the poet's practice.

new hampshire explodes into radio primary,
newspaper headlines & beer—
well-weathered tag-lines from lips of schoolchildren.
we triumph by not being clear.

—T. R. MAYERS, "(snap)shots"

4 Use consistent capitalization

When capitalization is flexible, be consistent within a document.

Complete sentence after a colon. When a *sentence* follows a colon (see 49b), you can use lowercase (as for other words after a colon) or capitalize.

OPTION 1
The population of New Brunswick is bilingual: **o**ne-third is French-speaking and the rest English-speaking.

OPTION 2
The population of New Brunswick is bilingual: **O**ne-third is French-speaking and the rest English-speaking.

Questions in a series. Capitalize or lowercase a sequence of questions.

OPTION 1
Should we order posters? **b**illboards? **f**lyers?

OPTION 2
Should we order posters? **B**illboards? **F**lyers?

Run-in lists. When items are not listed on separate lines, you may separate them with commas, semicolons (if they are complex), or periods (if they are sentences). Capitalize the first letters of sentences standing alone. Don't capitalize words, partial sentences, or a series of embedded sentences.

In estimating costs, remember the following: (a) **lab** facilities must be rented, (b) **utilities** are charged to the project's account, and (c) **measuring** equipment has to be leased.

In estimating costs, remember to include (a) **lab** facilities, (b) **utilities**, and (c) **measuring** equipment.

Vertical lists. Choose whether to capitalize words or partial sentences, but capitalize complete sentences except in an outline without periods.

OPTION 1
1. **L**ab facilities
2. **U**tilities
3. **M**easuring equipment

OPTION 2
1. **l**ab facilities
2. **u**tilities
3. **m**easuring equipment

54b Capitalizing proper names and titles

Capitalize the names of specific people, places, and things (**proper nouns**) as well as **proper adjectives** derived from them.

Brazil, Dickens   Brazilian music, Dickensian plot

In titles, capitalize the first word, the last word, and all words in between *except* articles (*a, an, the*), prepositions under five letters (*in, of, to*), and co-ordinating conjunctions (*and, but*). These rules apply to titles of long, short, and partial works as well as your own papers. Capitalize the first word after a colon that divides the title.

The Mill on the Floss   "Civil Rights: What Now?"

Developing a Growth Plan for a Small Business [your own title]

In an APA-style reference list, however, capitalize only proper nouns and the first letters of titles and subtitles of full works (books, articles) (see 27b).

CAPITALIZATION OF NOUNS AND ADJECTIVES

CAPITALIZED	LOWERCASE
INDIVIDUALS AND RELATIVES	
Georgia O'Keeffe	my teacher's father
Uncle Jack, Mother	my cousin, her dad
GROUPS OF PEOPLE AND LANGUAGES	
Maori, African American	the language, the people

(Continued)

CAPITALIZATION OF NOUNS AND ADJECTIVES (*continued*)

CAPITALIZED	LOWERCASE
TIME PERIODS AND SEASONS	
October, Easter, Ramadan	spring, summer, holiday
RELIGIONS AND RELATED SUBJECTS	
Buddhism, Catholic	catholic (meaning "universal")
Talmud, Bible, God	talmudic, biblical, a god
ORGANIZATIONS, INSTITUTIONS, AND MEMBERS	
U.S. Senate, Senator Hayes	a senator
Air Line Pilots Association	the union, a union member
PLACES, THEIR RESIDENTS, AND GEOGRAPHIC REGIONS	
Malaysia, Erie County	the country, the county
the Southwest, East Coast	southwestern, eastern
BUILDINGS AND MONUMENTS	
Taj Mahal, Getty Museum	the tower, a museum
HISTORICAL PERIODS, EVENTS, AND MOVEMENTS	
Algerian Revolution, Jazz Age	the revolution, a trend
Reformation	a reformation
ACADEMIC INSTITUTIONS AND COURSES	
Auburn University	a university, the college
Sociology 203, Art 101	sociology or art course
VEHICLES	
Chevrolet Impala	my car, an automobile
COMPANY NAMES AND TRADE NAMES	
Siemens, Kleenex	the company, tissues
SCIENTIFIC, TECHNICAL, AND MEDICAL TERMS	
Big Dipper, Earth (planet)	star, earth (ground)

55 Italicizing (Underlining)

Type that slants to the right—*italic type*—emphasizes words and ideas. In texts that are handwritten or typed, <u>underlining</u> is its equivalent: <u>The Color Purple</u> = *The Color Purple*. Texts prepared in MLA style (see 26c) should use italics.

ITALICS   Walker's novel *The Color Purple* has been praised since 1982.

       READER'S REACTION: **I can spot the book's title right away.**

Some readers, including many college instructors, prefer underlining because it's easy to see. Observe the conventions your community expects.

55a   Italics (underlining) in titles

     Italicize (underline) titles of most long works (books, magazines, films) and complete works (paintings, sculptures). Enclose titles of parts of works and short works (stories, reports, articles) in quotation marks (see 51b).

TREATMENT OF TITLES

ITALICS OR UNDERLINING	QUOTATION MARKS
BOOKS AND PAMPHLETS	
Maggie: A Girl of the Streets (book)	"Youth" (chapter in book)
Beetroot (story collection)	"The Purloined Letter" (story)
The White Album (essay collection)	"Once More to the Lake" (essay)
Guide for Surgery Patients (pamphlet)	"Anesthesia" (section of pamphlet)
POEMS	
Paradise Lost (long poem)	"Richard Cory" (short poem)
The One Day (long poem)	"Whoso list to hunt" (first line as title)
PLAYS AND FILMS	
King Lear (play)	
Star Wars (film)	
RADIO AND TELEVISION PROGRAMS	
The West Wing (TV series)	"Gone Quiet" (episode)
20/20 (TV news show)	"Binge Drinking" (news report)
PAINTINGS AND SCULPTURES	
Winged Victory (sculpture)	
MUSICAL WORKS	
Nutcracker Suite (work for orchestra)	"Waltz of the Flowers" (section of longer work)
Master of Puppets (CD)	"Orion" (song on CD)
Camille Saint-Saëns's *Organ Symphony*	BUT Saint-Saëns, Symphony no. 3 in C minor, op. 78

(Continued)

TREATMENT OF TITLES (*continued*)

MAGAZINES AND NEWSPAPERS

Discover (magazine)　　　　　　"How Baby Learns" (article)
Review of Contemporary Fiction　"Our Students Write with
　(scholarly journal)　　　　　　　Accents" (scholarly article)
the *Denver Post* (newspaper)　　"All the Rage" (article)

NO ITALICS, UNDERLINING, OR QUOTATION MARKS

SACRED BOOKS AND PUBLIC, LEGAL, OR WELL-KNOWN DOCUMENTS
Bible, Koran, Talmud, United States Constitution

TITLE OF YOUR OWN PAPER (UNLESS PUBLISHED)
Attitudes of College Students Toward Intramural Sports
Verbal Abuse in <u>The Color Purple</u> (title of work discussed is underlined)

55b Italics for specific terms

Italicize (underline) the names of specific ships, airplanes, trains, and spacecraft (*Voyager VI, Orient Express*) but not *types* of vehicles (Boeing 767, Chris Craft) or *USS* and *SS* (USS *Corpus Christi*). Italicize a foreign word or phrase that has not moved into common use (*omertà*) but not common words such as quiche, junta, taco, and kvetch. Italicize scientific names for plants (*Chrodus crispus*) and animals (*Gazella dorcas*) but not common names (seaweed, gazelle).

Focus attention on a word, letter, number as itself, or defined term by italicizing (underlining) it.

In Boston, *r* is pronounced *ah* so that the word *car* becomes *cah* and *park* becomes *pahk*.

A *piezoelectric crystal* is a piece of quartz or similar material that responds to pressure by producing electric current.

You may italicize a word or phrase for stylistic emphasis, but readers become annoyed if you do this too often.

EMPHASIS　　　　The letter's praise is *faint*, not fulsome.

55c Underlining for emphasis

Notes, personal letters, and other informal writing may use underlining to add "oral" emphasis. Avoid this in formal writing.

INFORMAL　　　　*Hand* the receipts to me.

MORE FORMAL　　Give the receipts to me personally.

56 Hyphenating

Readers expect hyphens to play two different roles—dividing words and tying them together.

CONFUSING   The Japanese language proposal is well prepared.

         READER'S REACTION: Is the proposal *in* Japanese or *about* the Japanese language?

CLARIFIED   The Japanese-language proposal is well prepared.

Type a hyphen as a *single* line (-) with no space on either side.

FAULTY HYPHEN   well ▬ trained engineer

EDITED   well▬trained engineer

56a Hyphenating to join words

Hyphens often tie together the elements of compound words and phrases. A **compound word** is made from two or more words tied together by hyphens (*double-decker*), combined as one word (*timekeeper*), or treated as separate words (*letter carrier*). These conventions may vary or change rapidly; check an academic style guide, observe accepted practice in public or work contexts, or use an up-to-date dictionary.

Numbers. In general writing, hyphenate numbers between twenty-one and ninety-nine, even if the number is part of a larger one. Academic and work-place readers in certain fields, however, expect numbers in figures (not spelled out) (see 57b).

     forty▬one   fifty▬eight thousand   sixty▬three million

Use a hyphen for inclusive numbers (pages 163▬78, volumes 9▬14) and generally for fractions spelled out (one▬half).

Prefixes and suffixes. Hyphenate a prefix that comes before a capitalized word or a number.

     Cro▬Magnon   non▬Euclidean   post▬Victorian   pre▬1989

Hyphenate with *ex-*, *self-*, *all-*, *-elect*, and *-odd*.

     self▬centered   all▬encompassing   president▬elect

Letters with words. Hyphenate a letter and a word forming a compound, except in music terms.

> A—frame   T—shirt   A minor   G sharp

Compound modifiers. Hyphenate two or more words working as a single modifier when you place them *before* a noun. When the modifiers come *after* a noun, generally do not hyphenate them.

BEFORE NOUN   The **second—largest** supplier of crude oil is Nigeria.

AFTER NOUN   Many cancer treatments are **nausea inducing**.

Do not hyphenate *-ly* adverbs or comparative and superlative forms.

> Our **highly regarded** research team developed them.

Hyphens help readers know which meaning to assign a compound.

> The scene required three **extra wild** monkeys.

> The scene required three **extra—wild** monkeys.

Strings of modifiers. Reduce repetition with hyphens that signal the suspension of an element until the end of a series of parallel compound modifiers. Leave a space after the hyphen and before *and*, but not before a comma.

> The process works with **oil— and water—based** compounds.

56b Hyphenating to divide words

> Hyphens help distinguish different words with the same spelling.

> For **recreation**, they staged a comic **re—creation** of events.

They clarify words with repeated combinations of letters.

> anti—imperialism   post—traumatic   co—owner

Traditionally you could use a hyphen to split a word at the end of a line, marking a break *between syllables*. Now word processors include **automatic hyphenation**, dividing words at the ends of lines but sometimes creating hard-to-read lines or splitting words incorrectly. Many writers turn off this feature, preferring a "ragged" (unjustified) right margin. Style guides such as MLA and APA advise the same.

- Divide words only between syllables (for example, *ad-just-able*).
- Check divisions in a dictionary (*ir-re-vo-ca-ble*, not *ir-rev-oc-able*).

- Leave more than one letter at the end of a line and more than two at the beginning (not *a-greement* or *disconnect-ed*).
- Divide at natural breaks between words in compounds (*Volks-wagen*, not *Volkswa-gen*) or after hyphens (*accident-prone*, not *acci-dent-prone*).
- Don't divide one-syllable words (*touched, drought, kicked, through*).
- Avoid confusing divisions that form distracting words (*sin-gle*).
- Don't split acronyms and abbreviations (*NATO, NCAA*), numerals (*100,000*), and contractions (*didn't*).
- Don't hyphenate an electronic address; simply divide it after a slash.

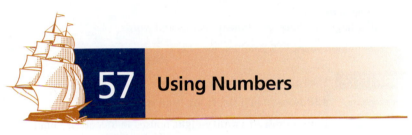

57 Using Numbers

You can convey numbers with numerals (*37, 18.6*), words (*eighty-one, two million*), or a combination (*7th, 2nd, 25 billion*).

GENERAL TEXT   These **fifty-nine** scientists represented **fourteen** states.

READER'S REACTION: In general academic or other texts, I expect most numbers to be spelled out.

TECHNICAL   These **59** scientists represented **14** states.

READER'S REACTION: When I read a scientific or technical report, I expect more numerals.

This chapter shows you how to present numbers in general writing. For conventions expected in specific technical, business, or scientific contexts, seek advice from your instructor, supervisor, colleagues, or style guide (see Chapters 26–29). Unconventional or inconsistent usage can mislead readers or undermine your authority as a writer.

57a Spelling out numbers

Spell out a number of one or two words, counting hyphenated compounds as a single word.

twenty-two computers   **seventy thousand** eggs   **306** books

Treat numbers in the same category consistently in a passage, either as numerals (if required for one number, use them for all) or as words.

CONSISTENT   Café Luna's menu soon expanded from **48** to **104** items.

Spell out numbers according to the following conventions.

DATES AND TIMES
October seventh   nineteenth century   the sixties
four o'clock, *not* 4 o'clock   four in the morning
half past eight, a quarter after one (rounded to the quarter hour)

ROUNDED NUMBERS OR ROUNDED AMOUNTS OF MONEY
three hundred thousand citizens   nearly eleven thousand dollars
sixty cents (and other small dollar or cent amounts)

LARGE NUMBERS
For large numbers, combine numerals and words.

75 million years   2.3 million members

STRATEGY   **Spell out an opening number, or rewrite.**

INAPPROPRIATE   **428** houses in Talcott are built on leased land.

DISTRACTING   **Four hundred twenty-eight** houses in Talcott are built on
leased land.

EASY TO READ   **In Talcott, 428** houses are built on leased land.

57b Using numerals

Use numerals according to the following conventions.

ADDRESSES, ROUTES
2450 Ridge Road, Alhambra, CA 91801   Interstate 6

DATES
September 7, 1976   1880–1910   from 1955 to 1957
1930s   class of '06   the '80s (informal)
486 BC (or BCE)   AD (or CE) 980

PARTS OF A WRITTEN WORK
Chapter 12   Genesis 1:1–6 *or* Gen. 1.1–6 (MLA style)
Macbeth 2.4.25–28 (*or* act II, scene iv, lines 25–28)

MEASUREMENTS WITH ABBREVIATIONS
55 mph   6'4"   47 psi   21 ml   80 kph

FRACTIONS, DECIMALS, PERCENTAGES
7 5/8   27.3   67 percent (*or* 67%)

TIME OF DAY
10:52   6:17 a.m.   12 p.m. (noon)   12 a.m. (midnight)

MONEY (SPECIFIC AMOUNTS)
$7,883 (*or* $7883) $4.29 $7.2 million (*or* $7,200,000)

SURVEYS, RATIOS, STATISTICS, SCORES
7 out of 10   3 to 1 (*or* 3:1)   a mean of 23
a standard deviation of 2.5   won 21 to 17

CLUSTERED NUMBERS
paragraphs 2, 9, and 13 through 15 (*or* 13–15)
units 23, 145, and 210

RANGES OF NUMBERS
LESS THAN 100   Supply the complete second number.

9–13   27–34   58–79   94–95

OVER 100   Simply supply the last two figures in the second number unless readers need more to avoid confusion. Do not use com-
mas in four-digit page numbers.

134–45   95–102 (*not* 95–02)   370–420
1534–620 (*not* 1534–20)   1007–09

YEARS   Supply all digits of both years in a range unless they belong
to the same century.

1890–1920   1770–86   476–823   42–38 BC

58 **Abbreviating**

When they are accepted by both writer and reader, abbreviations act
as a shorthand, making a sentence easy to write and read. Inappropriate or
badly placed abbreviations, however, can make a sentence *harder* to read.

CONFUSING   **Jg● Rich●** Posner was a **U of C** law **prof●**

READER'S REACTION: Am I supposed to know all these abbreviations?
What is "Jg."? Is "U of C" the University of California?

CLEAR   **Judge Richard** Posner was a **University of Chicago** law **professor**.

58a Familiar abbreviations

Many abbreviations are so widely used that readers have no trouble recognizing them. These abbreviations are acceptable in all kinds of writing as long as you present them in standard form.

1 Abbreviate titles with proper names

Abbreviate titles just before or after people's names.

Ms. Rutkowski   Cathy Harr, **D.V.M.**   James Guptil, **Sr.**

With a person's full name, you may abbreviate a title. Spell out a title used as *part of your reference to the person* or placed away from a proper name.

FAULTY   We invited **Prof.** Leves and **Rep.** Drew.

ACCEPTABLE   We invited **Professor** Leves and **Representative** Drew.

ALTERNATIVE   We invited **Prof. Roland** Leves and **Rep. John** Drew.

EXCEPTIONS   **Rev.** Mills and **Dr.** Smith were not invited.

Use only one form of a person's title at a time.

FAULTY   **Dr.** Vonetta McGee, **D.D.S.**

EDITED   **Dr.** Vonetta McGee *or* Vonetta McGee, **D.D.S.**

Abbreviated academic degrees such as *M.A.*, *Ph.D.*, *B.S.*, and *M.D.* can be used as titles or on their own.

ACCEPTABLE   The **Ed.D.** is designed for school administrators.

ESL ADVICE: ABBREVIATED TITLES

In some languages, abbreviated titles such as *Dr.* or *Mrs.* do not require periods as they do in English. If this is true in your first language, proofread carefully.

2 Abbreviate references to people and organizations

Readers generally accept abbreviations that are familiar (*3M*, *IBM*), simple (*AFL-CIO*), or standard in specific contexts (*FAFSA*). Abbreviations in which the letters are pronounced singly (*USDA*) and **acronyms** in which they form a pronounceable word (*NATO*) usually use capitals without periods (but note *laser, radar*).

ORGANIZATIONS	NAACP, AMA, NBA, FDA, NCAA, UNESCO, IBEW
CORPORATIONS	GTE, USX, PBS, GM, CNN, AT&T, CBS, BBC
COUNTRIES	USA (*or* U.S.A.), UK (*or* U.K.)
PEOPLE	JFK, LBJ, FDR, MLK
THINGS OR EVENTS	FM, AM, TB, MRI, AWOL, DUI, TGIF

STRATEGY Introduce an unfamiliar abbreviation.

Give the full term when you first use it; show the abbreviation in parentheses. From then on, use the abbreviation to avoid tedious repetition.

The **American Library Association (ALA)** has taken stands on access to information. For example, the **ALA** opposes book censorship.

3 Abbreviate terms with dates and numbers

Abbreviations that *specify* a number or amount may be used with dates and numbers; don't substitute them for general terms. For example, use *the morning*, not *the a.m.* (See 57b.)

ABBREVIATION	MEANING
AD	*anno Domini*, meaning "in the year of Our Lord"
BC	*before* Christ
BCE	*before* common *era* (alternative to BC)
CE	common *era* (alternative to AD)
a.m.	*ante meridiem* for "morning" (A.M. in print)
p.m.	*post meridiem* for "after noon" (P.M. in print)
no., $	number, dollars

58b Proofreading for appropriate abbreviations

In most formal writing, readers expect words in full form except for familiar abbreviations. In research, scientific, or technical writing, you can use more abbreviations to save space, particularly in documenting sources (see Chapters 26–29). Abbreviations may also be accepted in specific contexts—for example, OT (occupational therapy) in medical reports.

DAYS, MONTHS, AND HOLIDAYS

DRAFT	Thurs., Thur., Th.	Oct.	Xmas
EDITED	Thursday	October	Christmas

PLACES

DRAFT	Wasatch Mts.	Lk. Erie	Ont. Ave.
EDITED	Wasatch Mountains	Lake Erie	Ontario Avenue

EXCEPTION   988 Dunkerhook Road, Paramus, **NJ** 07652
Use accepted postal abbreviations in all addresses with zip codes.

COMPANY NAMES

QUESTIONABLE   LaForce Bros. Electrical Conts.

EDITED   LaForce Brothers Electrical Contractors
Use abbreviations only if they are part of the official name.

PEOPLE'S NAMES

DRAFT   Wm. and Kath. Newholtz will attend.

EDITED   William and Katherine Newholtz will attend.

DISCIPLINES AND PROFESSIONS

DRAFT	econ., bio.	poli. sci.	phys. ed.	PT
EDITED	economics, biology	political science	physical education	physical therapy

SYMBOLS AND UNITS OF MEASUREMENT

In general writing, reserve symbols (@, #, =, −, +) for tables or graphs. Spell out units of measurement (*mile*). Abbreviate phrases such as *rpm* and *mph*, with or without periods, but be consistent in a text.

AVOID IN TEXT	pt.	qt.	in.	mi.	kg.
USE IN TEXT	pint	quart	inch	mile	kilogram

PARTS OF WRITTEN WORKS

Follow your instructor's advice or the style guide for the field.

IN DOCUMENTATION	ch.	p.	pp.	fig.
IN WRITTEN TEXT	chapter	page	pages	figure

LATIN ABBREVIATIONS

Reserve these for documentation and parenthetical comments.

cf.	compare (*confer*)	i.e.	that is (*id est*)	e.g.	for example (*exempli gratia*)
N.B.	note well (*nota bene*)	et al.	and others (*et alii*)	etc.	and so forth (*et cetera*)

59 Spelling

Readers in academic, public, and work settings notice how accurately you spell.

INCORRECT   The city will not **except** any late bids for the project.

> **READER'S REACTION:** I get annoyed when careless or lazy writers won't correct their spelling.

PROOFREAD   The city will not **accept** any late bids for the project.

Readers may ignore or laugh at a newspaper misspelling. For academic and work documents, however, they may consider a writer who misspells lazy, ignorant, or disrespectful.

59a Starting with your spell checker

When you use a spelling checker, the computer compares the words in your text with those in its dictionary. If it finds a match, it assumes your word is correctly spelled. If it does *not* find a match, it questions the word so you can select an alternative spelling or make a correction. What it can't reveal are words properly spelled but used incorrectly, such as *lead* for *led*. When in doubt, check a dictionary.

STRATEGY   Go beyond the spelling checker.

- List as many possible spellings as you can. Look them up. Once you're in the right area in the dictionary, you may find the word.
- Try a special dictionary for poor spellers, listing words under both correct spelling (*phantom*) and likely misspellings (*fantom*).
- Try a thesaurus (see 47d); the word may be listed with a synonym.
- Ask classmates or coworkers about the preferred or correct spellings, especially for technical terms; verify their information in the dictionary.
- Check the indexes of books that treat the topic the word relates to.
- Look for the word in textbooks, company materials, or newspapers.
- Add tricky words to your own spelling list. Look for ways to recall them. For example, you might associate the two *z*'s in *quizzes* with boredom (*zzzz*).

59b Watching for common patterns of misspelling

If you can't remember all the rules and exceptions, try to remember the different kinds of patterns and check this handbook or a dictionary whenever you are unsure about a spelling.

1 Plurals

You form most plurals simply by adding -s (*novel, novels*).

- For words ending in a consonant plus -o, often add -es.

  ADD -es   potato, potatoes   hero, heroes

  ADD -s   cello, cellos   memo, memos

  When a vowel comes before the -o, add -s.

  ADD -s   stereo, stereos   video, videos

- For words ending in a consonant plus -y, change y to i, and add -es.

  etiology, etiologies   gallery, galleries   notary, notaries

  EXCEPTION   Add -s for proper nouns (*Kennedy, Kennedys*).

- For words ending in a vowel plus -y, keep the y, and add -s.

  day, days   journey, journeys   pulley, pulleys

- For words ending in -f or -fe, often change f to v, and add -s or -es.

  knife, knives   life, lives   self, selves

  Some words simply add -s.

  belief, beliefs   roof, roofs   turf, turfs

- For words ending with a hiss (-ch, -s, -ss, -sh, -x, -z), usually add -es.

  bench, benches   bus, buses   bush, bushes

  buzz, buzzes   fox, foxes   kiss, kisses

  One-syllable words may double a final -s or -z: *quiz, quizzes*.

- Words with foreign roots often follow the original language.

  alumna, alumnae   criterion, criteria   datum, data

- Some familiar plurals are irregular.

  foot, feet mouse, mice man, men

- In a compound, make the last word plural unless the first is more important.

  basketball, basketballs sister-in-law, sisters-in-law

2 Word beginnings and endings

Prefixes do not change the spelling of the root word that follows: *precut, post-traumatic, misspell.*

- *In-* and *im-* have the same meaning; use *im-* before *b*, *m*, and *p*.

USE *in-*	incorrect	inadequate	incumbent
USE *im-*	imbalance	immobile	impatient

Suffixes may change the root word that comes before, or they may pose spelling problems in themselves.

- Retain a word's final silent -*e* when a suffix begins with a consonant.

KEEP -*e*	fate, fateful	gentle, gentleness
EXCEPTIONS	words like *judgment, argument, truly,* and *ninth*	

- Drop the silent -*e* when a suffix begins with a vowel.

DROP -*e*	imagine, imaginary	decrease, decreasing
EXCEPTIONS	words like *noticeable* and *changeable*	

- Four familiar words end in -*ery*: *stationery* (paper), *cemetery, monastery, millinery.* Most others end in -*ary*: *stationary* (fixed in place), *secretary, primary, military, culinary.*
- Most words with a final "seed" sound end in -*cede*, such as *precede, recede,* and *intercede.* Only three are spelled -*ceed*: *proceed, succeed,* and *exceed.* One is spelled -*sede*: *supersede.*
- Add -*able* if word roots can stand on their own and -*ible* if they can't.

USE -*able*	charitable, habitable, advisable, mendable
	Drop the -*e* for word roots ending in one *e* (*comparable, debatable*). Keep it for words ending in double *e* (*agreeable*).
USE -*ible*	credible, irreducible

3 Words containing *ie* and *ei*

Most words follow the old rhyme: *I* before *e* / Except after *c*, / Or when sounding like *a* / As in n*ei*ghbor and w*ei*gh.

USE *ie*	believe, thief, grief, friend, chief, field, niece
USE *ei*	receive, deceit, perceive, ceiling, conceited
EXCEPTIONS	weird, seize, foreign, ancient, height, either, neither, their, leisure, forfeit

59c Proofreading for commonly misspelled words

Words that sound like each other but are spelled differently (*accept/except, assent/ascent*) are known as **homophones**.

COMMONLY MISSPELLED OR CONFUSED WORD PAIRS

WORD	MEANING
accept	receive
except	other than
affect	to influence; an emotional response
effect	result
all ready	prepared
already	by this time
allusion	indirect reference
illusion	faulty belief or perception
assure	state positively
ensure	make certain
insure	indemnify
bare	naked
bear	carry; an animal
board	get on; flat piece of wood
bored	not interested
brake	stop
break	shatter, destroy; a gap; a pause
capital	seat of government; monetary resources
capitol	building that houses government
cite	credit an authority
sight	ability to see; a view
site	a place
complement	to complete or supplement
compliment	to praise

COMMONLY MISSPELLED OR CONFUSED WORD PAIRS (*continued*)

WORD	MEANING
desert	abandon; sandy wasteland
dessert	sweet course at conclusion of meal
discreet	tactful, reserved
discrete	separate or distinct
elicit	draw out, evoke
illicit	illegal
eminent	well known, respected
immanent	inherent
imminent	about to happen
fair	lovely; light-colored; just
fare	fee for transportation
forth	forward
fourth	after *third*
gorilla	an ape
guerrilla	kind of soldier or warfare
hear	perceive sound
here	in this place
heard	past tense of *hear*
herd	group of animals
hole	opening
whole	complete
its	possessive form of *it*
it's	contraction for *it is*
know	understand or be aware of
no	negative
later	following in time
latter	last in a series
lessen	make less
lesson	something learned
loose	not tight
lose	misplace
passed	past tense of *pass*
past	after; events occurring at a prior time
patience	calm endurance
patients	people getting medical treatment
peace	calm or absence of war
piece	part of something

(*Continued*)

COMMONLY MISSPELLED OR CONFUSED WORD PAIRS (*continued*)

WORD	MEANING
plain	clear, unadorned
plane	woodworking tool; airplane
persecute	harass
prosecute	take legal action against
personal	relating to oneself
personnel	employees
precede	come before
proceed	go ahead, continue
principal	most important; head of a school
principle	basic truth, rule of behavior
raise	lift up or build up
raze	tear down
right	correct
rite	ritual
write	compose; put words into a text
scene	section of a play; setting of an action
seen	visible
stationary	fixed in place or still
stationery	paper for writing
straight	unbending
strait	water passageway
than	compared with
then	at that time; next
their	possessive form of *they*
there	in that place
they're	contraction for *they are*
to	toward
too	in addition, also
two	number after *one*
waist	middle of body
waste	leftover or discarded material
which	one of a group
witch	person with magical powers
who's	contraction for *who is*
whose	possessive of *who*
your	possessive of *you*
you're	contraction for *you are*

Assessing Writing, Glossary, and Index

TAKING IT ONLINE

COMMON ERRORS IN ENGLISH

http://www.wsu.edu/~brians/errors/

Devoted to errors in usage, this site lists hundreds of potentially troublesome words and expressions.

THE SLOT: A SPOT FOR COPY EDITORS

http://www.theslot.com/

Here, you can access usage issues and pesky expressions by searching the site.

THE VOCABULA REVIEW

http://www.vocabula.com/

This electronic publication regularly includes articles on word origins, common errors in grammar and usage, and advice about succinct and stylish writing. Its Language Links will connect you to a wide variety of sites—classics, language resources, periodicals, media sites, and quick references.

THE GLOSSARIST

http://www.glossarist.com

The site collects glossaries of terms for topics and fields—from Arts and Culture to World Regions, Countries, and Travel.

ENGLISH USAGE, STYLE, AND COMPOSITION

http://www.bartleby.com/usage

At this site, you can search for usage issues or access guides to language and usage.

GUIDE TO GRAMMAR AND STYLE

http://www.andromeda.rutgers.edu/~jlynch/Writing/index.html

Check here for grammar terms, comments on style, and usage notes.

ASSESSING YOUR WRITING

http://www.umuc.edu/prog/ugp/ewp_writingcenter/writinggde/chapter7/print7.shtml.

This site provides concrete advice for assessing your own writing along with checklists for all stages of the writing process.

Assessing Writing, Glossary, and Index

GLOSSARY OF USAGE **475**

Refer to the glossary for advice about how to use confusing words and expressions such as *a lot* or *fewer* and *less*. Terms are arranged alphabetically. Entries include explanations, examples, and cross-references to related sections in the book.

INDEX

Refer to the index to find topics and terms discussed in this handbook, including advice on writing, grammar, research, and documentation of sources.

60 Assessing Writing

You look over the essay or report you have been writing, and you ask yourself, "Should I revise this more? What's going to happen when my instructor or other people read this?" You are not grading your own writing, of course, nor are you making a final judgment about its quality. You are assessing it, nonetheless, by undertaking several of the important activities that fall under the heading **assessment**: evaluating, valuing, choosing, deciding, and predicting.

- **Assessing your own writing.** Should I revise or not? What should I change or add?
- **Assessing others' writing.** What elements of the writing do I (and probably other readers as well) evaluate either positively or negatively? What strategies will help me provide honest and useful feedback?
- **Understanding how others assess your writing.** What do readers notice? How do they evaluate and respond to what they are reading?
- **Assessing your portfolio.** Should I choose to present this work to others in a portfolio (or share it in some other way)? What changes should I make before presenting it? How should I introduce or explain my work to readers?

60a Assessing your own writing

Assessing your own writing requires that you stand "outside" the text, reading it as if you were not the author. Self-assessment can be difficult because you already know what you've written and because you bring more information to it than someone who doesn't share your knowledge and perspectives. If you write "my house" in a paper, the entire world of your house comes into view with all its details, but not so for your readers. The fact that they don't share what you know may not always be apparent to you.

1 Saying what you want to say

Writers often start out with a clear goal but lose their way while forming interesting and detailed sentences, developing effective examples and evidence, or explaining ideas. You may need to step back to remind yourself of what you want to say.

> **STRATEGY** **Focus on what you want to say.**

After completing a draft, try *saying* what you are trying to say, out loud. Or try writing a brief paragraph, without looking at your draft, describing what you're trying to say. Then reread the draft against what you just said or wrote. Are the two versions of your thinking the same? If not, prepare a plan for making your writing say what you want to say—from the beginning of the project to the end.

2 Sharing what you want to share

Self-assessment requires that you look at your draft through a lens of sincerity: Is this what you believe? Is this what happened? Is this a good reflection of who you are? Are the feelings and values you wish to share effectively presented? The following strategy can help you focus on emotions and values in your writing.

> **STRATEGY** **Share your feelings and values.**

Name your feelings in a numbered list, including your feelings toward your subject along with any feelings you hope readers will share. Start with a list of five, and then go to ten if you can. Do you have values or beliefs you want to convey or that you hope readers will share? Put them in another list. Next, look carefully over your draft, putting a corresponding number in the margin next to the place you communicate each feeling or value. Finally, assess how effectively you have shared each feeling or value.

3 Being honest about things that didn't work or shortcuts you took

Only you know how you assembled your writing project. As you review your draft, you can revise much more effectively if you are honest with yourself about those places that you know need more work.

> **STRATEGY** **Tackle the weak spots.**

Reread your draft. At any point where you know you took a shortcut, wrote too quickly, researched too minimally, or spent too little time reworking the material, place an asterisk. Be honest with yourself. You can then work on each asterisked section in manageable chunks of time.

4 Recognizing what you didn't understand

In writing based on external sources, you risk including information that you don't know with 100 percent confidence. Now is the time to assess the accuracy of quotations, paraphrases, summaries, and factual material.

5 Deciding on a revision plan

After reading a draft, you should have a good sense of what you need to do to improve it. You may also get feedback from other readers before revising. In either case, you will need a revision plan.

STRATEGY   **Set priorities for revision.**

- Write two or three sentences summing up the *most global changes* you need to make. These are large-scale *additions* or *deletions* of material, *reorganization* of major chunks of the work, or "ripple effect" changes such as altering the tone or voice of your writing (see 5a).
- Make these global changes first. There is no sense in working on smaller issues until you get the main text right.
- Now, *working directly on the revised draft*, begin *editing*, or looking for paragraph coherence, stylistic problems, and the like (see 5e). Identify areas that need improvement and come back to them later.

60b Assessing someone else's writing

Assessing someone else's writing, and providing helpful responses not only aids that person but also helps you learn how to revise for yourself.

1 Being sympathetic versus being helpful

Think carefully about the social dynamics of peer response before you get down to work. Because most people are reluctant to criticize others, they tend to say that someone else's writing is "OK" or "good" without offering much helpful response. It's fine to sympathize with a writer's struggles or offer a general endorsement, and your response can certainly start with the positives. But that won't improve your partner's paper. What's the most helpful information you can provide? Can you find a way to give that information in the form of a response as a reader, rather than an "expert"? (See 60b-2.)

2 Deciding what makes a difference for you as a reader

By far the best information you can give a writer is your direct response as a reader. Both you and your revision partner will feel much more comfortable if you don't alternate playing teacher or expert. Instead, provide direct feedback as a reader.

STRATEGY   **Be a reader, not a critic.**

- Come up with some images of your experience: "I felt like you were beating me over the head with your point on this page," or "Most of us know this basic information, so I felt a little condescended to here." It's up to the writer to figure out how to solve these problems.

- Place check marks in the margins where the writing works especially well for you, and use some other mark such as an asterisk where it feels choppy, unorganized, or confusing.
- Place exclamation marks next to information that interests or engages you, and add downward arrows where you lose focus or become bored.
- Compliment the writer on effective expression: clear phrases and sentences; well-designed paragraphs; or helpful headings, examples, or visuals.

3 Believing and doubting

A famous writing expert, Peter Elbow, has used the terms *believing game* and *doubting game* to refer to our attitudes as readers. When we play the believing game, we look for reasons to endorse what the writer is saying or go along with the narrative, explanation, or argument. When we play the doubting game, we constantly look for reasons not to trust the writer.

STRATEGY   **Believe and doubt.**

Start with the believing game. Read through a text making positive marginal comments at points where you agree with what the writer is saying or sharing, even if these are only small spaces in a thicket of disagreement. Point out what works: clear statements, powerful wording, well-developed paragraphs, compelling examples, or enlightening visuals.

Move to the doubting game. In the margins, raise questions or points of disagreement you feel the writer ought to address. Ask for further information or explanation. Point out where the writing is hard to follow and where extensive revision is needed.

4 Learning the language of assessment

The assessment of writing in academic settings has some unique language and terminology, such as *coherence, organization, paragraph structure, purpose statement, thesis, awareness of audience, appeal to logic, stance.* As you read your peers' drafts, try to use language that your instructor uses and that is explained in this book.

5 Prompting change

Although it's tempting to cover a paper with marks and corrections, writers revise most effectively when they get a few *meaningful* comments that prompt major, effective revisions. Writers can work on many of the small details later; they need your most important feedback first in order to make the most beneficial changes.

> **STRATEGY** **Look for big issues, not details.**
>
> - As you read a peer's writing, make a list of the three most important concerns that could lead to improvements. For example, if the writer has assumed a tone that is too clinical and removed from the subject, offer a comment about the whole paper's tone, perhaps anchored in a specific example.
> - If you notice a problem with a smaller detail, such as the use of commas, resist marking every case. Mark one and respond to it with a readerly comment: "This comma tricks me into thinking that the second part of the sentence is related to the first, but it's not." Then explain that this happens in other places in the writing, too.

6 Working with others

If you are working with a peer group on your writing, remember you are all collaborating and your goal is to improve each other's work. Try giving each other a sense of direction, and put aside your ego (see 5c).

> **STRATEGY** **Work productively with your group.**
>
> - Participate responsibly. If you need to circulate drafts by a certain date, do your part. Don't miss the meeting: your peers are counting on you. Prepare adequately; don't read papers at the last minute. Be sure to write responses on the drafts or separately to remind you of issues you want to discuss.
> - Keep apologies to a minimum. Don't bog down the meeting by spending a lot of time trying to save face.
> - As responder, strike a good tone. Be helpful and diplomatic, and avoid sarcasm, ridicule, or over-the-top criticism. As an author, accept criticism gratefully. Don't counter every concern with an explanation or become defensive. Listen, and write down your readers' responses, but make the final decision yourself.
> - Don't dominate, either with your comments or in the amount of time spent on your paper. Divide the time evenly, and stick to the time blocks for each paper.

60c How others assess your writing

The more you can anticipate how other readers will read and be affected by your writing, the more effectively you can write in the first place. Your peers can become good "trial" readers for you. But you also need to develop a kind of internal monitor for what readers like or dislike in the text they read.

1 Where readers start evaluating

Typically, readers begin sizing you up as a writer from the first line of your text—sometimes even before, as when they look at a page that is poorly designed. You need to make a good impression, so pay attention to your introduction. If your first paragraph is garbled, too general, or filled with errors, readers may not want to keep going.

2 How readers move through your writing

Although some readers skip around or skim as they read, most of the time they try to move through your prose from beginning to end. However, they need clues about where they're going. For longer papers, *headings* can help. For shorter papers, topic sentences and effective transitions are essential (see 6a–d).

3 How readers decide on evaluation standards

As soon as a reader knows the genre and context of a piece of writing, certain standards or expectations will come alive. When you read an account of an event on the front page of a newspaper, for example, you expect *accuracy, sufficient detail, lack of bias, reasonable brevity, journalistic style,* and a *structure* that usually moves from essential information first to greater detail later, so you can get the gist in the first few lines and skip the rest if you want. Or if you read a brief travelogue describing a vacation spot, your criteria will include at least some *evaluation* of the locale. Similarly, your readers will expect specific things from your writing, and if you are aware of these expectations, you can more effectively revise your writing to match them.

STRATEGY   Meet expectations.

- Make a list of the three most important expectations your readers will have of the particular genre, or type of writing, you are creating. Think of these as criteria for assessment.
- Work through your draft once for each expectation or criterion, judging how effectively you achieve it. If the genre calls for lots of visual detail, ask yourself just how detailed your writing is, and jot comments in the margins indicating where you can deepen the detail.

60d Assessing your portfolio

Portfolios are collections of your writing, assembled so people can read, understand, evaluate, and enjoy what you have to say. For example, portfolios may be simply collections of all the writing you have produced in a course (or on the job), or they may be presentations of your writing at its best, carefully chosen, revised, and introduced to readers. The rest of this section considers the role of assessment in creating this latter kind of portfolio.

1 Assessing to choose

You need to choose selections that represent you as a writer *at your best*. But what is your best? Your best may vary from one kind of writing to another. For a portfolio, you need to start with writing that may not represent your best right now but will do so after you have finished revising it. In short, you need to assess the possibilities: what your writing can become.

To assess your writing, you need to choose some criteria, that is, standards for judging what your writing is or can be.

> **STRATEGY** **Show your strengths.**
>
> Assemble the pieces of writing from which you plan to choose selections for your portfolio. For each, choose up to five terms you think could appropriately fill in the blank in this question.
>
> If I revised this selection, it could represent my writing at its
>
> _____.
>
> | | | |
> |---|---|---|
> | best | most informative | most convincing |
> | clearest | most imaginative | most surprising |
> | freshest | most improved | most innovative |
> | funniest | most detailed | most fully developed |
> | and many more possibilities . . . | | |

2 Assessing for variety

A successful portfolio also represents the range of your ability as a writer. For your portfolio, therefore, choose selections that differ in subject, strategy, and technique or in the demands and opportunities they present to readers.

> **STRATEGY** **Show your range.**
>
> Use the following qualities or categories to identify varied kinds of writing to include in a portfolio. Look for selections that differ according to qualities like these.
>
> | | | |
> |---|---|---|
> | purpose | arrangement | complexity |
> | style | feelings | use of sources |
> | values | subject matter | amount of detail |

3 Assessing to introduce

You introduce a portfolio with a brief essay that explains your choices, highlights the qualities of your writing, and helps readers approach the selections in ways that aid understanding and appreciation.

STRATEGY **Introduce yourself and your writing.**

Freewrite on topics like the following, thinking about ways your introduction can best help readers understand you as a writer with particular goals or aspirations and ways your introduction can help readers notice the most important features of your writing.

Contrasts among the selections in your portfolio

Ways the selections document your growth as a writer

Choices you made in revising

Things you learned about writing as you revised

Information or ideas you added

Reasons you included the selections

Features you think are worth noticing

Ways the selections try to alter or shape readers' perspectives

Choices you considered but rejected

Things you hope readers will remember from your portfolio

Information or ideas you cut

Reasons you excluded some selections

GLOSSARY OF USAGE

a, an When the word after *a* or *an* begins with a vowel sound, use *an: an outrageous film.* Use *a* before consonants: *a shocking film.* (See 30a.)

accept, except *Accept* means "to take or receive"; *except* means "excluding."

> Everyone **accepted** the invitation **except** Larry.

adverse, averse Someone opposed to something is *averse* to it; if conditions stand in opposition to achieving a goal, they are *adverse.*

advice, advise *Advice* is a noun meaning "counsel" or "recommendations." *Advise* is a verb meaning "to give counsel or recommendations."

> Raul wanted to **advise** his students, but they wanted no **advice**.

affect, effect *Affect* is a verb meaning "to influence." *Effect* is a noun meaning "a result." More rarely, *effect* is a verb meaning "to cause something to happen."

> CFCs may **affect** the deterioration of the ozone layer. The **effect** of that deterioration on global warming is uncertain. Lawmakers need to **effect** changes in public attitudes toward our environment.

aggravate, irritate *Aggravate* means "to worsen"; *irritate* means "to bother or pester."

ain't Although widely used, *ain't* is inappropriate in formal writing. Use *am not*, *is not*, or *are not*; the contracted forms *aren't* and *isn't* are more acceptable than *ain't* but may still be too informal in some contexts. (See 50b.)

all ready, already *All ready* means "prepared for"; *already* means "by that time."

> Sam was **all ready** for the meeting, but it had **already** started.

all right This expression is always spelled as two words, not as *alright.*

all together, altogether Use *all together* to mean "everyone"; use *altogether* to mean "completely."

> We were **all together** on our decision to support the center, but it was **altogether** too hard for us to organize a fund-raiser in a week.

allude, elude *Allude* means "hint at" or "refer to indirectly"; *elude* means "escape."

allusion, illusion An *allusion* is a reference to something; an *illusion* is a vision or a false belief.

a lot This expression is always spelled as two words, not as *alot.* Because *a lot* may be too informal for some writing, consider *many*, *much*, or another modifier instead.

a.m., p.m. These abbreviations may be capital or lowercase letters (see 58a).

among, between Use *between* to describe something involving two people, things, or ideas; use *among* to refer to three or more.

> The fight **between** the umpire and the catcher was followed by a discussion **among** the catcher, the umpire, and the managers.

amount, number Use *amount* for a quantity of something that can't be divided into separate units. Use *number* for countable objects.

> A large **number** of spices may be used in Thai dishes. This recipe calls for a small **amount** of coconut milk.

an, a (See **a, an**.)

and etc. (See **etc**.)

and/or Although widely used, *and/or* is usually imprecise and may distract your reader. Choose one of the words, or revise your sentence. (See 53e.)

ante-, anti- Use *ante-* as a prefix to mean "before" or "predating"; use *anti-* to mean "against" or "opposed."

anyone, any one *Anyone* as one word is an indefinite pronoun. Occasionally you may want to use *any* to modify *one*, in the sense of "any individual thing or person." (The same distinction applies to **everyone**, **every one**; **somebody**, **some body**; and **someone**, **some one**.)

> **Anyone** can learn to parachute without fear, but the instructors are told not to spend too much time with **any one** person.

anyplace Replace this term in formal writing with *anywhere*, or revise.

anyways, anywheres Avoid these incorrect versions of *anyway* and *anywhere*.

as, like Used as a preposition, *as* indicates a precise comparison. *Like* indicates a resemblance or similarity.

> Remembered **as** a man of habit, Kant took a walk at the same time each day. He, **like** many other philosophers, was thoughtful and intense.

as to *As to* is considered informal in many contexts.

> INFORMAL   The media speculated **as to** the film's success.
>
> EDITED   The media speculated **about** the film's success.

assure, ensure, insure Use *assure* to imply a promise; use *ensure* to imply a certain outcome. Use *insure* only when you imply something legal or financial.

> The surgeon **assured** the pianist that his fingers would heal in time for the concert. To **ensure** that, the pianist did not practice for three weeks and **insured** his hands with Lloyd's of London.

at In any writing, avoid using *at* in direct and indirect questions.

> COLLOQUIAL   Jones wondered where his attorney was **at**.
>
> EDITED   Jones wondered where his attorney **was.**

awful, awfully Use *awful* as an adjective modifying a noun or pronoun; use *awfully* as an adverb modifying a verb, adjective, or other adverb. (See 35b.)

> Sanders played **awfully at** the golf tournament. On the sixth hole, an **awful** shot landed his ball in the pond.

awhile, a while *Awhile* (as one word) functions as an adverb; it is not preceded by a preposition. *A while* functions as a noun (preceded by *a*, an article) and is often used in prepositional phrases.

> The shelter suggested that the homeless family stay **awhile**. It turned out that the children had not eaten for **a while.**

bad, badly Use *bad* as an adjective that modifies nouns or with a linking verb expressing feelings. Use *badly* as an adverb. (See 35b-3.)

because, since In general, avoid using *since* in place of *because*, which is more formal and precise. Use *since* to indicate time, not causality.

being as, being that Avoid both in formal writing when you mean *because*.

beside, besides Use *beside* as a preposition to mean "next to." Use *besides* as an adverb meaning "also" or an adjective meaning "except."

> Betsy placed the documents **beside** Mr. Klein. **Besides** being the best lawyer at the firm, Klein was also the most cautious.

better, had better Avoid using *better* or *had better* in place of *ought to* or *should* in formal writing.

> COLLOQUIAL — Fast-food chains **better** realize that Americans are more health-conscious today.
>
> EDITED — Fast-food chains **ought to** realize that Americans are more health-conscious today.

between, among (See **among, between**.)

bring, take *Bring* implies a movement from somewhere else to close at hand; *take* implies a movement in the opposite direction.

> Please **bring** me a coffee refill, and **take** away these leftover muffins.

broke *Broke* is the past tense of *break*; avoid using it as the past participle.

> DRAFT — The computer was **broke**.
>
> EDITED — The computer was **broken**.

burst, bursted *Burst* implies an outward explosion. Do not use the form *bursted* for the past tense.

> The gang of boys **burst** the balloon.

bust, busted Avoid the use of *bust* or *busted* to mean "broke."

> COLLOQUIAL — The senator's limousine **bust** down on the trip.
>
> EDITED — The senator's limousine **broke** down on the trip.

but however, but yet Choose one word of each pair, not both.

can, may *Can* implies ability; *may* implies permission or uncertainty.

> Bart **can** drive now, but his parents **may** not lend him their new car.

can't hardly, can't scarcely Use these pairs positively, not negatively: *can hardly* and *can scarcely*, or simply *can't*. (See 35b-4.)

capital, capitol *Capital* refers to a government center or to money; *capitol* refers to a government building.

censor, censure *Censor* means the act of shielding something from the public, such as a movie. *Censure* implies punishment or critical labeling.

center around Use *center on* or *focus on*, or reword as *revolve around*.

choose, chose Watch for spelling errors; use *choose* for the present tense form of the verb and *chose* for the past tense.

cite, site *Cite* means to acknowledge someone else's work; *site* means a place or location.

> Phil decided to **cite** Chomsky's theory of syntax.

> We chose the perfect **site** to pitch our tent.

climactic, climatic *Climactic* refers to the culmination of something; *climatic* refers to weather conditions.

compare to, compare with Use *compare to* when you want to imply similarities between two things—the phrase is close in meaning to *liken to*. Use *compare with* to imply both similarities and differences.

> The doctor **compared** the boy's virus **to** a tiny army in his body. **Compared with** his last illness, this one was mild.

complement, compliment *Complement* means "an accompaniment"; *compliment* means "words of praise."

> The diplomats **complimented** the ambassador on her menu. The dessert **complemented** the main course perfectly.

continual, continuous *Continual* implies that something is recurring; *continuous* implies that something is constant and unceasing.

> Local residents found the **continual** noise of landing jets less annoying than the traffic that **continuously** circled the airport.

could of, would of These incorrect pairs are common because they are often pronounced as if they are spelled this way. Use the correct verb forms *could have* and *would have*.

> DRAFT   I **could of** written a letter to the editor.

> EDITED   I **could have** written a letter to the editor.

couple, couple of In formal writing, use a *few* or *two* instead.

> COLLOQUIAL   Watson took a **couple of** days to examine the data.

> EDITED   Watson took **a few** days to examine the data.

criteria *Criteria* is the plural form of *criterion*. Make sure your verbs agree in number with this noun.

> SINGULAR   One **criterion** for the bonus was selling ten cars.

> PLURAL   The **criteria** were too strict to follow.

curriculum *Curriculum* is the singular form of this noun. For the plural, use either *curricula* or *curriculums*, but be consistent.

data Although widely used for both the singular and plural, *data* technically is a plural noun; *datum* refers to a single piece of data. If in doubt, use the formal distinction, and make sure your verbs agree in number.

> SINGULAR   This one **datum** was unexpected.

> PLURAL   These **data** are not very revealing.

different from, different than Use *different from* when an object follows, and use *different than* when an entire clause follows.

> Jack's proposal is **different from** Marlene's, but his ideas are now **different than** they were when he first joined the sales team.

discreet, discrete *Discreet* means "reserved or cautious"; *discrete* means "distinctive, different, or explicit."

disinterested, uninterested *disinterested* implies impartiality or objectivity; *uninterested* implies boredom or lack of interest.

done Avoid using *done* as a simple past tense; it is a *past participle* (see 32c).

DRAFT	The skater **done** the best she could at the Olympics.
EDITED	The skater **did** the best she could at the Olympics.

don't, doesn't Contractions like these may strike some readers as too informal. Err on the side of formality (*do not, does not*) when in doubt. (See 50b.)

due to When meaning "because," use *due to* only after some form of the verb *be*. Avoid *due to the fact that*, which is wordy.

DRAFT	The mayor collapsed **due to** campaign fatigue.
EDITED	The mayor's collapse was **due to** campaign fatigue.
EDITED	The mayor collapsed **because** of campaign fatigue.

effect, affect (See **affect, effect**.)

e.g. Avoid this abbreviation (from Latin, "for example") when possible. (See 58b.)

AWKWARD	Her positions on major issues, **e.g.**, gun control, abortion, and the death penalty, are very liberal.
EDITED	Her positions on major issues **such as** gun control, abortion, and the death penalty are very liberal.

emigrate from, immigrate to Foreigners *emigrate from* one country and *immigrate to* another. *Migrate* implies moving around (as in *migrant workers*) or settling temporarily.

ensure, assure, insure (See **assure, ensure, insure**.)

enthused Avoid *enthused* to mean *enthusiastic* in formal writing.

especially, specially *Especially* implies "in particular"; *specially* means "for a specific purpose."

> It is **especially** important that Jo follow her **specially** designed workouts.

etc. Avoid this abbreviation in formal writing by supplying a complete list of items or by using a phrase like *so forth*. (See 58b.)

INFORMAL	The Washington march was a disaster: it was cold and rainy, the protesters had no food, **etc.**
EDITED	The Washington march was a disaster: the protesters were cold, wet, and hungry.

eventually, ultimately Use *eventually* to imply that an outcome follows a series of events or a lapse of events. Use *ultimately* to imply that a final or culminating act ends a series of events.

Eventually, the rescue team managed to pull the last of the survivors from the wreck, and **ultimately** there were no casualties.

everyday, every day *Everyday* is an adjective that modifies a noun. *Every day* is a noun (*day*) modified by an adjective (*every*).

Every day in the Peace Corps, Monique faced the **everyday** task of boiling her drinking water.

everyone, every one *Everyone* is a pronoun. *Every one* is a noun (*one*) modified by an adjective (*every*). (See also **anyone, any one**.)

Everyone was tantalized by **every one** of the desserts on the menu.

exam In formal writing, some readers may be bothered by this abbreviation of *examination*.

except, accept (See **accept, except**.)

explicit, implicit *Explicit* means that something is outwardly or openly stated; *implicit* means that it is implied or suggested.

farther, further *Farther* implies a measurable distance; *further* implies something that cannot be measured.

The **farther** they trekked into the wilderness, the **further** their relationship deteriorated.

female, male Use these terms only when you want to call attention to gender specifically, as in a research report. Otherwise, use the simpler *man* and *woman* or *boy* and *girl* unless such usage is sexist (see 46b).

fewer, less Use *fewer* for things that can be counted, and use *less* for quantities that cannot be divided. (See 30a.)

The new bill had **fewer** supporters and **less** media coverage.

finalize Some readers object to adjectives and nouns that are turned into verbs ending in *-ize* (*finalize, prioritize, objectivize*). When in doubt, use *make final* or some other construction. (See also **-ize, -wise**.)

firstly Use *first, second, third*, and so forth when enumerating points in writing.

former, latter *Former* means "the one before" and *latter* means "the one after." They can be used only when referring to two things.

freshman, freshmen Many readers consider these terms sexist and archaic. Unless you are citing an established term or group (such as the Freshman Colloquium at Midwest University), use *first-year student* instead.

get Avoid imprecise or frequent use of *get* in formal writing.

INFORMAL	Martin Luther King had a premonition that he would **get** shot; his speeches before his death **got** nostalgic.
EDITED	Martin Luther King had a premonition that he would **be** shot; his speeches before his death **waxed** nostalgic.

go, say In very informal contexts, some speakers use **go** and **goes** to mean *say* and *says*. This usage is considered inappropriate in all writing.

INAPPROPRIATE	Hjalmar **goes** to Gregers, "I thought this was my account."
EDITED	Hjalmar **says** to Gregers, "I thought this was my account."

gone, went Do not use *went* (the past tense of *go*) in place of the past participle form *gone*. (See 32c–d.)

DRAFT	The officers **should have went** to their captain.
EDITED	The officers **should have gone** to their captain.

good, well *Good* is an adjective meaning "favorable" (a *good* trip). *Well* is an adverb meaning "done favorably." (See 35b-3.)

good and This is a colloquial term when used to mean "very" (*good and* tired; *good and* hot). Avoid it in formal writing.

got to Avoid the colloquial use of *got* or *got to* in place of *must* or *have to*.

COLLOQUIAL	I **got to** improve my ratings in the opinion polls.
EDITED	I **must** improve my ratings in the opinion polls.

great In formal writing, avoid using *great* as an adjective meaning "wonderful." Use *great* in the sense of "large" or "monumental."

hanged, hung Although the distinction between these terms is disappearing, some readers may expect you to use **hanged** exclusively to mean execution by hanging and **hung** to refer to anything else.

have, got (See **got to.**)

have, of (See **could of, would of.**)

he, she, he or she, his or her When you use gender-specific pronouns, be careful not to privilege the male versions (see 46b).

hopefully Although the word is widely used to modify entire clauses (as in "Hopefully, her condition will improve"), some readers may object. When in doubt, use *hopefully* only to mean "feeling hopeful."

Bystanders watched **hopefully** as the workers continued to dig.

however, yet, but (See **but however, but yet.**)

hung, hanged (See **hanged, hung.**)

if, whether Use *if* before a specific outcome (either stated or implied); use *whether* when you are considering alternatives.

If holographic technology can be perfected, we may soon be watching three-dimensional television. But **whether** we will be able to afford it is another question.

illusion, allusion (See **allusion, illusion.**)

immigrate to, emigrate from (See **emigrate from, immigrate to.**)

implicit, explicit (See **explicit, implicit.**)

in regard to Although it may sound sophisticated, *in regard to* is wordy. Use *about* instead.

inside of, outside of When you use *inside* or *outside* to mark locations, do not pair them with *of*.

UNNEEDED	**Inside of** the hut was a large stock of rootwater.
EDITED	**Inside** the hut was a large stock of rootwater.

insure, assure, ensure (See **assure, ensure, insure.**)

irregardless Avoid this erroneous form of the word *regardless*, commonly used because *regardless* and *irrespective* are often used synonymously.

irritate, aggravate (See **aggravate, irritate**.)

its, it's *Its* is a possessive pronoun, and *it's* contracts *it is* (33a and 50b). (Some readers may also object to *it's* for *it is* in formal writing.)

-ize, -wise Some readers object to nouns or adjectives turned into verbs by adding *-ize* (*finalize, itemize, computerize*). Also avoid adding *-wise* to words, as in "Weather-*wise*, it will be chilly."

kind, sort, type These words are singular nouns; precede them with *this*, not *these*. In general, use more precise words.

kind of, sort of Considered by most readers to be informal, these phrases should be avoided in academic and workplace writing.

latter, former (See **former, latter**.)

lay, lie *Lay* is a transitive verb requiring a direct object (but not the self). *Lie*, when used to mean "place in a resting position," refers to the self but takes the form *lay* in the past tense. (See 32f.)

less, fewer (See **fewer, less**.)

lie, lay (See **lay, lie**.)

like, as (See **as, like**.)

literally Avoid using *literally* in a figurative statement (one that is not true to fact). Even when used correctly, *literally* is redundant because the statement will be taken as fact anyway.

> DRAFT — The visitors **literally** died when they saw their hotel.
>
> REDUNDANT — The visitors **literally gasped** when they saw their hotel.
>
> EDITED — The visitors gasped when they saw their hotel.

loose, lose Commonly misspelled, these words are pronounced differently. *Loose* (rhyming with *moose*) is an adjective meaning "not tight." *Lose* (rhyming with *snooze*) is a present tense verb meaning "to misplace."

lots, lots of, a lot of (See **a lot**.)

may, can (See **can, may**.)

maybe, may be *Maybe* means *possibly*; *may be* is part of a verb structure.

> The President **may be** speaking now, so **maybe** we should turn on the news.

media, medium Technically, *media* is a plural noun requiring a verb that agrees in number. Many people now use *media* as a singular noun when referring to the press. *Medium* generally refers to a conduit or method of transmission.

> The **media** is not covering the story accurately.
>
> The telephone was not a good **medium** for reviewing the budget.

might of, may of (See **could of, would of**.)

mighty Avoid this adjective in formal writing; omit it or use *very*.

Ms. To avoid the sexist labeling of women as "married" or "unmarried" (a condition not marked in men's titles), use *Ms.* unless you have reason to use *Miss* or *Mrs.* (for example, when giving the name of a character such as *Mrs. Dalloway*).

Use professional titles when appropriate (*Doctor, Professor, Senator, Mayor*). (See 46b.)

must of, must have (See **could of, would of**.)

nor, or Use *nor* in negative constructions and *or* in positive ones.

| NEGATIVE | Neither rain **nor** snow will slow the team. |
| POSITIVE | Either rain **or** snow may delay the game. |

nothing like, nowhere near These are considered informal phases when used to compare two things (as in "Gibbon's position is **nowhere near** as justified as Carlyle's"). Avoid them in formal writing.

nowheres Use *nowhere* instead.

number, amount (See **amount, number**.)

of, have (See **could of, would of**.)

off of Simply use *off* instead.

OK When you write formally, use *OK* only in dialogue. If you mean "good" or "acceptable," use these terms.

on account of Avoid this expression in formal writing. Use *because* instead.

outside of, inside of (See **inside of, outside of**.)

per Use *per* only to mean "by the," as in *per hour* or *per day*. Avoid using it to mean "according to," as in "per your instructions."

percent, percentage Use *percent* only with numerical data. Use *percentage* for a statistical part of something, not simply to mean *some* or *part*.

Ten **percent** of the sample returned the questionnaire.

A large **percentage** of the parking revenue was stolen.

plus Avoid using *plus* as a conjunction joining two independent clauses.

| INFORMAL | The school saved money through its "lights off" campaign, **plus** it generated income by recycling aluminum cans. |
| EDITED | The school saved money through its "lights off" campaign and also generated income by recycling aluminum cans. |

Use *plus* only to mean "in addition to."

The wearisome campaign, **plus** the media pressures, exhausted her.

precede, proceed *Precede* means "come before"; *proceed* means "go ahead."

pretty Avoid using *pretty* (as in *pretty good, pretty hungry, pretty sad*) to mean "somewhat" or "rather." Use *pretty* in the sense of "attractive."

principal, principle *Principal* is a noun meaning "an authority" or "head of a school" or an adjective meaning "leading" ("a *principal* objection to the testimony"). *Principle* is a noun meaning "belief or conviction."

proceed, precede (See **precede, proceed**.)

quote, quotation Formally, *quote* is a verb and *quotation* is a noun. *Quote* is sometimes used as a short version of the noun *quotation*, but this may bother some readers. Use *quotation* instead.

raise, rise *Raise* is a transitive verb meaning "to lift up." *Rise* is an intransitive verb (it takes no object) meaning "to get up or move up."

> He **raised** his head and watched the fog **rise** from the lake.

rarely ever Use *rarely* alone, not paired with *ever*.

real, really Use *real* as an adjective and *really* as an adverb. (See 35b-3)

reason is because, reason is that Avoid these wordy phrases. (See 41b-3.)

regarding, in regard, with regard to (See **in regard to**.)

regardless, irregardless (See **irregardless**.)

respectfully, respectively *Respectfully* means "with respect"; *respectively* implies a certain order for events or things.

> The senior class **respectfully** submitted the planning document. The administration considered items 3, 6, and 10, **respectively**.

rise, raise (See **raise, rise**.)

says, goes (See **go, say**.)

set, sit *Set* means "to place"; *sit* means "to place oneself." (See 32f.)

should of (See **could of, would of**.)

since, because (See **because, since**.)

sit, set (See **set, sit**.)

site, cite (See **cite, site**.)

so Some readers object to the use of *so* in place of *very*.

> INFORMAL   The filmmaker is **so** thoughtful about his films' themes.

> EDITED   The filmmaker is **very** thoughtful about his films' themes.

somebody, some body (See **anyone, any one**.)

someone, some one (See **anyone, any one**.)

sometime, some time, sometimes *Sometime* refers to an indistinct time in the future; *sometimes* means "every once in a while." *Some time* is an adjective (*some*) modifying a noun (*time*).

> The probe will reach the nebula **sometime** in the next decade. **Sometimes** such probes fail to send back any data. It takes **some time** before images will return from Neptune.

sort, kind, type (See **kind, sort, type**.)

specially, especially (See **especially, specially**.)

stationary, stationery *Stationary* means "standing still"; *stationery* refers to writing paper.

such Some readers will expect you to avoid using *such* without *that*.

> INFORMAL   Anne Frank had **such** a difficult time.

> EDITED   Anne Frank had **such** a difficult time growing up **that** her diary writing became her only solace.

suppose to, supposed to The correct form of this phrase is *supposed to*; the *-d* is sometimes mistakenly left off because it is not always heard. (See 32c.)

sure, surely In formal writing, use *sure* to mean "certain." *Surely* is an adverb; don't use *sure* in its place. (See 35b-3.)

> He has **surely** studied hard for the exam; he is **sure** to pass.

sure and, try and With *sure* and *try*, replace *and* with *to*.

take, bring (See **bring, take**.)

than, then *Than* is used to compare; *then* implies a sequence of events or a causal relationship.

> West played harder **than** East, but **then** the rain began.

that, which Although the distinction between *that* and *which* is weakening in many contexts, formal writing often requires you to know the difference. Use *that* in a clause that is essential to the meaning of a sentence (restrictive modifier); use *which* with a clause that does not provide essential information (nonrestrictive modifier). (See 48c.)

theirself, theirselves, themself All these forms are incorrect; use *themselves* to refer to more than one person and *himself* or *herself* to refer to one.

them Avoid using *them* as a subject or to modify a subject, as in "*Them* are delicious" or "*Them* apples are very crisp."

then, than (See **than, then**.)

there, their, they're These forms are often confused in spelling because they all sound alike. *There* frequently indicates location; *their* indicates possession; *they're* is a contraction of *they* and *are*. (See 50b.)

> Look **over there**.

> **Their** car ran out of gas.

> **They're** not eager to hike to the nearest gas station.

thusly Avoid this term; use *thus* or *therefore* instead.

till, 'til, until Some readers will find *till* and *'til* too informal; use *until*.

to, too, two Because these words sound the same, they may be confused. *To* is a preposition indicating direction or location. *Too* means "also." *Two* is a number.

> The Birdsalls went **to** their lake cabin. They invited the Corbetts **too**. That made **two** trips so far this season.

toward, towards Prefer *toward* in formal writing. (You may see *towards* in England and Canada.)

try and, try to, sure and (See **sure and, try and**.)

ultimately, eventually (See **eventually, ultimately**.)

uninterested, disinterested (See **disinterested, uninterested**.)

unique Use *unique* alone, not *most unique* or *more unique*. (See 35b-4.)

until, till (See **till, 'til, until**.)

use to, used to Like *supposed to*, this phrase may be mistakenly written as *use to* because the *-d* is not always clearly pronounced. Write *used to*. (See 32c.)

wait for, wait on Use *wait on* only to refer to a clerk's or server's job; use *wait for* to mean "to await someone's arrival."

well, good (See **good, well**.)

went, gone (See **gone, went**.)

were, we're *Were* is the past plural form of *was; we're* contracts *we are*. (See 50b.)

> **We're** going to the ruins where the fiercest battles **were**.

where . . . at (See **at**.)

whether, if (See **if, whether**.)

which, that (See **that, which**.)

who, whom Although the distinction between these words is slowly disappearing from the language, many readers will expect you to use *whom* as the objective form. When in doubt, err on the side of formality. (Sometimes editing can eliminate the need to choose.) (See 33b-4.)

who's, whose *Who's* contracts *who is. Whose* indicates possession. (See 50b.)

> The programmer **who's** joining our division hunted for the person **whose** bag he took by mistake.

wise, -ize (See **-ize, -wise**.)

would of, could of (See **could of, would of**.)

yet, however, but (See **but however, but yet**.)

your, you're *Your* is a possessive pronoun; *you're* contracts *you are*. (See 33a-3 and 50b.)

> If **you're** going to take physics, you'd better know **your** math.

CREDITS

Page 2, From "Living with Wildlife in Coyote Country" from the Colorado Division of Wildlife web site, http://wildlife.state.co.us. Reprinted by permission of Colorado Division of Wildlife. *Photo:* Michael Seraphin, Colorado Division of Wildlife. *Page 31,* Jay Sankey, *Zen and the Art of Stand-Up Comedy.* New York: Routledge, 1998. *Page 34,* "Fast Track Recalls," *Consumer Product Safety Review,* Fall 1998, Vol. 3, No. 1. *Page 35,* John Berendt, "Class Acts," *Esquire,* 1991. *Page 36,* Christine Gorman "Sizing Up the Sexes," *Time,* January 20, 1992. *Page 37,* Deborah Tannen, *You Just Don't Understand: Women and Men in Conversation.* New York: Morrow, 1990. *Page 37,* Jennifer Finney Boylan, "The Bad Lumberjack," *Boston Review,* 1990. *Page 40,* Daniel Goleman, "Too Little, Too Late," *American Health,* 1992. *Page 53, Atlanta Journal-Constitution,* Staff Writer. From "Restrict Rights to Sue or We'll Pay in the End." Copyright © 2001 by Atlanta Journal-Constitution. Reproduced with permission of Atlanta Journal-Constitution in the format Textbook and Other Book via Copyright Clearance Center. *Page 70,* Open Society Institute, *Gun Control in the United States: A Comparative Survey of State Firearm Laws,* April 2000. *Page 71,* Graph / Fig 1 "Population Reference Bureau Estimates and UN (Medium Series) Long-range Projections of 1992" as appears in "Global and U.S. National Population Trends," *Consequences,* Vol. 1, No. 2 (1995), www.grico.org. The U.S. Global Change Research Information Office. *Page 106,* Anson Gonzalez, "Little Rosebud Girl." Copyright © 1972 by Anson Gonzalez. Reprinted by permission. *Page 113,* Screenshot from Inanimate.com, http://Inanimate.com/portfolio.html. Original web design by Jared Cole, jaredcole.com. Reprinted by permission. *Page 149,* Leo Reisberg, "Colleges Step Up Efforts to Combat Alcohol Abuse," *The Chronicle of Higher Education,* June 12, 1998. *Page 156,* Screen shot of search results for keywords *Afro-Cuban music* from HELIN Library Catalog. Used by permission of the HELIN Consortium. *Page 159,* Screen shot of detailed information for one entry under *Afro-Cuban music* from HELIN Library Catalog. Used by permission of the HELIN Consortium. *Page 161,* Screen shot for search terms "hydrogenated oils and food" from EBSCOHost *Academic Search Premier* online database. Reprinted by permission of EBSCO Publishing. *Page 162,* Screen shot for search results "Zero in on Hidden Fats" from EBSCOHost *Academic Search Premier* online database. Reprinted by permission of EBSCO Publishing. *Page 162,* Holly McCord and Gloria McVeigh, excerpt from "Zero in on Hidden Fats" from *Prevention,* February, 2003. Reprinted by permission of *Prevention* Magazine. Copyright 2003, Rodale Inc. All rights reserved. For more articles visit Prevention.com. For subscription information call 1-800-813-8070. *Page 164,* J. Edward Hunter, abstract from "Trans Fatty Acids: Effects and Alternatives," *Food Technology,* December 2002. Reprinted by permission of *Food Technology* Magazine. *Page 164,* From the online catalog of the Providence Public Library, Health & Wellness Resource Center. Reprinted by permission of the Providence Public Library, Providence, RI. Screen shot powered by InfoTrac from the online database Health Reference Center-Academic. Copyright © 2007. Reprinted by permission of Thomson Gale, a division of Thomson Learning: www.thomsonrights.com. *Page 167,* Google™Logo and Search Code Copyright © 2007 Google. The Google search code and Google Logo used on the main page of this site are provided by and are used with the permission of: http://www.google.com. *Page 173,* Google™Logo and Search Code Copyright © 2007 Google. The Google search code and Google Logo used on the main page of this site are provided by and are used with the permission of: http://www.google.com. *Page 194,* Excerpt from "The Black-Faced Sheep," from *Old and New Poems* by Donald Hall. Copyright © 1990 by Donald Hall. Reprinted by permission of Houghton Mifflin Company. All rights reserved. *Page 215,* Reprint of magazine page from *Journal of Cultural Geography* with excerpt from "Forget the Alamo: The Border as Place in John Sayles' *Lone Star*" by Daniel D. Arreola, *Journal of Cultural Geography,* Fall/Winter 2005. By permission of JCG Press, Oklahoma State University. *Page 222,* Screen shot from *Student Affairs On-Line,* Summer 2006, Vol. 7, No. 2 with excerpt from article "Student Affairs and Podcasting: The New Frontier?" by Stuart Brown. http://studentaffairs.com/ © 2007 StudentAffairs.com. All rights reserved. Used by permission of StudentAffairs.com LLC. *Page 227,* Screen shot of search results in html format from Blackwell Synergy online database for article "A Queen for Whose Time? Elizabeth I as Icon for the Twentieth Century" by David Grant, *Journal of Popular Culture,* 39 (2006). By permission of Blackwell Publishing. *Page 228,* Screen shot of search results in pdf format from Blackwell Synergy online database for article "A Queen for Whose Time? Elizabeth I as Icon for the Twentieth Century" by David Grant, *Journal of Popular Culture,* 39 (2006). By permission of Blackwell Publishing. *Page 250,* One page from *Journal of Broadcasting & Electronic Media,* June 2006. Copyright 2006. Excerpt from "Judging the Degree of Violence in Media Portrayals" by Karyn Riddle *et al.,* *Journal of Broadcasting & Electronic Media* 50(2), 2006, p. 270. Reproduced by permission of Taylor & Francis Group, LLC, http://www.taylorandfrancis.com. *Page 254,* From "What Students Want: Leave Me Alone . . . I'm Socializing" by Neal Starkman, *T.H.E. Journal,* March 2007 issue. Copyright © 2007. http://www.thejournal.com/articles/20336. Reprinted by permission of PARS International on behalf of T.H.E. Journal. *Photo:* Masterfile. *Page 257,* Screen shot for search result "Treatment Approaches for Sleep Difficulties in College Students" from EBSCOHost *Academic Search Premier* online database. Reprinted by permission of EBSCO Publishing. *Page 258,* Excerpt from "Treatment Approaches for Sleep Difficulties among College Students" by Walter C. Buboltz *et al.* from *Counselling Psychology Quarterly,* September 2002, Vol. 15, No. 2. Reprinted by permission of the publisher, Taylor & Francis Ltd, http://informaworld.com. *Page 272,* Copyright © 2001. From "Body Esteem Scale for Adults and Adolescents" by Mendelson, Mendelson, and White, *Journal of Personality Assessment,* 2001, 76 (1). Reproduced by permission of Society for Personality Assessment, http://www.personality.org. *Page 448,* Excerpt from "At the Barrier" from *Levering Avenue: Poems* by Robert Daseler. University of Evansville Press, 1998. Reprinted by permission. *Page 448,* T.R. Mayers, from "(snap)shots." Reprinted by permission of the author.

INDEX

Note: The index is sorted by word order. **Bold** page numbers indicate definitions in the text. Page numbers followed by *G* indicate entries in the glossary. (WWW) indicates the location of information about a specific Web site where additional information may be available. *See* references refer you to appropriate or related index entries.

GUIDE TO ESL ADVICE

If your first language is not English, look for special advice integrated throughout the handbook. Each ESL Advice section is labeled and highlighted.

ADJECTIVES AND ADVERBS

Adjective Forms (**30d**)
Adjective Clauses (**31c**)
Adjectives in a Series (**35a**)
Adverb Clauses (**31c**)

AGREEMENT

Pronoun-Antecedent Agreement (**34d**)
    Demonstrative Adjectives or
        Pronouns (**34d**)
Subject-Verb Agreement (**34b, 34c**)
    Other, Others, and *Another* (**34c**)
    Present Tense Verb Agreement
        (**34b**)
    Quantifiers (*each, one, many,*
        much, most) (**34c**)
    Separated Subjects and Verbs (**34c**)

ARTICLES AND NOUNS

Articles: *A, An,* and *The* (**30a**)
Noun Clauses (**31c**)

PREPOSITIONS

Prepositions (**30f**)
For and *Since* in Time Expressions (**30f**)
Prepositions of Place and Time: *At,*
    On, and *In* (**30f**)
Prepositions with Nouns, Verbs, and
    Adjectives (**30f**)
To or No Preposition to Express Going
    to a Place (**30f**)

PUNCTUATION AND MECHANICS

Abbreviated Titles (**58a**)
Quotation Marks (**51a**)

SENTENCES

Because and *Because of* (**37c**)
Coordination and Subordination
    (**31c, 37c, 43c**)
Position of Modifiers (**39a**)
There and *It* as Subjects (**7b**)

VERBALS

Gerunds (**31b**)
Gerunds vs. Infinitives (**31b**)
Infinitives (**31b**)

VERBS

Verb Forms (**32d**)
Conditional Statements (**32h**)
Helping Verbs (**32d**)
Passive Voice (**32i**)
Simple Present and Simple Past (**32a**)
Simple Present and Present
    Progressive Tenses (**32e**)
Subject-Verb Agreement (**34b, 34c**)
Third Person *–s* or *–es* Ending (**32b**)
Verb Tense and Expressions of Time
    (**32e, 40b**)

WORDS

Idioms in American English (**45b**)

WRITING

Clear and Forceful Details (**2a**)
Effective Writing (**1a**)
Semidrafting and Phrasing (**4a**)

SYMBOLS FOR REVISING AND EDITING

Boldface numbers refer to sections and chapters in the handbook.

abbrev	incorrect abbreviation, **58**	**¶**	new paragraph, **6**
add	information or detail needed, **6a, 6e–f**	**no ¶**	no new paragraph, **6**
		p	error in punctuation, **48–53**
agr	error in subject-verb or pronoun-antecedent agreement, **34**	**prep**	preposition error, **30f**
		pr ref	pronoun reference error, **38**
apos	lack of (or incorrect) possessive apostrophe, **50**	**proof?**	missing or inadequate evidence, **8b, 10d**
art	article used incorrectly, **30a**	**punc**	error in punctuation, **48–53**
awk	awkward construction, **7**	**⌃**	comma, **48**
cap	capital letter needed, **54**	**no ⌃**	no comma, **48i**
case	incorrect pronoun form, **33**	**;**	semicolon, **49a**
clear	clearer sentence needed, **7**	**:**	colon, **49b**
coh	paragraph or essay coherence needed, **6c–d**	**v̇**	apostrophe, **50**
		" "	quotation marks, **51**
coord	faulty coordination, **43**	**.**	period, **52a**
cs	comma splice, **37**	**?**	question mark, **52b**
cut	unnecessary material, **6a**	**!**	exclamation point, **52c**
dev	paragraph or essay development needed, **6a–f**	**( ) [ ] —**	parentheses, brackets, dashes,
		. . . /	ellipses, slashes, **53**
discrm	sexist or discriminatory language, **46**	**ref**	pronoun reference error, **38**
dm	dangling modifier, **39**	**reorg**	reorganize passage or section, **2b, 5a**
dneg	double negative, **35b-4**		
emph	emphasis needed, **7c**	**rep**	repetitious, **45**
focus	paragraph or essay focus needed, **6a–b**	**sent**	sentence revision needed, **5a–b, 7**
		shift	shift, **40**
frag	sentence fragment, **36**	**sp**	word spelled incorrectly, **59**
fs	fused sentence, **37**	**spell**	word spelled incorrectly, **59**
gap	more explanation or information needed, **8b–c, 10d–f**	**sub**	faulty subordination, **43b–c**
		t	wrong verb tense, **32a–g**
		tense	wrong verb tense, **32a–g**
hyph	hyphen (-) needed, **56**	**trans**	transition needed, **6d, 6f**
inc	incomplete sentence, **41**	**und**	underlining (italics), **55**
ital	italics (underlining), **55**	**us**	error in usage, **Glossary**
lc	lowercase letter needed, **54**	**var**	sentence variety needed, **7**
link	paragraph linkage needed, **6d, 6g**	**verb**	incorrect verb form, **32**
		wc	faulty word choice, **45**
log	faulty reasoning, **8, 10f**	**wordy**	unneeded words, **44**
mixed	grammatically mixed sentence, **41**	**ww**	wrong word, **45**
		^	insert
mm	misplaced modifier, **39**	**⌀**	delete
modif	incorrect adjective or adverb, **35**		close up space
		∿	transpose letters or words
num	incorrect numbering style, **57**	**#**	add a space
//	parallel elements needed, **42**	**X**	obvious error

Contents